Democracy in Scandinavia

MANCHESTER
1824

Manchester University Press

Democracy in Scandinavia

Consensual, majoritarian or mixed?

David Arter

Manchester University Press
Manchester and New York
distributed exclusively in the USA by Palgrave

Published by Manchester University Press
Oxford Road, Manchester M13 9NR, UK
and Room 400, 175 Fifth Avenue, New York, NY 10010, USA
www.manchesteruniversitypress.co.uk

Distributed exclusively in the USA by
Palgrave, 175 Fifth Avenue, New York,
NY 10010, USA

Distributed exclusively in Canada by
UBC Press, University of British Columbia, 2029 West Mall,
Vancouver, BC, Canada V6T 1Z2

British Library Cataloguing-in-Publication Data
A catalogue record for this book is available from the British Library

Library of Congress Cataloging-in-Publication Data applied for

ISBN 0 7190 7046 5 *hardback*
EAN 978 0 7190 7046 4

ISBN 0 7190 7047 3 *paperback*
EAN 978 0 7190 7047 1

First published 2006

15 14 13 12 11 10 09 08 07 06   10 9 8 7 6 5 4 3 2 1

Edited and typeset by
Frances Hackeson Freelance Publishing Services, Brinscall, Lancs
Printed in Great Britain
by Biddles Ltd, King's Lynn

Contents

Tables

Preface

Criminals, it is said, often return to the scene of their crime(s). Indeed, it might well be considered a 'criminal' act in an academic sense to return to the theme of Scandinavian government – and in particular classifying the democracies in the Nordic region – so relatively soon after my *Scandinavian Politics Today* (Manchester University Press, 1999). Why not simply revise that volume rather than re-open the whole Scandinavian file to extend the crime department metaphor? Two pieces of new evidence in particular have prompted the present investigation. First, there was the publication of Arend Lijphart's expanded study *Patterns of Democracy* (Yale University Press, 1999) in which he expressly confirms the status of the Scandinavian countries as 'consensus model democracies'. Second, there was the inception the same year of the devolved Scottish Parliament, which the architects clearly wanted to be an institution characterised by 'consensus politics'. I bring this point out in my study *The Scottish Parliament: A Scandinavian-Style Assembly?* (Frank Cass, 2004)

The Consultative Steering Group's document *Shaping Scotland's Parliament* (Scottish Office, 1999) is replete with references to Scandinavian legislative practices and it was this concern to import 'best practice' from the Nordic region, which prompted the first main question in this book. *What, if any, are the distinctive features of the Nordic political systems when compared with the Westminster model of democracy – the archetype of 'majoritarian democracy' in Lijphart's terms?* Knut Heidar has written (see chapter 1) that the notion of a Nordic model of government is "a useful catch phrase" and "a rough guide to certain aspects of the politics of the region". But what are these distinctive aspects? The first seven chapters seek to demythologise, demystify or at very least challenge the conventional accounts, which contain widespread reference to such things as 'the Swedish model' a 'Nordic model of government' and so on. A number of particular features are identified and, where possible, related to questions in the current political science debate.

One could never accuse the Scandinavians of complacency when it comes to their political systems. The 1982 Norwegian Power and Democracy Commission significantly antedated the present vogue for democratic auditing and, much more recently, there have been major 'democracy commissions' in Denmark, Norway and Sweden. Scandinavian academics, moreover, have pointed to evidence *inter alia* of declining electoral turnout, declining membership of parties and popular movements, along with declining trust in politicians. Can there really be a 'crisis of democracy' in the Scandinavian states? The second main question in this book is thus concerned with the state of democracy in Scandinavia and whether Scandinavian democracy is 'in a state'. It asks, 'How well do the recent power and democracy commissions suggest that Scandinavian democracy is working?' In other words, how well do the Scandinavians think their democracies are working? The findings are remarkable contradictory, something explained in no small measure by the contrasting normative and methodological approaches. For example, whereas the Danes are described as being "still democratically active" and their political institutions "democratically robust", Norway is labelled "a disintegrating democracy".

The third, overarching question – and the question in the sub-title of this book – is 'Is democracy in Scandinavia consensual, majoritarian or mixed?' Four chapters consider the region as an exemplar of 'consensus model democracy', explore the nature of legislative–executive relations in the Nordic countries and, in particular, focus on the role of parliamentary opposition and its involvement in policy-making. The fundamental question relates to the extent of consensual legislative practice. The central conclusion is that all the Nordic states are majoritarian democracies, albeit with varying amounts of consensual legislative behaviour. The empirical work draws on what prima facie are the sharply contrasting cases of Finland – a system with broad-based majority governments – and Sweden – a system with regular minority cabinets. In fact, the two countries fit nicely into a 'most similar design' schema, their parliamentary oppositions since 2002/03 displaying remarkable similarities. Interviews were conducted with the leaders and senior figures in the parliamentary opposition parties in the two countries over summer 2004.

In his review of *Scandinavian Politics Today* (*Political Studies* 48, 1, 2000), the Dane Mogens N. Pedersen, although complimentary, detected "some biases". "Swedish and Finnish politics are better covered than Danish, Icelandic and Norwegian politics", he wrote. I was reading recently that 36% of Copenhagen residents cycled to work compared with 27% who drive and 33% who use public transport. Evidently the City Council has set the target of 40% cycling to work by 2012. Extending the cycling analogy, my concern in this volume has certainly not been to 'pedal' old messages, but to break new ground in challenging the established status of the Scandinavian countries as 'consensus model democracies'. While the field-work concentrates on Finland and Sweden – cases of contrasting governments but comparable oppositions – it is hoped that the approach and conclusions have an application across the Nordic region and lead to future cross-national research. Meanwhile, where did I put that bike?

1

Analysing the Nordic region: a block of distinctive consensus model democracies?

It may well be an apocryphal story, but media interest was certainly aroused when it transpired that a leading member of the Scottish Parliament (MSP) had declined an invitation to accompany a distinguished foreign visitor to the official opening of the new Scottish Parliament building on 9 October 2004. He did so, it seems, in order to attend a vital Scotland–Norway World Cup qualifying football match that afternoon. The MSP reputedly changed his mind, however, when he learned that the guest was none other than the deputy prime minister of Norway, who in turn intended the leave the ceremonies early to get to the match at Hampden Park! Norway, incidentally, won 0–1.[1]

The Scots and Norwegians have, of course, much more in common than being 'fitba mad'. Most obviously, there have been extensive historical links between the two countries. It seems quite possible that the notorious raid on the Northumbrian island monastery of Lindisfarne in AD 793 was the work of Norwegian Vikings who had lost their way en route to the north of Scotland. But, in any event, records indicate that plundering began in the Hebrides in 798 and there were a series of seasonal raids in the west of Scotland until at least the 830s. Before the end of the ninth century, the Vikings had taken large tracts of land in north and west Scotland. Indeed, as Barbara Crawford has written (Crawford 1987), for a few centuries the northern and western coasts of Scotland were "a part of the Scandinavian world" in the sense that they were to a greater or lesser extent under "the parent political authority of Norway". (cited in Graham-Campbell and Batey 1998: 3) The Norse dialect *Norn*, a form of west Norwegian, survived as a living language in Orkney and Shetland until the eighteenth century.

There are, of course, far more recent historical connections between Scotland and Norway. Thus, in his powerful account of *The Shetland Bus*, David Howarth recalls how, "during the Nazi occupation of Norway between 1940–45, every Norwegian knew that small boats were constantly sailing from the Shetland Isles to Norway to land weapons and supplies and to rescue refugees.

The Norwegians who stayed in Norway and struggled there against the invaders were fortified by this knowledge".[2] (Howarth 2001) They referred to the traffic across the North Sea as 'taking the Shetland Bus' and this "became a synonym in Norway for escape when danger was overwhelming". The aim of the Shetland Bus, of course, was to maintain contact between the exiled Norwegian government in London and the (as yet) uncoordinated resistance during the German occupation.

Perhaps it was not altogether surprising, in view of the strong ties between Scotland and Norway, that the architects of the new devolved parliament 'north of the border' wanted to import a Scandinavian-style politics into Scotland. So much is evident from the document *Shaping Scotland's Parliament*, prepared by a Consultative Steering Group (CSG) set up in 1997 which, in making explicit references to legislative practice in Denmark, Norway and Sweden, is a *smörgåsbord* of Scandinavian influences. The CSG was impressed with the high quality information service provided by the Swedish Riksdag. (CSG 1999: 11) It referred to the way the powers vested in the Speaker of the Scandinavian parliaments to suspend sittings were written into the various Standing Orders. (CSG 1999: 46) It noted that, in determining the order of plenary speakers, the Norwegian practice, where members could register their interest to speak prior to the debate, might be appropriate. (CSG 1999: 47) The CSG also proposed that MSPs should be addressed simply by name, as, it claimed, had become the convention in the Danish Folketing. (CSG 1999: 49) Ironically, the present Speaker (Presiding Officer) of the Scottish Parliament, George Reid, has recounted how it was he who commissioned the Scandinavian evidence, as part of the CSG's deliberations, but because it took nine months to arrive the references to Scandinavian parliamentary practice in *Shaping Scotland's Parliament* are not evidence-based. (Arter 2004: 126–127)

At the time of the establishment of the devolved parliament in Edinburgh, there was widespread reference to the need to create a 'new politics' in Scotland. (Mitchell 2000: 605–621) This was to be a style of politics and an approach to politics diametrically different from the adversarial Westminster model of democracy. It was to be a politics predicated on a three-way sharing of power between government, parliament and civil society. It was in short to be something approximating a Scandinavian-style consensus democracy. This was in itself a perfectly worthy ambition. But for longstanding observers of the Scandinavian political scene it begged the need to re-address a series of fundamental questions. Are the Scandinavian countries really exemplary consensus model democracies? What exactly is the nature of the desired Scandinavian-style politics? Indeed, is there such a thing as a 'Scandinavian politics' and do all the 'Cs' associated with it – cooperation, compromise and comprehensive social engineering – represent a real or idealised picture? These are some of the questions tackled in the first seven chapters of this book.

Incidentally, the adjectives 'Nordic' and 'Scandinavian' are used interchangeably in this study. Elder, Thomas and Arter make the case. "It would be as pedantic to limit the latter to the geographical core-area concept (Denmark, Norway, Sweden) as to interpret the former in a strict anthropological sense as referring to the tall, blond dolicephalic race whose representatives are in a clear minority in the region anyway." (Elder, Thomas and Arter 1982: 2) However, the term 'metropolitan Scandinavia' refers more narrowly to Denmark, Norway and Sweden. True, Elder et al. allude only to the two former imperial powers of Denmark and Sweden as 'metropolitan states'. (Elder, Thomas and Arter 1982: 100–101) The term 'metropolitan Scandinavia' is none the less useful shorthand to distinguish the 'inner three' from the non-metropolitan states of Finland and Iceland, which, as we shall see, are 'outliers', not only geographically but in a significant political sense.

The Nordic region: common denominators

Studying the politics and government of the five Nordic states must involve making comparisons at two levels at least. First, there is the internal (intra-regional) perspective. For example, it seems reasonable to assert that the government–trade union relationship has been very different in Iceland (until recently, essentially adversarial) from say Norway (primarily co-operative). Second, there is the external perspective, which involves comparing practice in the Nordic states with one or more states outside the region. As a wholly random example, it is clear that the proportional voting systems in Scandinavia stand in sharp contrast to the simple plurality system used for British general elections. This is despite the fact that, outside Finland, there are national qualifying thresholds for representation of between 2–4%.

The internal comparison of the Nordic countries is a central theme in the present author's earlier volume *Scandinavian Politics Today* and it is not, therefore, intended to cover the same ground again in more than outline. It is, however, worth reminding ourselves of Giovanni Sartori's axiomatic proposition that it is impossible to compare stones and rabbits – impossible because they are two entirely different things and have nothing in common. The Nordic states are emphatically not like stones and rabbits and, despite their differences, have a number of common denominators that make them readily comparable.

First, they have overlapping histories and occupy adjacent geopolitical space. Norway did not gain full independence from Sweden until 1905, having until 1814 formed part of the Danish crown. Finland was part of the Czarist Russian Empire until 1917 while Iceland did not vote for full freedom from

Denmark until 1944. Accordingly, three of the five Nordic countries are relatively young nation-states.

Second, there are obvious cultural affinities between the Scandinavian countries, particularly through language. It was significant that in the current affairs magazine *Nordisk Kontakt*, which until the early 1990s was published
about nine times annually by the Nordic Council, only the coverage of Icelandic events was not in a national language. Reports on Iceland were mostly in
Danish, the former 'imperial tongue'. The section on Finland was in the second national language, Swedish – itself a reminder that, until the Napoleonic
Wars, Finland formed part of the Swedish crown. Over the last century, the
size of the Swedish language minority in Finland has declined appreciably to
about 5% of the total population. Indeed, it may be, as Kenneth McRae has
asserted, that "in spite of official bilingualism, contemporary Finland has become more homogenous linguistically than many official unilingual countries". (McRae 1997: 85)

Third, since the Second World War, in particular, there have developed
strong cross-national institutional linkages and networks across the Nordic
region. (Arter 1999: 7–20) Initially, these were concentrated on and in the
Nordic Council, an inter-parliamentary consultative organ, founded following a Danish initiative in 1952.[3] A Nordic Council of Ministers was created in
1971.[4] Today, three of the Scandinavian states, Denmark (from 1973) together with Sweden and Finland (from 1995) are members of the European
Union. There are also a variety of regional organs such as the Barents Euro-
Arctic Regional Council (BEAR) through which the Scandinavian states (along
with others) work to achieve desired goals. Their significance, however, should
not be exaggerated. Thus, in his study of politics and business in the Barents
region, Bo Svensson found that to date the perceived impact of transnational
regional co-operation in creating a conducive environment for cross-border
business development has been strictly limited. (Svensson 1998: 255–268)

Finally, there are common denominators in the size of the Scandinavian
states, which may be said to comprise a group of 'small democracies'. 'Small'
is, of course, an arbitrary notion. It might reasonably be objected that Sweden
with a population of 9 million is not really small. Iceland, moreover, with in
the order of 290,000 inhabitants, might best be thought of as a *micro-state*.
Clive Archer and Nigel Nugent, however, have argued persuasively that micro-
states not only have very small populations and geographical areas, but are
"heavily dependent on neighbouring states for diplomatic support". (Archer
and Nugent 2002: 5) States like Andorra, Monaco and San Marino do not
have an independent foreign policy. But this is emphatically not the case in
Iceland, which is the only Nordic state never to have applied for EC/EU

membership and, distinctively in the region, has a special relationship with the United States through its 1951 Defence Agreement.

Clearly, in defining a small state, population size is the most obvious criterion in determining, among other things, its representation on supranational bodies. Equally, Baldur Thorhallsson has noted, that the capacity of a small state and its behaviour in international relations is determined to a degree by the size and characteristics of the national administration. In 2001 Iceland's foreign service comprised 150 persons, compared with 1150 for Norway and 1163 for Denmark. (Thorhallsson 2004: 163) Thorhallsson contends that the exceptionally small size of the national administration has reduced Iceland's capacity to participate in European integration and also meant that the political elite has not been exposed to the ideological influences of the most enthusiastic pro-European elites in the original EU member states. (Thorhallsson 2004: 161–162)

Importantly, smallness has been linked to *policy style* and policy practice. Gunnel Gustafsson and Jeremy Richardson have defined policy style as "the standard operating procedures for handling issues which arrive on the political agenda" and depict the Swedish policy style as predominantly "consultative and radical" – radical in the sense of getting to the very roots of the problem. (Gustafsson and Richardson 1980: 21–37) Indeed, there are those who would argue that smallness has contributed significantly to a consultative and consensus-based Scandinavian-style politics. This brings us back nicely to what the architects of the Scottish Parliament – Scotland is broadly the same size as Denmark, Norway and Finland – wished to import. There was at least the hazy idea in Edinburgh that Scandinavian politics was constructive and consensual in a way that politics in Westminster was negative and adversarial.

There has been substantial support in the political science literature for the perception of the Scandinavian states as consensual democracies. In the 1980s, Elder, Thomas and Arter brought out the way "the shaping of economic policy is much less concertative in Britain than in Scandinavia" and they note that in the latter conflicting interests can be settled "by horse-trading, which may be regarded as a form of concertation". (Elder, Thomas and Arter 1982: 190–191) Olof Petersson claims that "to some extent at least, the Nordic countries have been able to develop their own particular ways of solving conflicts and making political decisions". He continues that "an emphasis on compromise and pragmatic solutions has led to the development of a political culture based on consensus". (Petersson 1994: 33) Arend Lijphart cites the Scandinavian states as evidence of a correspondence between the conceptual and geographical "as far as the consensus side of the executive-parties dimension is concerned". (Lijphart 1999: 250) The Americans Eric Einhorn and John Logue, moreover, argue that even during periods of single-party majority government, as in Norway between 1945–61, the Scandinavian states resemble Lijphart's consensus model. (Einhorn and Logue 2003: 42)

The broad consensus among political scientists (both Nordic and non-Nordic) about the consensual nature of Scandinavian politics and government does not in itself make the case. Indeed, definitions of consensual democracy have been scarce and the systematic application of a set of operational indicators conspicuous by its absence. Much has been impressionistic. True, Elder, Thomas and Arter have modelled consensual democracy along three complementary dimensions. 1) A liberal democratic polity, which is characterised by a low level of opposition to the framework of rules and regulations for the resolution of political conflict within the state. 2) A liberal democratic system characterised by a low level of conflict about the actual exercise of power within the state. 3) A liberal democratic system characterised by a high degree of concertation in the gestation of public policy. (Elder, Thomas and Arter 1982: 10–11) But their response to the seminal question 'Consensual Democracies?' is very 'broad brush': Finland and Iceland are becoming more consensual; Denmark, Norway and Sweden, less so (that, of course, was in the 1980s).

The Nordic states: distinctive politics?

This book is structured around three fundamental questions, each of which attempts to shed broad light on the practice of politics, government and democracy in the Nordic countries when viewed from an external perspective. The six chapters following this introduction seek to demystify and challenge the conventional accounts, which contain widespread reference to such things as 'the Swedish model', a 'Nordic model of government' and so on. The first central question is 'What, if any, are the distinctive features of the Nordic political systems when compared with the Westminster model of democracy' – the archetype of 'majoritarian democracy' in Lijphart's terms?

Distilling from a fairly substantial literature, the present author has, in an earlier volume, sought to portray the essential features of an ideal-type Nordic model of government. (Arter 1999: 144–172) Seven characteristics were identified. 1) Dominant or numerically strong social democratic parties working closely with the peak blue-collar trade-union federation. 2) Moderate 'working multi-party systems' – that is, parties able to work together effectively (whether from a position in government or opposition) to produce public policy. 3) A consensual rather than adversarial approach to policy-making. 4) Extensive and regular consultation with pressure groups and special interests in the consideration of public policy issues. 5) A centralised system of collective bargaining. 6) An active role for the state in regulating the market and in the provision of social protection. 7) The personalisation of relations among the political elites which, as a by-product of the 'politics of [the small] scale', conduces towards give-and-take pragmatic solutions.

Of course, in order to claim the existence of a Nordic model of government, it is necessary not only that the Nordic states should share the model's basic elements, but that the model should be unique. No other countries should fit the Nordic model. In practice, there have been problems of universal application within the Nordic region and the features of the model have not been manifest in all the Scandinavian states. For example, social democracy has not been dominant in Iceland, a numerically significant anti-system radical left has polarised Finnish politics and, in general, the model draws very heavily on the Swedish experience. Furthermore, it is not clear that the Nordic model of government is region-specific. Knut Heidar has observed that "if we focus on specific elements of the Nordic model, such as the strength of social democracy, the corporatist arrangements or pragmatic political culture, it is difficult to exclude Austria from the 'Nordic model'". (Heidar 2004: 265) In a similar vein, I have suggested earlier that "perhaps (and only perhaps) the extent of the consultation and by extension the exhaustive deliberations involved in the formulation of measures in some parts of Scandinavia represent a difference of degree if not kind from practice elsewhere in Western Europe". (Arter 1999: 169) Heidar concludes that the notion of a Nordic model is "a useful catch phrase" and "a rough guide to certain aspects of the politics of the region". (Heidar 2004: 263) But what are these distinctive aspects?

The six chapters that follow seek to identify those elements in the political practice of the Nordic states that appear somewhat different when viewed from an essentially 'Westminster model' perspective. They also strive to relate these particular features, where possible, to questions in the current political science debate.

At least when compared with the Westminster model of democracy, the Scandinavian political systems have a number of distinctive components. First, there are the varieties of preferential PR list voting systems that create a 'candidate vote' option in Denmark and Sweden and require an individual candidate ballot in Finland. Scandinavian political parties have received extensive public funding since the 1960s. But to what extent have these 'personalised' electoral arrangements constituted a challenge to the 'party democracy' model? Moreover, is there any basis in Scandinavia for Mark Hallerberg's hypothesis that the more candidate-centred the electoral system the higher the level of fragmentation within parliament or his assertion that "where the personal vote is high, restrictions on the behaviour of parliamentarians will be especially stringent"? (Hallerberg 2004: 20, 31)

Second, there existed in Scandinavia from the completion of mass democracy in the 1920s to the late 1960s a highly unidimensional form of multipartism, with the political parties readily located on a left–right continuum and, even more strikingly, high levels of class voting. Sweden was perhaps a limiting case in this respect since, as Hans Bergström has observed, "in no other country has the basic left-right scale accounted for such a great deal of party structure and electoral behaviour". (Bergström 1991: 8) But to what extent has *party system change* since 1970 meant the Scandinavian party systems are less unidimensional and, therefore, less distinctive? Moreover, how far has increased electoral volatility involved increased cross-class voting?

Third, probably the feature of the Scandinavian political landscape (outside Iceland) most remarked upon by foreign observers has been the electoral and governmental strength of the social democratic-labour parties. At various times since the 1930s the Danish, Norwegian and Swedish social democratic-labour parties have enjoyed dominant, even hegemonic status. Do these parties remain dominant or is there evidence of incipient 'social democratic decomposition' in Gøsta Esping-Andersen's phrase? (Esping-Andersen 1985) Portentously perhaps, for the first time in any of the mainland Scandinavian countries, the Danish Social Democrats in February 2005 failed for a second consecutive general election to gain the largest share of the vote. They were beaten into second place by Denmark's oldest party, the Liberals (*Venstre*).

Fourth, in the last four decades, the Nordic states have witnessed an exceptionally wide variety of types of coalition government. These have ranged from 'outsize' or 'surplus majority' coalitions in Finland to several (non-socialist) minority coalitions in Denmark, Norway and Sweden. The Danish four-party, non-socialist minority cabinet of Conservatives, Liberals, Christians and Centre Democrats – the so-called *four-leaf clover* – formed under Poul Schlüter in autumn 1982 stayed in power for almost six years (Elklit 1999: 78–79) Conspicuous by their absence have been single-party majority governments or 'minimal winning coalitions'. Has this diversity of coalition types had implications for the political culture of parliament and government?

Fifth, the frequency of minority governments has been a feature of legislative–executive relations in the 'metropolitan Scandinavian states' of Denmark, Norway and Sweden. Indeed, Denmark has been called 'the home of minority government'. Has this 'minority parliamentarism' – the far from felicitous term used by Scandinavian political scientists – been the principal component of a 'distinctively Scandinavian form of parliamentarism' in Anders Sannerstedt's phrase? (Sannerstedt 1996: 53–54)

Sixth, there has been a tradition in the Nordic states (outside Iceland) of power-sharing or corporatism in macro-economic policy management, fostered by the ruling Social Democrats and involving the main sectoral interest groups (social partners) and the government. But is the heyday of corporatism past? Has there been a 'retreat of corporatism' and evidence of a shift to 'lobbyism'? (Rommetvedt 2005)

Although the search thus far has been for the distinctive features of the politics and government of the Scandinavian states when viewed principally from a Westminster perspective, a reasonable case could be made for a growing institutional convergence between them. Cross-national divergence seems increasingly a thing of the past. Thus, since the Second World War, all the Nordic parliaments have become unicameral, with specialist standing committee systems. The adoption of a new constitution in March 2000, in formalising a reduced role for the president, effectively marked the end of 'Finnish exceptionalism'. It is no longer a case of 'semi-presidential government' other than in the minimalist sense of a "situation where a popularly-elected, fixed-term president exists alongside a prime minister and cabinet who are responsible to parliament". (Elgie 2004: 317) The head of state no longer possesses "quite significant powers" in Duverger's terms. (Duverger 1980: 165–187) Across the region the role of prime minister appears to have grown in importance. Chapter 7 considers the office of prime minister and asks more widely whether the Scandinavian states are *en route* to becoming (converging as) routine West European parliamentary democracies.

The Nordic states – democracies in good working order?

It is impossible to accuse the Scandinavians of becoming complacent about the working of their political systems and of basking in an Oxbridge-style 'effortless superiority' over other less lauded democracies. If anything, the reverse has been the case. There has existed an almost pathological introspection and concern to sustain and improve their democratic processes. Symptomatically, the 1982 Norwegian Power Commission considerably antedated the present vogue for democratic auditing. Much more recently, there have been major 'democracy commissions' in Denmark, Norway and Sweden. Indeed, publicly financed power studies have been very much a Scandinavian phenomenon. Three have been set up since 1997. 'An Analysis of Democracy and Power in Denmark' was instituted by the *Folketing* (parliament) against the backdrop of growing concern among many MPs about a decline in the legislative capacity of the national legislature. The 'Power and Democracy Commission' in Norway is a good example of policy transfer or institutional diffusion since it was motivated by a similar concern about an insidious erosion of parliament's legislative clout.

The Swedish Democracy Commission's report 'A Resilient Democracy', published in 2000 after three years of deliberations, should be seen in the

context of a trend towards declining political participation both through political parties and more immediately through the ballot boxes. Moreover, in
addition to the publicly appointed Democracy Commission, the private and
non-partisan Centre for Business and Policy Studies – SNS – has produced
annual reports on the state of democracy in Sweden. There has not been the
same history of power commissions in Finland and Iceland. However, influenced by the tradition of democratic auditing in 'metropolitan Scandinavia', a
'Policy Programme for Citizen Participation' was launched by the Vanhanen
government in Finland in summer 2003. The programme was designed to
consolidate representative democracy and promote active citizenship, based
on the notion of citizens as partners.

The various power commissions have mobilised armies of academics and
they in turn have amassed revealing evidence of declining electoral turnout,
declining party membership, declining membership of popular movements
(such as trade unions) and declining trust in politicians. Does this evidence
amount to a 'crisis of democracy' in the Scandinavian states? The second big
question in this book, therefore, is concerned with the state of Scandinavian
democracy and whether Scandinavian democracy is 'in a state'. It asks 'How
well do the recent "power and democracy" commissions suggest that Scandinavian democracy is working?' While the findings are remarkably contradictory – something explained in no small measure by the contrasting normative
and methodological approaches – the question is undoubtedly topical.

Symptomatically, during Iceland's Presidency of the Nordic Council in 2004,
the Icelandic minister for Nordic co-operation, Siv Friðleifsdóttir, launched a
Democracy Committee, which was charged with generating proposals on "how
to improve and develop the democratic processes" in the region as a whole.
Friðleifsdóttir emphasised the need to examine democracy in the context of
globalisation and the IT revolution, as well as considering how to integrate
immigrants, and increasingly women and young persons, into the decision-
making processes. She also expressed concern about declining turnout in several of the recent Nordic general elections.[5]

In a recent special issue of *Parliamentary Affairs* the present author suggested that a healthy democracy depended on at least five conditions – adapted
from David Beetham's 'best practice' approach – being met. (Arter 2004b:
581–600). 1) There should be a representative parliament that accurately reflects the will of the electorate at the polls. 2) There should be a representative
government, that is one which parliament can hold adequately to account. 3)
There should be responsive government in so far as the political executive
should be open and accessible and there should be regularised procedures for
public consultation in the formulation of measures. 4) There should be a

responsive parliament and linkage mechanisms allowing civil society a measure of influence on strategic parliamentary actors – especially the standing committees – when legislative proposals are being discussed, inquiries undertaken and public petitions lodged. 5) There should be a participative electorate.

The Danish commission evaluated the state of democracy by reference to the extent to which it approximated five core ideals. 1) The existence of equal political rights, based on universal suffrage, majority decisions and the protection of minorities. 2) The existence of the free formation of opinion based on open and diverse access to information. 3) The existence of broad and equal participation grounded in the broadly equal distribution of economic and social resources. 4) The existence of effective and responsible governance. 5) The existence of trust, tolerance and regard for the community. Clearly, a detailed analysis of either of these sets of 'performance indicators' – and the problem is that there is no consensus about the measures to be used in evaluating democracy – would require at least a book in its own right. However, all that chapter 8 seeks to do is to present the main conclusions of the various power studies in response to the question about how well the Scandinavians perceive Scandinavian democracy to be working.

The Nordic states – consensual democracies?

The last six chapters of this book revisit the generally accepted wisdom that the Scandinavian states have formed a distinct sub-species of representative democracy in the form of a block of consensual democracies. The focus is on the region as an exemplar of 'consensus model democracy', the nature of legislative–executive relations in the Nordic countries and, in particular, the role of the parliamentary opposition and its involvement in policy-making. The generic question runs 'Is democracy in Scandinavia consensual, majoritarian or mixed?' There are two integrally related sub-questions. 1) How consensual is legislative practice in the Nordic countries? 2) How, and to what effect, does the parliamentary opposition participate in the exercise of power in the Scandinavian countries and in the contrasting cases of Finland and Sweden in particular? In the former, broad-based majority government has become the norm whereas in the latter minority government has become routine.

The question of the extent to which legislative practice in the Nordic countries has been consensual raises a further issue. Has there been an essentially inclusive or exclusive approach to the exercise of power on the part of the government? In other words, are the Nordic states cases of what Kaare Strøm has described as *inclusionary democracy* in which policy influence may be gained without control of the executive branch or rather systems in which the governing parties tend to monopolise both office and policy benefits? (Müller and

Strøm 1999: 288) Re-stated, are the parties outside government in a strongly competitive relationship with the holders of cabinet office? Is there an adversarial relationship – a zero-sum approach – between government and opposition or instead evidence of consensual parliamentary practice?

As to the second sub-question about the extent to which the parliamentary opposition participates in the exercise of power, it seems reasonable to distinguish among the opposition parties. There are those whose support is necessary for a change in the legislative status quo and those parties which do not need to be consulted in the enactment of new policies because they are surplus to the functional dictates of majority-building. Drawing on the work of George Tsebelis the pertinent question would appear to be 'to what extent are non-veto players among the opposition parties consulted by the political executive and thus able to exert influence in the legislative agenda-setting process? This is viewed as the litmus test of consensual legislative behaviour in the fullest sense of the term or what I am going to refer to as 'extreme parliamentary consensualism'.

Clearly, it is important to trace the somewhat circuitous route from Lijphart's classical work on 'consensus model democracy' to the approach adopted in this book. Lijphart distinguishes two polar types of democracy. *Majoritarian democracy*, which he sees as best exemplified in Westminster, is characterised by, among other things, a simple plurality electoral system, a two-party system in parliament and a dominant executive, which concentrates power in its own hands. (Lijphart 1999: 3) Majoritarian democracy is, as David Judge has noted, "elitist, executive-centric government". (Judge 2004: 697) Moreover, Matthew Flinders' analysis of the impact of the British Labour Party's constitutional reforms since 1997 would suggest that British democracy remains as majoritarian as ever. Flinders notes that "it is clear from the analysis of Lijphart's variables that New Labour has taken greater care to implement its constitutional reforms, however precariously, within the traditional majoritarian structure of British government". (Flinders 2005: 86) He argues that Labour's constitutional reforms "represent moderate, and in some areas cosmetic adjustments to what is still quite clearly a majoritarian model of democracy". (Flinders 2005: 67) If anything, he concludes, executive dominance has increased since the advent of Labour in 1997.

In contrast to majoritarian democracy, Lijphart notes that a *consensus democracy* tries to share, disperse and limit power in a variety of ways. It is characterised by inclusiveness, bargaining and compromise and for this reason consensus democracy could also be termed "negotiation democracy". (Lijphart 1999: 2) Democratic systems are considered along two dimensions – the *executive-parties* dimension and the *federal– unitary* dimension. The five features of the consensus model of democracy in unitary states are 1) A PR electoral system 2) A multiparty system 3) Executive power-sharing in broad coalition cabinets 4) A balance of power between executive and legislature 5) Corporatist interest group systems designed to achieve compromise and concertation. (Lijphart 1999: 3)

'Majoritarian democracy' and 'consensus democracy' are viewed as ideal-types and it is argued that in reality most Western democracies will contain a mixture of majoritarian and consensual features. Manfred Schmidt, for example, notes that "in contrast to a majoritarian democracy, such as Britain or New Zealand prior to the introduction of proportional representation in 1993, the German polity involves a major non-majoritarian component [the upper chamber *Bundesrat*]. This transforms the political system of the country into a mix of majoritarian democracy and negotiation democracy". (Schmidt 2003: 102) Britain, however, may be more consensual than Schmidt appears to believe, albeit in an entirely different meaning of the term. Thus, Richard Heffernan notes strikingly that "consensus is not a particularly British phenomenon, although it has certain British peculiarities, particularly in light of the majoritarian features of Britain's non-consensual political regime. The adversarial nature of a one-dimensional, two party pluralist system, where Labour and Conservatives are deemed to stand off one against the other from behind opposed ideological redoubts, makes policy agreement theoretically unlikely. But successive forms of consensus politics demonstrates that policy association is possible". (Heffernan 2002: 744) Unlike Schmidt, who relates the non-majoritarian element in German democracy to the existence of institutional checks and balances on the executive, Heffernan views the consensual element in the majoritarian British system in terms of a prevailing set of policy ideas. Probing the notions of 'policy continuity' and 'policy change', he conceptualises consensus as a "framework in which policy is built around dominant ideas and where political choices are structured by a predominant policy paradigm". (Heffernan 2002: 743) At present, he claims, British governments work within a neo-liberal consensus in economic policy.[6]

It seems, therefore, that there will be majoritarian democracies with consensual elements and consensus democracies with majoritarian elements. The problem appears to lie in distinguishing which is which and how much there is of both and this task is not materially assisted by Lijphart's claim that "most democracies have significant or even predominantly consensual traits". (Lijphart 1999: 7) Take the case of the Irish Republic for example. Put baldly, this has three of Lijphart's five consensual features along the executive-parties dimension.

First, there is a multi-party Dáil in which six parties are represented – Fianna Fáil with 81 seats, Fine Gael 31, Labour 21, Progressive Democrats 8, Greens 5 (and 14 others). Next, there is a proportional electoral system based on single transferable voting. Third, there is a strongly corporatist approach to economic policy management, reflected in the so-called social partnership model. As Neil Collins has observed: "The consensual nature of politics is very much reflected in state-industry relations. Ireland has corporatist institutional arrangements of the type found in several small European countries. These bring together business, labour and government in a concerted effort to establish consensus on major economic policies". (Collins 2004: 603) However, Ireland has a stable majoritarian-style minimal winning coalition comprising Fianna Fáil and Progressive Democrats. In other words, there is not evidence of executive power-sharing in a broad governing coalition nor, given the stability of the coalition, is there evidence of an executive–legislative balance of power. So the question is: 'Is Ireland, applying Lijphart's criteria, a predominantly consensual or essentially majoritarian democracy? I shall return to the problem of 'fit' in relation to characterising the Scandinavian democracies shortly. In the Irish case, however, Marsh and Mitchell have absolutely no doubts. "Ireland has a Westminster-style system in which office is a pre-requisite for policy influence. In fact, the opportunities for the opposition to have policy influence are even more curtailed than in Westminster itself." (Marsh and Mitchell 1999: 37)

Perhaps the 'soul' of a democracy should be sought in the nature of its political culture since Lijphart claims that "a consensus democracy may not be able to take root and thrive unless it is supported by a consensual political culture". (Lijphart 1999: 306) Leif Lewin, analysing the Swedish case, brings out the differential normative base of the two democratic models. Majoritarian democracy stresses *accountable government*; consensus democracy, at least in its Swedish variant, gives priority to *representative government*. "By sharing power with the parties in opposition and including them in the rule of the country, the government is supposed to be regarded as representative of the people as a whole and consequently one that all can feel loyal to." (Lewin 1998: 203)

Clearly in Lijphart's schema, 'consensus democracy' is an empirically-derived ideal-type, which draws much of its inspiration from the small West European democracies. Yet, far from being uniform, the institutional and cleavage structures of the small continental democracies have varied appreciably. For example, none of the Nordic countries has a federal form of government, none has any longer a bicameral legislature and none has manifested linguistic or religious divisions on the scale of Lijphart's two examples of consensual democracy, Belgium and Switzerland. In his earlier work in the 1960s, the likes of Belgium, Holland and Austria are regarded as *consociational democracies* in which overarching elite co-operation serves to counter the potentially disruptive implications of highly segmented political societies. More recently, however, Lijphart has seemed to equate and conflate the terms 'consensus democracy' and 'consociational democracy' and, as a consequence, the consensus democracy category (leaving aside issues relating to the conceptual clarity of the term) has become too broad to be useful. All but a handful of Westminster-style majoritarian systems fall, if only by default, into the consensual category – Italy, for example!

Equally, two features of consensus democracy along the executive-parties dimension appear difficult to reconcile. The first posits that there is executive power-sharing in broad coalition cabinets. The consensus principle is to let all or most of the important parties share governmental power in a broad coalition. The second, however, refers to an executive–legislative balance of power. It is not obvious *prima facie*, and not really explained later, how a 'surplus majority' coalition – as say in Finland between 1995–2003 – can facilitate a more independent legislature and/or a legislative–executive equilibrium. In practice, the reverse would seem far more likely to be the case.

There are also problems of 'fit'. Although Lijphart regards the Nordic states as consensual democracies, they meet at best four and at worst only two of his five executive-parties features. Of course they all have PR electoral systems and multiparty assemblies. However, only Finland has a recent history of governing coalitions broader than the 'minimal winning' variety, corporatism appears in decline, at least in Denmark, Norway and Sweden, and it is not at all clear that there has been a balance of power between executive and legislature. Perhaps the crucial extra ingredient – the added value, so to speak – is the existence or otherwise of a consensual political culture (as Lewin has emphasised in the Swedish case). But this is difficult to define and operationalise and Lijphart does not do so. True, he adumbrates the consensual principle clearly enough. Whereas majoritarian democracy is based on government by the majority of the people, consensus democracy is based on government by as many people as possible. Majority rule is merely a minimum requirement. Rather, consensus democracy is characterised by inclusiveness, bargaining and compromise and these, it must be assumed, are the vital components of a consensual political culture.

Lijphart does not conceal his preference for consensus democracy. "Majoritarian democracies suffer not only from their in-built tendency towards a 'tyranny of the majority', but also from a tendency to produce conflict resolutions of the zero-sum type, such as in a winner-takes-all game. It is largely for these reasons that majoritarian democracies are hardly suitable for integrating opposition parties, nor are they particularly well equipped to integrate adversarial minorities." (Schmidt 2002: 151) As Rudy Andeweg has written, "a consensus democracy rather than a Westminster-style majoritarian democracy was necessary when Dutch society was still divided by deep social cleavages of class and religion" although he notes that "the social segmentation of the past has largely eroded". (Andeweg 2004: 569) In any event, reference to the integration of the opposition parties brings us back to the essential nature of the government–opposition relationship in consensual democracies and probably the most important, and problematical of Lijphart's five features along the executive-parties dimension, a balance of power between executive and legislature. As he himself observes, "the contrast between executive dominance and executive-legislative balance is a very important aspect of the difference between majoritarian and consensus forms of democracy". (Lijphart 2003: 20)

Executive dominance in short is regarded as incompatible with consensus democracy and the degree of executive dominance is measured by reference to the durability of cabinets. "A cabinet that stays in power for a long time is likely to be dominant vis-à-vis the legislature and a short-lived cabinet is likely to be relatively weak." (Lijphart 1999: 129) Clearly, however, when government stability is contingent on support from parties outside the cabinet – that is, a *legislative coalition* – the dependency relationship does not indicate executive dominance. Lijphart recognises this when stating that minority cabinets (and these have been both routine and relatively stable in metropolitan Scandinavia) "are by their very nature at the mercy of the legislature in parliamentary systems and can, therefore, not be expected to dominate their legislatures". (Lijphart 1999: 136) Equally, drawing on evidence of backbench rebellions in the House of Commons, Lijphart hypothesises that 'surplus majority' cabinets will encourage parliamentarians to vote against their own government in certain circumstances. In his words, "we can expect greater legislative independence when cabinets are oversized rather than minimal winning". (Lijphart 1999: 136)

Plainly, Lijphart's belief is that executive dominance is likely to be greatest when stable minimal winning coalitions or single-party majority cabinets are in power. The fact that (outside Iceland) both have been rare in the Nordic states in recent years would on the face of it suggest a lack of executive dominance. But have the relatively stable minority governments that have been routine in Denmark, Norway and Sweden over the last four decades led to a balance of power between executive and legislature? Furthermore, have the surplus majority cabinets that have been a feature in Finland since the mid-1960s really enhanced the independence of the legislature? "In real political life", Lijphart notes, "a variety of patterns [of legislative–executive relations] between complete balance and severe imbalance can occur". (Lijphart 1999: 116) Yet while executive dominance is the essence of the majoritarian model of democracy, it is not clear what a "more balanced executive-legislative relationship" is and when it may be said to exist.

Interestingly, the notion of a balanced relationship between executive and legislature is at the core of one of the three types of parliamentary democracy, which Alan Siaroff has identified. (Siaroff 2003: 445–464) There are those systems where there is "executive dominance over the legislature"; those polarised systems where there is "a central role for a fragmented parliament"; and those where there is "fused parliamentarism" with "co-operative policy-making diffusion". Significantly, Siaroff views Norway and indeed (since 1948) Sweden as cases of executive–legislative balance systems, which provide institutional checks and balances on cabinet dominance and conduce towards "co-operative policy-making diffusion" and increased policy consensus. He alludes to the importance, among other things, of corporatism, limits on the early dissolution of parliament (not possible in Norway), an institutionalised committee system, a proportionate sharing of committee chairs and the existence of an incompatibility rule preventing ministers from being at the same time MPs. However, he appears to underestimate the power of parties as cohesive legislative actors – vitiating to a degree the autonomy of standing committees – and the salience of the mathematics of the party balance in the assembly in determining the nature of the legislative–executive relationship.

In his influential work on 'veto players' in which he focuses on policy outcomes, George Tsebelis uses the term 'executive domination' to refer to the government's power to set the parliamentary agenda rather than using the variable 'government duration' à la Lijphart. It is a matter of 'agenda control', that is the government's ability to have its proposals accepted the way they are, as opposed to having them massively amended by parliament. The ability to control the agenda will relate to the existence of 'partisan veto players' and 'institutional veto players'. Veto players are "individual or collective actors whose agreement is necessary for a change of the status quo". (Tsebelis 2002: 2) *Institutional veto players* are generated by the constitution of a country and its prescription of the rules and structures of the political game. *Partisan veto players* are generated by the political game so that each country will have its own configuration of veto players. In analysing the extent of policy stability, Tsebelis brings out the relevance of a) the number of veto players b) the ideological distance between them and c) the extent to which they are internally cohesive.

Summing up, agenda control, Tsebelis contends, will obviously be contingent on positional (political factors) and will be facilitated when governments have a majority or are located at the centre of the policy space, able readily to work with groups to left and right. However, Tsebelis also argues that the interaction between executive and legislature is regulated by an institutional variable in the form of the rules defining legislative agenda-setting. (Tsebelis 2002: 92) For example, in exceptional circumstances, a government may make a piece of proposed legislation a matter of confidence. It may also have the exclusive right to introduce money bills, control the timetable of parliamentary committees and so on. Challengingly, Tsebelis goes so far as to argue that "minority governments are equipped with significant positional and institutional weapons that enable them (most of the time) to impose their will on parliament, just as majority governments do." (Tsebelis 2004: 175)

In Lijphart's schema consensus democracy is marked by a legislative–executive balance, which is not operationalised and is presumed to exist when there is not a situation of executive domination. There is no proxy for legislative–executive balance. Yet, as we shall examine fully in chapter 4, there are three possible configurations underpinning the relationship between government and parliament. There are *minimal winning coalitions* (including single-party governments in a two-party system); 'oversized' or *surplus majority coalitions*; and *minority governments*. In minimal winning and surplus majority coalitions, the participants in the *executive coalition* will be 'partisan veto players'. When minority governments hold office the participants in the *legislative coalition* will be partisan veto players. Equally, it seems reasonable to think that in practice during periods of minority government, the parliamentary opposition will comprise partisan veto players and parties that are not normally veto players.

Identifying veto players is no simple matter in qualitative research. It may be difficult in practice to distinguish between different types of veto players and their relative veto power. (Ganghof 2003: 17) Politics and policy-making are dynamic and circumstantial. None the less, it is clear that the rules relating to legislative enactment may limit the capacity of all but the very broadest-based governments to impose their preferences and, accordingly, oblige a measure of consultation with opposition groupings that are not normally veto players. For example, article 42 of the Danish constitution allows one-third of *Folketing* members to refer to a referendum a bill that has already completed its passage through parliament and only awaits the royal assent. The main exclusions under article 42 include finance, taxation (direct and indirect), naturalisation and expropriation bills. In his analysis of the impact of article 42, Mads Qvortrup insists that "the significance of the provision should not be measured solely by the single occasion – in 1963 – when it was brought into use. Rather, its infrequent use serves to emphasise that the provision has encouraged the search for consensus in Danish politics". (Qvortrup 2000: 18) Qvortrup's interviews with opposition party spokespersons, however, reveal that only the major opposition parties have found article 42 an efficient alternative to the upper chamber *Landstinget,* which was abolished as part of the constitutional reform in 1953. (Qvortrup 2000: 25) For the smaller opposition parties, the threshold of one-third of parliamentarians has simply been too high.

In Finland until 1992 a nexus of qualified majority rules compelled the government to consult with the leading opposition party on a range of important policy measures, including changes in the level of taxation that were designed to be in force for longer than a year. The qualified majority provisions were in large measure a legacy of Russification at the turn of the last century – that is, Czar Nicholas 11's attempt to reduce such basic Finnish institutions as the army, post office and currency as part of a wider programme of centralisation within the Empire. Their retention in the post-independence form of government reflected parliament's concern to protect citizens against any further violations of their fundamental rights and freedoms. (Arter 1987: 49–50)

Reference to the particular rules of legislative enactment – article 42 in Denmark or the qualified majority requirements in Finland until 1992 – leads to the final stage of our discussion and the method of classifying democracies adopted in this book. This draws on the approaches of Anthony McGann and particularly Steffen Ganghof, both of whom take Lijphart to task for conflating rules and behaviour. In emphasising a rules-based approach, McGann notes that Lijphart's distinction between 'majoritarian' and 'consensual' democracy confuses consensual outcomes with consensual institutions. He concludes that, "the consensual democracy literature portrays the consensual democracies as a different kind of democracy. However, the typical institutions of consensual democracy (proportional representation at the electoral stage, majority rule at the decision-making stage) are those dictated by the most democratic principles. Far from being a new form, the institutions of consensual democracy are the most basic type of democratic institutions. Rather than inventing a new species of democracy, it would be better to refer to it simply as *simple democracy*". (McGann 2004 – my italics)

Ganghof is particularly concerned to exclude observable patterns of elite interaction from the measurement of democratic structures. He identifies three types of democracy based exclusively on the formal institutional rules. First, *supermajoritarian democracies* are those in which the search for consensus is required by institutional minority vetoes. Next, *true majoritarian systems* combine PR and legislative majority rule and in these democracies the search for consensus may emerge as a by-product of the majoritarian legislative rules. Finally, a *pluralitarian democracy* combines a plurality electoral system, such as in the UK, with legislative majority rules. Two conclusions from Ganghof's critique of Lijphart need emphasis. Clearly, the logic of his analysis is that the notion of consensual democracy as a distinct sub-type should be abandoned. Moreover, majoritarian democracy, far from being incompatible with consensual parliamentary practices, will foster varying degrees of consensual legislative behaviour. In Ganghof's words, "legislative majority rule, if combined with electoral proportionality, does not necessarily prevent behavioural patterns generally perceived as consensual. On the contrary ... it can contribute to them". (Ganghof 2005)

Of course, it could reasonably be objected that in practice the dividing line between institutional rules and legislative behaviour can be difficult to draw. For example, Giliberto Capano and Marco Giuliani have argued in the case of the Italian Chamber of Deputies that consensual norms have become institutionalised and therefore *de facto* rules. They note that "twenty years of reform of internal procedures have proven incapable of substantially affecting the historically rooted consensual style that characterises parliamentary life". (Capano and Giuliani 2003: 15) They add that "consensual law-making persisted throughout the 1990s by simply changing its institutional setting (from the committee room to the plenum) whilst the decreasing number of laws approved in the permanent committees has been matched by an almost equivalent increase in the number of laws approved by assemblies with oversized majorities". (Capano and Giuliani 2003: 28)

Nonetheless, it is clear that, based on the formal institutional rules (PR + legislative majorities), most West European systems, including those in Scandinavia, are majoritarian democracies with varying degrees of consensual parliamentary practice. Accordingly, the broad focus of the final chapters of this book is the legislative–executive relationship and the central question of how consensual is legislative practice in the Nordic countries. The assumption is that it is possible to chart the extent of consensualism in the executive-legislative relationship on the basis of the degree and mode of inter-party negotiation across the government–opposition divide. Exclusionary government–opposition relations – in which the opposition is excluded from the legislative-building process and which are associated in Ganghof's schema with Westminster-style pluralitarian systems – are viewed as the antithesis of consensual legislative behaviour.

The suggestion is that it is possible to envisage a continuum of consensual legislative practice based on the size, scope and duration of the legislative coalitions formed between the party(ies) in government and one or more opposition parties. Inclusionary government–opposition relations involve building legislative coalitions that can be outsized or minimal winning, cover a broad spectrum of policies or be issue-based and have a short or longer lifespan. The following three types seek to combine all these elements, albeit in a rather impressionistic fashion. The qualitative adjective (ad hoc, binding, extreme) is a composite, which strives to incorporate all three dimensions of legislative coalitions, while bringing out the predominant trait.

Ad hoc parliamentary consensualism seeks to capture the essence of a style of legislative majority-building, which involves diverse, changing and flexible patterns of legislative alliances across the government–opposition divide. This type of *ad hoc* consensualism is characterised by fluctuating legislative coalitions, negotiated essentially on an issue-by-issue basis, which manifest a low degree of formalism, variable majorities and have a generally short duration. Among the Scandinavian countries, Norway would appear broadly to fit this pattern. (Christiansen 2005)

Binding parliamentary consensualism endeavours to depict the situation in which the government is reliant for its legislative majority on a pact with one or more opposition parties, which give it in practice a regular majority on a range of agreed policies. Binding consensualism involves policy-making on the basis of more or less formalised legislative coalitions, often described in a binding document, which will embrace a spectrum of policy areas and usually be minimal winning in character. So-called 'contract parliamentarism' in Sweden may well fit into this category. (Aylott and Bergman 2004)

A limiting case of consensual legislative practice would involve the incorporation into the legislative majority of opposition parties whose support is not numerically necessary to the functional dictates of majority-building. This type of broad-gauge or *extreme parliamentary consensualism* will typically witness the inclusion of non-veto playing opposition parties into 'surplus majority legislative coalitions', of both short or longer duration, albeit most typically negotiated on specific pieces of legislation. Denmark, with its 'package deal parliamentarism' would seem to fit this limiting type. Two-thirds of the package deal agreements (*forlig*) have comprised surplus majority legislative coalitions. (Christiansen 2005)

So, to sum up, this book does not view the Nordic states as consensual democracies. Rather, from a rules-based perspective, they are all majoritarian democracies, which display varying degrees of consensual legislative practice. In order to paint a more nuanced picture, the contrasting cases of Finland, a 'supermajoritarian democracy' until 1992, and Sweden, a majoritarian system but with a reputation for consensual decision-making, are explored in some detail. This is done primarily on the basis of interviews with the opposition party leaders and senior opposition politicians in both countries. The types and brief profiles of the opposition parties in these two states are presented, along with a discussion of the policy-making system in the parliamentary party groups of the opposition parties. There is then a case-study of a highly adversarial episode in Finnish politics, which came to be known as the 'Midsummer Bomb 2003'. Finally, there is an elaboration of the shifting majorities and multilateral opposition that have characterised Swedish politics over the last decade. The last chapter reviews the nature of consensual legislative practice, both in the two case-study countries and more widely in the Nordic region as a whole.

Notes

1   According to the results of a survey undertaken by 'Norway 2005' – the body responsible for co-ordinating the celebration of the centenary of Norwegian independence – the Danes believe that the Norwegians , with their "long ball game" threaten to kill football as a sport. 'Kysely: Norja on kylmä ja pimeä valaanpyynti maa' *Helsingin Sanomat* 22.9.2004

2   'Norwegians join islanders in homage to Shetland Bus' *Sunday Herald* 22.6.2003.

3   There are presently 87 members of the Nordic Council. Sweden and Norway have 20 seats each, Finland 18, Denmark 16 and Iceland 7. The Home Rule territories of Greenland, Faeroes and Åland have 2 seats each.

4   The responsible national ministers meet as the Nordic Council of Ministers. From January 2006 Nordic Council of Ministers' meetings will cover only 11 rather than the previous 18 policy sectors. They are the labour market and the working environment; business, industry, energy and regional policy; fisheries, agriculture, forestry and food; cultural co-operation; gender equality; legislation; environmental protection issues; social and health affairs; education, training and research; and economic and fiscal policy. The Ministers for Nordic Co-operation will make up an eleventh Council of Ministers. 'Norden – the Top of Europe' Electronic newsletter July 2005. http://www.norden.org/topofeurope.

5   Nordic Council and Council of Ministers, *Newsletter* 1, February 2004.

6   It might reasonably be argued that there are institutional checks and balances even in Westminster. The compromise forced on the Labour government during the enactment of the 'Prevention of Terrorism Bill' in March 2005 is a case in point. The *Sunday Herald* commented that "the only cause for optimism in the whole sorry mess was a reaffirmation of the value of the House of Lords, not just as a revising chamber, but as a safeguard against a government in love with the politics of the bulldozer". 'A 30-hour battle over anti-terror laws and it's still bad legislation' *Sunday Herald* 13.3.2005

References

Archer, Clive and Nigel Nugent 'Introduction: Small States and the European Union' *Current Politics and Economics of Europe* 11, 1, 2002, pp. 1–10
Andeweg, Rudy 'Parliamentary Democracy in the Netherlands' *Parliamentary Affairs*

57, 3, 2004, pp. 568–580

Arter, David *Politics and Policy-Making in Finland* (Wheatsheaf: Sussex, 1987)

Arter, David *Scandinavian Politics Today* (Manchester University Press: Manchester, 1999)

Arter, David *The Scottish Parliament: A Scandinavian-style Assembly?* (Frank Cass: London and Portland, OR, 2004)

Arter, David (2004b) 'Parliamentary Democracy in Scandinavia' *Parliamentary Affairs* 57, 3, 2004, pp. 581–600

Aylott, Nicholas and Torbjörn Bergman 'Almost in Government, But Not Quite: The Swedish Greens, Bargaining Constraints and the Rise of Contract Parliamentarism' ECPR Joint Sessions of Workshops, Uppsala, April 2004

Bergström, Hans 'Sweden's Politics and Party System at the Crossroads' *West European Politics* 14, 1, 1991, pp. 8–30

Capano, Giliberto and Marco Giuliani 'The Italian Parliament: In Search of a New Role?' *The Journal of Legislative Studies* 9, 2, 2003, pp. 8–34

Christiansen, Flemming Juul 'Inter-Party Co-operation in Scandinavia. Minority Parliamentarism and Strong Parliaments' ECPR Joint Sessions of Workshops, Granada, 14–19 April 2005

Collins, Neil 'Parliamentary Democracy in Ireland' *Parliamentary Affairs* 57, 3, 2004, pp. 601–612

Consultative Steering Group *Shaping Scotland's Parliament* (Scottish Office: Edinburgh, 1999)

Crawford, B. E. *Scandinavian Scotland* (Leicester University Press: Leicester, 1987)

Duverger, Maurice 'A New Political System Model: Semi-Presidential Government' *European Journal of Political Research* 8, 1980, pp. 165–187

Einhorn, Eric S. and John Logue *Modern Welfare States* Second Edition (Praeger: Westport, CT and London, 2003)

Elder, Neil, Alastair H. Thomas and David Arter *The Consensual Democracies? The Government and Politics of the Scandinavian States* (Martin Robertson: Oxford, 1982)

Elgie, Robert 'Semi-Presidentialism: Concepts, Consequences and Contesting Explanations' *Political Studies Review* 2, 3, 2004, pp. 314–330

Elklit, Jørgen 'Party Behaviour and the Formation of Minority Coalition Governments: Danish Experience from the 1970s and 1980s', in Wolfgang C. Müller and Kaare Strøm *Policy, Office or Votes?* (Cambridge University Press: Cambridge, 1999), pp. 63–88

Esping-Andersen, Gøsta *Politics against markets. The social democratic road to power.* (Princeton University Press: Princeton, NJ, 1985)

Flinders, Matthew 'Majoritarian Democracy in Britain: New Labour and the Constitution' *West European Politics* 28, 1, 2005, pp. 61–93

Ganghof, Steffen 'Promises and Pitfalls of Veto Player Analysis' *Swiss Political Science Review* 9, 2, 2003, pp. 1–25

Ganghof, Steffen 'Retrieving True Majoritarianism. On Mapping and Theorizing Parliamentary Democracies' MPI fg Discussion Paper (Max Planck Institute for the Study of Societies: Cologne, 2005)

Graham-Campbell, James and Colleen E. Batey *Vikings in Scotland* (Edinburgh University Press: Edinburgh, 1998)

Gustafsson, Gunnel and Jeremy Richardson 'Post-Industrial Changes in Policy Style' *Scandinavian Political Studies* 3, 1, 1980, pp. 21–37

Hallerberg, Mark 'Electoral Laws, Government and Parliament', in Herbert Döring and Mark Hallerberg (eds) *Patterns of Parliamentary Behaviour* (Ashgate: Aldershot, 2004), pp. 11–33

Heffernan, Richard "'The Possible as the Art of Politics' Understanding Consensus Politics" *Political Studies* 50, 2, 2002, pp. 742–760

Heidar, Knut 'Comparative Perspectives on the Northern Countries', in Knut Heidar (ed.) *Nordic Politics* Comparative Perspectives (Universitetsforlaget: Oslo, 2004), pp. 262–270

Howarth, David *The Shetland Bus* (The Lyons Press: New York, 2001)

Judge, David 'What happened to Parliamentary Democracy in the United Kingdom?' *Parliamentary Affairs* 57, 3, 2004, pp. 682–701

Lewin, Leif 'Majoritarian and Consensus Democracy: the Swedish Experience' *Scandinavian Political Studies* 21, 3, 1998, pp. 195–206

Lijphart, Arend *Patterns of Democracy: Government Forms and Performance in Thirty-Six Countries* (Yale University Press: New Haven and London, 1999)

Lijphart, Arend 'Negotiation Democracy versus Consensus Democracy. Parallel Conclusions and Recommendations' *European Journal of Political Research* 41, 1, 2002, pp. 107–113

Lijphart, Arend 'Measurement Validity and Institutional Engineering – Reflections on Rein Taagepera's Meta-Study' *Political Studies* 51, 1, 2003, pp. 20–25

Marsh, Michael and Paul Mitchell 'Office, Votes and then Policy: Hard Choices for Political Parties in the Republic of Ireland 1981–1992', in Wolfgang C. Müller and Kaare Strøm (eds) *Policy, Office or Votes?* (Cambridge University Press: Cambridge, 1999), pp. 36–62

McGann, Anthony J. 'The Calculus of Consensual Democracy' Paper presented at the Annual Meeting of the American Political Science Association, Chicago, IL, 2–5 September 2004

McRae, Kenneth D. *Conflict and Compromise in Multilingual Societies – Finland* (Wilfrid Laurier University Press: Waterloo, Ontario, Canada, 1997)

Mitchell, James 'New Parliament: New Politics in Scotland' *Parliamentary Affairs* 53, 3, 2000, pp. 605–621

Müller, Wolfgang C. and Kaare Strøm 'Conclusions: Party Behaviour and Representative Democracy', in Wolfgang C. Müller and Kaare Strøm (eds) *Policy, Office, or Votes? How Political Parties in Western Europe Make Hard Decisions* (Cambridge University Press: Cambridge, 1999), pp. 279–309

Qvortrup, Mads 'Checks and Balances in a Unicameral Parliament: The Case of the Danish Minority Referendum' *The Journal of Legislative Studies* 6, 3, 2000, pp. 15–28

Petersson, Olof *The Government and Politics of the Nordic Countries* (Fritz: Stockholm, 1994)

Rommetvedt, Hilmar 'Resources Count, but Votes Decide? From Neo-corporatist Representation to Neo-pluralist Parliamentarism: the Case of Norway' Paper presented at the ECPR Joint Sessions, Granada, 14–19 April 2005

Sannerstedt, Anders 'Negotiations in the Riksdag', in Lars-Göran Stenelo and Magnus Jerneck (eds), *The Bargaining Democracy* (Lund University Press: Lund, 1996), pp. 17–58

Schmidt, Manfred G. 'Political Performance and Types of Democracy. Findings from Comparative Studies' *European Journal of Political Research* 41, 1, 2002, pp. 147–163

Schmidt, Manfred G. *Political Institutions in the Federal Republic of Germany* (Oxford University Press: Oxford, 2003)

Siaroff, A. 'Varieties of Parliamentarism in the Advanced Industrial Democracies' *International Political Science Review* 24, 4, 2003, pp. 445–464

Svensson, Bo *Politics and Business in the Barents Region* (Fritzes: Stockholm, 1998)

Taagepera, Rein 'Arend Lijphart's Dimensions of Democracy: Logical Connections and Institutional Design' *Political Studies* 51, 1, 2003, pp. 1–19

Thorhallsson, Baldur (ed.) *Iceland and European Integration* (Routledge: London and New York, 2004)

Togeby, Lise, Jørgen Goul Andersen, Peter Munk Christiansen, Torben Beck Jørgensen and Signild Vallgårda *Power and Democracy in Denmark. Conclusions.* (Magtutredningen: Aarhus, 2003)

Tsebelis, George *Veto Players: How Political Institutions Work* (Russell Sage Foundation: New York, 2002)

Tsebelis, George 'Veto Players and Law Production', in Herbert Döring and Mark Hallerberg, *Patterns of Parliamentary Behaviour* (Ashgate: Aldershot, 2004), pp. 169–200

2

Preferential list voting systems in Denmark, Finland and Sweden: a challenge to the 'party democracy model'?

The next six chapters address the first of the three central questions posed in this book, namely 'what, if any, are the distinctive features of the Nordic political systems when compared with the Westminster model of democracy?' A number of obvious differences will be identified. 1) The existence of PR list electoral systems across the Nordic region – in contrast to the British single-member, simple plurality system – complemented by historic preferential voting provisions in Denmark and Finland and the recent introduction in Sweden of the option of voting for an individual candidate. 2) Since the introduction of PR and the completion of mass democracy, the existence of a notably uni-dimensional form of multipartism in Scandinavia underpinned, even more than in the UK, by strikingly high levels of class voting. 3) The traditional electoral strength of social democratic-labour parties in metropolitan Scandinavia reflected, particularly in Sweden, in a governmental presence far exceeding the tenure in office of the British Labour Party (even including the Blair cabinets since 1997). 4) Compared with the single-party cabinets in Westminster, the existence of an exceptionally wide variety of types of coalition governments in the Nordic states, ranging from the 'surplus majority' coalitions in Finland to minority coalitions in Denmark, Norway and Sweden. In Finland and Iceland, moreover, the majority coalitions have routinely involved both socialist and non-socialist parties. 5) Compared with the majority governments in Westminster, the frequency of minority governments has been a feature of legislative–executive relations in metropolitan Scandinavia. 6) Compared with the at times fractious, or at least strained relations between the government and the main interest groups in the UK, there has been a tradition in the Nordic states (outside Iceland) of power-sharing or corporatism in macro-economic policy management.

These points will be elaborated in the chapters that follow. However, despite the demonstrable differences between Scandinavia practice and the

Westminster model of majoritarian democracy, the differences do not *ipso facto* signify that the Scandinavian states are consensus model democracies – not, at least, if, as suggested in chapter 1, a rules-based approach is adopted. Nor is it suggested that the distinguishing features of political practice identified above indicate the existence of a 'Nordic model of government'. Some of the features apply to some of the Scandinavian states more than others, rather than being universal characteristics with equal validity across the region. Moreover, there appear to be common denominators between British and Nordic practice, particularly the growth in the importance of the role and office of prime minister. Finally, the intra-regional differences may be declining and the Scandinavian states converging as standard 'continental European' parliamentary democracies. This point will be taken up in chapter 7. However, the present chapter concentrates on electoral arrangements in the Nordic countries and in particular whether the preferential list voting systems have constituted a challenge to the 'party democracy model'.

All the Nordic states have standard 'continental' PR list voting systems in which as a basic principle the aggregate vote for a party list determines the allocation of seats to that list. True, the rules (divisor) for calculating the basic quota for successful candidates vary. However, Denmark, Finland and Sweden offer citizens a greater choice than the widespread practice of simply voting for a party list on which the ordering of successful candidates is predetermined by a party selectorate. In the three aforementioned Scandinavian countries, votes for individual candidates matter in the allocation of seats on the party list. In fact, in Finland since 1958 voters have been obliged to vote for a particular list candidate whereas in Denmark since 1920 and Sweden since 1998 they have had the option of doing so. In contrast, a proposal in 2003 to introduce personal preference voting for Norwegian general elections was rejected by parliament. The present discussion examines the working of the preferential list voting systems in Denmark, Finland and Sweden. Have they loosened the party stranglehold on elections and/or had other consequences for the behaviour of the political system?

In their analysis of conflict and consensus in the committees of the West European parliaments, Erik Damgaard and Ingvar Mattson assume, along with Gary Cox, that the political system becomes more competitive and, thus more conflictual, when voters have a chance to cast a ballot for individual candidates. They validate this assumption with the claim that: "If candidate votes are possible, then the level of conflict increases in parliament. We interpret this as a sign of an increased level of competition among parliamentarians". (Damgaard and Mattson 2004: 139) The ramifications (if any) of the existence of preferential list voting arrangements for the behaviour of parliamentarians remain systematically to be examined. However, anecdotal evidence of a greater 'individualisation' of the activities of MPs at the expense of collective deliberation and decision-making in the parliamentary party groups is noted elsewhere in this book. It is at least safe to suppose that the existence of a preferential list voting system will have implications for recruitment on to party lists, the electoral strategies of the political parties, the choice available to citizens between 'candidate voting' and 'party voting' and the type of candidate elected. Preferential voting might also increase civic interest in politics, which would in turn become less anonymous.

Finland: a "strong preferential list voting system"

Finland's system of *strong preferential list voting* is one of the oldest of its kind in the world. (Karvonen 2004: 203–226) The specifics of the present electoral system date back only to 1958, when the length of the parliamentary term was increased from three to four years.[1] But Finnish voters have for nearly a century been able – in reality had no choice but – to choose between candidates on party lists in electing the 200-seat Eduskunta. The introduction of a PR electoral system, which allowed voters to express preference between candidates, accompanied the shift to a unicameral legislature based on universal suffrage (including women) in 1906. Finland was then a Grand Duchy of the Czarist Russian empire and parliamentary and electoral reform were a by-product of Nicholas II's October Manifesto of 1905. Moreover, not only did the introduction of a preferential voting system antedate the emergence of mass parties in Finland, it also reflected a measure of suspicion towards parties, particularly in right-wing circles. The Election Act of 1906 did not contain a single reference to the word 'party'. As Klaus Törnudd has observed: "The organisational network of political parties was still imperfect and the drafters of the law apparently expected that many other groups of citizens would nominate candidates". (Törnudd 1968: 36)

Initially, citizens were afforded considerable personal discretion in casting their ballots. Until the electoral reform of 1935, they had three options. They could either support a list, alter the ordering of candidates on a list or even constitute a list of their own. This they did by setting out the names, occupations and addresses of not more than three eligible persons in the space provided on the ballot paper. (Törnudd 1968: 103) In addition to the personal choice element provided through candidate voting, the Finnish electoral system has displayed other distinctive features. For example, there has never been an electoral threshold (national or constituency-level) to qualify for parliamentary representation. In Norway and Sweden the threshold is presently 4% of the national vote and in Denmark 2%. Moreover, until the 1969 Electoral

Act, there was provision for multiple candidacies in Finland and small parties in particular sought to capitalise on this by running prominent figures in many constituencies. Multiple candidacies are in fact still permitted in Sweden and in 1998 the Christian Democrats' chair, Alf Svensson, stood in all twenty-nine constituencies. Finally, strategic electoral alliances, often between a large and a small party – an instrumental arrangement made purely for their mutual benefit – have typified electoral politics in Finland.[2] Memorably, in the 1930 general election, the Agrarians and Conservatives made an electoral alliance and then built a plywood tank, which they dragged around during the campaign with the slogan 'Filthy Communists Out of Finland'.

Despite the preferential voting system, Finns over the last half century appear to have given precedence to a political party over and above an individual candidate when making their voter choice. Pertti Pesonen's analysis of electoral behaviour in the industrial city of Tampere at the 1958 general election revealed that no less than 80% of those interviewed were guided first and foremost by party and only 15% placed a particular candidate before a political party. The corresponding figures for a national sample at the 1966 general election were 67% and 31% respectively. (Törnudd 1968: 110) By the early 1990s 'candidate voting' was apparently on the increase. After the March 1991 general election voters were asked 'What was ultimately more important in your voting decision, party or candidate?' Over two-fifths (43%) said 'candidate' compared with half (51%) 'party'. A narrow majority of those under thirty years of age, especially students, regarded the choice of candidate as more important than party. (Pesonen, Sänkiaho, Borg 1993: 76) However, it is important to note that there was no provision for saying both were equally important. In the same election year 1991, 24% of voters compared the candidates of different parties before coming to a decision compared with 42% who considered the candidates of one party and 34% who considered only one candidate.

In their study based on the 1991 general election, Pertti Pesonen, Risto Sänkiaho and Sami Borg conclude that "in the long term the primacy of party has significantly declined. But the tendency has not reached the point at which the majority of voters regard the choice of candidate as more important than the choice of party". (Pesonen, Sänkiaho, Borg 1993: 74) Moreover, they add that the increase in the proportion of voters placing candidate before party in their voting decision does not always appear to stem from an overriding concern to get a particular person elected. It is possible, they insist, that a segment of the electorate regards its choice of party as so self-evident as to place greater emphasis on choosing a candidate. Equally, the selection of a particular candidate may represent a statement of dissatisfaction with the party leadership. (Pesonen, Sänkiaho and Borg 1993: 354)

Clearly, the increased importance of individual candidate voting over party voting cannot be divorced from the general decline in the strength of party allegiance. Yet the relationship is neither simple nor causal. What is evident is that the choice of candidate is a decision taken most frequently quite separately from the choice of party and most commonly during the election campaign itself. Many strong party identifiers choose their candidate late, while many of those prioritising a candidate are voters for whom party is paramount and the selection of a candidate secondary. (Pesonen, Sänkiaho and Borg 1993: 354)

In the two most recent general elections in 1999 and 2003, there is *prima facie* evidence of a reversal of the trend of the early 1990s and a growth in 'party voting' over 'candidate voting'. According to *Suomen Gallup* surveys, 61% voted principally for a party in 1999 and 64% did so in 2003. However, in the last-mentioned year, 30% of respondents stated that the choice of the next prime minister had influenced either 'significantly' or 'decisively' their choice of party.[3] Outside the Helsinki constituency (where the two main prime minister candidates, Paavo Lipponen and Anneli Jäätteenmäki, were standing), voters were obliged to back a party first (Lipponen's Social Democrats or Jäätteenmäki's Centre) and then find a suitable candidate if they wanted to influence the race for the prime minister's post.

Preferential list voting has over the years facilitated the election of 'personalities' with no prior background or experience in politics. Indeed, many parties try to get a handful of such figures on their lists to give extra publicity to their campaigns. In attracting a personal vote, a protest vote or in simply mobilising previously passive sections of the citizenry, 'personalities' can have a significant effect. Tony Halme, an 'independent' standing on a True Finn (*perussuomalainen*) list in the Helsinki constituency in 2003, appealed to those age-groups – the 25–28 years and 29–34 age-cohorts – that had previously abstained. Turnout among these groups increased by a significant 12% compared with the 1999 general election, providing evidence to contradict the conventional wisdom that the 'life cycle effect' was not working in Finland.[4]

The propensity of the parties to field a number of 'personalities' on their lists raises the complex question of the relationship between preferential voting, candidate selection and the type of candidate elected to the Eduskunta. It stands to reason that in general terms one would expect preferential voting to accentuate the need for a balanced slate of candidates. Put another way, in order to maximise votes and seats, there appears an obvious functional logic in producing lists that are representative in a socio-demographic sense. Soile Kuitinen makes the point. "Party officials are not obliged to think in terms of safe, combative and hopeless list positions, but have to pay attention to the entire list being as representative as possible in relation to the proportion of important sub-groups in society." (Kuitinen 2002: 70) In practice, many other factors are at work in constituting a party list. For example, the territorial dimension – that is, fielding candidates that represent the various districts within the constituency – seems particularly salient at the selection stage.[5]

As to the impact of a candidate-centred electoral system on the type of candidate selected – and by extension elected – the existence of preferential list voting does appear *inter alia* to have contributed to the increased representation of women in the Eduskunta. Certainly in recent elections a narrow majority of women has voted for female candidates, whereas an overwhelming majority of men (74%) has voted first and foremost for male candidates. This evidence of gender-centred voting, coupled with the increased number of female candidates and the growing proportion of women voters among the active electorate have contributed to the rise in female representation in the Eduskunta. (Kuitinen 2002: 91)

There has been little or no debate in Finland about electoral reform for general elections. However, there have been advocates of change for European Parliament elections, not least because in 1999 turnout fell to only a little over 30%. Indeed, a proposal from the minister of justice Johannes Koskinen (Social Democrat) that closed party lists should be employed for European Parliament elections prompted a lively debate in parliament and the media both for and against. The main lines of the discourse may be traced briefly, since they raise many of the issues that were discussed in Sweden prior to the incorporation of a preferential voting option (not requirement) for the 1998 Riksdag election.

When his proposal came before parliament in February 2004, Koskinen supported a shift to closed lists by claiming that parties would then concentrate on policies rather than individuals. He was supported by, among others, Kimmo Kiljunen and Jukka Vihriälä, the latter insisting that [in strong defence of the 'party democracy model'] "party power is people power".[6] However, Ben Zyskowicz, the parliamentary party group leader of the main opposition Conservative Party, rejected Koskinen's premise that closed lists would deter 'personality candidates' and get more 'competent candidates' elected. He believed that closed lists would lower the turnout still further.

The debate about electoral reform for European Parliament elections also extended to the pages of the national daily *Helsingin Sanomat*. Two contributions in particular warrant a note. The first came from Ensio Laaksonen from Vantaa near Helsinki. He stated that if closed lists were introduced he would stop voting and he added that he had voted at every level since the early 1960s. Moreover, Laaksonen emphasised that he had always voted for a candidate, not a party. Since 90% of the population does not belong to a political party, he argued, the rank ordering of candidates by a tiny selectorate based on the result of a primary was profoundly undemocratic. Furthermore, he held that the electoral law needed to be amended so as to conform to article six of the 2000 constitution. This states that no one should be placed on a different footing on the basis of age, gender, ethnicity, language, religious conviction, mental or physical health, disability or any other particularity. Laaksonen concluded that the electoral law should be modified so as to break party cartels and allow the genuine and open wish of the people to be expressed and represented.[7]

A second *Helsingin Sanomat* contribution came from Jarmo Törneblom, a recently retired civil servant with responsibilities for electoral organisation, who made a vigorous defence of closed party lists for European Parliament elections. His central contention was that open lists make elections very expensive and favour 'personality candidates' whereas a shift to closed lists would oblige the parties to produce 'proper election programmes'[8] Paavo Lipponen, the former prime minister, in an interview in the weekly *Suomen Kuvalehti*, also favoured closed party lists. He insisted that they would promote policy alternatives and raise turnout. He then used the curious line that closed lists would improve Finland's chances of gaining leading positions in the European Parliament. Committee chairs, he pointed out, are negotiated well before the election on the basis of who is in first place on closed lists. For the most part it is clear who will be elected from Germany, France and Sweden. He concluded that: "The open list system weakens Finland's chances of having an impact. Positions are divided up between those whose election is certain".[9]

None the less, outside the Leftist Alliance, which has appeared willing to experiment, there has been little support for the introduction of closed party lists for European Parliament elections. The Greens in particular have been reluctant to sanction a further increase in the power of political parties. Their objection has not been dissimilar to Laaksonen's letter, which contained a strong critique of the 'party democracy model'. In any event, turnout at the 2004 European Parliament election rose to 40.4%, less than impressive in a comparative perspective but doubtless sufficient to justify the *status quo ante* of preferential list voting.

Denmark and Sweden: "weak preferential list voting systems"

The Danish Election Act of 1920 represented a compromise, which sought to combine one of the perceived advantages of the previous plurality system – the possibility of personal voting for a candidate in a particular electoral district – with a standard PR list system. (Pedersen 2002: 47) It was agreed between the Social Liberals' (*Radikale Venstre*) minister of the interior, Ove Rode, and the Conservative, Asger Karstensen, and, as Jørgen Elklit has noted, it is remarkable how few changes to the electoral system there have been since then. (Elklit 2003: 30) As early as the first general election conducted under the new electoral system in 1920, the parties instructed voters to back them and not individual candidates and in many ways that approach has changed relatively little since. (Pedersen 1966: 173–174; Pedersen 2002: 48; Tonsgaard 1986: 381) Nonetheless, there has been a recent increase in the incidence of candidate voting. Torben Worre describes the way the number of personal votes fell significantly from 70% in 1945 to only 39% in 1966. However, by 1988 the level had risen again to 49%. He points to the way it has been lowest in the case of new parties whose local candidates are less well known to voters. (Worre 1989: 76) Erik Damgaard comments that the evidence suggests that today on average just over half of all votes are cast for parties and that there has been relatively little variation in this respect since the shift to a unicameral Folketing in 1953. It follows that just under half of all votes are given as a personal vote for a candidate on a party list, a fact, which appears to have increased competition between candidates of the same party. (Damgaard 2003: 23–24)

Turnout in Danish elections is high in a comparative perspective and has not fallen over the last fifty years. This is in contrast to developments in Norway, Sweden and particularly Finland. Only in Iceland in the Nordic region has there been a comparably high and sustained turnout as in Denmark. In the 1990s average turnout in Denmark was approximately 85%, which is a couple of percentage points lower than in the period 1960–90, but a couple higher than in the 1950s. At the 2001 general election turnout was an impressive 87% and was almost 85% in February 2005 when, following a short, three-week election campaign the Liberal (*Venstre*) prime minister, Anders Fogh Rasmussen was returned to power. Clearly then the complexities of the electoral system have not depressed levels of electoral participation. Yet when compared with the Finnish system described above, the method of presenting candidates and the various qualifying thresholds for representation in the Folketing appear complicated at very least.

In Denmark there are three main ways of arranging candidates at parliamentary elections, although since 1971 combinations of the three have been possible. First, parties may present a 'party list of candidates' (*partiliste*). The constituency party organisation (there are seventeen constituencies nationally) puts up a slate of rank-ordered candidates, albeit with the candidates selected by each of the electoral districts or 'nomination districts' (*opstillingskredse*) within the constituency placed at the top of the list in that district. There are 103 electoral districts in Denmark as a whole. Voters then cast a ballot either for the party, the candidate put up by the electoral district or one of the other candidates in the constituency. The impact of personal voting is least in the case of party lists and they are relatively uncommon today. Only really the Socialist People's Party (SF), the Red–Green Alliance (*Enhedslisten*) and the anti-immigrant Danish People's Party (DFP) run party lists in some districts.

Second, a party may present voters with an 'electoral district list' (*kredsvis opstilling*). The party's electoral district organisation selects one and only one prioritised candidate, who appears in bold type on the ballot paper. The other candidates follow in alphabetical order, and in smaller print. The 'electoral district list' is also less common than it used to be.

Finally, there is the 'co-ordinated constituency list' (*sideordnet opstilling*). All the candidates, who are presented alphabetically and bracketed together, are listed in all the electoral districts in a particular constituency. They are, in short, given parity of standing by the party. Voters then place a cross either against the name of a party or that of a particular candidate. The personal vote is for the candidate, whereas party votes are divided up among all the candidates in proportion to the number of personal votes they have received. Mogens Pedersen has referred to voting for a candidate on a co-ordinated constituency list as *effective personal voting*. (Pedersen 2002: 48) Moreover, as Damgaard has observed, the trend is towards co-ordinated constituency lists becoming the predominant form and, accordingly, the voters' influence through personal voting has increased. Conversely, the local/constituency party organisation has diminished influence over which of their candidates is elected. (Damgaard 2003: 33) The thrust of the recent Danish electoral analysis, moreover, is that co-ordinated constituency lists favour candidates who are able to attract personal votes. While this does not violate the basic representative principle, it appears to have led to heightened internal competition between candidates of the same party.

At this point a distinction must be drawn between the increased incidence and the increased impact of personal voting. Indeed, there probably remains much basic truth in Pedersen's assertion from the mid-1960s that for ordinary citizens it is difficult to gauge the likely effect of casting a personal ballot. "Even for the voter who knows a great deal about the Danish electoral system, it may be said that his possibility for judging if and to what degree a personal vote can exercise any influence on the election of candidates is extremely minimal." (Pedersen 1966: 173) There is some evidence, as in Finland, that incumbent MPs and, increasingly, women are favoured by preferential voting. Equally, the impact of preferential voting in heightening competition between candidates of the same party can easily be exaggerated. Normally (party leaders are the exception), candidates will only campaign within the boundaries of their own electoral district, a norm which is particularly strong in the Social Democratic Party. (Pedersen 2002: 46)

In a recent article, Jørgen Elklit has submitted the Danish electoral system to a brief 'democratic audit'. He identifies a variety of practical anomalies that need correcting, albeit not through legislation. For example, in order for a party to participate in a parliamentary election, it must either have been represented in the previous Folketing election or collected a number of signatures equivalent to 1/175th of the total number of valid votes cast at the previous general election. In 2001 this was just under twenty thousand. While Elklit regards these conditions as perfectly reasonable he notes that a number of changes in the collection and approval procedures have complicated the task of getting the necessary number of signatures. (Elklit 2001: 25)

He sees no case either for changing all three of the rules relating to representation in the national assembly. To qualify for the Folketing's 135 'regular seats', a party must either have gained a constituency seat or 2% of the national vote. In order to qualify for the 40 'supplementary seats' a party must have attained the average number of votes per seat in two of the three main regions – the capital city, the islands and Jutland. In relation to the first rule, no party since 1961 with less than 2% of the national vote has gained a constituency seat. However, as Elklit describes, in connection with the 1998 Folketing election, there was talk of applying this rule if the Progress Party candidate Kirsten Jacobsen performed as well as expected in North Jutland and her party fell below the qualifying threshold at the national level. In the event, the Progress Party managed 2.4% of the national vote and Jacobsen's success had, therefore, no wider significance. Even so, Elklit insists there are no grounds for abolishing the 'constituency seat' rule.

All in all, Elklit does not advocate major surgery on the present electoral system. However, from our perspective, it is significant that one of his six recommendations for electoral reform concerns increasing the salience of personal vote totals in selecting successful candidates. His recommendations in full are 1) Voting rights should be extended to incorporate Danes living abroad and the question of franchise rights for non-Danish subjects with a fixed address in Denmark postponed until a wider discussion of constitutional change. 2) The need for 150–200 supporters for non-party candidates should be increased to 3,000–4,000. 3) The qualifying threshold for 'supplementary seats' should be fixed at 1/175th of the valid national vote and not the average number of votes per seat in two of the three main regions. 4) The three large constituencies should be combined into one with a corresponding allocation of parliamentary seats. 5) The selection of the quota of elected candidates should proceed on the basis of personal votes (except of course on party lists). 6) The present number of electoral districts should be retained in view of the decline in party membership. The amalgamation of electoral districts into larger units could complicate the recruitment/nomination process.

Until 1998 Sweden had one of the most party-based electoral systems in the world. Voters voted for a party list and not an individual candidate, although they did have the (largely symbolic) right to cross out the names of those candidates on the list which they did not want elected. Moves to introduce a measure of preferential voting, however, antedated the shift to unicameralism in 1970. A Constitutional Commission proposed a system of obligatory voting for individual candidates as early as 1963. Its recommendation was not acted upon. However, a commission of inquiry (*utredning*) into preferential voting, which reported in 1993, revisited the question of voting for individual candidates, albeit within the narrow remit that "elections shall continue to be of the nature of elections between parties". (Karvonen 1999: 117) This excluded consideration of the Finnish system, it was argued, because a ballot paper that did not indicate a preference for an individual candidate was ruled invalid. In other words, it is not possible in Finland simply to vote for a party and its slate of candidates. (Karvonen 1999: 136) In fact, the Swedish electoral reform proposed by the 1993 commission, which backed a limited form of preferential voting, was largely modelled on Danish practice.

While none of the political parties was enthusiastic, and the Leftists and Greens were in practice opposed, preferential candidate voting was given a trial run at the local government elections in 1994 and European Parliament elections the following year before being introduced at the 1998 general election. A voter places a cross against the name of a candidate on the party list. If he/she gains at least 8% of the party vote in that constituency they will be eligible to be elected, irrespective of the prior ordering of candidates, providing of course that they have more votes than those placed ahead on the list. For local government and European Parliament elections, the personal vote threshold is set at 5%.

The electoral reform introduced for the 1998 general election was a compromise, which lacked active supporters among the parties. (Karvonen 1999: 116) However, in the lively media debate three main arguments were adduced in support of preferential voting. First, it was said that citizens needed to be able to identify with their elected representatives. Second, it was claimed that democracy needed to be revitalised, preferential voting would increase civic interest and politics would become less anonymous. Finally, it was held that voters would be able to call their elected representatives directly to account. (Karvonen 1999: 128) The commission on preferential voting had devoted much attention to the impact of candidate voting on female representation and here the Finnish case appears to have played an important role. (Karvonen 1999: 124) There were those who favoured the Finnish system and pointed out, along with Lauri Karvonen, that "there is no obvious contradiction between compulsory voting for individual candidates and the primary character of elections as elections between parties". (Karvonen 1999: 137) However, critics of the Finnish system held that 'personalities', known for other things than their political merits, were advantaged by preferential voting. It was argued too that there was a risk that external financial interests could affect the outcome of the election by pouring money into individual campaigns. The Finnish system was also said to lead to unhealthy conflicts between candidates on the same party list. (Karvonen 1999: 137–138) Interestingly, in the general media debate, there was scarcely a mention of the importance of being able to vote for the candidate best placed to promote the interests of the voter's own locality.

Thus far, the option of casting a preferential vote has had only a limited impact in Sweden. In 1998 30% of the active electorate availed themselves of the personal vote facility and this fell to 26% at the following general election in 2002. Moreover, the preference vote has had relatively limited effect on the number of MPs elected. In 1998 twelve candidates improved their positions on the party list and were returned on the strength of their personal vote; in 2002, the figure was ten. Advocates of strengthening the personal vote element point to the way in densely populated constituencies, 8% of the party vote represents a high hurdle. In Stockholm county in 2002, for example, a Social Democratic candidate needed slightly more than 16,500 personal votes to change the ordering of candidates. The preferential vote has, therefore, had a greater significance in the smaller constituencies and for the smaller parties.

Although the Swedish electorate used the personal vote provision relatively sparingly when it was introduced in 1998, it attracted substantial media attention. Perhaps the most publicised case was that of Kent Härstedt, a survivor of the Estonia car-ferry disaster in 1994 and a social democrat in Helsingborg in the West Skåne constituency of southern Sweden. Härstedt finished third in his party's pre-election primary, was ultimately dropped down to sixth on his party's list, but following a vigorous campaign he emerged as the leading social democrat with almost 20% of the party's total vote. Under the previous system, Härstedt would not have been elected since the Social Democrats' total poll in West Skåne entitled it to only four MPs. (Arter 1999: 296–300) Cases like that of Härstedt made a powerful case for preferential voting.

Indeed, in order to strengthen the personal vote element, the 1999 Constitutional Commission, led by Ulf Lönnquist, considered splitting up the three largest constituencies of Stockholm county, Stockholm city and Göteborg county. In the event, this was not recommended. However, on 20 February 2004, Pär Nuder presented the main findings of a Social Democratic consultation exercise on constitutional matters, which included questions on preferential voting. The questionnaire was circulated to local party branches, the public at large and a variety of organisations. The responses on preferential voting are worth a brief note, although they did not throw up anything particularly new on either side of the argument.

Perhaps the most enthusiastic proponent of preferential list voting was the local Social Democratic (SAP) branch in Örebro (*Örebro arbetarekommun*), which stated unequivocally that "the time of anonymous party voting is past". It canvassed smaller parliamentary constituencies and a consolidated personal vote element. SAP's Student Organisation was not only committed to retaining the personal vote provision, but also to investigating the possibility of voting for more than one candidate, as well as reducing the qualifying threshold of 8%. To prevent the distortions caused by big business backing particular individuals, however, every candidate should be obliged to account for her/his campaign expenditure in a public register. A commission of inquiry should also be set up to examine ways of equalising the resources available to candidates.[10]

The SAP local branch organisation in Jakobsberg south made perhaps the most persuasive case for the *status quo ante* – that is, the existing mix of party voting and candidate voting. It noted nonetheless that the British system had much to commend it, particularly in making members of parliament better known in their constituencies and, by extension, obliging them to be more active locally throughout the parliamentary term. The Jakobsberg south branch also held that the personal vote threshold of 8% was too high and wondered why there was one threshold for parties (4% of the national vote) and another for individual candidates. The Vara local branch was typical of many submissions favouring the continued use of preferential voting. It maintained that preferential voting was a way of giving voters greater influence and offsetting the power of narrow party selectorates. It also provided an opportunity for candidates with strong individual qualities to get elected and, in providing interest for the mass media, contributed to keeping turnout at a high level. The Tullen-Bytorps branch in Borås insisted that the preferential vote had in fact had a positive effect in that candidates presented themselves better and stayed in closer touch with the people. In all these submissions, however, candidate voting was viewed as an alternative to, rather than a replacement for party voting.

Perhaps the most reactionary view of preferential voting came from the Study Circle of SAP women in Borlänge, which recommended a return to the previous system of crossing out 'undesirable candidates'. It went on that "our experience is that electors abstain from voting because, among other things, they cannot strike from the list a candidate they do not sympathise with". There were similarly strong feelings elsewhere. The Kungsbacka local branch was typical of many in arguing that "we will not accept a system in which those with wealth are able to take advantage of it. And this applies too when so-called 'personalities' engage in politics solely on the strength of their celebrity status – that is, they do a 'Schwartzenegger'. We cannot accept either that personal campaigns are sponsored on condition that candidates promote the views of economic interest groups and other organisations".

In a similar vein, the Skogsberg branch stated simply that "we do not like the preference vote and feel uneasy about any development where money can increase influence (as in the United States) and one can buy votes and influence". The potential 'Americanisation' of Swedish politics was something extensively debated when the commission on preferential voting reported in 1993. The Ängelholm local branch submitted that a personal campaign ran the risk of becoming populist and that preferential voting was a 'bourgeois project', which should not be pursued. Several SAP branches pointed to the way the preferential element in the voting system promoted individualism on the part of MPs (a variation on the Damgaard-Mattson-Cox hypothesis here), which in turn could complicate internal party work. All in all, it was clear from the feedback on the SAP consultation exercise (*rådslag*) on constitutional matters that the party was fairly evenly split on the question of the preferential voting option.

SAP has also been deeply split on 'Europe' and opposition from a section of SAP voters was the biggest contributory factor in bringing about the referendum majority against EMU membership in autumn 2003. At the 2004 European Parliament elections, preferential voting propelled the one 'Eurosceptic' on SAP's national list to success in quite sensational fashion. Anna Hedh, a young woman largely unknown outside her home district in rural south Öland, competed for one of Sweden's nineteen seats in the European Parliament in June 2004. She was placed a lowly thirty-first on SAP's national list of candidates and on the reverse side of the ballot paper. A vociferous critic of the EU and EMU, the intention of the party hierarchy was clearly that she would not be elected.[11] Yet she comfortably cleared the 5% threshold to gain over thirty thousand personal votes and a seat in the European Parliament. This was in spite of what she claimed to be harassment of her personal campaign – the removal of posters, stolen election material etc – and interference which, she believed, emanated from the Cabinet Office itself.[12] In a highly individual campaign, Hedh presented herself as a 'watchdog', guarding that no more power flowed from Sweden to Brussels. She attacked the ambitions to create an EU superstate, condemned the proposed EU constitution and criticised her own party for selling out on Swedish sovereignty. Above all, she indicted SAP with being blind to the fundamental failings of the welfare system and for having no policy at all to get unemployment down below 4%.[13]

Hedh is a relative of the EU and EMU critic, Margareta Winberg, the former SAP deputy prime minister, who was dismissed from the cabinet and despatched as Swedish ambassador to Brazil after the EMU referendum. She gained financial support from the large Trade and Transport Union and backing in general from EU critics in the labour movement. Hedh's estimate that possibly as many as one-quarter of those who voted for the anti-EU 'June List' were social democrats is hard to verify. But clearly her remarkable and much-publicised success suggests some support for the view that preferential list voting can contribute to exposing and reinforcing internal party division, albeit in this case on an issue ('Europe'), which had strained cohesion in SAP's ranks for well over a decade.

Incidentally, three women were elected as Swedish MEPs in June 2004 on the strength of their personal vote. In addition to Anna Hedh, Åsa Westlund, a previous chair of SAP's Student Organisation, who was supported in her campaign by the former prime minister Ingvar Carlsson, was successful. So, too, was the *Dagens Nyheter* journalist, Maria Carlshamre.

In Finland, then, voters must opt for a particular candidate; in Denmark and Sweden they may do so. Finland has a system of strong preferential voting because, while the aggregate list vote determines its allocation of seats, those returned to parliament are decided purely on the basis of their personal vote totals. Denmark and Sweden have weak preferential voting systems because there is no requirement to vote for an individual candidate and the determination of successful candidates is not exclusively (or in the Swedish case primarily) on the basis of personal vote scores. Finland has a so-called 'open list' system whereas this is not the case in Denmark and Sweden. Nonetheless, preferential voting has been possible in Denmark for over eight decades and in Sweden since 1998. In contrast, a proposal in 2003 to introduce personal preference voting in Norwegian general elections failed to obtain a majority in the Storting.[14] It is, however, possible in local elections.

A new electoral system was introduced in Iceland for the 2003 Alþingi election. Sixty-three MPs are elected in six constituencies. Supplementary seats are available and to qualify for these a party must receive at least 5% of the national vote. Preference voting is allowed, but only in so far as voters can cross out the names of individual candidates and/or change the rank order of candidates (much as in Sweden before 1998). However, as Svanur Kristjánsson notes, alterations to party lists have had no real impact on the selection of MPs. "The rules are like a huge sledge-hammer. They look threatening but are in fact too heavy for practical use." (Kristjánsson 2004: 157) He concludes that the political parties have repeatedly changed the electoral rules so as to eliminate any real impact of the personal vote. (Kristjánsson 204: 170)

As to a possible connection between preferential voting and turnout, Finland, the country with the longest experience of personal voting and the strongest preferential voting system, has witnessed the greatest decline in national turnout in recent decades. Turnout at the Finnish general election in 1999 fell to 68.3%. That it rose slightly in 2003 (to 69.6%) was due in some measure to the highly personalised nature of the contest between the prime minister (Lipponen) and leader of the opposition (Jäätteenmäki), both standing in the Helsinki constituency. Also standing in Helsinki was the 'loose cannon' Tony Halme, who as an independent True Finn was able to mobilise previously passive voters, especially young voters, in such working-class suburbs in the east of the city as Jakomäki. (Arter 2003: 161) Individual candidates, profiting from personal voting arrangements, can it seems raise interest and turnout at the margins, although plainly not enough to offset the weight of the general factors working to reduce levels of electoral participation. This is something we will return to when discussing the evidence of 'spectator democracy' in Scandinavia in chapter 8 of this book.

Conclusions: a challenge to the party democracy model?

In general, electoral systems serve the interests of the larger parties and the Scandinavian voting systems are no exception. In three of the five Nordic states, the largest parties at the general elections between 2001–03 were over-represented – the Finnish Centre (+6), the Swedish Social Democrats (+5) and the Norwegian Labour Party (+3) – in terms of their parliamentary seats relative to their popular vote. Equally, the smallest parliamentary parties were not under-represented on the basis of their popular vote at the polls in this same period. Only Steinar Bastesen's Coastal Party in Norway, which ran candidates in only a few constituencies but won 1.7% of the national vote, ended up with two less seats than a strictly proportional result would have yielded (it failed to select any MPs in 2005).

Nonetheless, outside Finland, small parties have to negotiate an electoral threshold to gain representation in the national legislature and the 4% barrier in Norway and Sweden and 5% in Iceland represent high hurdles when viewed in a comparative perspective. For small parties, strategic electoral alliances – that is, running joint lists of candidates – with other parties offer a possible pathway to parliament. The Finnish Christian League MP, Raimo Westerholm, was elected in 1970 from a joint list with the Centre Party in the Mikkeli constituency. Similarly, the first Swedish Christian Democratic MP, Alf Svensson, was elected in 1985 from a joint list with the Centre in Jönköping constituency. Preferential list voting can also assist small parties if they can attract a well-known public figure as a candidate. Tony Halme's success, standing as an Independent on the Real Finn list for Helsinki at the 2003 Finnish general election is the best recent example. Moreover, his celebrity status un-doubtedly benefited the (previously unelected) True Finn leader, Timo Soini, who was returned to parliament for the neighbouring constituency of Uusimaa.

Halme may have been elected as an Independent (he promptly joined the Real Finn parliamentary group), but have preferential list voting systems chal-lenged the 'party democracy model' in the sense of weakening the party strangle-hold on elections? One of the arguments expressed in the earlier discussion by advocates of personalised proportional representation – that is, open lists – was precisely that it increased voter influence and served to offset the power of narrow party selectorates.

Two immediate responses are in order. First, there is no necessary contra-diction between compulsory voting for individual candidates and the primary character of elections as a choice between parties. The Finnish evidence bears this out. The survey data indicate that a section of the electorate views its party option as so self-evident as to place greater emphasis on selecting a candidate. In any event, there is no evidence in Scandinavia in recent decades, even in the strong Finnish preferential voting system, that a majority of voters view the choice of candidate as more important than the choice of party. Second, the success of a particular candidate may represent a statement of dissatisfaction with the national party leadership and/or local party selectorate. In other words, in certain circumstances, preferential voting systems may promote or facilitate protest voting. Beyond that, it is hazardous to proceed, although preferential systems will clearly affect party selection strategies in that there are no 'hope-less positions' on the list.

Virtually all Scandinavian parliamentarians are members of party. But do elected representatives represent their parties first and foremost or do prefer-ential list voting systems (strong or weak) encourage MPs, concerned to be re-elected, to attach particular importance to constituency interests? After all, the regional dimension is symbolically expressed in the regional seating of MPs in the Swedish Riksdag and Norwegian Storting. It is not uncommon for 're-gion' to be placed ahead of 'party' in the Nordic parliaments. As Hanne Marthe Narud has observed, moreover, MPs "for peripheral parts of the territory are more alert to problems of a regional character than are representatives for central constituencies". (Narud 2004: 122) What is not clear is that personalised

PR is a significant causal variable in explaining 'constituency voting behaviour' in the Scandinavian legislatures. As Peter Esaiasson has noted, "the relatively strong support for constituency representation shows that old traditions live in the Nordic parliaments *irrespective of electoral system* or cohesive national parties". (Narud 2004: 119 – my italics). In short, Scandinavian party democracy has an accentuated territorial dimension, which is reflected in legislative behaviour, although party voting, both in the country at large and in parliament, is the norm.

Notes

1 The shift from three- to four-year parliamentary terms was approved in parliament by 140–40 votes on 11 May 1954. It was opposed by the Communists, who argued that it was an attempt to restrict democracy on the part of the representatives of large-scale capital, giving them longer to serve the interests of big business. 'Vaalikausi 4-vuotiseksi 140 äänellä 40 vastaan' *Helsingin Sanomat* 12.5.1954.

2 For small parties in particular electoral alliances can make a significant difference. For example at the 2003 general election, the Christian Democrats polled their best parliamentary result of 5.3% but, without the electoral alliance they had with the Centre in 1999, they lost three seats. 'Kallis on vaikea korvata' *Helsingin Sanomat* 17.6.2004.

3 'Pääministerivaali pakotti monet äänestämään puoluetta' *Helsingin Sanomat* 7.6.2003.

4 'Tony Halme herätti vaaleissa aiemmin nukkuneita ikäryhmi' *Helsingin Sanomat* 27.12.2003.

5 The 1975 Election Act requires parties to select their candidates through primaries, which were to be conducted in accordance with electoral law and internal party rules. In practice, the party statutes have taken precedence over the legal provisions.

6 'Kansanedustajat sanailevat pitkistä listoisa' *Helsingin Sanomat* 11.2.2004.

7 Ensio Laaksonen, 'Listavaali on selvästi epädemokraattinen' *Helsingin Sanomat* 18.2.2004.

8 'Lähes kaikki puolueet vastustavat listavaalia EU-vaaleissa' *Helsingin Sanomat* 27.2.2004.

9 'Lipponen kannattaa listavaalia' *Helsingin Sanomat* 27.2.2004.

10 For the responses to the Social Democratic consultation exercise on constitutional matters, including preferential voting, see *Sammanställning av synpunkter till rådslaget om fördjupat folkstyre och författningsfrågor.*

11 'Val på parti eller person' *Dagens Nyheter* 17.6.2004.

12 'Straffad för sin Eu-linje' *Dagens Nyheter* 16.6.2004.

13 'Min kampanj bromsade väljarras' *Dagens Nyheter* 17.6.2004.

14 For the relevant debate, see Odelstinget. Møte onsdag den 4.juni kl. 14.10, 2003.

Innstilling fra kontroll- og konstitusjonskomiteen om lov om endringer i lov 28. Juni 2002 nr. 57 om valg to fylkesting og kommunestyrer (valloven). (Innst. O. nr. 102 2002-2003), jf Ot. Prp.nr.45 (2001-2002 – regler som spesielt gjelder valg til Stortinget.

References

Arter, David 'The Swedish General Election of 20th September 1998: a Victory for Values over Policies?' *Electoral Studies* 18, 2, 1999, pp. 296–300

Arter, David 'From the "Rainbow Coalition" Back Down to "Red Earth"? The 2003 Finnish General Election' *West European Politics* 26, 3, 2003, pp. 153–162

Damgaard, Erik *Folkets Styre. Magt og ansvar i Dansk politik* (Aarhus Universitetsforlaget: Aarhus 2003)

Damgaard, Erik and Ingvar Mattson 'Conflict and Consensus in Committees', in Herbert Döring and Mark Hallerberg (eds) *Patterns of Parliamentary Behaviour* (Ashgate: Aldershot, 2004), pp. 113–139

Elklit, Jørgen 'Bør folketingsvalgloven revideres?' *Politica* 33, 1, 2001, pp. 19–32

Elklit, Jørgen *Dansk valgsystemer: Fordelingsmetoder, spærregler, analyseredskaber* (Aarhus Universitet: Aarhus, 2003)

Karvonen, Lauri 'Why Vote for Individual Candidates?', in Olof Petersson, Klaus von Beyme, Lauri Karvonen, Birgitta Nedelmans and Eivind Smith *Democracy the Swedish Way. Report from the Democratic Audit of Sweden 1999* (SNS: Stockholm, 1999)

Karvonen, Lauri 'Preferential Voting: Incidence and Effects' *International Political Science Review* 25, 2, 2004, pp. 203–226

Kristjánsson, Svanur 'Iceland: Searching for Democracy along Three Dimensions of Citizen Control' *Scandinavian Political Studies* 27, 2, 2004, pp. 153–174

Kuitinen, Soile 'Finland: Formalized Procedures with Member Predominance', in Hanne Marthe Narud, Mogens N. Pedersen and Henry Valen (eds) *Party Sovereignty and Citizen Control* (University Press of Southern Denmark: Odense, 2002), pp. 63–104

Narud, Hanne Marthe 'Parliamentary Nominations and Political Representation – Group Representation or Party Mandates?', in Knut Heidar (ed.) *Nordic Politics. Comparative Perspectives* (Universitetsforlaget: Oslo, 2004), pp. 108–126

Pedersen, Mogens N. 'Preferential Voting in Denmark: The Voters' Influence on the Election of Folketing Candidates' *Scandinavian Political Studies* 1, 1966, pp. 167–187

Pedersen, Mogens N. 'Denmark: The Interplay of Nominations and Elections in Danish Politics', in Hanne Marthe Narud, Mogens N. Pedersen and Henry Valen (eds) *Party Sovereignty and Citizen Control* (University Press of Southern Denmark: Odense, 2002), pp. 29–61

Pesonen, Pertti, Risto Sänkiaho and Sami Borg, *Vaalikansan äänivalta* (WSOY: Porvoo-Helsinki-Juva, 1993)

Petersson, Olof, Klaus von Beyme, Lauri Karvonen, Birgitta Nedelmans and Eivind Smith *Democracy the Swedish Way. Report from the Democratic Audit of Sweden*

1999 (SNS: Stockholm, 1999)

Tonsgaard, Ole 'Vallovgivningen – en kritisk gennemgang', in Jørgen Elklit and Ole Tonsgaard (eds) *Valg og Vælgeradfærd* (Forlaget Politica: Aarhus, 1986), pp. 369–382

Törnudd, Klaus *The Electoral System of Finland* (Hugh Evelyn: London, 1968)

Worre Torben *Det politiske system i Danmark* (Akademisk Forlag: Odense, 1989)

3

The Scandinavian party system(s) since 1970: less unidimensional and less distinctive?

Parties, it is often said, rarely go out of business. Indeed several of the present Scandinavian parliamentary parties can trace a history going back nearly a century and a half. Take the Danish *Venstre* for example – the name literally means 'Left' – which emerged, like the Radical Party in the Third French Republic, as a party of the nineteenth-century non-socialist Left. *Venstre* was the largest party until 1924, added the suffix 'Denmark's Liberal Party' in 1970, adopted a neo-liberal programme in the 1980s, which placed it to the right of the Conservatives, and in 2001 became the largest party in Denmark again. (Goul Andersen and Jensen 2001: 96–131) It maintained its position as the largest Danish party at the February 2005 general election. Similarly, the Finnish Agrarian Party was founded in 1906, changed its name to Centre Party in 1965 and at the last general election in 2003 was the largest single party, narrowly surpassing the Social Democrats' poll. Ironically, a former farmers' party is presently the leading governing party in the 'high-tech' society and Nokia-led economy of Finland in the new millennium. Parties then adapt and change to survive and there is a substantial *party change* literature presenting both analytical frameworks and case-studies of change in individual parties.

Of course, not all parties prove as durable as the two mentioned above. The Finnish Rural Party was a classic example of what Harmel and Svåsand refer to as an *entrepreneurial issue party*. (Harmel and Svåsand 1993: 67–88) Founded by Veikko Vennamo, who was succeeded by his son Pekka, the Rural Party broke into parliament in 1970 with 10.5% of the vote. It emerged as a populist-protest party, which, however, lost its radical appeal when it entered a governing coalition in 1983. The party effectively died when Pekka jumped ship and left his ministerial post in 1990 for a senior management position in the central administration. More short-lived was the populist-protest New Democracy in Sweden, which gained 6.7% at its first Riksdag election in 1991 but failed to return a single member of parliament three years later.

While many parties adapt and change, at least some hit the electoral buffers and go out of business.

Chapter 4 focuses on the distinctive strength of social democratic-labour parties on mainland Scandinavia and analyses, among other things, the extent of party change in these historically dominant parties. The present discussion, however, concentrates not on party change, but on the extent of *party system change*. It poses two basic questions: 1) Has the Scandinavian party system been distinctive in a comparative perspective? 2) How much has it changed and has it become more or less distinctive? It deploys the two main approaches to assessing the extent of party system change. First, there is the focus on the *core electoral features* of the party system. Thus, Gordon Smith has devised various categories of change – including 'temporary fluctuations', 'restricted change' and 'general change' – based on the amount of sustained variation in the relative support for the parties. A timescale of three general elections is regarded as a minimum assessment period. (Smith 1989: 157–168) Second, there is the importance of changes in the *structure of party competition*, that is changes in patterns of elite interaction. This is broadly the approach of Peter Mair. (Mair 1997) Clearly, changes in inter-party relationships at the parliamentary level are likely to be reflected in the process of building legislative majorities, but may not mirror significant shifts in the relative electoral standing of the parties.

The Scandinavian party system or party systems?

The historic process of party building in the Nordic countries and the relative strengths of the various party families are discussed at length in my book *Scandinavian Politics Today* and there is little reason to cover the same ground. (Arter 1999: 70–95) It is nonetheless worth reminding ourselves that the completion of mass democracy by the 1920s spawned a highly unidimensional form of multipartism in mainland Scandinavia. The political parties could readily be located on a left–right continuum. The basic formula was a bifurcated left (Social Democrats and Communists) and three parties of the centre-right (Agrarians, Liberals and Conservatives). Two plus three equals Berglund and Lindström's 'five-party Scandinavian party system model' (Berglund and Lindström 1978), best exemplified in the Swedish case. As Hans Bergström has noted: "In no other country has the basic left-right scale accounted for such a great deal of party structure and electoral behaviour." (Bergström 1991: 8)

Bergström may well overstate his case somewhat. It is true that at the 1952 Swedish general election, the five historic parties contrived a remarkable 99.9% of the total vote (see table 3.1). Yet in Denmark in 1950 the combined vote for the five 'left to right' parties was 91.5% and this was depressed only by a record poll of 8.2% for the Justice Party, which was inspired by the ideas of Henry George (see table 3.2). Moreover, in Britain in the late 1940s and 1950s – "the apogee of the Westminster model" in David Marquand's phrase – the left–right scale, that is, support for the Labour and Conservative parties, accounted for about 9 in 10 voters. (Marquand 1979 cited in Madgwick, Steeds and Williams 1982: 136) In 1951 the two-party share of the vote was 96.8%. Indeed, it might well be argued that it was not so much the unidimensionality of the Swedish party system that was distinctive as the high political cohesion of the three main social classes – workers, farmers and middle class. The vast majority of workers voted for the parties of the left; the vast majority of the farmers for the farmers' parties (Arter 2001); and the vast majority of the middle class (admittedly a heterogeneous category) for one of the parties of the centre-right. The incidence of cross-class voting was relatively low. Comparable data are not readily available. However, in Britain in the 1950s, 30% of the 'solid working class' and 35% of the 'upper working class' – in Mark Abrams' terms – voted Conservative (Madgwick, Steeds and Williams 1982: 203). In contrast, working-class support for the Conservatives in Scandinavia in the 1960s ranged from 6% in Finland and 5% in Denmark and Norway to a mere 2% in Sweden (Berglund and Lindström 1978: 108)

Table 3.1 *The distribution of the party vote at the 1952 Swedish general election (%)*

Communists	Social Democrats	Agrarians	Liberals	Conservatives
4.3	46.1	10.7	24.4	14.4

Table 3.2 *The distribution of the party vote at the 1950 Danish general election (%)*

Communists	Social Democrats	Social Liberals*	Liberals	Conservatives
4.6	39.6	8.2	21.3	17.8

*   Social Liberals translates the Danish *Radikale Venstre*

The unidimensionality of the party system in Finland was compromised to a degree from the outset by the existence of an *ethno-regionalist party* in the form of the Swedish People's Party, which in the early years of universal suffrage polled about one-tenth of the vote. The Swedish People's Party emerged as the mouthpiece of the national language minority and at the first democratic election in 1907 92% of those communes where it polled between three-quarters and all the votes were Swedish-speaking. (Sundberg 1985: 53). The Swedish People's Party has been a broad church – an historic catchall party – embracing the farmers in Ostrobothnia (*Pohjanmaa*) in the north-west, the fishermen in the south-western archipelago and the professional and industrial class in the towns and capital city in particular. In short, the political cohesion of the Swedish-speaking population has been high, although from the earliest elections a small proportion of the Swedish-speaking blue-collar workforce has voted for the class party of the workers, the Social Democrats. The Swedish People's Party averaged as much as 11.3% of the vote in inter-war elections, but declined sharply thereafter in line with a fall in the numbers speaking the second national language (see table 3.3).

Table 3.3 *The distribution of the party vote at the 1951 Finnish general election (%)*

Communists*	Social Democrats	Agrarians	Liberals	Swedish People's	Conservatives
21.6	26.5	23.3	5.7	7.6	14.6

*   Strictly speaking, the Communists operated as part of an umbrella organisation called the Finnish People's Democratic League

Table 3:4 *The distribution of the party vote at the 1953 Norwegian general election (%)*

Communists	Labour	Agrarians	Christians	People's Liberals	Conservatives
5.1	46.7	9.0	10.5	10.0	18.8

The unidimensionality of the Norwegian party system was also reduced, albeit in the period after the Second World War, by the appearance on the national scene of a *confessional party* in the form of the Christian People's Party. In fact, the Christian People's Party emerged in the 'Bible Belt' area of southwest Norway in 1933 and reflected growing dissatisfaction with the Liberal Party. In particular there was disquiet at the way the latter had reneged on its strict prohibitionist stance by presiding over the reopening of liquor outlets (some 300 in Bergen). But the Norwegians Christians did not contest elections on a national scale until 1945 (see table 3.4).

However, it is probably fair to assert that from the completion of mass democracy in the 1920s to the late 1960s, the class base of the Scandinavian party systems was distinctive in a comparative perspective. Torben Worre refers to their domination by "three big class parties" and concludes that "the Scandinavian party systems are [were] more strongly connected to the economic aspects of the social structure than those of any other democratic country". (Worre 1980: 319) To adapt Peter Pultzer's classical characterisation of electoral behaviour in Britain in the late 1960s, one could say that even more so in Scandinavia at the same time, 'class was the basis of party politics, all else was embellishment and detail'. In particular, there was a generally high level of electoral stability between the parties of the left and those of the centre-right. What volatility there was occurred within, rather than between the blocs.

All in all, despite the minor deviations of an ethno-regionalist party in Finland and confessional party in Norway, it seems appropriate to speak of a Scandinavian party system in the singular between the completion of mass democracy in the 1920s and the late 1960s. The five 'old parties' – four in Denmark where the Communists were only intermittently a parliamentary party – could relatively easily be placed on a left–right continuum. The significant deviation from the 'Scandinavian party system model' was on the non-socialist side in Iceland. The Progressive Party was essentially an agrarian party but to its right the Independence Party was from its origins in the late 1920s a catchall party comparable to the British Conservatives in attracting sizeable support from the working class. At the 1953 Icelandic general election, only four parties gained parliamentary representation, all easy to locate on a left–right continuum. There were two leftist parties, the Social Democrats and the People's Alliance, the centrist Progressive Party and the centre-right Independent Party, which polled over two-fifths of the valid vote (see table 3.5)

Table 3.5 The distribution of the party vote at the 1953 Icelandic general election (%)

People's Alliance	Social Democrats	Progressive Party	Independence Party
16.0*	15.6	27.9	40.4

*   Strictly speaking, the various radical leftist groupings, including the Communists, did not come together as the People's Alliance until 1956

Changes in the core electoral features of the Nordic party system since 1970

The period 1970–73 witnessed a series of 'earthquake elections', which shook support for the 'old parties' in Finland, Denmark and Norway. Ironically, the tremors were felt as far away as Britain and the mould of the two-party system there appeared to crack. At the February 1974 UK general election, the Liberals polled nearly 20% of the vote, while the ethno-regionalist Scottish National Party gained nearly one-third of the electorate 'north of the border'. The combined vote of Labour and Conservatives plummeted to 75.1% in February 1974. In Denmark, Finland and Norway, however, the 'Scandinavian party systems' that had 'frozen' for the forty years following the completion of the formative period of party building in the late 1920s, (Lipset and Rokkan 1967) 'thawed' suddenly and new parties flooded into parliament. But while the number of parliamentary parties rose significantly, it is important to assess the significance of these new parties in changing the *core electoral features* of the Scandinavian party system. Several of the new parties proved both small and short-lived.

Nonetheless, since the 1970s there has been an increased polarisation of the Scandinavian party systems. Numerically significant populist-protest parties (admittedly ephemeral in their support in the cases of the Finnish Rural Party and New Democracy in Sweden) have occupied a space on the radical right for really the first time. In recent years, their common denominator has been opposition to immigration. (Arter 1999: 98–117) While Sweden has been a multicultural society since the late 1960s – when large numbers of Finns, Turks and others poured in – the other mainland Scandinavian countries have witnessed increased levels of immigration only relatively recently. Nonetheless, the numbers have grown sharply. Norway, for example, has today the highest level of immigration in Europe and, significantly, much of that immigration is *fremmedkulturell*, that is, it involves the penetration of a 'foreign culture' (Islam). In Oslo immigrants make up about 20% of the population. Similarly in Denmark about 8% of the total population of 5.4 million comprises immigrants and their descendants.

The Norwegian Progress Party, led since 1978 by Carl I. Hagen, gained 15.3% of the vote at the 1997 general election and 22.1% in 2005.[5] Importantly, it was not until the mid-1980s that the Progress Party turned immigration into a significant political issue. By 1995, however, when immigration was a major question in the local government election campaign, 47% of Progress Party supporters held that immigration was *the most important issue* in their voting behaviour. (Hagelund 2003: 48) Thereafter, with governments viring North Sea oil and gas revenues into a 'rainy day fund', the Progress Party combined its anti-immigration appeal (the costs of immigrants and the problems of managing multiculturalism) with *welfare chauvinism* and a demand for spending on the elderly, young-parent families, hospitals etc). In short, there was a not unsuccessful attempt to steal the traditional clothes of the Labour Party. Survey research in 2001 showed that 26% of respondents (the highest of any of the parties) believed that 'Hagen's Party' was best equipped to solve the problems of the elderly, while 38% held it had the best immigration policy.

In the last three general elections, the Danish People's Party, founded in 1995 under Pia Kjærsgaard, polled 7.2% in 1998, 12% in 2001 and 13.2% in 2005. In contrast, Mogens Glistrup's Progress Party, which had gained 15.9% in 1973, failed to elect a single MP. Jens Rydgren argues that the Progress Party and the People's Party belong to two different party families. The Progress Party was "a tax-populist, anti-bureaucracy, protest party" while he claims the People's Party is "a pure radical right-wing populist party" in the sense of embracing the notion of ethno-nationalism. (Rydgren 2004: 474). He emphasises the close links between the People's Party and the Danish Association (*Den Danske Forening*), which was founded in 1987 and in turn adopted many of the ideas of the *Front National* in France. Prominent Danish Association members, Søren Krarup and Jesper Langbelle were both elected People's Party MPs in 2001. (Rydgren 2004: 483) In addition to its anti-immigrant stance, the People's Party demands that Denmark should leave the EU. All in all, then, numerically significant radical rightist parties in Norway and Denmark constitute a new feature of the party systems in these countries. The Progress Party (Norway) and People's Party (Denmark) are the second and third largest parties in their respective countries.

Social structural change has served to erode the traditional class base of the Scandinavian party systems and the historic parties have been obliged with varying degrees of success to seek support outside their *classe gardée*. With the exception of the Finnish case, the Agrarian parties that became Centre parties – with a capital 'C' – in the period 1957–65 have not succeeded in building a significantly broader support base. At the same time, support for the Social Democratic-Labour parties appears in slow decline, a matter that will be examined fully in the next chapter. The Conservatives (and Liberals in Denmark), on the other hand, profiting from 'new middle-class' support, have generally gained ground, although experiencing at times significant fluctuations in their support levels. Equally, the emergence of durable new party families such as the Christian Democrats across the region and the Greens in Finland, Sweden and Iceland has vested the Scandinavian party systems with a heightened multi-dimensionality.

For example, the activists and core voters of the new Christian parties have largely comprised religious fundamentalists, both within the Lutheran Church (various revivalist groups) and outside it (Free Church, Baptists etc). Typically, the Christian Democratic Minister for Ecclesiastical Affairs in Bildt's four-party non-socialist coalition in Sweden between 1991–94 had close personal links with the Pentecostalist movement. (Knutsen 2004: 97–128; Gustafsson 2003: 51–72) Many of these religious fundamentalists were simply not active politically before the emergence of Christian parties in the 1950s and 1960s. In short, there is a *prima facie* case for arguing that, viewed from an electoral perspective, the Scandinavian party systems are less distinctive and that there have been significant changes in their core electoral features.

There is unquestionably evidence of increased volatility and its corollary declining partisan identification. From the early 1970s there have been a number of 'high volatility elections' on mainland Scandinavia. Aggregate electoral volatility, calculated on the basis of the total gains of the winning parties, reached no less than 21.2 in Denmark in 1973. Moreover, Anders Todal Jenssen has observed that in the Norwegian case "even among the hard core of party identifiers, volatility has become notable" and he remarks that the group of "firm believers" is shrinking and "the commitment among the partisans is not what it used to be". (Todal Jenssen 1999: 22–23) The bulk of the electoral volatility remains intra-bloc mobility. For example, almost one-third (30%) of the Swedish Leftist Party's best-ever poll of 12% in 1998 comprised former social democratic voters. However, there was also evidence of increased inter-bloc mobility during the 1990s. At the same 1998 general election in Sweden, 9% of the Christian Democrats' record performance of 11.8% came from the Social Democrats. (Möller 1999: 261–276) Crucially, the radical rightist parties in Denmark and Norway have attracted significant working-class support from the Social Democrats.

The causes of increased electoral volatility are, of course, many and complex. They include long-term social structural change and the aforementioned erosion of the old class contours of politics. In addition, there has been the decline in membership and active involvement in political parties, the impact of big and sensitive issues (EU, nuclear power, immigration etc) and a perception among the electorate of a generally reduced ideological distance between the 'old parties'. Hans Jørgen Nielsen develops this last point in the Danish case. Nielsen emphasises the importance of educational level in determining the propensity for voting for one of the radical rightist parties. While highly educated voters seem to be "immunized against the new right tendencies", voters with an average level of education are just as likely to support the 'new right' as voters with a low level of education. (Nielsen 1999: 76) However, Nielsen canvasses against viewing electoral mobility as primarily an expression of anti-party protest. He argues that it is probably the result of a combination of "a multiplicity of parties and the *weak voter differentiation between them*" rather than "negativism towards the parties". (Nielsen 1999: 80 – my italics)

Todal Jenssen brings out the way party identification has dropped dramatically in Norway since the mid-1980s, something which, he notes, is not exclusively bound up with the issue of EU membership. True, he admits that the intense debate over EU membership weakened the formation of partisan identification in the periods preceding the referendums in 1972 and 1994. But Todal Jenssen argues that the observed decline in party identification is a long-term change linked to the fading of the old cleavages and the decline of parties as mass organisations. (Todal Jenssen 1999: 1–27)

Importantly, the consolidation of sizeable radical rightist parties in Denmark and Norway has significantly reduced the explanatory power of class as the primary determinant of voting behaviour. In the 1990s, the three anti-immigrant parties in Denmark (Progress and People's Party) and Norway (Progress) gained a higher proportion of workers among their electorates than any other party, including the Social Democrats (Bjørklund and Andersen 2002: 119). At the 2001 general election, 56% of Danish People's Party voters (cf. 49% in 1998) comprised workers, compared with 43% of workers among the Social Democrats' electorate. (Rydgren 2004: 490) At the 2001 Norwegian general election, blue-collar workers made up only 14% of the Labour Party's electorate, compared with 22% of those voting for the Progress Party.

In addition to strong support among manual workers, there has been a marked male dominance among radical rightist voters in Norway and Denmark. In the case of the Norwegian Progress Party, there has been a distinctive *age*, as well as *gender* profile among its supporters. At the time of the 1981 general election approximately 10% of young males under 30 backed the Progress Party – more than twice the party's national vote – as did 10% of those on the lowest incomes. (Pettersen and Rose 2004: 11) When the Progress Party's vote rose sharply to 13% at the 1989 Storting election, the under 30 men continued to be 'overrepresented' and 18.2% of its support belonged to this youngest male age cohort. (Pettersen and Rose 2004: 31) As Per Arnt Pettersen and Lawrence Rose attest, "the Progress Party was at the outset a protest party attracting support from young men". (Pettersen and Rose 2004: 33) In 1997, when the Progress Party gained its second best result of 15.3%, young men still comprised the largest support group, although the party's age and gender profile had broadened significantly by then.

Despite increased electoral volatility, declining partisan identification and the rise of new parties, particularly the radical right, the traditional class parties have proved resilient and electorally adaptable, albeit to varying degrees, expanding their core constituencies to become catchall parties. In this connection, Jan Sundberg refers to the "enduring Scandinavian party system" (Sundberg 1999: 221–241). Sundberg analyses the support for the "three pole

parties" – Social Democrats, Agrarian-Centre and Conservatives – the "remaining two parties" in the five-party system – the Liberals and Communists
– and the "other parties" in all the mainland Scandinavian countries between
the late 1940s and the mid 1990s. He points to a "remarkable stability among
the three pole parties", which have managed to retain their electoral dominance after the Second World War. Put another way, Sundberg highlights "the
frozen part of the party system", which on average boasts 63% of the electorate in Finland, 70% in Denmark and Norway and 77% in Sweden. He concludes that, given the stability of the three pole parties, "the free space for new
parties to compete in elections seems to be no more than 40% of the vote".
(Sundberg 1999: 230) The thrust of Sundberg's submission is plain. The three
pole parties have proved relatively adaptable in a competitive electoral marketplace, and the political cohesion of their core class support remains high.
Viewed from a bottom-up electoral perspective in short the extent of party
system change in mainland Scandinavia should not be exaggerated. At the
same time, the heightened polarisation of the Danish and Norwegian party
systems – with the emergence and, more importantly, consolidation of a numerically significant radical right – and the increased multidimensionality created across the region by the likes of the Greens and Christian Democrats
should be acknowledged. At the first general elections in the new millennium
support for the 'pole parties' was 65.1% in Denmark, 67.8% in Finland, 61.2%
in Sweden, but only 53.3% in Norway (see table 3.6)

Table 3.6 Support for the three 'pole parties' on mainland Scandinavia at the 2001–05
general elections (%)

	Denmark (2005)	Finland (2003)	Norway (2005)	Sweden (2002)
Social Democrats	25.8	24.5	32.7	39.9
Centre	29.0*	24.7	6.5	6.2
Conservatives	10.3	18.6	14.1	15.1
Total	65.1	67.8	53.3	61.2

*   This is Agrarian Liberals (*Venstre*)

Changes in the structure of party competition in Scandinavia since 1970

Party system change in Scandinavia can also be viewed from a top-down perspective by examining changes in the *structure of party competition* at the elite
(parliamentary and governmental) level. In the absence (in Scandinavia) of a

single party with an absolute plurality of parliamentary seats, legislative majority building must necessary involve inter-party co-operation, either in the form of executive coalitions or legislative coalitions (regularised or ad hoc) between the government and one or more opposition parties. In analysing changing patterns of party competition, moreover, an adequate time span is important. In addition, there is the problem of how to characterise party system change at the elite level. If the dynamics of legislative majority building have changed, has the process become less unidimensional? In other words, have legislative majorities broadly conformed to the left–right (socialist/non-socialist) axis of the traditional Scandinavian party system model and what difference have the new parties made? Since the size and composition of cabinets and govern-ment–opposition relations will be discussed fully later in this book, only a few brief points are in order at this stage.

First, it is important to emphasise that there has been a tradition of 'cross class' co-operation between the parties at the elite level in the form of both executive and legislative coalitions. Thus, co-operation between the two big class parties, the Social Democrats and Agrarians, to meet the challenges of economic recession, spawned red–green deals across mainland Scandinavia in the 1930s, which laid the foundations for important social welfare legislation. Historically, in short, legislative majorities in Scandinavia have not observed a unidimensional left–right pattern. Particularly in Finland, moreover, but also in Iceland and Denmark, cabinets have routinely comprised parties "across the blocs". The Agrarians and Social Democrats formed the core of Finnish coalitions for fifty years until 1987.

Second, the advent of new parliamentary parties since the 1970s – the Greens, Christians, post-communist Left etc – has meant an increase in the number of 'relevant parties' (in Sartori's sense of parties with either *coalition potential* or *blackmail potential*) and greater diversity in the composition of both executive and legislative coalitions. (Sartori 1966) Legislative majorities are more multidimensional in terms of their partisan composition than ear-lier. For example, the Swedish Greens (considered a left-of-centre party) have formed part of a legislative coalition with the ruling Social Democrats since 1998. The Finnish Greens (considered a non-socialist party) participated in a broad Social Democrat-led cabinet between 1995–2002.

Third, in addition to the increase in the number of 'relevant' new parties, it might be argued that the single most important development in Scandinavian party politics since around 1970 has been the way the historic non-socialist parties have acquired an enhanced role as coalition parties, both individually and collectively. (Arter 1999: 148). Non-socialist cabinets have been more frequent across the region since the 'earthquake elections' than before them (see table 3.7). Moreover, in the Swedish case at least, the core electoral features may be said to have changed less than the structure of party competition since 1970. Thus, from 1976 Sweden acquired the bipolar dynamics of Sartori's moderate multipartism and the transition from a one-party dominant system occurred within the existing framework of the five-party system model underpinned by relatively minor electoral shifts between the competing party blocs.

Table 3.7 Non-Socialist cabinets in Scandinavia since 1972

Denmark	1982–93	2001–			
Finland	1991–95				
Iceland	1974–78	1983–87	1995–		
Norway	1972–73	1981–86	1989–90	1997–2000	2001–05
Sweden	1976–82	1991–94			

Fourth, in both Sweden and Norway, the structure of party competition has largely followed 'bloc lines' (left versus centre-right) and there has been a strong preference for the Social Democrats to govern on a minority basis and to forge legislative coalitions with opposition parties to the left-of-centre. Conversely, the formation of non-socialist cabinets has been complicated by the historic competition between three 'old' non-socialist parties in Sweden and four in Norway. The number of non-socialist coalitions has grown, but several have proved short-lived. Nonetheless, particularly in Sweden, it seems possible to speak of 'crunch co-operation' between the parties on the centre-right. First in 1976, after forty-four years of social democratic rule, and again in 1991 the non-socialists combined forces to break the Social Democrats' monopoly of power. (Arter 1999: 155) In other words, if there has been party system change at the elite level in Sweden, it has been in the direction of an accentuated bi-polarity and emphasised 'bloc politics'. When in autumn 2004 the leaders of the four non-socialist parties launched six policy working groups to lay the foundations for a common election manifesto for the 2006 Riksdag election, this was tantamount to the emergence of a shadow cabinet in Sweden for really the first time in its history. Although the term 'shadow cabinet' was not used at the press conference, it was clear that the convenors of the six working groups and the four party leaders expected to form the core of a non-socialist coalition after the 2006 general election (see chapter 13).

Focusing on the impact of the radical right on party system change in Denmark and Norway, Tim Bale arrives at a similar conclusion – that is, he discerns a tendency towards increased bipolarity – albeit by a different route.

Bale begins with the bold assertion that "West European party systems may be thawing, but there is no fluid free-for-all. Indeed, the much touted fragmentation and polarisation under way is occurring alongside a trend towards two bloc electoral competition" and bi-polarising party systems. (Bale 2003: 69). He goes on to say that where there is a significant or potentially significant radical right, the centre-right has exploited its existence in order to regain office and, once there, implement policies (notably on immigration) traditionally associated with the radical right. (Bale 2003: 84–85) The centre-right, by including the radical right, either as a coalition partner or a support party, has ended a situation in which radical right votes were effectively wasted. (Bale 2003: 69) Bale's thrust – or at least the inference to be drawn from his argument – would appear to be that the presence of a sizeable radical right in Denmark and Norway has reinforced the tendency to bi-polarisation in these party systems. Both in Denmark and Norway radical rightist parties have sustained minority centre-right governments in power. However, in Sweden, the bi-polarisation of the party system is not indebted to the emergence of a radical right, although the short-lived parliamentary presence of New Democracy (1991–94), in taking votes off the Social Democrats, contributed to facilitating a four-party non-socialist coalition under Carl Bildt.

Elsewhere in the region, governments have formed 'across the blocs' with varying degrees of frequency. Finland is a limiting case in this regard. For only four of the last forty years have Finnish cabinets not comprised the Social Democrats together with one of the two main non-socialist parties (Agrarian-Centre or Conservatives). The greater multi-dimensionality of the Finnish party system at the electoral level has also been reflected in composition of governments. Since 1983 the (now moribund) Finnish Rural Party, the Greens, Christian Democrats and Leftists have all held ministerial portfolios. Inter-party co-operation in Finland has proceeded on very much an 'anything goes' basis, something reflected in the so-called 'rainbow coalition' between 1995–2002, which comprised Social Democrats, Conservatives, Leftists, Greens and the Swedish People's Party!

Conclusions

Summing up, the electoral features of the Scandinavian party systems since 1970 have manifested a mixture of 'persistence' and 'change'. Support for the three 'pole parties' has remained strong and relatively stable in the post-war period. Indeed, the persistence of the most important electoral features has meant at best 'restricted change' rather than 'general change' in Gordon Smith's terms. In truth, the precise difference between the two is not clearly delineated in Smith's work. However, there has been increased voter volatility, both intra-bloc and, more recently, inter-bloc mobility. Moreover, a heightened multi-dimensionality in electoral behaviour has been reflected in the consolidation of a numerically significant radical right in Norway and Denmark and support more widely for new parties such as the Greens and Christians, which cannot easily be located on a left–right continuum. Viewed from the perspective of their core electoral features, the Scandinavian party systems are less distinctive than in the 'frozen years' between the 1920s and 1960s.

Peter Mair has noted that "electoral change should be seen to lead to party system change only when it brings about a shift from one type of party system to another" and herein lies a problem. (Mair 1997: 44–45) Clearly, examining the structure and dynamics of party competition in the governmental and parliamentary arenas represents a vital complementary, top-down perspective on party system change. But the reliance in the literature on Sartori's classification of party systems does little to illuminate the Scandinavian case. True, some impressions can be noted.

Writing in the mid-1960s, Sartori referred to Sweden, along with the Irish Republic, as a 'one-party dominant' or *predominant party system*. (Sartori 1966) It was a case of one party, the Social Democrats, repeatedly winning elections and dominating governments despite the existence of open competition for power. However, the fundamental bloc logistics of party politics since the early 1970s makes a solid case for considering Sweden as having moved from the category of one-party dominant to become a *moderate multiparty system*. Viewed in terms of the structure of party competition, Sweden today appears more typical of the West European party systems as a whole.

In Norway, superficial appearances are deceptive. The existence of in excess of five 'relevant parties', including the radical (if hardly anti-systemic) Progress Party, along with, between 2001–05, a numerically weak, centre-based minority government, suggests extreme multipartism. Yet Norway does not exhibit the features of polarised pluralism and the Christian-led coalition forged legislative coalitions with parties on the left and right to enact a legislative programme. Indeed, in Bale's terms, an important consequence of the emergence of a significant radical right in Scandinavia has been to accentuate the tendency towards bi-polarity in the party system – the main feature of Sartori's moderate multipartism – and to make Norway and Denmark, like Sweden, relatively typical of West European party systems in general.

In Iceland the merger in 1999 of the Social Democrats, People's Alliance and the Women's Party as the Democratic Alliance, which polled over 30% of the vote at the 2003 general election, represented an attempt to offer the electorate a cohesive left-of-centre alternative to Independence Party-led cabinets. A radical left, in the form of the Left Greens, a miscellaneous assortment of feminists, environmentalists and maverick elements, remained outside the new formation. However, the idea behind the Alliance was to create the realistic possibility of the type 'alternation of power' associated with the Westminster model. It was 'crunch co-operation' on the left – paralleling that of the Swedish non-socialists in 1976 and 1991 – and while it has affected the core electoral features of the Icelandic party system, it has thus far failed significantly to alter the basic pattern of inter-elite relations between the parties. The Independence Party and the Progressive have co-operated in government for over ten years.

As for Finland, Sartori considered it in the 1960s a possible case of *extreme multipartism*. Yet, at least since the 1980s, all the parties have been 'relevant' and most have governed together in recent years. Finland is emphatically not a case of polarised pluralism. Nor, lacking a fundamental bi-polarity, and with cabinets routinely comprising parties 'across the blocs' is it a moderate multi-party system. Indeed, while it is clear that there have been significant shifts in patterns of inter-party co-operation and competition in Finland (as elsewhere in Scandinavia), it is considerably less clear how to characterise these changes. The impression in Finland is of a *consociational party system* with governments reflecting overarching elite co-operation. However, sharper evaluative criteria are clearly needed.

References

Arter, David *Scandinavian Politics Today* (Manchester University Press: Manchester, 1999)

Arter, David "Party System Change in Scandinavia since 1970: 'Restricted Change' or 'General Change'?" *West European Politics* 22, 3, 1999, pp. 139–158

Arter, David (ed.) *From Farmyard to City Square. The Electoral Adaptation of the Nordic Agrarian Parties* (Ashgate: Aldershot, 2001)

Bale, Tim 'Cinderella and Her Ugly Sisters: The Mainstream and Extreme Right in Europe's Bipolarising Party Systems' *West European Politics* 26, 3, 2003, pp. 67–90

Berglund, Sten and Ulf Lindström *The Scandinavian Party System(s)* (Studentlitteratur: Lund, 1978)

Bergström, Hans 'Sweden's Politics and Party System at the Crossroads' *West European Politics* 14, 1, 1991, pp. 8–30

Bjørklund, Tor and Jørgen Goul Andersen 'Anti-Immigration Parties in Denmark and Norway: The Progress Parties and the Danish People's Party', in Martin Schain, Aristide Zolberg and Patrick Hossay (eds) *Shadows over Europe: The Development and Impact of the Extreme Right in Western Europe* (Palgrave Macmillan: Basingstoke, 2002), pp. 107–136

Esping-Andersen, Gøsta *Politics against Markets. The Social Democratic Road to Power* (Princeton University Press: Princeton, NJ, 1985)

Glans, Ingemar 'Denmark: The 1964 Folketing Election' *Scandinavian Political Studies* 1, 1966, pp. 231–236

Goul Andersen, Jørgen and Jan Bendix Jensen 'The Danish Venstre: Liberal, Agrarian or Centrist', in D. Arter (ed.), *From Farmyard to City Square?* (Ashgate: Aldershot, 2001), pp. 96–131

Gustafsson, Göran 'Church-State Separation Swedish-Style' *West European Politics* 26, 1, 2003, pp. 51–72

Hadenius, Stig *Modern svensk politisk historia* (Hjalmarson & Högberg: Stockholm, 2003)

Hagelund, Annika 'A Matter of Decency? The Progress Party in Norwegian Immigration Politics' *Journal of Ethnic and Migration Studies* 23, 1, 2003, pp. 47–65

Harmel, Robert and Lars Svåsand 'Party Leadership and Party Institutionalisation: Three Phases of Development' *West European Politics* 16, 2, 1993, pp. 67–88

Jenkins, Roy *Nine Men of Power* (Hamish Hamilton: London, 1974), pp. 30–59

Jenssen, Anders Todal "All that is Solid Melts into Air: Party Identification in Norway' *Scandinavian Political Studies* 22, 1, 1999, pp. 1–27

Knutsen, Oddbjørn *Generations, Age Groups and Voting Behaviour in the Scandinavian Countries. A Comparative Study* (University of Oslo, Research report 4/2003)

Knutsen, Oddbjørn 'Religious Denomination and Party Choice in Western Europe: A Comparative Longitudinal Study from Eight Countries, 1970–97' *International Political Science Review* 25, 1, 2004, pp. 97–128

Lipset, S. M. and S. Rokkan (eds) *Voter Systems and Party Alignments* (Free Press: New York, 1967)

Madgwick, P. J., D. Steeds and L. J. Williams *Britain since 1945* (Hutchinson: London, 1982)

Mair, Peter *Party System Change* (Clarendon Press: Oxford, 1997)

Marquand, David 'The Devolution Debate' *The Listener* 8.3.1979, pp. 3–4.

Möller, Tommy 'The Swedish Election 1998: A Protest Vote and the Birth of a New Political Landscape' *Scandinavian Political Studies* 22, 3, 1999, pp. 261–276

Nielsen, Hans Jørgen 'The Danish Election 1998' *Scandinavian Political Studies* 22, 1, 1999, pp. 67–81

Pettersen, Per Arnt and Lawrence E. Rose 'Høyrebølgene – de store og små: Velgerprofilene til Høyre og Fremskrittspartiet i flo og fjære' *Norsk Statsvitenskapelig Tidskrift* 20, 3, 2004, pp. 3–37

Rydgren, Jens 'Explaining the Emergence of Radical Right-Wing Populist Parties: The Case of Denmark' *West European Politics* 27, 3, 2004, pp. 474–502

Särlvik, Bo 'Political Stability and Change in the Swedish Electorate' *Scandinavian Political Studies* 1, 1966, pp. 188–222

Sartori, Giovanni 'European Political Parties: The Case of Polarized Pluralism', in J. LaPalombara and M. Weiner (eds) *Political Parties and Political Development* (Princeton University Press: Princeton, NJ, 1966)

Smith, Gordon 'Core Persistence: System Change and the "People's Party"' *West European Politics* 12, 4, 1989, pp. 157–168

Sundberg, Jan *Svenskhetens dilemma i Finland* (Finska Vetenskaps-Societeten:

Helsingfors, 1985)

Sundberg, Jan 'The Enduring Scandinavian Party System' *Scandinavian Political Studies* 22, 3, 1999, pp. 221–241

Thomas, Alastair H. 'Social Democracy in Denmark', in William E. Paterson and Alastair H. Thomas (eds) *Social Democratic Parties in Western Europe* (Croom Helm: London, 1977), pp. 234–271

Worre, Torben 'Class Parties and Class Voting in the Scandinavian Countries' *Scandinavian Political Studies* 3, 4, 1980, pp. 299–320

4

The strength of Social Democracy on mainland Scandinavia: continued dominance or incipient decomposition?

In 1968, at the last election to the Second Chamber of the Riksdag before the shift to unicameralism in 1970, the Swedish Social Democrats polled 50.1% of the active electorate. It was the second time in their history they had gained an absolute majority of the vote. Eight years later the unthinkable happened and the Social Democrats lost power. In 1975 the controversial wage-earner funds scheme had been launched. Then, amid much publicity, the celebrated film director, Ingmar Bergman, sought tax exile in Monaco. In spring 1976, Astrid Lindgren, the well-known author of children's books, wrote a strong attack on the long-serving Social Democratic minister of finance, Gunnar Sträng, in the form of a fable in an evening newspaper. Finally, three weeks before the September 1976 general election, Lindgren wrote an open letter to the governing Social Democrats in which, having again criticised the demoralising effects of high income taxation, she signed herself 'formerly a Social Democrat, now simply a Democrat'. (Elder 1977) The time it seems had come for a change and, although the Social Democrats lost only 0.9% of the vote and the aggregate gain for the three non-socialist parties amounted to only 2%, the Social Democrats were forced into opposition for the first time in forty-four years.

For over four decades – from 1932–76 – the Swedish Social Democratic Party had participated in government, mostly on its own. Bo Rothstein described it as simply "the world's most successful social democratic party in electoral terms". (Rothstein 1996: 3) It was small wonder too that Sartori, writing in the 1960s, described Sweden as a 'one-party dominant system', matched only by the supremacy of Fianna Fáil in the Irish Republic. (Sartori 1966) Norway's first Labour government in 1928 lasted only a paltry eighteen days before substantial pressure from the banking sector prompted its resignation. However, Labour regained power in 1935 and retained it for three decades, although the government operated in exile during the German occupation of Norway between 1940–45. In Knut Heidar's words, "the Labour Party became the hegemonic party in Norwegian politics". (Heidar 2001: 25) Indeed, the strength of social democracy has appeared a distinctive feature of the politics and government of the Scandinavian countries. Thus, Olof Petersson notes that "in political terms it is social democracy that has been chiefly characteristic of the Nordic model and it has dominated the exercise of power over long periods". (Petersson 1994: 34)

The present chapter concentrates on the electoral strength of Scandinavian social democracy. Remarkably, in only five Nordic general elections since the Second World War (excluding Iceland) have social democratic-labour parties not emerged as the largest party. The first section presents the briefest of electoral profiles of each of the mainland social democratic parties, bringing out the extent of their support in a wider party system perspective. There is then a discussion of the social structure of Scandinavian social democracy, that is the anatomy of its support base. The final section considers the main question in this chapter, namely 'are there signs of incipient decline or even decomposition in the Scandinavian social democratic party electorates?'

Brief electoral profiles of the mainland Scandinavian Social Democratic parties

The Finnish Social Democratic Party was the largest parliamentary party of its kind in Western Europe in 1907 in one of the most agrarian societies. It claimed two-fifths of the Eduskunta seats and 37% of the vote. This had reached 40% of the electorate by 1910, 43.1% in 1913 and 47.3% in 1916, when the Social Democrats also gained an absolute majority of 103 of the 200 parliamentary seats. This is the only time any Finnish party has gained overall control of the Eduskunta. The arbitrary dissolution of the Finnish parliament by the Russian Czar – the head of state in the Grand Duchy – meant the 1916 election was the seventh general election in nine years, a fact reflected in the turnout of only 55.5%. None the less, it was the possibility of a repetition of the 1916 result, which prompted the political Right to press for the creation of a strong head of state during the constitutional debates of 1918–1919. The Finnish Right viewed the president as a counterweight to a Social Democrat-controlled legislature and, ironically, the office was vested with powers comparable to those exercised by the Russian Czar before Finland gained independence in December 1917.

Independence was followed by civil war over the first months of 1918, defeat for the forces of the left and the creation in Moscow of the Finnish Communist Party by Red exiles in August that same year.[1] The split on the political Left was reflected in reduced support for the Social Democrats. True, in the first general election of the independence period in July 1919, the Social Democrats polled 38%, twice that of the second largest party, the Agrarians. But during the 1920s, competition from the Socialist Workers' Party, coordinated from Moscow by Finnish Communists, meant the Social Democratic vote never exceeded 30%. It recovered in the 1930s, following a ban on the radical left, and in 1939 (the year Stalin's attack on Finland led to the Winter War) the Social Democrats polled fractionally under two-fifths of the vote.

The re-legalisation of the radical left as part of the armistice with the Soviet Union in August 1944, and the emergence of a Communist-dominated Finnish People's Democratic League (SKDL), which enjoyed in its prime over one-fifth of the vote, created two relatively evenly-matched left-wing parties in post-war Finland. Indeed, in 1958 the Social Democrats and SKDL both polled 23.2% and shared the position of largest party. At the time, division in the ranks of the former had led to the creation of a breakaway Social Democratic Opposition (TPSL) and in 1962 the Social Democratic vote fell below one-fifth of the active electorate for the first and only time in its history. The (reputedly right-wing) Social Democratic leadership was viewed with suspicion in Moscow, which was solidly behind the (former Agrarian) president Urho Kekkonen. In 1966 the Social Democrats recovered to 27.2% and in 1995 gained 28.3%. In the thirty-four general elections since the introduction of universal suffrage in 1907, the Social Democrats have polled the highest vote in all but three – 1962, 1991 and 2003 – when on each occasion the Agrarian-Centre has fared better.

Summing up, three points warrant emphasis. First, the heyday of Finnish social democracy was in the decade before independence, when the party averaged over two-fifths of the vote. It is a fair bet that had it not been for the civil war and the split on the political Left, Finnish social democracy would have matched the level of its counterparts in Sweden and Norway. Second, competition from the Communists, in the guise of the Socialist Workers' Party in the 1920s and SKDL after the Second World War, significantly undercut social democratic support. In the two decades after 1945, the Social Democrats averaged just under one-quarter of the vote. Third, since the first of the Scandinavian 'earthquake elections' in March 1970, the Finnish Social Democrats have maintained the support of about 25% of the electorate (see table 4.1). Unlike their sister parties in Denmark and Norway, the advent of new (and several protest) parties has not led to electoral decline. But neither do the Finnish Social Democrats appear to have profited from the factionalisation and slow decline of the radical left.

Table 4.1 Support for the Finnish Social Democrats, 1907–2003

	Average Social Democrat vote (%)	Average winning margin (%)
1907–17	41.3	17.9
1919–39	33.1	10.4
1945–66	24.9	1.3
1970–2003	24.7	3.4

Founded by the trade union movement in 1887, the Norwegian Labour Party did not gain its first seats in the Storting until 1903, two years before Norway gained independence from Sweden. Moreover, although significantly consolidating its parliamentary position, Labour did not become the largest Storting party immediately following the introduction of PR in 1921. It was substantially underrepresented by the French-style single-member, double ballot system, which was used between 1906–18. By 1921 Norwegian social democracy had split into two parties over its stance towards Moscow in the wake of the Russian Revolution. In 1919 a narrow Labour majority voted to join the Comintern, precisely as a majority of the SFIO had done at the 1920 Congress of Tours, when Léon Blum was left to defend *la vieille maison*. (Jenkins 1974: 29–59) Two years later, a moderate wing formed the Norwegian Social Democratic Workers' Party. Labour left the Comintern in 1923 (although a splinter group formed the Norwegian Communist Party) and the two social democratic-labour parties reunited in 1927. Since that year, Labour has been the largest party in every Storting election.

In its heyday between 1945–69, the Norwegian Labour Party's average support of 45.4% was only one and a half percentage points below that of its celebrated Swedish counterpart in the same period (see table 4.2). The electoral dominance of Labour can also be seen in terms of its winning margin, that is the average differential in support between Labour and the next best-supported party. In the period 1945–69, which was dominated by the long-serving chair and prime minister, Einar Gerhardsen, the winning margin was no less than 26.4 percentage points. Put another way, Labour has been approximately twice as large as the second party (until recently) the Conservatives. This was the era of what has been described as the "social democratic order". (Heidar 2001: 4)

In the nine Storting elections since the seismic general election of September 1973, Labour's average support has fallen back to an average of 35.4% and its winning margin to an average 13.0%. The 'European issue' split the party in the 1970s and 1990s and there is also evidence of some 'generational decomposition' of its support base. In 2001, Labour polled its worst result (24.3%) since 1909 and although it recovered to 32.7% in 2005, this was still its second lowest vote since 1930.

Table 4.2 Support for the Norwegian Labour Party, 1921–2005

	Average Labour use (%)	*Average winning margin (%)*
1921–36	34.8	7.1
1945–69	45.4	26.4
1973–2005	35.4	13.0

Summing up, the electoral dominance of the Norwegian Labour Party was greatest, as in Sweden, in the 1950s and 1960s and in 1957 it polled a record 48.3%. Although performing badly in 2001 the Labour Party, unlike its Finnish counterpart in 1962, 1991 and 2003, still kept its nose in front of the second strongest party, the Conservatives. Since the mid-1970s, however, Labour has also faced an intermittently significant challenge from the red–green radical left which, in the form of the Socialist Left Party, polled 12.5% in 2001.

The electoral dominance of the Danish Social Democratic Party, the oldest of the Scandinavian social democratic parties, can be seen in the fact that it was the largest party in every Folketing election between 1924–98. Its average poll exceeded that of the Finnish and Norwegian parties in the pre-1945 period, when it also achieved its best election results. Contesting the 1935 general election using the slogan 'Stauning [the party chairman] or chaos' the Danish Social Democrats achieved their best-ever result of 46.1%, and their winning margin of 28.3% over the second largest parties (both the Liberals and Conservatives polled 17.8%) was also their highest on record. The 1930s appear to have been the "golden age" of Danish social democracy. (Thomas 1977: 234)

The Danish party attracted a significantly lower poll in the period 1945–73 than the social democratic-labour parties in Norway and Sweden (see table 4.3). Its average winning margin of 16.9% – although impressive enough – was nearly ten percentage points lower than the Norwegian party and over 10% lower than that achieved by the Swedish party. Nonetheless, the average winning margin exceeded the 11.2% it managed in the period 1920–43.

Table 4.3 *Support for the Danish Social Democrats, 1920–2005*

	Average Social Democrat vote (%)	Average winning margin (%)
1920–43	38.3	11.2
1945–71	38.8	16.9
1973–2005	32.1	11.5

Since the 1973 'earthquake election' the Danish Social Democrats' electoral dominance has been challenged by a mixture of increased party competition, heightened electoral volatility and an ageing support base. The increased party competition came in particular from the breakaway Centre Democrats in the 1970s, the radical leftist Socialist People's Party in the 1980s (which polled an average 12.6% in the four elections between 1981–88) and a resurgent Liberal Party in the 1990s. In six of the thirteen general elections since 1973, the Danish Social Democrats have polled under thirty per cent of the vote and in 2001 they were surpassed as the largest single party by the Liberals. The February 2005 general election in Denmark made history. It was the first time on mainland Scandinavia that the Social Democrats had failed in consecutive elections to emerge as the largest party. Under the leadership of Mogens Lykketoft, the Danish Social Democrats polled only 26.6% of the vote, second again to Anders Fogh Rasmussen's Liberals.

Unlike its sister parties in Denmark, Finland and Norway, the Swedish Social Democratic Party (SAP), which was founded in 1889, has been the largest party in every Riksdag election since the completion of mass democracy in 1921. Unlike its Danish and Norwegian counterparts, SAP was the largest party throughout the 1920s, a period of 'minority parliamentarism' in Sweden (see table 4.4). Thus, in the first general election with universal suffrage in 1921 SAP gained 36.2% of the vote, despite competition from two splinter groups to its left – the Left Socialists and Communists – which polled a combined 7.8%. Throughout the 1920s, SAP had to face a barrage of hostile propaganda from the non-socialists, and the Conservatives (*högern*) in particular, insinuating that at heart the Social Democrats were a revolutionary socialist party. During the so-called 'Cossack election' of 1928, one Conservative poster read: "Anybody who votes for the workers' party votes for Moscow". Another, directed at female voters claimed that a social democratic vote would mean the "dissolution of family ties, unruly children and the wholesale collapse of standards"! (Hadenius 2003: 53)

Table 4.4 Support for the Swedish Social Democrats, 1920–2002

	Average Social Democrat vote (%)	*Average winning margin (%)*
1920–40	40.8	16.0
1944–68	46.9	27.3
1970–2002	42.5	21.1

Uniquely among the Nordic social democratic parties, SAP has on two occasions – 1940 and 1968 – won an absolute majority of the vote. The September 1940 general election, at which SAP recorded its best-ever result of 53.8%, was staged in exceptional circumstances and was exceptional too in that the parties largely refrained from criticising one another. Instead, they came together in defence of Swedish territorial sovereignty and the government's line of highly pragmatic neutrality.[2]

SAP's narrow absolute majority of 50.1% in 1968 was achieved at the last general election before the introduction of a single-chamber Riksdag and the last fought by the long-serving SAP prime minister Tage Erlander. It represented an 8.1% increase (and over half a million extra votes) compared with the SAP result in the 1966 local government election, when the non-socialists displayed a significantly greater unity of purpose and the Communists polled their best result of 6.4% since 1948. SAP's winning margin of 34.4 percentage points over the second-placed Centre is the greatest winning margin achieved by any political party in the Nordic region. Several factors may be adduced to explain the Social Democrats' success in winning over half the active electorate.

First, there was SAP's promotion of a new industrial policy, which involved a more active role for the state in supporting and stimulating business development. 1967, for example, saw the creation of a State Investment Bank providing ready access to venture capital. Second, despite closer co-operation between the so-called 'middle parties' – and even talk of a merger between the Centre and Liberals – promoted by the Centre leader Gunnar Hedlund, the non-socialist parties conspicuously failed to campaign on an alternative government programme. Third, there appeared to be something of a popular reaction against the radical student movement in Stockholm in spring 1968, which was triggered in large part by the anti-Vietnam demonstrations in the USA and across Western Europe and developed a broad critique of the social democratic order. This assault on 'welfare capitalism' was not shared by the majority of the citizenry. Indeed, the reaction to it probably contributed to mobilising SAP voters and the turnout reached an all-time record of 89.3%.

Fourth, the Soviet invasion of Czechoslovakia on 21 August 1968 to snuff out Dubcek's "communism with a human face" provoked outrage in Sweden and reduced the Communists to a mere 3.0% of the vote. Finally, the role played by the veteran SAP prime minister, Tage Erlander, was also important given the events preceding the election. He embodied continuity, certainty and the "Swedish way" for an electorate that largely eschewed the Americanised campaign style of the new Liberal and Conservative leaders. Moreover, it was widely known that this would be Erlander's last election. (Hadenius 2003: 133–135)

The social structure of Scandinavian Social Democracy

The rise of the Scandinavian social democratic-labour parties to a position of electoral dominance by the 1930s was predicated first and foremost on the high level of political cohesion among the working class. The social democratic parties emerged and developed as class parties, albeit by no means in the same heavy industrialised mould as the British Labour Party. A few brief observations on the regional strength of the parties in the early 1930s will give a reasonably reliable indication of the social composition of the social democrats' core support base.

A general contextual factor was the differential rate and impact of economic modernisation, which would go some considerable way to explaining why Danish social democracy emerged as much more an urban phenomenon than its sister parties in the region. Denmark experienced industrialisation half a century before Norway and Sweden and by the end of the First World War about one-quarter of the entire population lived in the greater Copenhagen area, the industrial centre of the country. Accordingly, the Danish Social Democrats were "dominated by and run from Copenhagen" (Berglund and Lindström 1978: 34) They also had pockets of electoral strength in eastern Jutland and Zealand, but the party was weak in the predominantly agricultural north, south and west Jutland.

In contrast, the Finnish Social Democrats attracted significant support from the rural proletariat of southern, central and eastern Finland – the agricultural workers, scrapholders, tenants and crofters – in the pre-independence period. Thereafter, an extensive land reform programme in the 1920s created land for the landless, boosted support for the Agrarians, whose growing dominance in the countryside was challenged in the 1920s (and again after the second world war) by the radical left, not the Social Democrats. By the 1930s Finnish social democracy drew essentially on the urbanised and industrialised south, along with sections of the Swedish-speaking blue-collar workforce in Helsinki and its environs.

The strongholds of the Norwegian Labour Party by the 1930s were in the capital Oslo and eastern Norway, on the one hand, and northern Norway, on the other. Its support in short pivoted on an urban–rural axis. The party attracted significant numbers of farm-fishermen in the north – Berglund and Lindström have estimated that about 45% of voters in northern Norway in the 1930s backed Labour (Berglund and Lindström 1978: 122) But its strength none the less lay in the cities. Its 'blind spots' were in southern and western Norway, where barely one-quarter of the electorate supported Labour.

The regional variation in the Swedish Social Democrats' electoral support in the 1930s was relatively limited. Mikael Gilljam has estimated that SAP's variation coefficient – calculated as the overall standard deviation divided by the average based on the constituency – fell from 0.30 in 1924 to 0.16 in 1936. (Gilljam 1993: 216–221)[3] However, Ingemar Wörlund's study of regional variation in SAP's support between 1921–40 revealed that the Social Democrats were strong in the 'deep south' – that is, southern Skåne – along with much of central Sweden, the Stockholm area and West Norrland. Their 'Achilles heel' (in relative terms!) was in the 'far north' (Norrbotten and Västerbotten), parts of the south-west and the island of Gotland. (Wörlund 1986: 90) Wörlund notes, however, that variation in SAP's support did not always follow county boundaries, while he also observes a rural–urban dimension. SAP was strong in about 80% of all cities.

Clearly then, a number of regions have traditionally been more difficult for the social democratic-labour parties to penetrate and in these there appears to have been a degree of 'cultural resistance' to socialism seemingly moulded by factors such as religion, ethnicity and a temperance tradition. These cultural factors, however, are probably best thought of as largely reinforcing the electoral logic of the socio-economic structure of the region. Thus, in Denmark the low church 'Inner Mission' has been strong in Western Jutland where the Social Democrats have been weak, but this is largely a farming area and natural terrain for the agrarian Liberals (*Venstre*). Similarly, the Finnish Social Democrats have struggled in the Swedish-speaking towns and villages of Ostrobothnia (in Western Finland) but, as in Western Jutland, the economy is essentially farm-based and, as such, largely impervious to social democracy. Significantly, the non-Swedish speaking countryside of Ostrobothnia (inland rather than the coastal fringe) has overwhelmingly backed the Agrarian-Centre.

Perhaps more directly linked to cultural factors has been the relative Labour weakness in the so-called 'Bible Belt' area of south-west Norway. Even in the late 1960s, the Norwegian Labour Party managed only 36% of the active electorate in the sparsely-populated districts in the south-west (compared with 52% in the densely-populated areas in the east of the country) and by 1985 this figure had fallen to 22%. (Aardal and Valen 1989: 225, 319) Similarly, SAP in Sweden has performed below its national average in the Jönköping constituency, where the Pentecostalist movement is strong and along the West coast, where the temperance movement has deep historical roots. Moreover, Västerbotten has had a very strong free church, teetotal tradition (*frisinnad*) of support for liberalism.

In these cases, a 'competitive' organisational infrastructure antedated both social democracy and mass democracy. In contrast, in its stronghold areas in the 1930s, the mass membership character of the Scandinavian social democratic parties was very much in evidence. There was a high member–voter ratio, close links to the trade union movement and a network of clubs, cooperative shops and newspapers reinforcing a sub-culture of labour solidarity. Comparative data are not readily available, but on the basis of Edvard Thermeanius' figures, SAP's membership in 1932 stood at 296,507 and its vote 1,040, 673. (Thermeanius 1933: 192, 194) This would make a social democratic member–voter ratio in Sweden of 1:3.

By the 1960s that solidarity remained very much in evidence, contributing to the striking stability of the social democratic electorate. For example, 89% of those who voted for SAP in 1960 claimed they had never voted for another party, whereas the figure for the three Swedish non-socialist parties was lower than 60% in each case. (Särlvik 1966: 196) However, two trends reflected an expansion of the social democratic electorate beyond its solidary, core blue-collar constituency in the early post-war decades. First, by the early 1960s there had been something of *a nationalisation of the social democratic-labour vote*, that is a reduction in the support differential between its strong and weaker areas. For instance, in the 1960 and 1964 general elections, the Danish Social Democrats were the largest party in all the constituencies in the capital city and Island regions *and* also in over half the constituencies of Jutland. In the three large provincial cities of Aarhus, Odense and Aalborg, the Social Democrats polled an absolute majority of the vote. (Glans 1966: 235)

Second, by the 1960s and early 1970s there had been something of *an embourgeoisment of the social democratic electorate.* According to Torben Worre's figures – based on survey research undertaken before the 'earthquake elections' of 1973 – between just under one-quarter of the middle class in Denmark (24%), one-third in Norway and somewhat under two-fifths in Sweden supported social democratic-labour parties. (Worre 1980: 302) The greatest support came from the lower middle class, almost half of which backed SAP in Sweden, particularly those with a working-class background. As many as 54% of the middle class where the father was working-class backed SAP and 49% the Norwegian Labour Party. (Worre 1980: 307) In short, by the 1960s the Scandinavian social democratic labour parties had to varying degrees evolved from class to catchall parties by attracting significant support from the so-called 'new middle class' in the vastly expanded public sector.

Scandinavian Social Democracy: continued dominance or incipient decomposition?

Half a century later, the case for the continuing electoral dominance of Scandinavian social democracy is hardly difficult to make. Excluding Iceland, there were 108 general elections in the Nordic region between 1919–2005 and in 92% of these social democratic-labour parties were the largest party. Moreover, half of the ten general elections in which a non-socialist party claimed the highest percentage poll occurred in the 1920s. Since the Second World War, only in Finland in 1962, 1991 and 2003, and in Denmark in 2001 and 2005 have the social democrats not been the largest party.

The degree of the electoral dominance of social democracy has, however, varied across mainland Scandinavia. The 'winning margin' between the social democrats and the second largest party has ranged from 26–28 percentage points in Sweden and Norway between 1945–69 to only 1.3 percentage points in Finland in the same period.

The electoral 'peak years' of the Scandinavian social democratic parties have also varied. The heyday of Finnish social democracy was in the decade before independence, when the party averaged two-fifths of the vote. The 1930s represented the 'golden age' of Danish social democracy and in 1935 the party recorded its best-ever poll of 46.1%. In its 'best years' between 1945–69, the Norwegian Labour Party averaged 45.4% of the electorate. The track record of the Swedish social democrats is unique. The Social Democrats have been the largest party in every Riksdag election since the introduction of PR and universal suffrage in 1921. However, the electoral prime of Swedish social democracy was the high economic growth period in the 1950s and 1960s when the party averaged over 45% of the vote.[4]

The electoral peak of Scandinavian social democracy appears past. The 'winning margin' of the Danish, Swedish and especially Norwegian social democratic labour parties is substantially smaller than it was. In Denmark and Norway the 'earthquake elections' of 1973 marked something of a watershed. Indeed, the winning margin of the Norwegian Labour Party between 1973 and the 2005 general election at 13.0% was barely half that of the 1945–69 period. The hegemonic ruling status of the Swedish and Norwegian social democratic-labour parties, marked by continuous periods of governmental incumbency lasting for three or four decades also appears very much in the past.

Taking the post-war period as a whole, the Finnish Social Democratic Party has been neither electorally nor governmentally as dominant as its sister parties in Scandinavia. However, in only three general elections since 1945 has it not emerged as the largest party and since 1966 it can reasonably lay claim to be the natural governing party in Finland. Put another way, in nearly four decades since 1966 the Finnish social democrats have failed to participate in only one party political government – the non-socialist coalition led by Esko Aho (Centre) between 1991–95 – and have remained in opposition for only 8.5% of the time. While prima facie this would suggest that over the last forty years the Finnish Social Democrats have enjoyed greater governmental dominance than their better-known Swedish and Norwegian counterparts – and they have boasted the prime minister for much of the period – appearances are a little deceptive. Whereas until 2005 the Norwegian Labour Party had never governed in coalition, and in the post-war period the Swedish Social Democrats have only once done so – with the Agrarians between 1951–57 – the Finnish Social Democrats have only once in the last four decades governed on their own. That was as a single-party minority cabinet in 1972 under Rafael Paasio. Moreover, the Finnish Social Democrats have never led a left-wing government with the radical left and have always co-operated in coalition with one of the two other larger parties, the Centre or Conservatives. In short, although the Finnish Social Democrats have been in power more than their sister parties in Norway and Sweden since the mid-1960s, they have routinely shared power with non-socialist parties 'across the blocs'.

The striking exception to the strength of Scandinavian social democracy has been Iceland. In the eighteen general elections between 1942–95 the Social Democrats averaged only 14.6% of the vote and in June 1974 their poll dropped to 9.1%. Even when they gained their best result of 22% in June 1978 the Social Democrats were only the third largest of the four old parties. However, things might be changing. As noted in chapter 3, the Democratic Alliance formed in 1999 from a merger of the Women's List, Radical Left and Social Democrats polled 31% at the 2003 general election. In so doing, it became the only party apart from the Independence Party to exceed 30% of the vote for over seventy years.

Although the Social Democrats were the largest party in all four mainland Nordic countries in the mid-1980s, Gøsta Esping-Andersen none the less made arresting reference to the phenomenon of 'social democratic party decomposition'. (Esping-Andersen 1985) Over twenty years later, a number of factors would appear to account for the (largely) gradual erosion of electoral support for the social democrats. Of course, the emphasis in any analysis will depend to a large extent on the particular disciplinary perspective.

Political sociologists would doubtless focus on the way social structural change has blurred the traditional class contours of politics, reduced the relative size of the Scandinavian Social Democrats' core working-class base and led by extension to an accentuated 'embourgeoisment' of their members and voters. On the changing background of the party membership, Knut Heidar has noted that at the Norwegian Labour Party conference in 1985, 57% of delegates were public employees, only 12% came from industry and 46% had a university-level education. (Heidar 1994: 107) As to voters, it would be expected that the changing balance between blue-collar social democrats and white-collar social democrats would be reflected (minimally and somewhat crudely) in a decline in the Alford class index of voting. In this respect, Denmark appears a limiting case among the Scandinavian countries. Thus, Johannes Andersen and Jørgen Goul Andersen have shown how between 1966–2001 the Alford index in Denmark plummeted from +52 in 1966 – on a par with Sweden – to a mere +6 in 2001. Re-stated, 81% of Danish workers supported a workers' party in 1966 whereas by 2001 only 42% did so. (Andersen and Andersen 200: 209) In the same period the proportion of the middle class voting for the left rose, albeit not dramatically, from 28–36% (see table 4.5).

There is unmistakable evidence of a decline in class voting in Norway and Sweden too. Henry Valen's figures – see table 4.6 – indicate that the Alford index fell in Norway from +49 in 1949 to +36 in 1973, the 'earthquake election' year. It fell further to only +18 in 1989, when the Progress Party gained nearly ten percentage points to poll 13% of the electorate. (Valen 1995: 139) Some caution should be exercised in interpreting the data, however, since voters have been simply dichotomised into 'workers' and 'others' and the figures are for leftist parties in general and not just Labour. Nonetheless, the downtrend is clear enough.

So it is in Sweden, too, since as table 4.7 illustrates, the class index of voting fell from +51 in 1956 to +25 in 1991 – Sweden's 'earthquake election' year. In the latter year, 8% of the working class voted for the populist New Democracy party, although this soon imploded and disappeared from parliament almost as quickly as it had arrived on the scene. In contrast to Denmark, however, class voting in Sweden rose marginally over the course of the 1990s.

Although never electorally dominant in the Independence period in the manner of its metropolitan Scandinavian counterparts, the Finnish Social Democratic Party has mirrored the social structural changes that followed the rapid economic modernisation of the country in the second half of the twentieth century. Finland was transformed from a predominantly agrarian society in the late 1940s to an essentially post-industrial society by the start of the new millennium. During that period the Social Democrats evolved from being a class party to one in which the working-class component in its support was in a narrow minority. Risto Sänkiaho has shown that in 1948 76% of the Social Democrats' support came from blue-collar workers, but this fell to 63% in 1982 and 52% in 1991. (Sänkiaho 1995: 71)

Table 4.5 The decline in class voting in Denmark, 1964–2001

| | Support for socialist parties (%) | | |
	Workers	Middle class	Alford index
1964	78	28	50
1966	81	29	52
1968	71	24	47
1971	74	31	43
1973	56	21	35
1975	62	27	35
1977	64	37	27
1979	66	40	26
1981	64	38	26
1984	64	38	26
1987	67	44	23
1988	62	39	23
1990	71	42	29
1994	57	39	18
1998	54	41	13
2001	42	36	6

Source: Johannes Andersen and Jørgen Goul Andersen, 'Klassernes forsvinden', in Andersen and Borre (2003), p. 209

Table 4.6 Class voting in Norway, 1949–89

	Workers	Others	Alford index
1949	83	34	49
1957	78	34	44
1965	76	32	44
1969	74	34	40
1973	68	32	36
1977	70	33	37
1989	59	41	18

Source: Henry Valen, *Valg og Politikk – et samfunn i endring* (1995), p. 139

A *political sociology perspective* would also point to the failure of the party system adequately to respond to the imperatives of social structural change, the phenomenon of so-called 'partisan dealignment' and its corollary, rising electoral volatility and increased abstentionism. In the social democratic context, evidence would be sought *inter alia* in the reduced electoral stability of the party's core working-class electorate. There is no doubt that since the 'earthquake elections' of 1970–73, electoral volatility has risen sharply and affected blue-collar voters as much, if not more than others. In the period 1966–2001 the proportion of Danish workers supporting one of the non-socialist parties rose from 14–52%. (Andersen and Andersen 2003: 209) At the Danish general election in 2001, the working-class share of the Social Democrats' vote at 48.2% was easily exceeded by the 58.8% of the Progress Party and 61.2% of the Danish People's Party. (Andersen and Andersen 2003: 217) Similarly, at the 2001 Norwegian general election, blue-collar workers made up only 14% of the Labour Party's support, compared with 22% for the Progress Party. (Pettersen and Rose 2004: 12)

A *party organisation perspective* would tend to focus on conflict and cohesion within parties. It would view them as 'internal coalitions', comprising factions and tendencies that operate in all or some of the party's arenas – the party in parliament, the party in the country etc. In the Scandinavian social democratic party context, the solidarity of early decades gave way to the rise of factionalism in the 1960s. Simplifying somewhat, this had at its heart tensions between the older generation of traditional (often working-class) socialists and younger, more educated middle-class elements. In the Norwegian Labour Party, for example, internal opposition emerged –mainly within the youth organisation – as a by-product of the international reaction against the Vietnam war. Then the EC membership issue pitted the pro-membership leadership, trade union movement and parliamentary party group majority against an internal opposition group, the 'Information Committee Against Membership' formed in 1971. (Heidar 1994: 98) A majority of its leaders, although not rank-and-file, subsequently left the Labour Party to join the Socialist Electoral Alliance. But a legacy of factionalisation remained, fuelled by environmental issues and, not least, the decision to store equipment for the US military in Norway. (Heidar 1994: 96–111)

A *party change perspective* would concentrate *inter alia* on the evolution of a party's programme and its stance on the important issues of the day. From a Scandinavian social democratic standpoint, at least two observations might be made. First, the 'metropolitan' social democratic-labour parties have been deeply divided on such high-profile issues as the EU, EMU and the future of nuclear energy. For example, among those who supported the Social Democrats at the 2002 Swedish general election, 42% voted in favour of EMU membership at the 2003 referendum and 56% voted against, with 2% voting 'blank'.

(Holmberg 2004: 81–99) Second, the exigencies of macro-economic policy management have conspired to limit the Social Democrats' traditional capacity to institutionalise their own power base through the pursuit of reformist policies. In Sweden, for example, policies such as the controversial supplementary (income-related) pensions' project in the late 1950s were successful in transforming SAP into a wage-earner's party. By the 1960s, as Esping-Andersen has remarked, "SAP had managed to build a welfare state that pleased the workers and the middle class". (Esping-Andersen 1990: 57) However, managing Sweden out of recession during the mid–1990s largely prevented the ruling Social Democrats from pursuing a traditionally expansionist welfare programme. Austerity measures led to the appearance of a *neo-liberalisation of social democracy* and prompted vote defection to the Leftist Party, which claimed a record 12% of the poll in 1998. (Arter 2003: 233)

Table 4.7 Class voting in Sweden, 1956–98

	Working class (%)	Middle class (%)	Alford index
1956	75	24	51
1960	80	28	52
1964	78	31	47
1968	76	35	41
1970	70	32	38
1973	73	30	43
1976	69	32	37
1979	71	33	38
1982	72	35	37
1985	71	35	36
1988	70	39	31
1991	57	32	25
1994	70	41	29
1998	67	38	29

Source: Maria Oskarson, *Klassröstning i Sverige – rationalitet, lojalitet eller bara slentrian?* (1994), p. 42. Sören Holmberg, *Välja parti* (2000), pp. 66–67

Ironically, it was much the same story in Norway, despite the very strong economy. When the Labour leader Jens Stoltenberg became prime minister in spring 2000, he pursued a tight fiscal policy, placing a chunk of oil and gas revenues into a 'rainy day fund' and emphasising the importance of a sustainable welfare state. It was by no means coincidental, therefore, that at the general election the following year Labour, with 24.4% of the vote, experienced its worst result since 1924. In contrast, the Socialist Left Party, under the female leadership of Kristin Halvorsen, canvassing an expansion of the public sector, gained its best result of 12.4%. There was a significant defection of Labour support to the Socialist Left, especially on the part of young women.

From a *decline of party* perspective, reference could well be made to the growing personalisation of social democratic politics and the loss of many of its 'movemental characteristics'. Put another way, evidence of an erosion in the traditional organisational infrastructure of social democracy would be sought. Membership of the Swedish party, for instance, has fallen sharply, not least because, since 1990, trade union members have no longer automatically been SAP members. From the Second World War to the 1970s, during the era of so-called 'collective (automatic) membership', between 34–39% of the central blue-collar federation Landorganisationen's (LO) members were SAP members. (Widfeldt 2001: 68–69) By the mid-1990s, when collective membership had been abolished, this figure had fallen to 7.6%. In Norway, too, LO branches could decide to join the Labour Party and individual LO members would then automatically become party members. Unlike Sweden, however, collective membership was in decline when it was abolished in Norway in 1992. For example, it fell from 50% to just 24% of the Labour Party's total membership between 1971–89. In Denmark there have never been collective membership arrangements between LO and the Social Democrats, although many blue-collar workers have traditionally been members of both.

Some movemental elements remain. Thus, the Christian social democrats in Sweden have their own organisation, 'The Brotherhood' (*Broderskapet*), which was formed in 1929 and is officially a subsidiary of the party. Unlike trade union members, all members of The Brotherhood are automatically members of SAP. Membership figures are difficult to obtain, although it is safe to assume the figure of 6–8,000 in the 1990s has subsequently fallen. While small, 'The Brotherhood' is by no means insignificant and its conference every second year is usually addressed by a senior party figure. In 1965, for example, Olof Palme gave a speech there, which was widely regarded as the starting point of his vigorous criticism of US policy in Vietnam. However, it is probably safe to say that the lines of influence in the social democratic-labour parties run from the top down and that the character and electoral perception of social democracy are determined increasingly by the party chairman and his close advisers.

An analysis of social democratic party decomposition from a psephological perspective would focus, among other things, on the *political socialisation of age cohorts* and the impact of 'period effects'. Generational turnover has confronted the Social Democrats with an increasingly ageing support base. Put another way, the evidence suggests that in the three 'metropolitan Scandinavian' states, the social democratic-labour parties have increasingly struggled to appeal to young voters. It may be that for the new cohorts "the Social Democrats represent 'the Establishment' by virtue of their long-term position in government, and their focus on an issue agenda that is not central to their values". (Knutsen 2003: 60) In any event, the average differences in support for the social democratic-labour parties in Denmark, Norway and Sweden between the oldest and youngest age-cohorts in the 1970s–1990s are set out in table 4: 8. It is evident that the social democratic parties have lower support among the younger age-groups than the older ones in all three countries – the differential is particularly marked in Norway – although the tendency varies over time and place. It is strongest in Denmark and Norway in the 1980s and Sweden in the 1990s. (Knutsen 2003: 148) Oddbjørn Knutsen concludes that "the 1970s and 1980s are characterised by only minor age differences in support for the Swedish Social Democrats. This accords well with Esping-Andersen's perspective of only slight party decomposition among Sweden's Social Democrats. On the other hand, we can note general support for the perspective of an age decomposition in the 1990s". (Knutsen 2003: 135–136) Clearly, a foremost challenge for social democratic parties across the region is generational renewal.

Table 4.8 The difference in support between the oldest and youngest age-cohorts for the 'metropolitan Scandinavian' Social Democratic-Labour parties, 1970s–90s*

	Denmark	Norway	Sweden
Average 1970s	3.9	9.8	5.3
Average 1980s	12.4	14.3	7.5
Average 1990s	7.8	10.1	12.1

*   Calculated on the basis of the average percentage differences in support for the social democratic-labour parties between the oldest two age cohorts – 60–69 years and 70+ – and the two youngest – 18–24 years and 25–29 years.

Source: Oddbjørn Knutsen, Generations, Age Groups and Voting Behaviour in the Scandinavian Countries. A Comparative Survey (2003), pp. 118, 129, 144

Finally, from a *party system change perspective*, changes in the structure of party competition have meant increased co-operation among the non-socialist parties (especially in Sweden) and heightened competition for power from a centre-right bloc of parties. This is not, of course, strictly relevant to the decomposition of the social democratic vote, but is likely to have at least short-term implications for it. Earlier, the Social Democrats could operate on a 'divide and rule' basis, forging legislative coalitions with one or more of the opposition-based non-socialists (Liberals or Centre) to create a parliamentary majority for measures. Particularly in Sweden this is becoming increasingly difficult.

In a wide-ranging analysis, Herbert Kitschelt sees West European social democracy facing twin challenges (Kitschelt 1994). It must respond credibly to the pressures of managing the economy and welfare state in an era of globalisation, while also reacting to the sharpened sensitivities of the electorate to issues associated with the new social movements. The problem for the Scandinavian social-democratic labour parties, albeit in varying electoral degrees, has been that policies of fiscal orthodoxy (at times austerity) have allowed parties on the radical left to espouse the politics of redistribution and the traditional 'tax-and-spend' welfarism of 1960s social democracy. However, responding to the post-materialist agenda has also proved problematical for the Scandinavian social democrats. This is in part because the traditional blue-collar support has been alienated from the 'new politics', especially such things as feminism and environmentalism, which threaten the material interests of male trade unionists.

So what would be a reasonable response to the question in the title of this chapter 'Continued dominance or incipient decomposition?' Writing in 2005, social democratic-labour parties are the largest party in only two of the four mainland Nordic countries and even in Sweden SAP has struggled to be the '40% party' it has always regarded itself as. It has not surmounted the 40% barrier for the last two Riksdag elections. In the short term, at least, the case for the electoral dominance of Scandinavian social democracy really cannot be made. But what of the longer-term trends?

Maria Oskarson in her doctoral dissertation on 'Class Voting in Sweden' added the rider question – 'rationality, loyalty or simply habit'? From the evidence presented, we can, by appropriating her terms, say at least three things with reasonable confidence. 1) The proportion of 'habitual social democratic voters' in Scandinavia is greatest among the older age cohorts and there is variable evidence of an 'age decomposition' among the social democratic electorates. There are fewer 'habitual social democrats' among younger voters and one manifestation of this heightened electoral volatility has been the extent of young (especially male) working-class support for the radical rightist parties. 2) The number of 'loyal (working-class) social democratic voters' has fallen as class identification has weakened and social and geographical mobility increased.

The point should not be exaggerated, since in Sweden Holmberg has estimated that in 1998 just under half (47%) of SAP voters came from the working class. (Holmberg 2000: 65) Nonetheless, the evidence of a decline in class
voting is incontrovertible. Moreover, there has been a particularly sharp reduction in support for the social democratic-labour parties from blue-collar
trade union members – from 81% in 1956 to 55% in 1998 in Sweden, for
example. (Holmberg 2000: 68–69) 3) The number of 'rational social democratic voters' – that is, those motivated to support a social democratic party
primarily out of considerations of economic self-interest – may well have fallen
as the social democrats have pursued fiscal policies more closely associated
with the political Right and appeared to abandon the traditional politics of
redistribution. This is obviously a highly speculative point. On firmer empirical ground, it may be said that a foremost challenge of Scandinavian social
democracy is generational renewal. This, of course, is not peculiar to the Scandinavian social democrats, nor is there a simple formula for success.

Notes

1   The 25 August 1918 Finnish Communist Party programme was based on five
    principles. They were that the workers' movement would be exclusively prepared
    for an armed revolution; that only actively promoting revolution was legitimate;
    that in the revolution all power would be taken into the hands of the proletariat;
    that there would be an immediate expropriation of the capitalists; and that the
    new party would be a branch of an international revolutionary front dedicated to
    the defence of the Bolshevik revolution. (Upton 1980: 519)
2   'Strict neutrality' inclined towards 'semi-neutrality' – in Hans Mouritzen's phrase
    – when in June 1940 the Swedish government (which from December 1939
    contained all the political parties except the Communists) felt obliged to accede
    to a German request to allow the transit of Nazi troops journeying on leave from
    Norway through Sweden to Germany. (Mouritzen 1988: 166–218)
3   The variation coefficient can range between 0 (no variation at all) to 5.2 (maxi-
    mum variation). The latter is based on the square root of all units of analysis (the
    twenty-eight Swedish constituencies) minus one, i.e. the square root of 27 = 5.196.
    (Gilljam 1993: 216–221)
4   Indeed, in the period 1945–87, the Swedish Social Democrats were the best sup-
    ported party in Western Europe – not just among its fraternal parties – narrowly
    surpassing the performance of Fianna Fáil in the Irish Republic.

References

Aardal, Bernt and Henry Valen *Velgere, Partier og Politisk Avstand* (Statistisk Sentralbyrå:
    Oslo, 1989)
Andersen, Jørgen Goul and Ole Borre (eds) *Politisk Forandring* (Systime Academic:

Århus, 2003)

Andersen, Johannes and Jørgen Goul Andersen 'Klassernes forsvinden' in Jørgen Goul Andersen and Ole Borre (eds) *Politisk Forandring* (Systime Academic: Århus, 2003), pp. 207–222)

Arter, David *Scandinavian Politics Today* (Manchester University Press: Manchester, 1999)

Arter, David 'Party System Change in Scandinavia since 1970: "Restricted Change" or "General Change"?' *West European Politics* 22, 3, 1999, pp. 139–158

Arter, David '"Communists we are no longer, Social Democrats we can never be": the Evolution of the Leftist Parties in Finland and Sweden', in Joan Botella and Luis Ramiro (eds) *The Crisis of Communism and Party Change. The Evolution of West European Communist and Post-Communist Parties* (ICPS: Barcelona, 2003), pp. 211–236

Berglund, Sten and Ulf Lindström *The Scandinavian Party System(s)* (Studentlitteratur: Lund, 1978)

Bergström, Hans 'Sweden's Politics and Party System at the Crossroads' *West European Politics* 14, 1, 1991, pp. 8–30

Bjørklund, Tor and Jørgen Goul Andersen 'Anti-Immigration Parties in Denmark and Norway: The Progress Parties and the Danish People's Party', in Martin Schain, Aristide Zolberg and Patrick Hossay (eds) *Shadows over Europe: The Development and Impact of the Extreme Right in Western Europe* (Palgrave Macmillan: Basingstoke, 2002), pp. 107–136

Borg, Sami and Risto Sänkiaho *The Finnish Voter* (The Finnish Political Science Association: Tampere, 1995), pp. 66–87

Elder, Neil 'The Swedish General Election of 1976' *Parliamentary Affairs* 2, 1977

Esping-Andersen, Gøsta *Politics against Markets. The Social Democratic Road to Power* (Princeton University Press: Princeton, NJ, 1985)

Esping-Andersen, Gøsta 'Single-party Dominance in Sweden: The Saga of Social Democracy', in T. J. Pempel (ed.) *Uncommon Democracies* (Cornell University: Ithaca NY, 1990), pp. 33–57

Gilljam, Mikael 'Sveriges politiska geografi', in Sören Holmberg and Mikael Gilljam *Väljarna inför 90-talet* (Norstedts juridik: Stockholm, 1993), pp. 216–221

Glans, Ingemar 'Denmark: The 1964 Folketing Election' *Scandinavian Political Studies* 1, 1966, pp. 231–236

Gustafsson, Göran 'Church-State Separation Swedish-Style' *West European Politics* 26, 1, 2003, pp. 51–72

Hadenius, Stig *Modern svensk politisk historia* (Hjalmarson & Högberg: Stockholm, 2003)

Hagelund, Annika 'A Matter of Decency? The Progress Party in Norwegian Immigration Politics' *Journal of Ethnic and Migration Studies* 23, 1, 2003, pp. 47–65

Heidar, Knut 'Towards Party Irrelevance? The Decline of Both Conflict and Cohesion in the Norwegian Labour Party', in David S. Bell and Eric Shaw (eds) *Conflict and Cohesion in Western European Social Democratic Parties* (Pinter: London and New York, 1994), pp. 96–111

Heidar, Knut *Norway. Elites on Trial* (Westview: Boulder, CO, 2001)

Holmberg, Sören 'Ännu inte marginaliserade partier', in Henrik Oscarsson and Sören Holmberg (eds) *Kampen on euro* (Göteborgs universitet: Göteborg, 2004), pp. 81–99)

Holmberg, Sören *Välja parti* (Norstedts Juridik: Stockholm, 2000)

Jenkins, Roy *Nine Men of Power* (Hamish Hamilton: London, 1974), pp. 30–59

Jenssen, Anders Todal 'All that is Solid Melts into Air: Party Identification in Norway' *Scandinavian Political Studies* 22, 1, 1999, pp. 1–27

Kitschelt, Herbert *The Transformation of European Social Democracy* (Cambridge University Press: Cambridge, 1994)

Knutsen, Oddbjørn *Generations, Age Groups and Voting Behaviour in the Scandinavian Countries. A Comparative Study* (University of Oslo, Research report 4/2003)

Knutsen, Oddbjørn 'Religious Denomination and Party Choice in Western Europe: A Comparative Longitudinal Study from Eight Countries, 1970–97' *International Political Science Review* 25, 1, 2004, pp. 97–128

Lipset, S. M. and S. Rokkan (eds) *Voter Systems and Party Alignments* (Free Press: New York, 1967)

Mair, Peter *Party System Change* (Clarendon Press: Oxford, 1997)

Möller, Tommy 'The Swedish Election 1998: A Protest Vote and the Birth of a New Political Landscape' *Scandinavian Political Studies* 22, 3, 1999, pp. 261–276

Mouritzen, Hans *Finlandization: Towards a General Theory of Adaptive Politics* (Avebury: Aldershot, 1988)

Nielsen, Hans Jørgen 'The Danish Election 1998' *Scandinavian Political Studies* 22, 1, 1999, pp. 67–81

Oskarson, Maria *Klassröstning i Sverige: rationalitet, lojalitet eller bara slentrian* (Nerenius och Santérus förlag, 1994)

Petersson, Olof *The Government and Politics of the Nordic Countries* (Fritzes: Stockholm, 1994)

Pettersen, Per Arnt and Lawrence E. Rose 'Høyrebølgene – de store og små: Velgerprofilene til Høyre og Fremskrittspartiet i flo og fjære' *Norsk Statsvitenskapelig Tidskrift* 20, 3, 2004, pp. 3–37

Rothstein, Bo *The Social Democratic State* (University of Pittsburgh Press: Pittsburgh and London, 1996)

Rydgren, Jens 'Explaining the Emergence of Radical Right-Wing Populist Parties: The Case of Denmark' *West European Politics* 27, 3, 2004, pp. 474–502

Sänkiaho, Risto 'The Social Basis for Party Support', in Sami Borg and Risto Sänkiaho *The Finnish Voter* (The Finnish Political Science Association: Tampere, 1995), pp. 66–87

Särlvik, Bo 'Political Stability and Change in the Swedish Electorate' *Scandinavian Political Studies* 1, 1966, pp. 188–222

Sartori, Giovanni 'European Political Parties: The Case of Polarized Pluralism', in J. LaPalombara and M. Weiner (eds) *Political Parties and Political Development* (Princeton University Press: Princeton, NJ, 1966)

Smith, Gordon 'Core Persistence: System Change and the "People's Party"' *West*

European Politics 12, 4, 1989, pp. 157–168

Sundberg, Jan 'The Enduring Scandinavian Party System' *Scandinavian Political Studies* 22, 3, 1999, pp. 221–241

Thermeanius, Edvard *Sveriges Politiska Partier* (Hugo Gebers förlag: Stockholm, 1933)

Thomas, Alastair H. 'Social Democracy in Denmark', in William E. Paterson and Alastair H. Thomas (eds) *Social Democratic Parties in Western Europe* (Croom Helm: London, 1977), pp. 234–271

Upton, Anthony F. *The Finnish Revolution 1917–1918* (University of Minnesota Press: Minneapolis, 1980)

Valen, Henry *Valg og Politikk – et samfunn i endring* (NKS-Forlaget: Oslo, 1995)

Widfeldt, Anders 'Sweden: Weakening Links Between Political Parties and Interest Organisations', in Clive S. Thomas (ed.) *Political Parties and Interest Groups: Shaping Democratic Governance* (Lynne Rienner: Boulder, CO, 2001), pp. 63–78

Wörlund, Ingemar 'Socialdemokratins politiska geografi 1921–1940', in Sten Berglund and Jan Åke Dellenbrant (eds) *Svenska Partiregionalism* (Liber: Stockholm, 1986), pp. 74–98)

Worre, Torben 'Class Parties and Class Voting in the Scandinavian Countries' *Scandinavian Political Studies* 3, 4, 1980, pp. 299–320

Worre, Torben *Dansk Vælgeradfærd* (Akadeemisk forlag: Copenhagen, 1987)

5

The diversity of coalition types and the frequency of minority governments: a distinctively Scandinavian form of parliamentarism?

There can be fewer more striking contrasts in the Nordic region than in the size and composition of governments. In the 'metropolitan' Scandinavian states of Denmark, Norway and Sweden, minority cabinets have become the norm and policy-making has proceeded on the basis of *legislative coalitions*, regularised or ad hoc, with one or more of the opposition parties. The last majority government in Denmark was in 1993–94, and in Sweden 1979–81. The present Stoltenberg coalition is the first majority government in Norway for 20 years. Moreover, in addition to the frequency of single-party minority cabinets (mostly Social Democratic), minority coalitions have not been uncommon and have been almost exclusively of the 'ideologically connected type', following the lines of socialist–non-socialist bloc politics. In Finland and Iceland, in contrast, majority governments have been the norm – in the former often 'surplus majority' governments – and cabinets have brought together parties 'across the blocs'. There have been only two minority coalitions in Iceland since 1979 and only one in Finland in the same period. Furthermore, coalitions have frequently been 'unconnected' in an ideological sense, bringing together the right-of-centre Independence Party and Social Democrats in Iceland, for example, and the Conservatives and Social Democrats in Finland. All in all, the Nordic region has exhibited a remarkable variety of types of coalition government, from 'surplus majority' to minority and, while Denmark has become known as the 'home of minority governments', the same could equally well be said of Norway and Sweden.

The focus of this chapter is on the *executive-parties dimension* in Lijphart's terms. (Lijphart 1999) In view of the diversity of coalition types and the frequency of minority governments, it poses three basic questions. 1) Why have outsize coalitions been commonplace in Finland and minority governments the norm in 'metropolitan Scandinavia'? 2) Does the Nordic experience indicate that minority governments are necessarily weak and majority governments necessarily strong? 3) Is there a distinctively Scandinavian form of parliamentarism? The discussion is in three parts. The first explores the Finnish experience of 'surplus majority' governments and in particular the reasons for the formation of Paavo Lipponen's so-called 'rainbow coalition' in April 1995. The second reviews the minority cabinets in metropolitan Scandinavia and the factors underpinning their formation. The concluding part considers the issue of strength and weakness in the Nordic governments and the essence of Scandinavian parliamentarism.

Majority governments 'across the blocs': Finland and Iceland

In terms of the size of Finnish governments, 1966 was a watershed year; in terms of their stability, it was 1983. Throughout the post-war period, however, Finnish government coalitions have been formed 'across the blocs' and from 1966–81 they regularly included the Communist-dominated Finnish People's Democratic League. Between 1995–2003 Finland was governed by a unique 'rainbow coalition', which incorporated the Social Democrats, Conservatives, Leftists, Greens and Swedish People's Party. Minimal winning coalitions à la William Riker in short have emphatically not been the norm. (Riker 1962) The three-party coalition led by the Centre chairman, Matti Vanhanen, in Finland since June 2003 is a case in point. The two major coalition parties, the Centre (with 55 seats) and Social Democrats (with 53) together hold a majority of seats in the 200-seat Eduskunta. However, despite a poor showing at the polls, the Swedish People's Party representing the national language minority, which elected nine members of parliament, was included. Indeed, the Swedish People's Party has been in every Finnish government since 1979.

Ideologically disparate, 'surplus majority' coalitions have become something of a post-war Finnish speciality and a number will be cited in due course. However, as an extreme example of the genre, the various factors surrounding the formation of the 1995 'rainbow coalition' will be explored in some detail. Before that, however, it is important to emphasise that Finland has not always boasted stable, broad-based government. (Jungar 2002: 57–83)

On at least three counts, Finnish governments before 1966 were regarded as notably weak in comparative perspective. First, the constitutional competence of cabinets was relatively limited. Legislative authority under the 1919 constitution was vested jointly in the president and parliament and the primary duty of the government was to execute presidential decisions. Second, the polarised nature of the party system complicated the process of forming governments. There was a numerically strong anti-system party of the radical left (the Communists, it will be recalled, were re-legalised under the armistice with the Soviet Union in 1944) and an endemic fragmentation in the non-socialist camp. Third, the qualified majority rules (explained shortly), which applied to much economic legislation meant that governments to be effective needed the support of at least two-thirds of the Eduskunta. (Arter 1987: 50–51)

Yet it was not perhaps the fact that they were constitutionally and often numerically weak that was the distinctive feature of Finnish cabinets between 1945–66. Rather, it was that they were short-lived. There were 22 governments in the 21 years between 1945–66 and their average life was 399 days. Cabinet crises were a fact of political life and convoluted and often protracted negotiations preceded the formation of a new government. Nonetheless, in the first two post-war decades there was a remarkable diversity in the types of government in Finland. Some 50% of cabinets between 1945–66 were majority governments and 18% of all governments in that period comprised large or 'surplus majority' coalitions with the backing of over two-thirds of the Eduskunta seats.

Some of these 'surplus majority' cabinets were more successful than others. The broad centre-left coalition between 1946–48, headed by Mauno Pekkala of the Communist-dominated Finnish People's Democratic League, proved stable and effective. These were the so-called 'danger years' (*vaaran vuodet*) when the threat of a Communist takeover, backed from Moscow, bulked large. However, according to one contemporary politician (the Agrarian MP Jussi Niukkanen), Pekkala, who had defected from the Social Democrats, was simply "too lazy to bring about a revolution"! (Virolainen 1969: 21)

A broad-based government in 1958, led by the Social Democrat K.A. Fagerholm, which included the Conservatives and Agrarians but excluded the Communists, fared considerably less well. The Communists had polled 23.2% at the 1958 general election to become the largest party (polling exactly the same amount as the Social Democrats).[1] The Communists' exclusion from the Fagerholm cabinet at the expense of two parties, the Social Democrats and Conservatives, who were both mistrusted in the Kremlin, prompted the Soviet ambassador to leave without warning. Trade between the two countries virtually stalled. This was the so-called 'Night Frost' crisis and it provided the clearest evidence yet of Soviet interference in Finnish domestic politics. Only when the Agrarians withdrew from the government, which soon afterwards collapsed, did Finno-Soviet relations return to normal. (Jussila, Hentilä and Nevakivi 1999: 276–278)

Majority and 'surplus majority' cabinets aside, half of all Finnish governments between 1945–66 comprised either single-party minority cabinets or 'caretaker' governments of officials. There were no less than seven of these stop-gap 'caretakers' – composed of civil servants, experts and occasionally interest-group leaders – and they were appointed by the president and in practice responsible to him rather than parliament. The high incidence of caretaker cabinets in the first three post-war decades made this form of crisis government very much a Finnish peculiarity.

The year 1966 was a watershed in the history of Finnish governments. It marked the first of a number of broad centre-left, so-called 'Popular Front' coalitions embracing the Social Democrats, Communists and the Agrarian-Centre. The Koivisto 1 coalition between 1968–70 had the backing of no less than 164 of the 200 Eduskunta seats. These 'surplus majority' governments were vigorously supported by the long-serving president Urho Kekkonen (1956–81) who played an active role in coalition-building and coalition maintenance. For example, over summer 1972 Kekkonen descended unannounced on an executive meeting of his former party, the Agrarian-Centre, to make plain that if it did not co-operate in government with the Social Democrats its future claims to government would be seriously jeopardised. This threatened sanction ultimately achieved its purpose and almost a year of political instability ended on 4 September 1972 with the formation of a Social Democrat-Centre coalition led by Kalevi Sorsa. (Arter 1987: 95) Moreover, in autumn 1975, Kekkonen drummed up a so-called 'Government of National Emergency' under Martti Miettunen to deal with rising unemployment when, after inconclusive elections, the parties were dragging their heels.

Following Kekkonen's retirement through ill-health in 1981, subsequent presidents have played a less public, if not always less decisive role in the formation and preservation of cabinets. Mauno Koivisto (1982–94), for example, acted single-mindedly to torpedo a secret pre-1987 election agreement between the leaders of three non-socialist parties (Centre, Conservatives and Swedish People's Party) to form a non-socialist coalition after the election, which would have excluded the Social Democrats. In so doing, Koivisto broke the Agrarian-Centre's historic stranglehold on government office. In 1993 Koivisto also almost certainly helped to sustain the prime minister Esko Aho in office following an attempt by his foreign secretary (and party colleague!), Paavo Väyrynen, to replace him (Aho 1998: 96–109). The process of constitutional change, which quickened in the 1990s, was in many ways a reaction against Kekkonen-style interventionism in the affairs of government and the new 2000 constitution effectively removed the head of state from the government formation process.

Every Finnish cabinet since 1983 has been a majority cabinet, which has served its full four-year term and, with the exception of the Aho-led non-socialist coalition between 1991–95, every cabinet has comprised parties 'across the blocs'. As mentioned, an extreme example of a 'surplus majority' government, exhibiting an unprecedented degree of ideological diversity, was the 'rainbow coalition' formed under the Social Democrat, Paavo Lipponen, in

April 1995. Not least because of its novelty, it warrants a more detailed note.

In his book *Ministerikyyti* ('Ministerial Ride'), the former Green leader, Osmo Soininvaara, paints a depressing picture of the irresponsible nature of parliamentary opposition in Finland. He argues that in recent years government–opposition relations have involved the cabinet steering a responsible and viable course in the face of unbridled populism from the leading opposition party. (Soininvaara 2002: 135) This was the case, he claims, during the period of non-socialist coalition led by Esko Aho between 1991–95, when the Social Democrats were in opposition. The latter inveighed against the need for, and content of the austerity measures introduced by the Aho government to deal with economic recession. But as soon as the Social Democrats gained power, they announced further savings worth FM 20 billion. (Soininvaara 2002: 135) Soininvaara's submission makes a prima facie case for regarding Finland as characterised by British-style adversarial legislative-executive relations. The presumption is of 'Westminster politics' in which the primary task of the leading opposition party is to oppose at all costs and hope to make electoral capital out of that opposition. At the 'earthquake election' of 1970 and the 'mini-quake' election of 1983, a small populist party, the Finnish Rural Party, rather than the leading opposition Conservatives made spectacular gains.[2] However, it was the leading opposition party, the Social Democrats, which served as the main channel for voter disaffection in March 1995 (Arter 1995: 201). They achieved their biggest post-war victory with 28.3% of the poll and would clearly lead the next government. Few, however, envisaged the shape of things to come.

Indeed, the 'rainbow coalition' exhibited a number of novel features. First, there was its *size*. The Lipponen 1 government (1995–99) commanded 145 or nearly three-quarters of the Eduskunta seats. Admittedly, this was less than the broad-based centre-left Koivisto 1 cabinet of 1968–70, but it reduced the opposition to the Centre, Christian League and two very small groupings well to the right. It was formed, moreover, at a time when Finland was emerging from the deepest recession in its history and the worst to affect any OECD member state since the Second World War.

Between 1990–93 the Finnish economy shrank by no less than 15%. The crisis was precipitated by a collapse in Finno-Soviet trade which, at its peak in the mid-1980s, constituted just over one-quarter of Finland's total trade. Then, when the demise of the Soviet Union facilitated an application for full EU membership in March 1992, the onset of international recession meant that Finland's traditional export outlets in Western Europe went into the doldrums. On the domestic economic front, there was a legacy of the serious overheating in the late 1980s, together with an unrestricted credit boom, fuelled in part by financial deregulation. As interest rates shot up and asset values collapsed, hundreds of companies went bankrupt. At the very time the banks incurred huge credit losses – and were bailed out by the government – the cost of rising unemployment spiralled. In 1990 unemployment in Finland was 3.4%, one of the lowest figures in Europe. By March 1995, 20% of the economically active population was out of work, a level exceeded only by Spain among the EU states. The added burden of maintaining an expensive welfare state led the government deep into the red and on the eve of the 1995 general election the state debt stood at 70% of GDP. (Arter 1995: 195)

Economic necessity, therefore, became the mother of the counter-cyclical fiscal policy pursued by the Aho government as the economy began to revive in 1994. Economists who observed the customers in transport cafés noted that by 1994 truckers were now indulging in the traditional Finnish bun – *pulla* – with their coffee rather than managing on coffee alone as two years earlier! *Pulla* consumption became an index of economic recovery. Nonetheless, there was broad cross-party agreement during the 1995 election campaign that further stringent spending cuts would be necessary. The rhetoric of the day preached the need for a government of national unity to deal with the severe economic challenges ahead, *inter alia* of meeting the 'convergence criteria' for EMU membership. In reality, however, as we shall see, there were more prosaic reasons for the broad-based composition of the 'rainbow coalition' and the door was firmly shut in the face of a Swiss-style 'all-party government' including the Centre. There were personal differences between Lipponen and Aho, while relations between the Centre and the Conservatives had deteriorated over the four years they had been together in government.

A second novel feature of the 'rainbow coalition' was the *policy space* covering the governing parties. Led by the Social Democrats under Lipponen, which was the *formateur party*, the rainbow coalition included the Conservatives, which, as mentioned, had been part of the Aho coalition, the Swedish People's Party representing the language minority (also in the Aho government), the post-communist Leftist Alliance (formed in April 1990) and the Greens. Never before had a party of the radical left and the Conservatives formed part of the same cabinet, although in 1979, in a vain attempt to end its long period in the opposition 'wilderness', the Conservatives had stated that they were not against such co-operation in principle.

Third, the rainbow coalition contained some *novice members*. Neither the Leftists nor the Greens had previously participated in government. Indeed, the Greens became the first West European member of that party family to enter a national government. Two Greens had been elected to the Eduskunta in 1983 and it was formed as a party in 1987. There had even been negotiations on joining the Aho coalition in 1991, although the Greens finally ruled themselves out by taking a hard line on energy policy. In any event, the Green Pekka Haavisto became the minister of the environment in the Lipponen 1 government. The Leftist Alliance's predecessor, the Communist-dominated Finnish People's Democratic League had participated in a number of centre-left coalitions between 1966–81. However, deepening division in the Communists' ranks meant that by the early 1980s there was the unusual spectacle of the majority ('Eurocommunist') wing forming part of the government and the pro-Moscow minority wing (the so-called *taistolaiset* after their leader Taisto Sinisalo) operating in opposition.

Finally, the 'rainbow coalition' proved exceptionally stable and for the first time in Finnish history the same configuration of parties came together again as the Lipponen 2 government after the March 1999 general election. This continued in office until 2003 although the Greens resigned in spring 2002. Throughout the eight years of 'rainbow' government, the core axis was that between the prime minister Lipponen and the Conservative finance minister and party leader, Sauli Niinistö.

Until 1992 a minimal winning coalition in Finland was one that contained two-thirds plus one – that is, 134 – seats in the Eduskunta. This was because of the existence of a nexus of historic qualified majority rules designed, among other things, to protect basic minority rights, including private property rights. The existence of these historic minority veto provisions meant that until the early 1990s Finland was a supermajoritarian democracy (see chapter 1 and the Conclusion). These distinctive institutional rules, moreover, clearly had implications for legislative behaviour. Two of them in particular, both dating back to 1906, affected the nature of government–opposition relations.

First, one-third of parliamentarians could 'lay to rest' (to translate from the Finnish) an adopted bill, which could not be taken up again until the second annual Eduskunta session after the one in which the decision to 'rest it' had been taken. It could then be enacted only if approved unchanged. Second, fundamental constitution-level laws, once accepted by a parliamentary majority, were laid to rest until after the next general election and then required a two-thirds majority for approval. They could be enacted in the lifetime of the existing Eduskunta, but only if a five-sixths majority declared them 'urgent' and they then gained a two-thirds majority. The qualified majority rules particularly tied the hands of the government in the management of the economy. For example, a two-thirds majority was necessary for any changes in taxation that were designed to be in force for longer than one year. This meant that on major pieces of economic legislation, including the budget, the leading opposition party – the Conservatives between 1966–87 – had to be consulted.

True, the legislative increment of this consultation should not be exaggerated. The long-serving Conservative parliamentarian, Kimmo Sasi, commented that his party usually won only minor concessions and could be judged 'guilty by association' with the government's economic policy in the eyes of the electorate. In any event, he insisted, the effect of the qualified majority rules was to weaken the lines of accountability between government and opposition.[3] Nonetheless, in order to facilitate the government's management of the economy through recession – that is, to enact austerity measures without being beholden to the opposition-based Social Democrats and Leftist Alliance – the Aho cabinet abolished most of the qualified majority rules in 1992. True, at the 1991 general election the combined vote for the Social Democrats and Leftist Alliance produced the lowest representation for the left in the entire Independence period. But the two leftist parties still narrowly obtained the one-third of the Eduskunta seats necessary to block major economic legislation. They also used this fact in the early 1990s systematically to obstruct attempts to cut public spending. (Mattila 1997: 332) This was part of the 'irresponsible opposition' to which Soininvaara had referred.

Following the removal of the qualified majority requirements, a minimal winning coalition of 50% + 1 of the parliamentary seats – that is, the backing of 101 members of parliament – after the 1995 general election would in principle have sufficed. Finland had shifted from a supermajoritarian to a straightforward majoritarian democracy. This, of course, begs the central question: 'why was a "rainbow coalition" formed, which violated all the conventional theories of coalition-building?' The question can be narrowed down.

In recent years Finnish cabinets have comprised two of the three larger parties, the Social Democrats, Conservatives and Centre. While flying in the face of the 'adjacency principles' in coalition-building – closely associated with Abram de Swaan – the leading left-wing party, the Social Democrats, and leading right-wing party, the Conservatives, were in fact renewing earlier governmental co-operation (De Swaan 1973). They formed the 'blue-red' core of a coalition led by the Conservative Harri Holkeri between 1987–91. As noted earlier, there was a secret agreement before the 1987 election (*kassakaapisopimus*), involving the leaders of the Centre (Paavo Väyrynen), Conservatives (Ilkka Suominen) and Swedish People's Party (Christoffer Taxell) to ditch the Social Democrats and form a non-socialist coalition after it. This was scuppered when the president Mauno Koivisto got wind of it. Since the Conservatives and Social Democrats (and indeed Swedish People's Party) had worked together previously in government, it must be presumed that the Leftist Alliance and Greens were the 'surplus parties'. So the central question can be reduced to: 'Why were the Leftists and Greens included in the "rainbow coalition" when neither, severally or jointly, had the power to bring the government down?' They were not 'veto players' in that most crucial sense.

Clearly, it is necessary to view the question from the standpoint of the formateur party and that of the 'surplus parties'. In respect of the former, a useful point of departure is the conclusion of Ann-Cathrine Jungar's case-study analysis of the formation of the Lipponen 1 government. "Surplus size is best explained by parties' strategic considerations", she contends, "that is the broad government is a consequence of the formateur party obtaining more benefits by including surplus members in the cabinet than not doing so." (Jungar 2002: 78) So, why did it serve the Social Democrats' interests to in-clude the Leftist Alliance and Greens rather than leave them in opposition?

A fundamental element in the equation was the Conservatives' statement at the outset that they would not participate in a government in which the left-wing parties controlled a majority of seats. There was a non-socialist majority in the Eduskunta of 115–85 seats and there should be at least non-socialist parity in the cabinet. Unlike the Swedish Greens, which by the early 1990s had positioned themselves as a left-of-centre party, the Finnish Greens were considered for the sake of coalition-building as a non-socialist party. Conse-quently, the Greens and Swedish People's Party could be incorporated into the cabinet at no 'office cost' to the Social Democrats. They were part of the non-socialists' allocation of portfolios.

The inclusion of the Leftist Alliance stood in contrast to the fate of the Leftist Party in Sweden, which the previous year (1994) had entered a *legis-lative coalition* with the ruling Social Democrats, but had not obtained min-isterial seats. Put simply, the Finnish Social Democrats calculated that it was easier to manage the economy and promote neo-corporatism when the Left-ist Alliance was in government than when it was not. This was an extension or revival of the [president] Kekkonen logic for including the Communists in the Popular Front governments of the late 1960s, which also saw the birth of an income policy system. Lipponen wished to rebuild an incomes policy system in order to stabilise the economy and reduce unemployment and for this the acquiescence of the trade union movement, including the former communist-dominated unions, was essential. In short, the Leftist Alliance's participation in government would, it was thought, facilitate corporate chan-nel consensus.

There were also doubtless electoral considerations underpinning Lipponen and the Social Democrats' decision to include the Leftist Alliance in the 'rain-bow coalition'. It was important to avoid replicating the situation in Sweden in 1998 when the Leftist Party made significant electoral gains to achieve its record poll of 12%. This was in part because the Social Democratic government appeared to be pursuing neo-liberal policies of fiscal austerity rather than its traditional line of redistribution (as discussed at the end of chapter 4). Put another way, it was important to deny the Finnish Leftist Alliance a similar opportunity to make electoral capital by stealing the Social Democrats' traditional welfare spending clothes. At the 1991 general election, the Social Democrats, following four years of cabinet co-operation with the Conservatives, had lost two percentage points – and its position as the largest single party – to poll 22.1%. The Leftist Alliance could not be allowed the luxury of sniping at the government from opposition and attracting disaffected social democratic voters.

The former Green leader, Osmo Soininvaara, has claimed genuinely not to know why the Greens were included in the rainbow coalition in 1995.[4] However, he made two interesting speculations. First, he drew on the analogy of the Centre, which effectively drew the electoral teeth of the populist Finnish Rural Party by incorporating it into the governing coalition under the Social Democrat prime minister, Kalevi Sorsa, in 1983 (the Rural Party remained in the cabinet until August 1990). Soininvaara suggested that, in similar fashion, Lipponen wanted to take the radical 'sting' out of the Greens by making them appear an Establishment party.[5] The Greens undoubtedly constituted an electoral challenge to the Social Democrats in attracting a younger generation of radical urban voters. In 1995 nearly three-quarters of Green supporters were under 39 years and over two-fifths under 29 and every second Green voter lived either in Helsinki (where it was the third largest party) or adjoining Uusimaa. Second, Soininvaara also offered the possibility that two surplus parties, or 'risk parties' as he called them, were better from Lipponen's standpoint than one, because one of them could withdraw without seriously disrupting the government. (Certainly when the Greens did resign in spring 2002 over the approval of an application to construct a fifth nuclear power plant, the coalition continued almost as if nothing had happened.) However, it might have been more persuasive to argue that including both the Leftist Alliance and Greens meant that neither would profit at the polls in 1999 from an appreciable 'opposition bonus'.

Viewed from the perspective of the surplus parties, there is much to commend Jungar's statement that "for the VIHR [Greens] the main issue was to gain credibility among the voters whereas VAS [the Leftist Alliance] wanted to guarantee governmental credibility". (Jungar 2002: 74) The driving force behind the Leftist Alliance's involvement in the 'rainbow coalition' was the party secretary, Matti Viialainen. However, the very narrow majority in its parliamentary party group in favour of this outcome was reflected in the nomination of Terttu Huttu-Juntunen, a first-time member of parliament, as the party's second cabinet minister. The case for Leftist Alliance participation in government in 1995 rested principally on the proposition that the Social Democrats had abandoned their core blue-collar electorate and were targetting the 'new middle class' in the urban south. The Leftist Alliance, therefore, it was implied, was the only party promoting the interests of the disadvantaged (and could do so more effectively in than out of government) and could also speak for the rural north and east of Finland, where most of its support was located. (Arter 2002: 1–28) Its leader Claes Andersson insisted that the Leftist Alliance had to be seen to be willing to assume the responsibility of governing or, otherwise, it would forfeit credibility, self-confidence and dynamism. Crucially, too, in view of its historical legacy of internecine division, it had to appear united (when it was not) over the decision to join the Lipponen coalition in 1995.

For the Greens, entering government was designed above all to signal to voters that supporting them was a constructive way of influencing policy and not simply a 'plague on all your houses' protest. The Greens laid down stiff conditions for participation. Indeed, it has been argued that Lipponen would not have got the Greens into government if he had not agreed with them that no further nuclear power stations would be built between 1995–99. (Uimonen 1998: 250)

From the standpoint of the 'surplus parties' there was doubtless a basic supposition in their calculus, namely that the policy influence that could be exercised from remaining in opposition would be low. Re-stated, the combination of majority government and the abolition of the qualified majority rules was likely to mean that the opposition would be politically weak, if not necessarily numerically so. The Finnish political science literature, moreover, suggested that, when viewed from a comparative perspective, the opposition had long lacked the cohesion necessary to generate effective policy alternatives. (Anckar 1992: 171) Of course, an effective opposition does not necessarily generate policy alternatives or exert a significant measure of policy influence. It may simply be effective in pointing up the shortcomings of government policy. But an opposition comprising about one-third of all MPs, divided between one larger and one or more smaller parties, would be unlikely effectively to challenge the government.[6]

A final point needs emphasis. Minority governments have been said to work best where they are most common and the same could be said for outsize coalitions. Re-stated, surplus majority coalitions function best where they are most common and in Finland they have been very common. Accordingly, there has developed a presumption in favour of broad-based coalitions. A consensual culture stemming from the wide-ranging Popular Front governments of the late 1960s doubtless facilitated the building of a broad-based 'rainbow coalition' committed to implementing an unattractive programme, which involved a number of public sector cuts.

Since 1983 the composition of Finnish governments has become less stable, and of the eight parties represented in the 2003–07 Eduskunta all have participated in government with the exception of the miniscule True Finn Party (and even then its predecessor, the Finnish Rural Party, did so). Similarly, the composition of the parliamentary opposition has become less stable. All three of the larger parties and all the smaller parties except the Swedish People's Party have experienced periods in opposition since the late 1980s. In this respect, the 'rainbow coalition', first formed in April 1995, reflected, as well of course as reinforcing an existing trend towards the greater accessibility and compositional diversity of cabinets. Plainly, the composition of the Lipponen 'rainbow coalitions' between 1995–2003 was *sui generis*. But in many ways it expressed, albeit in accentuated form, many of the features of Finnish coalitions that dated back to the mid-1960s. The two rainbow coalitions were broad-based governments, formed 'across the blocs', which proved remarkably durable. Stable majority government has become the norm in Finland over the last two decades and more.

Majority governments have an even longer pedigree in Iceland, where have they have been in power for 90% of the period since the achievement of independence in 1944. Moreover, like the metropolitan Scandinavian states, there has been a dominant electoral and governing party, albeit in the shape of the right-of-centre Independence Party rather than the Social Democrats. In the eighteen Icelandic general elections between 1944–2003, the Independence Party has averaged 38.4% of the Alþingi seats and over the six decades of independence, the Independence Party has been in government for 82% of the time. In sharp contrast to the Social Democratic-Labour Parties in Norway and Sweden, however, the Independence Party has normally governed in a coalition. Not only that, but it has co-operated in government with all the other parliamentary parties including, between 1980–83, the radical leftist People's Alliance. The 'across the blocs' character of Icelandic coalitions is illustrated in the fact that the Independence Party and Social Democrats have co-operated in office for exactly one-third of the independence period. In recent times, moreover, stable coalition government has been complemented by strong political leadership. The Independence Party chairman, Davíð Oddsson was prime minister between 1991–2004, longer than any other West European head of government except Helmut Kohl (1982–98).

The home of minority governments: 'metropolitan Scandinavia'

Minority governments are in many ways a counter-intuitive phenomenon, especially when viewed from a Westminster perspective. They tend to be seen as weak, aberrant and, therefore, undesirable. Yet, as Erik Damgaard has noted: "Minority governments are not as rare and abnormal as hitherto assumed, but on the other hand they do appear to be concentrated in a limited number of West European countries, not least the three Scandinavian countries". (Damgaard 2000: 365) Indeed, of the 43 governments in Denmark, Norway and Sweden between 1970/71–2005, 38 or 88% have been minority governments (see table 5.1). Majority governments in short have been highly exceptional in the metropolitan Scandinavian states.

Table 5.1 Minority governments in the metropolitan Scandinavian states, 1970/71–2005

	Number of governments	Minority	Single-party minority
Denmark	13	12	5
Norway	15	13	9
Sweden	15	13	11
Total	43	38	25

In Denmark there has been only one majority coalition since 1971, the four-party Social Democrat, Social Liberal, Centre Democrat and Christian People's Party coalition under the Social Democrat Poul Nyrup Rasmussen, and that survived only a year between 1993–94. Similarly, the only majority governments in Norway since 1971 have been the four-party, non-socialist cabinet under the Conservative Kåre Willoch between 1983–85 and the Stoltenberg Labour-led coalition formed in autumn 2005. In Sweden, both non-socialist majority coalitions, 1976–78 and 1979–81, were led by Thorbjörn Fälldin (Centre) but proved short-lived. The first collapsed over energy policy (the future of nuclear power) and the second over taxation policy.

While minority government has been the norm in recent decades in Denmark, Norway and Sweden, there has been variation in the types of minority government. Single-party minority governments have predominated in Sweden and Norway: 73% of all governments in Sweden and 60% in Norway since 1970/71 have been single-party minority cabinets. The vast majority of these have been single-party Social Democrat/Labour cabinets. The exception in Norway was the single-party Conservative minority under Willoch between 1981–83. The exception in Sweden was the 'stop-gap' or caretaker Liberal minority cabinet under Ola Ullsten, which held the fort until the 1979 general election following the disintegration of the Fälldin 1 government. In contrast, just over half (54%) of all Danish governments since 1971 have been minority coalitions and almost all of these have been of the 'ideologically connected type'. The striking exception was the short-lived left-right Social Democratic-Liberal coalition under the Social Democrat Anker Jørgensen between 1978–79. Both the minority coalitions in Sweden have been ideologically connected and the same has been true of all the Norwegian minority coalitions.

Minority governments in metropolitan Scandinavia, then, are both routine and relatively durable and there is not the same presumption in favour of majority government as in Westminster. Since 1982 every government in Sweden has been a minority government and yet every one has lasted its full parliamentary term (three years until 1994, four thereafter). In Denmark in the same period (1982–2005), the average life of minority coalitions has been just under four years. It has been shorter in Norway at two and a half years, although between 1990–97 the Labour Party governed as a single-party minority under Gro Harlem Brundtland (1990–96) and Thorbjørn Jagland (1996–97).

But why are minority governments so common in Denmark, Norway and Sweden? Kåre Strøm argues that minority governments should be viewed in rational cost-benefit terms and that for some parties participation in government is not necessarily their best strategy. When there is a likely long-term electoral dividend from remaining in opposition and significant policy influence can be exerted from opposition, minority governments are the likely outcome. In his words: "Minority governments are likely to form when parties value voters and policy highly compared to office". (Strøm 1990: 242) In the latter context, Strøm coins the term *policy influence differential* to describe the difference in policy terms between the governing party(ies) and the opposition parties. When this is low, minority governments will ensue. He adds that Norwegian political parties do not in comparative terms sacrifice a great deal of policy influence when they forego governmental participation. (Strøm 1990: 211)

There is a broad consensus in the literature that a corollary of regularised minority government has been a policy-making style characterised by constant bargaining and negotiation between the government and opposition parties. Damgaard observes in relation to Denmark that "since the early 1980s, all governments have had to make deals with opposition parties to ensure the passage of the budget and that almost every conceivable ad hoc coalition of parties has been practised in the last two decades". (Damgaard 2004: 118) Moreover, when the mathematics of the executive–legislative balance incline heavily in favour of the opposition, it is possible in extreme cases to witness government by an 'alternative majority' not including the government parties.

This was intermittently the situation in Denmark in the late 1980s and it meant, in Damgaard's words, that a "grouping of opposition parties commanding a majority could in effect 'govern' while the government in effect is in opposition to the non-governmental parties". (Damgaard 2004: 118)

However, it is important to differentiate between types of minority government and to recognise the variability in the nature and extent of the negotiation between government and opposition concomitant on the different types. Strøm notes that in Norway the typical practice has been "government by ad hoc and disaggregated legislative coalitions, often involving different opposition parties on different issues". (Strøm 1990: 224) In such a situation, constant and flexible inter-party negotiation and bargaining are a sine qua non of the enactment of a legislative programme. In contrast, where, as in Sweden, there have been in Anders Sannerstedt's phrase *minority governments with a bloc majority* – Strøm calls them "majority governments in disguise" – the main negotiation will take place at the government-building stage. (Ström 1990: 221; Sannerstedt 1996: 17–58) Indeed, the existence of a comprehensive legislative coalition between a minority cabinet and one or more 'support parties' will minimise the need to consult with the 'out-and-out' opposition parties (that is, those lacking 'veto player' status). In other words, minority governments with a bloc majority, based on a pre-negotiated and broad-ranging legislative agreement with 'support parties' – as in Sweden since 1998 – may exhibit many of the features of majoritarian government.

Strøm's argument is in many ways persuasive. The 'policy influence differential' between government and opposition may be relatively small and there may be considerable potential for opposition parties to influence through the parliamentary standing committee system. His assertion that "minority governments are promoted by institutions that enhance the power of the parliamentary opposition vis-à-vis the government" appears plausible. (Strøm 1990: 238) Yet Strøm talks only of "potential opposition influence" and, as noted, when minority governments command majority support within the terms of a pre-negotiated agreement, and where parties are cohesive, the incidence of anti-government coalitions on the parliamentary committees is likely to be rare.

Take Sweden in October 2002 for example. Following the general election the previous month a minority government was formed despite the fact that all six opposition parties (with the possible exception of the Conservatives) wanted to participate in government. Lars Leijonborg, whose Liberal Party had made significant gains at the polls, tried to form a minority coalition of the three centre-based non-socialist parties (Liberals, Centre and Christian Democrats) plus the Greens. The Greens and Leftist Party, both of which had worked in a legislative coalition with the minority Social Democratic government between 1998–2002, pressed hard for cabinet seats in a left-of-centre majority coalition. Only the Centre, which pulled out of the Leijonborg talks, may be said to have been concerned about the long-term electoral costs of governing à la Strøm. (The Leijonborg coalition initiative is discussed further in chapter 12).

So why then have minority governments been so common in the period beginning with the shift to unicameralism in Sweden and the 'earthquake elections' in Denmark and Norway? Viewed from the perspective of the structure and dynamics of the party system, three factors in particular would appear to explain the succession of minority governments in Sweden.

First, there has been the existence of a large Social Democratic party, which, although short of commanding an absolute majority of parliamentary seats, has been reluctant to share power in government. Strøm focuses on why parties do not always choose to enter government, presuming this to be an option. But a common denominator in Sweden and Norway and, to a lesser degree, Denmark has been the presence of a dominant Social Democratic-Labour Party, falling short of an overall majority of seats but nonetheless able to call the shots. In Sweden in 2002 the Social Democrats' 'winning margin' over the second-placed Conservatives was a massive 24.8 percentage points.

Second, there has been a radical left – the Left Party Communists until 1990 and Leftist Party thereafter – mostly unwilling to face the electoral consequences of toppling a socialist government. True, in the 1980s the Left Party Communists became less automatic and more demanding in their support of the ruling Social Democrats. But while the Leftist leadership has pressed hard for a coalition with the Social Democrats, a significant element in the party has preferred to remain in opposition so as not to compromise the party's radical credentials.

Third, there has been a fragmented bloc of non-socialist parties for which, in view of their policy differences, the benefits of sustaining a minority Social Democratic government have been seen to outweigh the costs of striving for governmental co-operation among themselves. The Centre's legislative deal with the Social Democrats in 1995–97 is a case in point. Majority-building among the non-socialist parties, hardly facilitated by at times serious issue divisions, was further complicated by the emergence of a short-lived radical right – New Democracy in the 1991–94 Riksdag – which was deemed unacceptable as a coalition partner.

In sum, it appears that minority governments in Sweden have largely resulted from the fact that the Social Democrats have wanted, and been able to govern as a single-party minority. This is far from the banal conclusion it may seem, since there is little or no evidence to suggest that the perception of a small policy influence differential has persuaded prospective governing parties to remain in opposition. The reverse has in fact been the case. Moreover, the inter-party negotiation between the governing Social Democrats and the parliamentary opposition has been almost exclusively with their 'support parties' – the Greens and Leftists since 1998 – and then primarily at the stage of building the legislative coalition.

This analysis is broadly in line with that of Bjørn Erik Rasch, although it places greater, or at least more explicit emphasis on the volitional aspects of the Social Democrats' approach to government-building – that is, the Social Democrats' strategic decision to monopolise cabinet posts. Rasch notes, when referring to all three metropolitan Scandinavian states, that "in a fragmented assembly without a majority party, if one party has a far larger share of the seats than any other party, it is likely to have a strong bargaining position". (Rasch 2004: 138–139) He adds that "minority governments are more likely in systems with one centrally positioned, relatively large party". (Rasch 2004: 140)

Torbjörn Bergman suggests five reasons for the frequency of Social Democratic minority cabinets in Sweden, which have a somewhat different orientation or perspective, but a substantially similar content. First, he emphasises the way inter-party competition has operated mainly, though not exclusively along a left–right dimension, implying that only ideologically connected cabinets have been possible. Second, the Social Democratic Party's electoral strength has given it a strong bargaining position. Third, rather than considering a coalition with a non-socialist party, the Communist Party has been willing to provide support for Social Democratic minority cabinets. Fourth, policy disagreements within the non-socialist bloc have enabled the Social Democrats readily to form ad hoc legislative coalitions with one or more of these parties. Finally, the absence of a minimum size threshold has facilitated the formation of minority governments, which once in place have been sustained in office by the requirement for an absolute majority of parliamentarians to pass a vote of no confidence. (Bergman 2003: 225)

In the Danish case, Mogens Pedersen notes that minority coalitions have been invariably of the ideologically connected type. "They are either 'Left-Centre' or 'Right-Centre' in their ideological position." (Pedersen 2000: 372) He also adduces four reasons for the frequency of minority coalitions. First, there is the fragmented party system where the centre of politics has been occupied by a number of small parties. This fragmentation, of course, increased from the 'earthquake election' of 1973. Second, the traditional political blocs and individual parties have rarely, if ever, been able to muster a majority of their own. Pedersen's third factor in explaining the frequency of Danish minority coalitions lends support to Torbjörn Bergman's thesis that "variations in the rules of government formation create variations in the logic of coalition bargaining". (Bergman 1993: 62) It is the principle of negative parliamentarism (common to Norway and Sweden too), which does not require an incoming government to obtain a vote of confidence. Minority governments in Denmark, Norway and Sweden need only the tolerance of parliament.[7] Finally, Pedersen brings out the way opposition parties can profit from legislative coalitions.

In Norway Narud and Strøm conclude that "the inclination towards [Labour] minority cabinets and ad hoc legislative coalescence seems to reflect the ease of informal majority building rather than the frustrations of full-blown coalescence". (Narud and Strøm 2003: 189) Put another way, the Labour Party has not needed (until 2005) to build executive coalitions in order to govern effectively. As Narud and Strøm note, "the failure to coalesce is a general and striking feature of Norwegian party politics". (Narud and Strøm 2003: 170)

A distinctively Scandinavian form of parliamentarism?

According to Rasch, the Scandinavian form of parliamentarism has two features – the prevalence of minority governments and the frequency of single-party cabinets. (Rasch 2004: 131) Minority governments have unquestionably become the norm in metropolitan Scandinavia and the last majority coalition in Denmark, for example, left office in 1994. There had not been a majority government in metropolitan Scandinavia for over ten years. In addition to single-party minority governments, moreover, minority coalitions have also been a feature of the political executive in Denmark, Norway and Sweden and they have been almost entirely of the 'ideologically connected type'. Indeed, until the Stoltenberg majority in Norway in autumn 2005, the preponderance of minority governments since the early 1970s has led Scandinavian political scientists to refer to the somewhat opaque term 'minority parliamentarism', presumably meaning that the government does not *in its own right* command majority support in the legislature. In one sense 'minority parliamentarism' has been seen to necessitate inter-party negotiations between government and opposition parties and these have been viewed as the central dynamic of a *distinctly Scandinavian form of parliamentarism*. In another sense, critics, especially in Norway, have inferred that 'minority parliamentarism' has created a significant 'democratic deficit' and prompted feelings of low subjective competence on the part of ordinary citizens. Critical statements from Stein Ringen, Hanne Marthe Narud and Kaare Strøm will illustrate the point.

According to Ringen "the Norwegian experience of 'minority parliamentarism' is that this is a form of disorder that voters dislike. Perpetual negotiations between government and Storting over budgets and legislation are seen to be quibble and governance without direction. Voters determine the composition of the Storting, but discover they are without direct influence in the formation of governments. On several occasions they have had to swallow the humiliation of seeing parties which they have punished with defeat in the elections go on to win cabinet power" (Ringen 2003). It might reasonably be objected that this was not a finding to emerge from the final report of the Norwegian 'Power and Democracy Commission' in 2003 (see chapter 8). It could also be said to apply equally well to many systems of 'majority parliamentarism', not least the 'surplus majority' cabinets in Finland. Nonetheless, Narud and Strøm provide indirect support for Ringen's view: "In Norway there is only a weak link between election results and subsequent government formation. In the post-war period, parties that have lost votes have entered government just as often as parties that have gained votes." (Narud and Strøm 2004: 191)

The phenomenon of 'unrepresentative cabinets' is probably best viewed as endemic to coalition-building in multi-party systems, since the composition of governments is determined first and foremost by patterns of elite cooperation and the structure of party competition in Mair's terms. What can be argued on the basis of the Scandinavian evidence, however, is that minority governments are by no means necessarily weak and, conversely, majority governments are by no means always strong.

Of course, strength and weakness in government is ultimately a matter of judgement and, to a degree, it is dictated by circumstances. Governments must be viewed in the particular context in which they find themselves. Nonetheless, *legislative capacity* might be a useful notion in assessing the efficacy of governments. Thus, a strong government could be regarded as one that possesses sufficient legislative capacity to enact its legislative programme. At least four vital *legislative resources* are integral to legislative capacity. They are *policies*, that is something to deliver; *time*, that is, a sufficient period in which to deliver it; *unity*, that is, the collective will to proceed with (controversial) policies; and *support*, that is, parliamentary backing for these policies. These legislative resources translate into a number of basic *properties of a strong government*, that is, a determinate programme, stability, cohesion and a reliable parliamentary majority.

Minority governments have often possessed the legislative resources to govern rather effectively, particularly in relation to legislative majority building. They may be numerically weak as in Norway. The Bondevik centre-right minority coalition of Christians, Liberals and Conservatives, formed after the 2001 general election, held only 62 of the 165 Storting seats. But legislative majority building did not prove difficult and the government, where necessary, used the 26 seats of the radical rightist Progress Party to pass vital legislation, including the budget. Of course, the Bondevik coalition was happy to give the Progress Party 'dog' a bad name, so to speak, and to present its views on immigration as the antithesis of decency. However, as Anniken Hagelund has observed, "when the indecency of the Progress Party is restricted to their immigration policies, two functions can be satisfied. On the one hand the party is kept outside the political circles of respectability, providing a negative image of what decent immigration politics should not be. On the other hand, when issues other than immigration are at stake its numerical strength in the Storting can be made use of in the ever-important search for compromise and coalitions that characterise a parliamentary system under minority governments". (Hagelund 2003: 62)

Furthermore, when minority governments have the backing of stable legislative coalitions, they may approximate majority government in disguise. Thus, an openly expressed criticism of the Göran Persson-led Social Democratic cabinets in Sweden since 1996 has been that, although possessing only a minority of Riksdag seats, they have acted like majority governments. Perhaps, with a winning margin since 2002 of nearly 25 percentage points over the next largest party, the Conservatives, and the backing since 1998 of the Left Party and Greens, it is not surprising. Certainly since 1998 Sweden has been a classic case of Sannerstedt's "minority government with a bloc majority". Nonetheless, whether the minority government has commanded a de facto majority or not, *the distinctively Scandinavian form of parliamentarism has involved policy-making by legislative coalitions.*

The size of these legislative coalitions, and the extent to which they are formalised (pre-negotiated, written and made public), has varied across the region. A feature of Danish politics has been the custom of governments to conclude pre-negotiated legislative agreements on major policy packages – the so-called *politisk forlig* – which often involve negotiation at the leadership level and require the unanimous parliamentary backing of all the parties concerned. In the three decades since the 1973 'earthquake election', moreover, approximately two-thirds of the formal (written) package deals have been *surplus majority legislative coalitions.* (Christiansen 2005) Parties previously viewed as 'beyond the pale' now participate in legislative coalitions and the general trend towards a variety of permutations and configurations in Danish legislative coalitions has been referred to as 'flexible minority parliamentarism'. In short, parties at either end of the political spectrum, such as the Socialist People's Party and the Danish People's Party, now have demonstrable *legislative coalition potential* (to adapt a Sartori term).

All in all, it is clear that minority governments work best where they are most common and there is not a strong expectation that majority cabinets will be formed. On the subject of majority governments, there can be fewer more striking contrasts in the Nordic region than in the size and composition of governments. In contrast to metropolitan Scandinavia, majority government is the norm in Finland and Iceland where cabinets have routinely brought together parties 'across the blocs'. In Finland the turning point was the formation of the so-called Popular Front government under the social democrat Rafael Paasio in 1966. Thereafter, majority and often surplus majority governments have become the norm. Majority governments, especially the outsize governments in Finland, are not necessarily strong and may suffer at times from low levels of internal cohesion. However, it may be hypothesised, when surplus majority governments are in office, the policy influence of the parliamentary opposition is invariably weak.

In recent years, Finland may well have appeared to approach the 'all-party government model' advocated by the Centre leader Johannes Virolainen in a speech in March 1977. Virolainen suggested that the cabinet should consist of a fixed number of ministries, with each party entitled to one portfolio for every 10 seats in the 200-member Eduskunta. (Arter 1978: 67) His proposal was designed to create government stability and generate greater cross-party consensus against the backdrop of the historic cabinet instability and polarised politics in Finland. It might well be suggested that the surplus majority governments of recent decades, together with the impressive cabinet stability since 1983, have rendered the 'all-party government model' considerably less salient. In any event, one of the three 'pole parties' – the Social Democrats, Centre and Conservatives – has always formed part of the opposition over the last twenty years or so. Indeed, it seems a distinctive feature of Finland's 'majority parliamentarism' that one of the three larger parties has led a numerically weak and fragmented opposition.

Notes

1   Since Communists comprised the overwhelming majority in, and controlled the Finnish People's Democratic League, the term 'Communists' is preferred here to the cumbersome 'Finnish People's Democratic League'.

2   In fact, the Conservatives also gained ground in 1970, advancing by over four percentage points compared with the previous general election in 1966 to become the largest non-socialist party. Their leader, Juha Rihtniemi, tried to form a minority coalition, which would have included the Finnish Rural Party, but the attempt was doomed from the start, not least because of opposition from Kekkonen and Moscow.

3   Interview with Kimmo Sasi MP, 12 May 2004.
4   Soininvaara lost the Green leadership following a ballot of members at the 2005
    party conference.
5   Interview with Osmo Soininvaara MP, 11 May 2004.
6   Tapio Raunio has asserted that "not surprisingly, the oversized coalitions have
    ruled without much effective opposition from the Eduskunta" and that "strong
    majority governments have ruled without much effective opposition since the
    early 1980s". (Raunio 2004: 15, 143) Such sweeping statements about the inef-
    fectuality of the Finnish opposition will be considered in the later chapters of this
    study.
7   In Sweden, unless the old government has resigned, there is no automatic vote of
    investiture after the election. If, however, the government has resigned, as Ingvar
    Carlsson (Social Democrat) and Carl Bildt (Conservative) did in 1991 and 1994
    respectively, then the new government will be subject to a vote of investiture,
    albeit with the tolerance rules applying. In other words, the government will be
    approved unless more than half the members of the Riksdag have voted against it.

References

Aho, Esko *Pääministeri* (Otava: Helsinki, 1998)
Anckar, Dag 'Finland: Dualism and Consensual Rule', in Erik Damgaard (ed.) *Parlia-
    mentary Change in the Nordic Countries* (Scandinavian University Press: Oslo, 1992),
    pp. 151–190
Arter, David 'All-Party Government for Finland?' *Parliamentary Affairs* 31, 1, 1978,
    pp. 67–85
Arter, David *Politics and Policy-Making in Finland* (Wheatsheaf: Sussex, 1987)
Arter, David 'The March 1995 Finnish Election: The Social Democrats Storm Back'
    West European Politics 18, 4, 1995, pp. 194–204
Arter, David '"Communists We are no Longer, Social Democrats We Can Never Be":
    the Evolution of the Leftist Parties in Finland and Sweden' *The Journal of Commu-
    nist and Transition Studies* 18, 3, 2002, pp. 1–28
Bergman, Torbjörn 'Formation Rules and Minority Governments' *European Journal of
    Political Research* 23, 1993, pp. 55–66
Bergman, Torbjörn 'Sweden: When Minority Cabinets Are the Rule and Majority
    Coalitions the Exception', in Wolfgang C. Müller and Kaare Strøm *Coalition Gov-
    ernments in Western Europe* (Oxford University Press: Oxford, 2003), pp. 192–
    230)
Christiansen, Flemming Juul 'Inter-party Co-operation in Scandinavia. Minority
    Parliamentarism and Strong Parliaments' Paper presented at the ECPR Joint Ses-
    sions of Workshops, Granada, 14–19 April 2005
Damgaard, Erik 'Minority Governments', in Lauri Karvonen and Krister Ståhlberg
    (eds) *Festschrift for Dag Anckar on his 60th Birthday on February 12, 2000* (Åbo
    Akademis Förlag: Åbo, 2000), pp. 353–369
Damgaard, Erik 'Developments in Danish Parliamentary Democracy: Accountability,

108 Democracy in Scandinavia

Parties and External Constraints' *Scandinavian Political Studies* 27, 2, 2004, pp. 115–131

De Swaan, Abram *Coalition Theories and Cabinet Formation* (Elsevier: Amsterdam, 1973)

Hagelund, Anniken 'A Matter of Decency? The Progress Party in Norwegian Immigration Politics' *Journal of Ethnic and Migration Studies* 23, 1, 2003, pp. 47–65

Jungar, Ann-Cathrine 'A Case of a Surplus Majority Government: The Finnish Rainbow Coalition' *Scandinavian Political Studies* 25, 1, 2002, pp. 57–83

Jussila, Osmo, Seppo Hentilä and Jukka Nevakivi *From Grand Duchy to a Modern State* (Hurst: London, 1999)

Lijphart, Arend *Patterns of Democracy* (Yale University Press: New Haven and London, 1999)

Mattila, Mikko 'From Qualified Majority to Simple Majority: The Effects of the 1992 Change in the Finnish Constitution' *Scandinavian Political Studies* 20, 4, 1997, pp. 331–345

Narud, Hanne Marthe and Kaare Strøm 'Norway. A Fragile Coalitional Order', in Wolfgang C. Müller and Kaare Strøm *Coalition Governments in Western Europe* (Oxford University Press: Oxford, 2003), pp. 158–191

Narud, Hanne Marthe and Kaare Strøm 'Norway: Madisonianism Reborn' *Scandinavian Political Studies* 27, 2, 2004, pp. 175–201

Pedersen, Mogens N. 'Coalition Formation Processes in Danish Politics: Reflections on Norms, Procedures and Processes', in Lauri Karvonen and Krister Ståhlberg (eds) *Festschrift for Dag Anckar on his 60th Birthday on February 12, 2000* (Åbo Akademis Förlag: Åbo, 2000), pp. 371–384

Rasch, Bjørn Erik, 'Parliamentary Government', in Knut Heidar (ed.) *Nordic Politics* (Universitetsforlaget: Oslo, 2004), pp. 127–141

Raunio, Tapio 'The Changing Finnish Democracy: Strong Parliamentary Accountability, Coalescing Political Parties and Weaker External Constraints' *Scandinavian Political Studies* 27, 2, 2004, pp. 133–152

Riker, William H. *The Theory of Political Coalitions* (Yale University Press: New Haven, 1962)

Ringen, Stein 'Where Now, Democracy?' *Times Literary Supplement* 13.2.2003

Sannerstedt, Anders 'Negotiations in the Riksdag', in Lars-Göran Stenelo and Magnus Jerneck (eds) *The Bargaining Democracy* (Lund University Press: Lund, 1996), pp. 17–58

Soininvaara, Osmo *Ministerikyyti* (WSOY: Helsinki, 2002)

Strøm, Kaare *Minority Government and Majority Rule* (Cambridge University Press: Cambridge, New York, Port Chester, Melbourne, Sydney, 1990)

Uimonen, Risto *Häntä heiluttaa koiraa. Suomen Demokratian Häiriötila 1983–2000?* (WSOY: Porvoo-Helsinki-Juva, 1998)

Virolainen, Johannes *Pääministerinä suomessa* (Kirjayhtymä: Helsinki, 1969)

6

Corporatist interest group systems: (still) a distinctive Scandinavian trait?

One of the five differences on the 'executive–parties dimension' which Lijphart identifies when distinguishing between the Westminster majoritarian democracy and the consensus model democracy concerns the nature of the government–interest group relationship. In the former, he writes, there are "pluralist interest group systems with free-for-all competition among groups". In the latter, consensual democracy, there are "corporatist interest group systems aimed at compromise and concertation". (Lijphart 1999: 3) It may not be obvious how the contrasting types of government-group practice are related to the other features of the two types of democracy on the executive–parties dimension, since these appear linked to the electoral rules and the dynamics of the party system. Nonetheless, it is clear that corporatist interest group systems have been closely associated with policy-making in several small West European democracies and Scandinavia in particular. Stretching the point, moreover, Scandinavian political scientists may be said almost to have 'invented' corporatist practice in pluralist democracies. Is this then the single most important characteristic of politics and government in the Nordic countries when compared with the Westminster model? Possibly so, if we follow Eric Einhorn and John Logue. They note that "although corporatism has declined after 1980, the Scandinavian countries remain strikingly corporatist to Anglo-American observers". (Einhorn and Logue 2003: 136) Michele Micheletti appears less convinced, at least in the Swedish case, and in an article discussing "corporatism at the crossroads" she asks whether Sweden has already become a nation among others "without an enviable uniqueness"? (Micheletti 1991: 161)

On the theme of "enviable uniqueness" or otherwise, the focus in this chapter is on the Scandinavian interest group systems. It poses two main questions. 1) Why has what Peter Katzenstein described as 'democratic corporatism' been seen as a distinctive feature of Scandinavian policy-making? Katzenstein defines 'democratic corporatism' as "the voluntary, co-operative regulation of conflicts over economic and social issues through highly structured and interpenetrating political relationships between business, trade unions and the state, augmented by political parties". (Katzenstein 1985: 32) 2) Have there been significant changes in the government–group relationship since the heyday of corporatism in the 1960s? This is by far the more difficult question of the two, as Peter Munk Christiansen and Asbjørn Sonne Nørgaard's conclusion on Denmark illustrates. "Relations between interest organisations and civil servants have never been purely pluralist and open or completely corporatist and closed. They have been more corporatist than pluralist for long periods and in recent decades more pluralist than earlier." (Christiansen and Nørgaard 2003: 219) Clearly, only qualified conclusions are in order!

'Peak corporatism'

As to the first question of democratic corporatism, a substantial part of the explanation of the close association of corporatism with 'metropolitan Scandinavia' undoubtedly lies in the impact of Stein Rokkan's model of *corporate pluralism* in which he conceptualised the role and influence of interest groups in 1960s Norway. (Rokkan 1966) Rokkan devised a policy-making schema based on a synthesis of pluralist and corporatist elements. He identified two distinct channels of influence in the policy process. The *electoral channel* is grounded in the pluralist principle. Voters exert influence through the ballot boxes and so determine the balance of power between the parties in parliament and by extension the composition of the government. This is *numerical democracy*.

Then there is the influence exerted by organised interests through their routinised involvement in the policy-making process. This is what Rokkan called the *corporate channel*. He proceeded to insist that, in the Norwegian case, the corporate channel has exercised the decisive influence over the electoral channel. The vital economic decisions affecting the pockets of ordinary Norwegians [in the 1960s] were seldom taken by the parties or in the Storting, but over the bargaining table where the public authorities met directly with the trade union leaders, the farmers, fishermen and employers' organisations. (Rokkan 1966: 197) Rokkan's basic argument became axiomatic: *votes count, but resources decide*. By 'resources' he meant the economic resources and resources of expertise possessed by the major sectoral interest groups. For Rokkan and many others, the corporatist equation has involved the relatively greater influence in policy-making of non-elected over elected elements. It might be surmised that the high rate of associationalism – that is the solidary (high) membership of a number of monolithic sectoral interest groups – legitimised to a degree this type of incomes policy management style.

The validity of Rokkan's proposition about 'resources deciding' is, as Knut Heidar has pointed out, empirically questionable. Major fiscal decisions have been worked out in the ministry of finance and are debated both in government and parliament before constituting a broad framework for the biennial incomes policy talks. (Heidar 2001: 75) The electoral-numerical channel, it is argued, has been more important in fiscal policy than Rokkan's conceptualisation allowed. However, the salient point is that the practice that Rokkan was describing is what I have termed 'summit-level corporatism' or 'peak corporatism'. By peak corporatism I mean a regularised and culturally entrenched system of macro-economic management, which involves the government working closely with the peak sectoral interest groups to achieve national incomes policy settlements that are compatible with the government's overall fiscal policy objectives. The overall package will complement the annual Finance Bill (budget) and the government will be either a player (directly involved in the negotiations with the peak groups) and/or a facilitator. In the latter role the government might provide incentives towards the achievement of the type of centralised agreement it desires – containing only modest wage increases for example – in the form of ancillary legislative measures relating say to housing benefits or holiday entitlements.

Klaus Armingeon has remarked on the extent of the summit-level co-operation between the trade unions, employers' organisations and government in Finland, Norway and formerly in Sweden. He adds that "in a corporatist system government, employers and unions are – together and directly – concerned with the development of working conditions, prices, employment and any public policy relevant to the economic system". (Armingeon 2002: 84) However, while peak corporatism may have the merit of efficiency, it has traditionally (witness Rokkan's work) been seen to reduce parliament to the role of a rubber-stamp dutifully approving any measures in the incomes policy package that need the force of law. Indeed, as recently as September 2004 *Helsingin Sanomat* wrote that: "In the Finnish corporatist system, parliament has had to become accustomed to approving laws associated with agreements between government and the peak labour-market organisations without touching their content".[1]

One of the claims made in support of peak corporatism has been that it militates towards consensus and moderation in economic policy management. Peter Katzenstein has noted that a distinctive feature of corporatism is "an ideology of social partnership" and the absence of "a winner-takes-all mentality". (Katzenstein 1985; Lijphart 1999: 171–184) Related to this is the probable development of an *incomes policy culture*, that is an expectation among elites and citizens alike that, nothwithstanding their differences, the actors involved in the peak negotiations will ultimately reach a comprehensive agreement. It has also been argued that peak corporatism has been a significant factor in the strong economic performance of the small European states. Katzenstein's central thesis is that small European states construct their economic strategies on the twin pillars of free trade and democratic corporatism. The second is a pre-condition of the first in that corporatism has enabled the small states to mitigate the social costs of highly open economies while also promoting high-technological export competitiveness. (Katzenstein 1985) Restated, corporatist arrangements have allowed small states to combine economic flexibility and political stability. In Olli Rehn's words, "flexible adjustment is produced by external economic liberalism leading to market-driven restructuring on the one hand, and by domestic compensation safeguarding social peace and legitimacy, on the other". (Rehn 1996: 72)

Peak corporatism in the metropolitan Scandinavian states may well be regarded as distinctive on three counts – its origins, functional logic and essentially non-institutionalised character. On the first point, the origins of peak corporatism can be traced back to the economic recession of the 1930s and, in the Danish case, earlier than that. Peak corporatism has long roots. Put another way, the historic compromises between capital and labour, which laid the foundations for centralised negotiations between the two sides of industry, were achieved in Denmark in the late nineteenth century and in Norway and Sweden before the Second World War. The 'September Compromise' in Denmark in 1899 between the trade union confederation and the employers was in fact the first agreement of its kind in the world, while similar agreements were reached in Norway in 1936 and notably at Saltsjöbaden in Sweden in 1938. (Kjellberg 1992: 89) The social democratic dominance of the trade union movement was an essential pre-condition for the class co-operation that created the basis for peak corporatism. Indeed, Anders Kjellberg has noted that it was government pressure – reinforced by the close relationship between the central trade union confederation LO and the social democrats – that promoted the policy of co-operation between LO and the central employers' organisation SAF, manifested in the 1938 Saltsjöbaden agreement. (Kjellberg 1992: 99)

Peak corporatism originated in Finland in very different circumstances, in that the centralised collective bargaining system can be traced back to the climate of solidarity generated by the nation's military struggle against the Soviet Union in the Winter War of November 1939–March 1940. On 23 January 1940 a first agreement between the central trade union federation and employers – the so-called 'January Engagement' – was concluded. The commitment of these two organisations to resolve differences in a spirit of mutual understanding was renewed in the form of a General Agreement in May 1946. (Arter 1987: 204–205)

Second, peak corporatism had a distinctive functional logic in metropolitan Scandinavia. It did not emerge as an overarching mechanism with which to regulate conflict between sectoral interests that were divided along religious and linguistic lines such as in Austria, Holland and Belgium. It was not part of a consociational system in that sense. Rather, peak corporatism was a by-product of a momentous class compromise between workers, farmers and subsequently employers in essentially homogenous societies. As Einhorn and Logue have observed: "In Scandinavia, corporatist institutions reflect not the balance sought in a segmented society, but the political hegemony of well-organised democratic popular movements – agrarian and labor". (Einhorn and Logue 2003: 336) The red–green deals in the early and mid-1930s made possible the social democratic consolidation of power, which in turn facilitated historic agreements between labour and capital just before the Second World War.

Third, peak corporatism in metropolitan Scandinavia and Finland has been non-institutionalised in the sense that the summit negotiations between government and groups have not generally taken place in formal settings such as the celebrated Social and Economic Council in Holland or the Economic Councils in France and Italy. Rather, the approach has been less structured. Thus, in Sweden, the celebrated *Harpsund Democracy*, which culminated in 1959, took its name from a series of informal gatherings of the main economic interest organisations at the prime minister's [Tage Erlander] country residence. However, the extent of state involvement in the centralised negotiations between employers and unions has varied across metropolitan Scandinavia and over time. In Denmark and Norway the government has intervened much more actively in collective bargaining than in Sweden, where until the 1980s self-regulation was the established formula.

On the question of government (state) involvement, Gary Marks has distinguished between two ideal-types of incomes policy system. A *compulsory incomes policy* is imposed, narrow in scope and enforced unilaterally by the state, as in the case of the statutory wage freeze in Denmark between 1976–80. A *consensual incomes policy* in contrast is the product of bargaining, is wide in scope and enforced by the participating organisations themselves – as, for example, in Norway between 1962–76. (Marks 1986: 71–83) The Finnish incomes policy system, generally known by the acronym TUPO, has been of the consensual variety. A high level of unionisation, highly centralised trade union structures and the shift from the mid-1960s to broad-based governing coalitions, including the Communists, created a favourable set of conditions. The broad-based nature of governments in particular was an important facilitating factor in achieving incomes policy settlements, while the implied threat to the stability of incomes policy sustained a succession of centre-left coalitions in office during the 1970s and early 1980s. (Arter 1987: 222) A distinctive feature of the Finnish TUPO system has been the active role of the state in promoting and often brokering a deal between the leading sectoral interest groups. In 1970 the authority of the presidential office and the highly public intervention of the head of state, Urho Kekkonen, were necessary to secure an incomes agreement.

The economic climate favouring the practice of peak corporatism has also varied. In metropolitan Scandinavia it might be regarded as something of a 'fair weather phenomenon'. Put another way, the heyday of peak corporatism in Norway and Sweden coincided with the years of social democratic dominance and strong economic growth. In Finland peak corporatism has been more a 'foul weather phenomenon' in that it had its origins (in the late 1960s) and greatest significance (in the late 1990s) at times of reduced or even minimal economic growth.

Routine corporatism

'Routine corporatism' – Trond Norby describes it as 'corporatism linked to the administration' – has also been closely associated with Scandinavian practice through the writings *inter alia* of Robert Kvavik. (Nordby 2004: 104–106) Kvavik refers to Norway as a *co-optive polity* in which relevant interests are co-opted on to the committees and commissions engaged in the policy-making process at the pre-parliamentary stage. (Kvavik 1996) However, the suspicion is that routine corporatism in Scandinavia, unlike the peak variety, is not that distinctive when viewed in a comparative perspective – at least as minimally defined by Leif Lewin. Lewin states that corporatism is "the officially sanctioned participation of organisations in decisions governing the affairs of state or in their administration". (Lewin 1999: 59)

Routine corporatism may, however, be older in Scandinavia than many other West European countries. Indeed, the incorporation of interest organisations into the process of policy formulation in the 'metropolitan' Scandinavian countries dates back to the seventeenth century in Sweden and the nineteenth and early decades of the twentieth century in Norway and Denmark. Routine corporatism in short considerably preceded the completion of mass democracy, that is, the introduction of universal suffrage and the development of mass membership parties. Plainly too, to take Denmark as an example, government–group consultation on the preparatory committees of the central administration substantially antedated the growth of the welfare state after the Second World War. In the period 1913–27 in Denmark, at least two-thirds and as much as eight-tenths of the policy formulating committees contained interest group representation, as Table 6.1 illustrates. (Christiansen and

Nørgaard 2003: 46) However, the real expansion in the institution of routine corporatism occurred after the Second World War contiguous with the growth in the scale and scope of government. Between 1946–75 interest groups were represented on about three-fifths of the Danish commissions preparing laws (*lovforberende kommissioner*) and approximately half the commissions of inquiry (those with a wider investigative function – *utredningsopgaver*). Munk Christiansen and Nørgaard in fact refer to the period from the late 1950s to the late 1960s as the "golden period of classical Danish corporatism". (Christiansen and Nørgaard 2003: 46) Their allusion to a 'golden period of Danish corporatism' raises the wider question – 'Has routine corporatism in Scandinavia represented a difference in degree or kind from practice elsewhere in Western Europe?'[2]

The implication in much of the literature is that the difference in degree during the golden years of routine corporatism was such as in practice to constitute a difference in kind. Corporatism, the argument went, denoted the extensive incorporation of interest groups into the policy-making process and the inference was that in Scandinavia there was a greater degree of integration of organised interests into public policy-making – both at the formulation and implementation stages – than elsewhere. Scandinavian corporatism was distinguished, it was said, by the degree of the institutionalisation of group incorporation, that is the formalisation of their role. The access afforded interest groups through the commission system and on central boards in Sweden for example featured particularly prominently in the literature.

Table 6.1 '*Routine corporatism' in Denmark, 1913–2000*

Interest groups on preparatory committees, 1913–27 (%)						
	1913	1916	1921	1926	1927	
All preparatory commissions	78	80	84	63	66	
	1946	1955	1965	1975		
Preparatory commissions	57	58	60	63		
Commissions of inquiry	35	51	50	47		
	1975	1980	1985	1990	1995	2000
All preparatory commissions	50	70	70	74	71	60

Source: Peter Munk Christiansen and Asbjørn Sonne Nørgaard, *Faste Forhold – Flygtige Forbindelser* (2003), pp. 46, 60, 101

True, even in the prime of routine corporatism there were marked differences between policy areas with respect to the extent of regularised interest group involvement in decision-making. Per Lægreid and Paul G. Roness for example have noted in the Norwegian context that the government departments most concerned with economic policy developed the most elaborate co-optive structures. (Lægreid and Roness 1997: 167–190) However, for Christiansen and Rommetvedt, the degree of institutionalisation has been crucial, for when relations between interest groups and the state are informal and ad hoc they speak of *lobbyism*. The less regularised and less structured the government-group relationship, the more the phenomenon is lobbyism. (Christiansen and Rommetvedt 2003: 134–158)

In short, at the heart of routine corporatism has been a special relationship between state and organised interests, which grants the latter privileged, regularised and formalised access to the central decision-making structures of the state. Lewin identifies four forms or modes of routine corporatism – or what he calls "officially sanctioned participation" – in the Swedish case. 1) The representation of groups on commissions of inquiry. 2) The involvement of groups in the consideration of commission reports – the so-called *remiss* process. 3) The representation of groups on the boards of state agencies – that is, at the policy implementation stage. 4) The representation of groups in the local government policy process. The commission system in particular has attracted much non-Nordic interest.

In its prime in the 1960s and 1970s, the Swedish commission system was distinctive in giving interest groups – and distinctively parliamentarians – both a highly institutionalised and notably transparent role in policy formulation. In their heyday, commissions represented what the Riksdag Speaker, Birgitta Dahl, referred to as "the first stage in Sweden's negotiating democracy". (Arter 2000: 110) They were an essential part of Thomas Anton's depiction of Swedish policy-making as "open, rationalistic, consensual and extraordinarily deliberative". (Anton 1969: 88–102) There could be in the order of three hundred commissions sitting at any one time, covering things as different as the level of free language tuition for immigrants, the medical helicopter service in the north of the country, the availability of affordable housing and the taxation of summer cottages. It was typical for commissions to take three to four years to produce a set of recommendations, which were then sent out 'on remiss' for feedback and final comments from the relevant organised interests. Interest groups in short had two bites of the cherry: they would participate in the commission and later have the opportunity of responding to its final report (drafted by the commission chair, usually a civil servant).

The commission system has changed since the early 1980s. Seniority is less important and relevant expertise more so in recruiting parliamentary members. Achieving a gender balance has become vital, while among the opposition parties, especially the Conservatives, there is increasingly the view that top politicians should not be placed on commissions dealing with matters of 'high politics'. In other words, there is resistance to the government's strategy of involving opposition politicians in the pre-parliamentary consensus-building process. Nonetheless, for younger MPs commission work performs a valuable socialisation function and can advance a political career. Indeed, it remains broadly true that "commissions have taught MPs to work with civil servants and outside experts and educated a generation of Swedish politicians to go further than simply legislation". (Arter 2000: 110)

All in all, there has been the undoubted supposition that in the golden years of routine corporatism pressure groups exerted significant, possibly at times even decisive influence in the policy process. True, that influence was exercised subject to operating within the terms of reference —the negotiating framework – laid down by the government. As noted earlier, it is a ministerial decision to create a commission of inquiry (although a parliamentary majority demanding one will be very difficult to resist) and it is the minister who determines its composition, guidelines and schedule for completion. Indeed, Nordby puts the arresting question 'who governs whom?' and concludes that, in its prime, corporatism was in no small measure a mechanism of state control. (Nordby 2004: 99) The incorporation of groups enabled governments to govern in the way they wanted. Clearly, the fundamental problem lies in the futility of attempting to generalise about the balance of influence between government and groups on the myriad corporatist structures of the central administration. It was symptomatic that, having reviewed the substantial academic literature in the early 1980s, Dag Anckar and Voitto Helander concluded that "no structured picture of the policy impact of corporatism has emerged from the years of research". (Anckar and Helander 1985: 132) Nordby notes that "despite wider differences, especially concerning the state's role, the *impression* of a strongly corporatist structure to the Norwegian settlement arrangement remains solidly in place". (Nordby 2004: 104 – my italics) Nonetheless, by the 1990s there was extensive reference in the Nordic literature to a 'retreat of corporatism' or 'decorporativisation'.

Corporatism in retreat?

In fact, even before Scandinavian political scientists began to challenge the corporatist orthodoxy in the 1990s, it was possible to construct a persuasive *counter-corporatist case*. In other words, it was reasonable to challenge the presumption that the privileged access afforded interest groups allowed them to exercise at times decisive influence in the decision-making process. First, as already noted, Rokkan's thesis that peak corporatism enabled the major sectoral interests to play the paramount role in economic policy-making has lacked systematic empirical support [in Norway at least]. Rather, it appears to underestimate the discretion of the cabinet and particularly the officials and experts in the ministries of finance to set the parameters of government–group negotiations.

Second, the inference that co-optation has allowed pressure groups to exert a decisive influence in the formulation of public policy may well confuse participation and influence. The fact that, as stated earlier, the government appoints the chair, lays down the guidelines and determines the composition of commissions normally permits it to keep matters in hand. In this connection, Johan P. Olsen, writing on Norway, has noted the importance of civil servants at the formulation stage, a view supported by the leaders and senior personnel of the main sectoral interest groups. (Olsen 1980: 203–255) In short, routine corporatism does not *ipso facto* allow interest groups routinely to dominate the pre-parliamentary stage of decision-making.

Third, the argument that, when co-optation was at its most extensive, pressure group involvement in the rigorous examination of issues on commissions of inquiry undermined the deliberative role of parliament may well have underestimated both the formal and informal influence that MPs can exert in the generation of legislative measures. The extensive representation of Swedish parliamentarians – both on the government and opposition side – on commissions has been distinctive, although Danish MPs sat on commissions at least until the mid-1960s. But, across the region, parliamentary pressure has led directly or indirectly to the creation of commissions, while MPs have been able to exert influence through representatives of their party and/or related interest group on the commission – a type of absentee representation. Importantly too, the shift to minority government in metropolitan Scandinavia has meant an increased role for parliament in the deliberation and amendment of legislation. The limited evidence suggests that interest groups have increased their contacts with parliamentary standing committees, parliamentary party groups (PPGs) and individual MPs. Munk Christiansen and Rommetvedt have described how in Denmark and Norway "parliamentary lobbyism has increased as traditional corporatism has declined in scope and intensity". (Christiansen and Rommetvedt 2003: 147) It certainly appears plausible to explain the changes in the focus of corporatist interest group activity as partly at least the consequence of the increased power of parliaments vis-à-vis the executives.

The counter-corporatist case was not heard during the halcyon years of Scandinavian corporatism. However, more recently, the conventional wisdom has been challenged and the prevailing view appears to be that both peak corporatism and routine corporatism are in retreat. It is not the place here to examine the 'decline factors' in any depth, although a brief note on the main explanatory variables may be helpful. Evidence of a decline in routine corporatism has been found in the reduction in the number of preparatory committees and the number of committees with interest groups on them. The extent of co-optation, it is argued, has declined. The contraction of the Swedish commission system is particularly emphasised.

Table 6.2 The composition of Swedish commissions, 1981–97

	Parliamentary commissions	Others	One-person	Total
1981	134	110	165	409
	(33%)	(27%)	(40%)	(100%)
1986	73	40	105	218
	(33%)	(18%)	(48%)	(100%)
1991	45	36	103	184
	(24%)	(20%)	(56%)	(100%)
1995	44	47	181	272
	(16%)	(17%)	(67%)	(100%)
1997	51	45	181	277
	(18%)	(16%)	(65%)	(100%)

Source: *Riksdagens Revisorer, rapport 1996/97*, 6, p. 57

The overall importance of the commission system in the Swedish policy process has undoubtedly declined since 1981 (see table 6.2) and the timetable for the completion of their reports has been substantially shortened. Moreover, the views of the parliamentary opposition towards commissions have tended to become increasingly sceptical, not least because it is felt that proceedings have become increasingly party politicised. The internationalisation of the parliamentarian's role has led to problems of attendance and of devoting sufficient time to commission work. More fundamentally, commissions are increasingly viewed as ponderous instruments in policy preparation, which cannot react and report quickly enough in an era when 'quick-fire decisions' have become the norm. (Arter 2000: 110–116) All in all, a much more cost-effective approach to policy formulation has been sought and this has meant that fewer commissions are appointed and that among the new ones there is a growing number of 'one person civil service' commissions.

Table 6.2 illustrates the way the Swedish government's control over the commission system has increased since the early 1980s. First, the number of commissions has fallen – from 409 in 1981 to 277 in 1997. Second, the number of one-person civil service commissions, which began to rise in the 1970s, increased steadily in the two subsequent decades. In 1981 one-person commissions constituted two-fifths of the total number of commissions; by the mid-1990s this had risen to about two-thirds. Third, the number of 'parliamentary commissions' – classified as those with at least two active MPs as members – fell from one-third of the total in 1981 to just under one-fifth in 1997. The representation of interest groups has remained broadly stable, with a presence on about one-third of Swedish commissions over the last quarter of a century or so. (Riksdagens Revisorer raport 1996/97, 6: 80) Significantly, the commissions have a narrower remit than earlier and focus on more technical questions.

Similar tendencies to rationalise and streamline the process of policy preparation and reduce the involvement of interest groups have been observed in Norway and Denmark. (Heidar 2001: 76) In Norway the machinery of corporatist consultation appears more limited than earlier. Thus, reporting the conclusion of the Norwegian 'Power and Democracy' commission in August 2003 – see chapter 8 – Steinar Haugsvær commented that routine corporatism continues to function, although the number of committees and commissions has been significantly reduced. Accordingly, Norwegian interest groups have built up a more professional information and communications apparatus with a view to targetting decision-makers and the mass media. "Corporatism has declined rather than been strengthened over the last decade." (Haugsvær 2003)

The main thrust of the 'retreat debate', however, has been on those factors conspiring to erode peak corporatist practices. In the Swedish case, five in particular appear prominently in the literature. (Micheletti 1991: 144–165; Arter 1999: 165–167). First, there has been the impact of social structural change, the relative decline in the size of the blue-collar workforce and the growth in the so-called 'new middle class' working in the much-expanded public sector. These developments have combined to produce more heterogeneous structures of interest group representation. Particularly marked has been the growth in the number of white-collar unions representing the majority of the economically active population now employed in the service sector. Half a century or so ago peak corporatist bargaining proceeded on the basis of 'institutional tripartism' involving the central labour federation, the employers and the government (directly or indirectly). Today there are many more economic interest organisations to be accommodated, while tensions between groups representing public and private sides of the same economic sector have created an increasingly pluralistic picture.

Second, there has been the impact of new production methods on the level of social solidarity and unionisation among the workforce. The use of sophisticated technology, including the robotisation of factories, has meant the displacement of labour, generally smaller and more dispersed workforces and the phenomenon of so-called 'disorganised capitalism'. Put another way, unionisation has generally fallen, class solidarity weakened, levels of structural unemployment and social exclusion risen and the gulf between public and private sector unions expanded.

Third, there was the impact of the so-called 'rightist wave' in the 1980s, influenced of course by the neo-liberalism of Thatcher and Reagan. This professed the 'counter-ideology' of flexible structures and decentralised wage bargaining in contrast to the centralised corporatism of ruling social democracy. Electorally, unlike Denmark, neo-liberalism in Sweden and the Conservatives' demand for a 'shift in the system' made little significant headway, although a non-socialist minority government was formed in 1991. However, from the early 1980s, the export-oriented employers in the engineering sector pressed for more decentralised forms of wage bargaining. (Kunkel and Pontusson 1998: 3) Moreover, anti-corporatist attitudes hardened among strategic (middle-level) decision-takers in the central employers' organisation SAF. There was particular opposition to the 'solidary wage policy' promoted by the Social Democrats and LO since, in principle, this required wage increases across the board regardless of differential output and productivity. At the time of substantially reduced economic growth (Sweden was heading from an overheating economy in the late 1980s into the deepest recession in its history by the early 1990s) and a widening imbalance between private and public sectors, this was felt to be simply unsustainable. As early as 1985, SAF's executive recommended the abolition of formal interest group representation on the decision-making bodies of the central government boards (*verk*) charged with the implementation of public policy. (Johansson 2003: 320) Six years later, SAF decided unilaterally to withdraw from the National Labour Market Board (AMS), the National Board of Occupational Safety and Health (ASS) and many other government agencies. Significantly, in 1992, the non-socialist majority in the Riksdag [the four-party, Conservative-led coalition plus the opposition-based New Democracy] changed the composition of the boards, alluding to the withdrawal of SAF (Johansson 2003: 308). Accordingly, LO and the white-collar TCO lost the right to be represented.

A fourth factor challenging the operation of peak corporatism has been the

process of European integration. Superimposed on a period of economic recession, which pointed up the need for fundamental restructuring, Sweden's
application for EU membership meant the need to meet the so-called convergence criteria to qualify for membership of the economic and monetary union
(rejected of course in a referendum in 2003). This placed a premium on a
programme of fiscal austerity and severe curbs on the traditional politics of
redistribution. However, there was only gradual and grudging recognition by
the Social Democrats when they returned to power in 1994 that Sweden could
not spend its way out of recession on the back of foreign loans. In Finland in
similar circumstances, the incomes policy system collapsed during the non-
socialist coalition of Esko Aho (1991–95), only to be revived with the advent
of the 'rainbow coalition' in 1995. In Sweden the dictates of the economic
climate and the imperative of cutting state spending [on welfare and benefits]
exacerbated existing tensions between the main corporate actors. There have
been few signs of a revival in peak corporatism in recent years.

    Finally, globalisation has allowed the large Swedish multi-nationals to
threaten to relocate shop-floor production to lower labour-cost countries and,
in this way, to hold a gun to the heads of the government and trade unions.
Moderate and decentralised wage settlements in short have been seen as a sine
qua non of the multinationals continuing to employ a significant domestic
workforce. Clearly, in these circumstances, the balance of power between the
two sides of industry has swung away from the increasingly fragmented trade
union movement towards big business, which has favoured decentralised and
flexible structures of wage bargaining and conflict resolution. While the above
analysis has focused largely on Sweden, many of the points would be equally
valid for Norway and Denmark.

    In the Danish case, economic necessity was in large part the mother of a
move towards more flexible and decentralised wage bargaining practices in the
late 1980s. Put another way, the problems of the Danish economy pointed up
the need to adapt a peak corporatist system that had become dysfunctional in
promoting excessive wage gains when there was only a weak capacity to export
and high (import) consumption. The twin maladies of a long-term current
account deficit and severe debt servicing problems (on foreign loans) were
integrally bound up with an economy with a distinctively large and low-tech
small- and medium-sized firms (SME) sector, which did not engage in long
production runs of standardised goods. As Herman Schwartz has noted
colourfully: "Denmark entered the 1980s on a fast train to macro-economic
hell, albeit in the first class coach". (Schwartz 2000: 3) To what extent the
turn-round in the 1990s – the Danish 'miracle' of current account surpluses,
high employment levels etc – was the result of 'luck' (fortuitous environmental

change) or 'pluck' (strategic choice) – Schwartz's terms – must remain an open question. It may that that it was 'stuck' to, or was the by-product of specific and existing institutional structures. Whatever the case, the salient point is that the macro-economic circumstances dictated a shift in the late 1980s away from centralised collective bargaining practices towards *enterprise bargaining* and there were rising numbers of locally negotiated work contracts.

In Finland, a centralised collective bargaining system developed relatively late at the end of the 1960s, but it has proved remarkably resilient. Nonetheless, the consensus about the desirability of consensual incomes' policy solutions has been intermittently challenged on economic grounds. In the 1970s, for example, the governor of the Bank of Finland, Mauno Koivisto, attacked the two-year incomes packages as viscose and unable adequately to respond to the dictates of rapidly changing economic circumstances. He also pointed to the inherent tension between safeguarding the vested interests of the participating organisations and the demands of economic realism. In July 1975 Koivisto wrote that: "The orchestrated support for centralised incomes policy packages has led to a situation in which increases in real earnings are secured without regard to the level of production and productivity." (Koivisto 1978: 88) His was then seen as something of a maverick voice.

However, when in August 2004, the minister of finance, Antti Kalliomäki, announced his ambition to secure an unprecedented three-year incomes policy package (in return for tax cuts), the 'noise level' of the 'dissenters' grew. The general thrust of their critique was that institutional tripartism or peak corporatism was a problem-solving mechanism rather than an end in its own right and that a model which linked wage increases to average productivity contained in-built inefficiencies. There was widespread reference to the need to meet the challenges of globalisation and the continued need to improve economic competitiveness.[3] No lesser a body than the IMF, pointing to the rapid ageing of the Finnish population, urged the need for more decentralised bargaining practices and the abandonment of a solidary wage policy in favour of productivity-based increases. The head of Nokia, Jorma Ollila, likened Finland's situation in 2004 to the one he confronted at the Salo plant (in south-west Finland) when he took over in February 1990. Nokia was then anything but a global brand and the workforce wanted a return to single-shift arrangements following the introduction of a two-shift system in autumn 1989. Instead, in the teeth of strong opposition, Ollila instituted a three-shift day and the success this brought meant that the 4,500 employees presently working in the Salo plant is broadly the same number as Nokia employs in the whole of China.[4] Ollila's inference was clear: tough decisions were needed to confront the challenge of keeping Finland economically competitive.

The 'dissent' did not abate when in December 2004 an unprecedented three-year central incomes policy deal was successfully negotiated. The former trade and industry minister, Seppo Lindblom, for example, reasserted the need for the central incomes policy system to adapt in order to negotiate the 'environmental turbulence' caused by globalisation, the introduction of new technology and the related changes to work patterns. His basic thesis was that the time had come to emphasise micro-economic efficiency at the expense of macro-economic coordination. Traditionally, incomes policy in Finland, Lindblom noted, had been effective in combatting inflation in the wake of currency devaluation and in creating conditions of economic stability. However, the three-year incomes agreement, catalysed by the government's commitment to tax reductions, had been secured against the backdrop of exceptionally low levels of domestic investment and a paucity of risk-taking, employment-generating firms to fuel growth and sustain the welfare state. He concluded that wage moderation and the fight against inflation were unduly modest goals for the central incomes policy agreement, which in the future should form part of the government's wider social policy objectives.[5] Incidentally, in the parliamentary debate on the attendant tax reductions, the [then] Green leader, Osmo Soininvaara, also rued the lack of open debate about incomes policy. He claimed that it was not possible to question incomes policy without being branded an opponent. "This is worse than the [Finlandised] Finland of the Friendship, Co-operation and Mutual Assistance Treaty [with the Soviet Union] era", he insisted.[6]

The classical 'corporatist thesis' was predicated on the existence of a nexus of highly integrated interest groups exercising significant influence in policy formulation and it probably exaggerated that influence. Equally, it is not clear that the 'decorporativisation thesis' has demonstrated a subsequent loss of group influence; indeed, it may well have exaggerated the extent of the loss of influence. It was significant that in a survey of recent empirical work on Scandinavian corporatism Jens Blom-Hansen leaves open the question of any changes in the relative influence of interest groups. (Blom-Hansen 2000: 157–181) According to Blom-Hansen: "Interactions between the state and organised interests are becoming less formal in terms of factors such as presence in formal decision-making arenas and occupation of formal veto points. Interactions with the state seem to have taken a more lobbyist character. However, what this implies for the influence of organised interests is less certain". (Blom-Hansen 2000: 177) In a similar vein, Heidar comments that "the degree to which there has been a 'de-corporation' of Norwegian politics during the latter decades is an open question". (Heidar 2001: 76). The fundamental problem remains deriving conclusions about influence from (changing) patterns of interest group participation in the work of the political executive.

For example, it was evident from the conclusions of the 'Power and Democracy' commission in Denmark, which reported in 2003, that a decline in the formal participation of groups (the extent of their co-optation) does not necessarily lead to a significant loss of influence. It is clear from the commission's work that the corporatist interest group system in Denmark gradually weakened from the 1970s onwards. Groups were no longer included to the same extent in the preparation of legislation. There were fewer policy formulating committees set up and even the larger groups were not invited to be represented on them. Even decisions on labour market matters were increasingly taken without including the central trade union confederation and the central employers' organisation. However, informal contacts between groups and civil servants and groups and the Folketing appear to have become very extensive. Moreover, groups have ample opportunity to mobilise resistance to proposals that deleteriously affect their members' interests and have on occasions succeeded in doing so. As the Power and Democracy Commission concluded: "Interest groups continue to enjoy close relations with the authorities and in many cases they have significant influence on legislation". (Togeby 2003: 25)

In sharp contrast, Erik Oddvar Eriksen has argued that the *post-corporate state* may represent a new order and continues that "the state cannot any longer trust the corporate arrangements to secure the government's interest". (Eriksen 1990: 346) The risk here is of throwing the baby out with the bathwater. There is still evidence of strong corporatist structures, but they appear to have declined in scope and intensity. In short, Scandinavian corporatism probably appeared at best a difference in degree rather than kind when compared with other West European interest group systems and that degree may well have been significantly reduced in recent years.

Conclusions

The close association of corporatism and policy-making in Scandinavia owes much to the analyses of Norwegian practices in the 1960s by Rokkan (on peak corporatism) and 1970s by Kvavik (on routine corporatism) respectively. The claim is that the distinctive element in the government–group relationship lay in the extent and intensity of the consultation with organised interests. The essential logic of corporatism is legitimisation by incorporation. Thus, Micheletti notes that the general practice has been for the state to legitimise antagonistic interests by incorporating them into government. (Micheletti 1991: 148) She adds that "dialogue between opposing political actors became a Swedish institutional tradition". (Micheletti 1991: 148)

The non-institutional character of peak corporatism in Scandinavia appears distinctive in a comparative perspective. In the Nordic region peak corporatism has involved negotiations conducted in informal settings à la Harpsund rather than formalised in Economic Councils. The scale and scope of the 'lower-level' consultation between the government and interest groups – that is, routine corporatism – through commissions and committees at the formulation stage of public policy is possibly (rather than probably) distinctive. However, simple conclusions about interest group influence based on the extent of their participation on relevant committees would be treacherous. It may be sufficient to emphasise the propensity to compromise and reach a consensus and the absence of a zero-sum culture in the bargaining process.

There is evidence of change in the corporatist interest group systems, both in peak corporatist and routine corporatist arrangements. At the summit level the 'flank countries' of Finland and Iceland again appear deviant cases. In Finland peak corporatism developed later than in metropolitan Scandinavia – that is, in the late 1960s – but has proved remarkably resilient. After a brief hiatus in the early 1990s, the incomes policy system has been restored with renewed vigour. Iceland has taken only modest steps in a corporatist direction. The formula of a large centre-right party, the Independence Party, opposed by a divided left and fragmented trade union movement hugely complicated the task of macro-economic management. The creation of the Alliance (social democrats, women's list and radical left) in 1999 and its concomitant, greater cohesion in the labour movement, have militated towards a form of 'embryonic corporatism', which is none the less fragile. In metropolitan Scandinavia centralised collective bargaining has largely given way to decentralised practices. There has also been a contraction in the machinery for routine corporatist exchanges – particularly the commission system – with the result that "Sweden is gradually being decorporatised". (Micheletti 1991: 154) Like the corporatist case, so the decorporativisation case is largely a matter of degree.

Notes

1 'Kunnallisvaalit antavat potkua eduskunnan syksyä' *Helsingin Sanomat* 11.9.2004.
2 Until the mid-1960s politicians – and in particular parliamentarians – were also well represented on the Danish committee system. In 1916, and also in 1921, there were parliamentarians on broadly half the preparatory committees. Even in 1965, the figure stood at 22%, although by 1975 it had fallen to 12%. (Christiansen and Nørgaard 2003: 46, 59) In 1972 Denmark shifted from a British-style bill committee system in the Folketing to a system of specialist standing committees. Parliamentarians became increasingly involved in their work.
3 By 'globalisation' here is meant 1) the growth of multi-national companies and

their share of world trade 2) the growth of money markets beyond government control 3) the increased mobility of capital.

4 Janne Virkkunen, 'Suomi, Salo ja muutos' *Helsingin Sanomat* 31.10.2004.
5 Seppo Lindblom, 'Suomalainen tulopolitiikka on tullut tienhaaraan' *Helsingin Sanomat* 4.12.2004.
6 'Tuloratkaisun verolait heti riidan aiheena eduskunnassa' *Helsingin Sanomat* 4.12.2004.

References

Anckar, Dag and Voitto Helander 'Corporatism and Representative Government in the Nordic Countries', in Risto Alapuro et al. (eds) *Small States in Comparative Perspective* (Norwegian University Press: Oslo, Bergen and Tromsø, 1985), pp. 124–137

Anton, Thomas J. 'Policy-Making and Political Culture in Sweden' *Scandinavian Political Studies* 4, 1969, pp. 88–102

Armingeon, Klaus 'The Effects of Negotiation Democracy: a Comparative Analysis' *European Journal of Political Research* 41, 1, 2002, pp. 81–105

Arter, David *Politics and Policy-Making in Finland* (Wheatsheaf: Sussex, 1987)

Arter, David *Scandinavian Politics Today* (Manchester University Press: Manchester, 1999)

Arter, David 'Change in the Swedish Riksdag: From a Part-Time Parliament to a Professionalised Assembly?' *The Journal of Legislative Studies* 6, 3, 2000, pp. 93–116

Blom-Hansen, Jens 'Still Corporatism in Scandinavia? A Survey of Recent Empirical Findings' *Scandinavian Political Studies* 23, 2, 2000, pp. 157–181

Christiansen, Peter Munk and Asbjørn Sonne Nørgaard *Faste Forhold – Flygtige Forbindelser. Stat og Interesseorganisationer in Danmark i det 20 århundrede* (Aarhus Universitetsforlag: Århus, 2003)

Christiansen, Peter Munk and Hilmar Rommetvedt 'From Corporatism to Lobbyism? Parliaments, Executives and Organised Interests in Denmark and Norway', in Hilmar Rommetvedt *The Rise of the Norwegian Parliament* (Frank Cass: London and Portland, OR 2003), pp. 134–158

Einhorn, Eric S. and John Logue *Modern Welfare States. Second Edition* (Praeger: Westport, CT and London, 2003)

Eriksen, Erik Oddvar 'Towards the Post-Corporate State?' *Scandinavian Political Studies* 13, 4, 1990, pp. 345–364

Haugsvær, Steinar *Maktutredningar* www.sv.uio.no/mutr/aktuelt/aktuelt/maktutredningens_hovedkonklusjoner_kort.html

Heidar, Knut *Norway. Elites on Trial* (Westview: Boulder, CO, 2001)

Johansson, Joakim 'Mid-Level Officials as Policy-Makers: Anti-Corporatist Policy Change in the Swedish Employers' Confederation 1982–85' *Scandinavian Political Studies* 26, 4, 2003, pp. 307–325

Katzenstein, Peter J. *Small States in World Markets. Industrial Policy in Europe* (Cornell University Press: Ithaca, 1985)

Kjellberg, Anders 'Sweden: Can the Model Survive?', in Anthony Ferner and Richard Hyman (eds) *Industrial Relations in the New Europe* (Blackwell: Oxford, 1992), pp. 88–142

Koivisto, Mauno *Väärää politiikkaa* (Kirjayhtymä: Helsinki, 1978)

Kunkel, Christoph and Jonas Pontusson 'Corporatism versus Social Democracy: Divergent Fortunes of the Austrian and Swedish Labour Movements' *West European Politics* 21, 2, 1998, pp. 1–31

Kvavik, Robert *Interest Groups in Norwegian Politics* (Universitetsforlaget: Oslo, Bergen and Tromsø, 1976)

Lewin, Leif 'The Rise and Decline of Corporatism: The Case of Sweden' *European Journal of Political Research* 26, 1, 1994, pp. 59–79

Lijphart, Arend *Patterns of Democracy* (Yale University Press: New Haven and London, 1999)

Lægreid, Per and Paul G. Roness 'Political Parties, Bureaucracies and Corporatism', in Kaare Strøm and Lars Svåsand (eds) *Challenges to Political Parties* (University of Michigan: Ann Arbor, MI, 1997), pp. 167–190

Marks, Gary 'Neocorporatism and Incomes Policy in Western Europe and North America' *Comparative Politics* 18, 3, 1986, pp. 71–83

Micheletti, Michele 'Swedish Corporatism at a Crossroads: The Impact of New Politics and New Social Movements' *West European Politics* 14, 3, 1991, pp. 144–165

Nordby, Trond 'Patterns of Corporatist Intermediation', in Knut Heidar (ed.) *Nordic Politics. Comparative Perspectives* (Universitetsforlaget: Oslo, 2004), pp. 98–107

Olsen, Johan P. 'Governing Norway: Segmentation, Anticipation and Consensus Formation', in Richard Rose and Ezra N. Suleiman (eds) *Presidents and Prime Ministers* (American Enterprise Institute for Public Policy Research: Washington DC, 1980), pp. 203–255

Rehn, Olli *Corporatism and Industrial Competitiveness in Small European States: Austria, Finland and Sweden, 1945–95* (University of Oxford, 1996)

Riksdagens Revisorer raport 1996/97, 6: 80

Rokkan, Stein 'Norway: Numerical Democracy and Corporate Pluralism', in Robert A. Dahl (ed.) *Political Oppositions in Western Democracies* (Yale University Press: New Haven, 1966)

Schwartz, Herman 'The Danish "Miracle": Luck, Pluck or Stuck?' *Comparative Political Studies*, 2000

Togeby, Lise, Jørgen Goul Andersen, Peter Munk Christiansen, Torben Beck Jørgensen and Signild Vallgårda *Power and Democracy in Denmark. Conclusions* (University of Aarhus: Aarhus, 2003)

7

A common denominator between Westminster and the Nordic region? The growing importance of the office of prime minister

The last five chapters have sought to identify those elements in the Nordic political systems which have appeared distinctive when viewed primarily from a Westminster perspective. Consideration has been given to the varieties of preferential PR voting systems in Denmark, Sweden and Finland; the unidimensionality and pronounced class base of the historic multi-party systems, notably in Sweden; the electoral strength (outside Iceland) of social democracy; the range of coalition types, particularly the 'surplus majority' coalitions in Finland; the frequency of minority governments, both coalitions and, more frequently, single-party; and the existence of corporatist interest group systems. The extent to which these distinguishing features have become more or less distinctive over the years has also been assessed. It should be obvious, of course, that there has been a good deal of intra-regional variation in Nordic political practice. We have already noted marked contrasts in cabinet types, as well as in the dynamics of the party systems at the elite level. The 'bloc-oriented' states of Denmark, Norway and Sweden and the 'across the bloc' systems of Finland and Iceland are cases in point.

It should be equally obvious that the features that distinguish the practice of politics and government in *Norden* do not in themselves signify that the Scandinavian states are 'consensus model democracies'. There may in fact be more common denominators between Lijphart's two types of democracy – or at least between the British and Scandinavian systems – than is generally allowed. For example, there have been periods –see chapter 12 – when government–opposition relations in Scandinavia have been at least as adversarial as in the two-party Westminster model. Moreover, government–group relations in Britain may be more corporatist – at least of the 'routine corporatism' variety – than the "pluralist free for all" suggested by Lijphart. (Lijphart 1999: 3) As early as the 1980s, Richardson and Jordan were able to apply the analytical frameworks of Scandinavian political scientists to their study of pressure groups in Britain. They note, for example, the way Robert Kvavik's description of the co-optation of Norwegian interest groups onto the policy-formulating committees and commissions of central government (Kvavik 1976) is "strikingly similar to our description of Britain". (Richardson and Jordan 1979: 165) This chapter, however, focuses on perhaps the most striking common denominator of all – the apparent growth in the role and importance of the prime minister. The basic question relates to whether it is possible to speak of something approximating 'prime ministerial government' in Scandinavia. The precise formulation draws on Johan P. Olsen's assertion a quarter of a century ago that "a Norwegian prime minister … is unlikely to achieve a position as superstar". (Olsen 1980: 213) It asks 'have the Nordic prime ministers today become superstars or are they essentially supervisors?'

The first part examines the limited constitutional prerogatives of the Nordic prime ministers and the relatively recent creation of a prime minister's office. Remarkably, for example, until 1935 and the advent of Thorvald Stauning, the Danish prime minister was responsible for a specific ministry, in addition to his responsibilities as prime minister and the modern prime minister's office was not created until 1964.[1] The second section examines the prime minister's role in supervising the work of the government. It considers the main constraints on his/her freedom of maneouvre and the validity in the Nordic region of Clay Clemens' characterisation of the German Chancellor as a "moderator within and between parties". (Clemens 1994: 47) The final section challenges Richard Rose's view that in most of Scandinavia the prime minister tends to represent the lowest common denominator of inter-party agreement (Rose 1991) and considers the case for the growing importance of the office of prime minister. Have the incumbents achieved 'superstar' status?

The constitutional prerogatives of the Nordic prime ministers

Outside Finland – and then only since 2000 – the constitutional prerogatives of the Nordic prime ministers are few and the *de jure* specification of the role very limited. The Danish and Icelandic constitutions make it clear that the prime minister is the chief spokesperson of the government in the major plenary debates. In Iceland the only reference to the prime minister in the constitution is in fact article 73, which refers to the 'prime minister's policy speech' at the start of each Alþingi session in October. This is followed by a general debate. Also in Denmark virtually the only reference to the prime minister in the 1953 constitution is contained in paragraph 5 article 38. This states that at the first meeting of the new Folketing year, the prime minister will present a review of the state of the realm and the measures planned by the government – *redegørelse for rigets almindelige stilling*. This will preface the 'opening debate' at which the length of speeches will be the same as for the first reading of the budget.

The 1814 Eidsvoll Constitution in Norway and the 1974 Swedish Constitution stipulate a lower limit on the number of ministers that must be present at a cabinet meeting and so, in practice, a minimum size of the cabinet. In Sweden the figure is five ministers and in Norway the prime minister plus at least seven other ministers. In Norway, moreover, the counter-signature of the prime minister is required on cabinet decisions. The Norwegian prime minister also has an extra vote if the King is not in attendance at the Council of State and has the right to obtain any information he requires from government departments.[2] But there is nothing comparable in Scandinavia to the 'constructive vote of no confidence' found in Germany and Spain, designed to fortify an existing government. In Norway, which distinctively in Western Europe has fixed-term parliaments, there is in fact no provision for the prime minister to dissolve parliament and call an early election. This was originally intended to protect the Storting against arbitrary dismissal by the Swedish King (during the Union with Sweden between 1815–1905), although it has in practice tended to sustain governments against irresponsible oppositions. As in Germany, the opposition cannot simply vote no confidence in the cabinet, but must come up with an alternative government. (This in fact happened in March 2000 when the Labour leader, Jens Stoltenberg, replaced a centre-led minority cabinet led by Kjell-Magne Bondevik of the Christian People's Party.)[3]

In Finland the dissolution of parliament was for long a presidential preserve. This is no longer the case. Indeed, the change in the legal status of the prime minister's office has been most marked in Finland. So much is evident *inter alia* from paragraph 66 of the 2000 constitution, according to which "the prime minister leads the work of the government and is responsible for the co-ordination of the preparation and deliberation of those matters falling within its remit". It also states that the prime minister leads the debate – that is, chairs – the 'general sittings' of the cabinet (held on Thursdays).

In contrast to the role of the Icelandic president which, with the achievement of full independence from Denmark in 1944, was modelled on the (by then) largely ceremonial duties of the Danish monarch (Kristinsson 1999: 86–103), the 1919 Finnish constitution prescribed a dual executive and a semi-presidential form of government. (Arter 1999: 48–66) The head of state was vested with significant powers, including the right to nominate and dismiss governments, dissolve parliament, make wide-ranging appointments and direct relations with foreign states. The president in short acquired many of the powers the Russian Czar had exercised in the Grand Duchy of Finland before the achievement of Finnish independence in 1917. During the post-war presidencies of J. K. Paasikivi (1946–56) and particularly the long-serving Urho Kekkonen (1956–81), the prime minister operated in the shadow of the head of state. The prime minister was chosen by the president and on occasions was removed by him; cabinets were mainly short-lived; and the president, in conducting foreign policy, accrued enormous influence through his personalised and successful management of Finno-Soviet relations. The president was the dominant political figure – the present author even referred to Finland under Kekkonen as "enlightened despotism" (Arter 1981: 219–234) – and brooked no competitors.[4] As late as 1994 Jaakko Nousiainen could write that "as the aura of national leader belongs to the president, the prime minister has a rather prosaic role of organiser and arbitrator rather than a policy activist". (Nousiainen 1994: 98)

Even so, in 1981, the Social Democrat Mauno Koivisto, became the first prime minister successfully to defy the attempt of (a by now ageing) Kekkonen to destabilise his government, insisting simply that his cabinet had not lost the confidence of parliament. When, the following year, Koivisto himself was elected president, he engineered a series of piecemeal reforms, which, collectively, did much to reduce the powers of the presidency and increase those of the prime minister. Ultimately, these powers were formalised in the March 2000 constitution (*hallitusmuoto*) and a revised Council of State Law (*valtioneuvostonlaki*), which took effect in April 2003. Importantly, the president was excluded from the government formation process. The head of state could become involved in coalition building only as a last resort if the parties could not reach agreement. In Max Jakobson's words, [today] "the prime minister is no longer chosen by the president and dependent on the president, but is the independent leader of the government".[5]

The new constitution also limited the president's powers of foreign policy management. She or he no longer determines Finland's relations with other states, but directs foreign policy in conjunction with the government. In this connection, Finnish membership of the EU in 1995 has seen the prime minister represent Finland at European Council meetings. The prime minister's formal power was further increased when in 2001 the influential EU secretariat was transferred from the foreign ministry to the prime minister's office. All in all, Finland can today no longer be described as a semi-presidential system, although the head of state is by no means a purely ceremonial figure.[6]

Iceland has never been a semi-presidential system in practice, although the 1944 constitution bestows considerable powers on the head of state. Indeed, Svanur Kristjánsson has spoken of the 'political presidency' of Ólafur Grímsson since 1996 – in sharp contrast to Vigdis Finnbogadóttir (1980–96) who would not even discuss politics in public – and in 2004 Grímsson refused controversially to ratify a new law designed to prevent media monopolies.[7] This was the first time that an Icelandic president had exercised his right not to ratify a law (which accordingly went to a popular referendum). Grímsson was elected for a third consecutive term of office in June 2004, with 85% of the votes for the three candidates. But, since 20% of all ballot papers were blank and the turnout was the lowest since 1919, it seems reasonable to think that there was a section of the electorate that was not happy with the president's action.[8]

The prime minister's role in supervising the work of the government

While the constitutional prerogatives of the office are limited, the Nordic prime ministers combine two essential roles – they manage the work of the government and they head their party, which is usually, though not always the largest party in the government. Managing the work of a coalition government, or a minority cabinet dependent on 'support parties', will clearly involve meeting challenges in the inter-party arena. Managing his/her own ministerial team, not to mention the parliamentary party group and beyond that the broader party membership, will entail intra-party skills. Obviously, each prime minister will have his/her own management style, dictated partly by the particular set of political circumstances and partly by the temperament and personality of the incumbent. Even the most forceful personality, however, will find their room for maneouvre constrained in appointing a ministerial team, carrying the parliamentary party group and, in coalition cabinets, handling relations with the other governing parties. It was against this backdrop that Clemens described the role of the German Chancellor as "a moderator within and between parties". (Clemens 1994: 47) This second section concentrates on the 'work environment' of the Nordic prime ministers and the nature of their task in supervising the work of the government.

There have been 70 prime ministers in the Nordic countries since the Second World War – or, in the Icelandic case, the achievement of independence in 1944 (see tables 7.1–7.5). The numbers have ranged from only eight in Sweden to twenty-two in Finland where, until 1975, there were numerous stop-gap caretaker and civil service cabinets. Longevity of tenure has been greatest in the case of Swedish Social Democratic prime ministers, since none in the post-war period has served less than seven years in the job. Indeed, no post-war Social Democratic prime minister in Sweden has ultimately relinquished the post as a result of an election defeat. Tage Erlander retired voluntarily in 1969 after a momentous two decades in office, Ingvar Carlsson did likewise in 1996 (being replaced by the current prime minister Göran Persson), while Olof Palme was assassinated in a Stockholm street in February 1986.

Table 7.1 *Swedish prime ministers since 1945*

Per Albin Hansson	Social Democrat	1945–46
Tage Erlander	Social Democrat	1946–69
Thorbjörn Fälldin	Centre	1976–78, 1979–82
Ola Ullsten	Liberal	1978–79
Olof Palme	Social Democrat	1969–76, 1982–86
Ingvar Carlsson	Social Democrat	1986–91, 1994–96
Carl Bildt	Conservative	1991–94
Göran Persson	Social Democrat	1996–

Table 7.2 *Danish prime ministers since 1945*

Knud Kristensen	Liberal	1945–47
Hans Hedtoft	Social Democrat	1947–50, 1953–55
Erik Eriksen	Liberal	1950–53
H. C. Hansen	Social Democrat	1955–57, 1957–60
Viggo Kampmann	Social Democrat	1960–62
Jens Otto Krag	Social Democrat	1962–68, 1971–72
Hilmar Baunsgaard	Social Liberal	1968–71
Anker Jørgensen	Social Democrat	1972–73, 1975–82
Poul Hartling	Liberal	1973–75
Poul Schlüter	Conservative	1982–93
Poul Nyrup Rasmussen	Social Democrat	1993–2001
Anders Fogh Rasmussen	Liberal	2001–

Table 7.3 *Finnish prime ministers since 1946*

Mauno Pekkala	Finnish People's Democratic League	1946–48
K. A. Fagerholm	Social Democrat	1948–50, 1956–57, 1958–59
Urho Kekkonen	Agrarian Party	1950–53, 1954–56
Sakari Tuomioja	non-party	1953–54
Ralf Törngren	Swedish People's Party	1954
V. J. Sukselainen	Agrarian Party 1957,	1959–61
Rainer von Fieandt	non-party	1957–58
Reino Kuuskoski	non-party	1958
Martti Miettunen	Agrarian-Centre	1961–62, 1975–77
Ahti Karjalainen	Agrarian-Centre	1962–63, 1970–71
Reino Lehto	non-party	1963–64
Johannes Virolainen	Agrarian-Centre	1964–66
Rafael Paasio	Social Democrat	1966–68, 1972
Mauno Koivisto	Social Democrat	1968–70, 1979–82

Teuvo Aura	non-party	1970, 1971–72
Kalevi Sorsa	Social Democrat	1972–75, 1977–79, 1982–87
Keijo Liinamaa	non-party	1975
Harri Holkeri	Conservative	1987–91
Esko Aho	Centre	1991–95
Paavo Lipponen	Social Democrat	1995–2003
Anneli Jäätteenmäki	Centre	2003
Matti Vanhanen	Centre	2003–

Table 7.4 Prime ministers in Norway since 1945

Einar Gerhardsen	Labour	1945–51, 1955–63, 1963–65
Oscar Torp	Labour	1951–55
Jon Lyng	Conservative	1963
Per Borten	Agrarian-Centre	1965–71
Trygve Bratteli	Labour	1971–72, 1973–76
Lars Korvald	Christian People's Party	1972–73
Odvar Nordli	Labour	1976–81
Gro Harlem Brundtland	Labour	1981, 1986–89, 1990–97
Kåre Willoch	Conservative	1981–86
Jan P. Syse	Conservative	1989–90
Thorbjørn Jagland	Labour	1996–97
Kjell Magne Bondevik	Christian People's Party	1997–2000, 2001–05
Jens Stoltenberg	Labour	2000–01, 2005–

Table 7.5 Prime ministers in Iceland since independence in 1944

Ólafur Thors	Independence Party	1944–47, 1949–50, 1953–56, 1959–63
Stefán Jóhann Stefánsson	Social Democrats	1947–49
Steingrímur Steinthórsson	Progressive Party	1950–53
Herman Jónasson	Progressive Party	1956–58
Emil Jónsson	Social Democrats	1958–59
Bjarni Benediktsson	Independence Party	1963–70
Jóhann Hafstein	Independence Party	1970–71
Ólafur Jóhannesson	Progressives	1971–74, 1978–79
Geir Hallgrímsson	Independence Party	1974–78
Benedikt Gröndal	Social Democrat	1979–80
Gunnar Thoroddsen	Independence Party	1980–83
Steingrímur Hermannsson	Progressives	1983–87, 1988–91
Thorsteinn Pálsson	Independence Party	1987–88
Davið Oddsson	Independence Party	1991–2004
Halldór Ásgrímsson	Progressives	2004–

There have also been some notably long-serving prime ministers outside Sweden. In Norway the Labour leader Einar Gerhardsen held the post for seventeen years, whilst Gro Harlem Brundtland, also Labour and Norway's first female prime minister, held the office for over eleven years in the 1980s and 1990s. In Finland the Social Democrat, Kalevi Sorsa, served as prime minister for ten years during the 1970s and 1980s, but the prime minister with the longest record of continuous service is Paavo Lipponen, who headed two 'rainbow coalitions' between 1995–2003. Denmark has been distinctive in that, although the Social Democrats have been the largest party in all but two post-war elections (2001 and 2005), the longest-serving prime minister has been a Conservative, Poul Schlüter. He led a series of non-socialist minority cabinets between 1982–93. In Iceland the most durable prime ministers have belonged to the largest grouping, the Independence Party. Ólafur Thors served as premier for nearly twelve years between independence from Denmark and 1963. However, the longest single stretch as prime minister was that of Davið Oððsson between 1991–2004. At the other extreme the first post-war non-socialist government in Norway under Jon Lyng survived only three weeks in 1963.

The background of the post-war Nordic prime ministers has been enormously varied. The long-serving Norwegian prime minister Gerhardsen, who was born in 1897, fits, as Johan P. Olsen has noted, "the Weberian ideal of a political generalist with politics as a vocation" (Olsen 1980: 213) He had only elementary schooling and was a road worker from the ages of seventeen to twenty-four. Oscar Torp, who was born in 1983, also had no higher education and had worked as an electrician whilst Trygve Bratteli had broadly similar working class 'credentials'. In fact, no less than eight of the post-war Norwegian prime ministers have not had a university degree and all but one of these, Lars Korvald of the Christian People's Party, has represented the Labour Party. In Denmark, the Social Democrat, Anker Jørgensen, who was the prime minister on five occasions between 1972–82 was a non-graduate. So, too, was Rafael Paasio, a journalist, who led the first so-called Popular Front (centre-left) government in Finland between 1966–68. The most notable exception to the rule of non-university educated prime ministers emanating from the social democratic-labour ranks was the Swedish Centre leader, Thorbjörn Fälldin, who headed three non-socialist coalitions between 1976–82. Fälldin claimed memorably that "parliament [the Riksdag] was my university".[9]

In Iceland, where the lion's share of the twenty-five prime ministers since the achievement of Home Rule in 1904 have hailed from the two non-socialist parties, their academic qualifications have been striking. No less than fifteen have held law degrees – one at the doctoral level – three have had engineering degrees, two graduated in theology and one each in history and agronomy. The present prime minister Halldór Ásgrímsson trained as an accountant. In other words, in over one hundred years, only two Icelandic prime ministers have not possessed university degrees.

Background, education and partisanship aside, the task of the prime minister is to lead the work of the government – that is, to direct the ministerial team that makes up the cabinet. Each prime minister will, of course, chair cabinet meetings in his or her own particular style. Johannes Virolainen has described the extremely forceful manner of Urho Kekkonen, who was Finnish prime minister on five occasions in the early 1950s. Kekkonen would sit at the top of the table, invite various ministers to have their say on the matter under discussion, but always end the dialogue in the same way. "Fine, that's clear then, we'll do it as I proposed"! (Virolainen 1969: 123) The prime minister may also chair cabinet committee meetings, although in Sweden these have existed only during the non-socialist coalitions of 1976–82 and 1991–94. (Bergman 2003: 213) There will also be extensive informal contacts with ministers. Most notably, there has been the celebrated Finnish 'evening class' (*iltakoulu*) or informal gathering of ministers (and increasingly officials and even interest group representatives) on Wednesday nights, prior to the full cabinet sitting on Thursdays. The institution of the 'evening class' declined, however during the 1970s and effectively disappeared under Lipponen between 1995–2003. In Sweden, too, the previously daily cabinet lunches are now occasional and poorly attended. In both countries EU membership, and the general internationalisation of politics, have dictated that several ministers will be abroad at any one time and unable to attend.

One meeting the prime minister does not chair is the formal Council of State. A ceremonial legacy of past times, these meetings are essentially rubber-stamping exercises. Indeed, the former Danish prime minister, Anker Jørgensen, has recorded amusingly how he particularly liked Council of State meetings because it was the only time he could be certain of getting half an hour's rest! (Miller 1991: 54–55)

The individual management style of the prime minister will reflect not only the personality of the incumbent, but also the particular size and partisan composition of the government. Managing a broad 'surplus majority' coalition of the 'rainbow' variety will entail different challenges from holding together a numerically weak minority coalition. Yet, while generalisation is inevitably risky, it is probably fair to assert that the tendency has been towards a decentralisation and sectoralisation of the work of Scandinavian governments. Ministers are largely left to develop policy within their particular area of responsibility, ministers and the prime minister increasingly engage in bilateral discussions (the prime minister–finance minister axis is crucial) and the effective deliberation takes place within cabinet committees and informal working groups. Full cabinet meetings have become short, increasingly ritualistic and devoid of real debate. As Jørgen Grønnegard Christensen noted fully twenty years ago, "like the cabinets in Denmark's neighbouring countries, the cabinet [in Denmark] is neither a forum for policy discussions nor the real decision-making centre in central government". (Christensen 1985: 119)

On the basis of interviews with fourteen ministers in the Lipponen 11 'rainbow coalition' (1999–2003), Minna Tiili concluded that there existed only a weak sense of collegiality and that there was relatively little collective cabinet discussion. Interestingly, the paucity of collective discussion was viewed as a problem by some, but by no means all ministers. (Tiili 2004: 137–142) One minister who clearly did view it as a problem was Arja Alho, the second (deputy) finance minister in the Lipponen 1 'rainbow coalition' between 1995–97. In her doctoral dissertation 'Silent Democracy, Noisy Media', Alho relates how, despite her ministerial portfolio, her central position in the Social Democratic Party, and long years of parliamentary experience, including a period as chair of the Constitutional Committee, she was completely excluded from any meaningful discussion of the proposed Finnish membership of EMU. (Alho 2004) Decisions on this and other important issues were taken by the prime minister and an inner cabinet.[10]

From a prime minister's perspective a lack of collective deliberation could, of course, mean a lack of collective disagreement. In any event, it seems there has been more debate in the Vanhanen government (2003–) than in the Lipponen governments, both in cabinet committees and in full cabinet. Difficult matters are nonetheless resolved in an informal 'inner cabinet' between the three party leaders Vanhanen, the minister of finance Euro Heinäluoma (Social Democrat) and the minister of the environment Jan-Erik Enestam (Swedish People's Party), together with the prime minister's adviser.[11]

Outside the cabinet room and the various cabinet committees, the prime minister is the cabinet's chief spokesperson on the floor of parliament. He accounts for the actions of his government through the medium of plenary account debates, mostly prompted by questions and interpellations. However, compared with its Westminster counterpart, Question Time in the Nordic parliaments is quietist and almost deferential. Ingvar Mattson sums up on Sweden. "The prime minister rarely receives and answers questions. Question Time does not, as in Great Britain, provide an opportunity where the head of government faces his or her political opponents … to answer critical follow-up questions he may not have prepared for." (Mattson 1994: 334) A mediocre performance by the prime minister on the floor of parliament will, of course, do nothing for his reputation, but unless a question leads to a vote of no confidence, the government would normally expect to survive.

The risk of not surviving is greatest in 'metropolitan Scandinavia' where minority governments (both single-party and coalitions) have become the norm. Yet minority governments are in fact routinely defeated on legislative amendments and remain in office unless the prime minister makes an issue a matter of confidence. For example, the cabinets led by Gro Harlem Brundtland (the first female Norwegian prime minister) in the 1990s incurred parliamentary defeats with increasing regularity while becoming more not less ensconced. (Narud and Strøm 2003: 167) There is not the same presumption in favour of majority arrangements as in Westminster. Majority coalitions, especially the 'surplus majority' coalitions in Finland in recent years, can often withstand the resignation of one of the minor parties on a matter of principle, as long as they retain a plurality of parliamentarians behind them.

In both minority and majority coalitions, of course, the prime minister must work to accommodate the 'partner parties' and to achieve a satisfactory level of cabinet cohesion. This may be particularly challenging when the prime minister does not come from the largest coalition party. The Conservatives, not the prime minister's own party the Centre, were the largest party in the Fälldin coalition in Sweden between 1979–81 and matters were further complicated by the fact that it had an overall majority of only one in the Riksdag. In only six of the nine post-war Norwegian coalitions (all but one non-socialist) has the prime minister come from the largest coalition party. As Narud and Strøm observe, the fact that this has not happened in one-third of all Norwegian coalitions may be noteworthy by international standards. (Narud and Strøm 2003: 181)

Clearly then, executive leadership must be viewed in the context of the complex and dynamic power relationships that exist between the prime minister and his or her parliamentary party group (PPG) on the one hand and their relationship with the party leaders of the support parties on the other. The support parties may be involved in a formal *executive coalition* (an inter-party sharing of ministerial portfolios) or a *legislative coalition* (a pact with opposition parties, as in Sweden since 1998).

In her classical essay on Germany, Renate Mayntz wrote that: "The most important basis of the Chancellor's power is his position within his political party". (Mayntz 1980: 148) In Scandinavia, as in Germany, the prime minister is the leader of her or his party, as well as leader of the government. Thus, from the start of Mauno Koivisto's presidency in 1982, all the Finnish prime ministers, with the exception of the Conservative Harri Holkeri (1987–91), have also been chairs of their parties. Matti Vanhanen, who replaced Jäätteenmäki as Finnish prime minister in June 2003, was only deputy chair of the Centre, but he became chair within a few months of taking office. Historically, there has been a particularly strong conjunction between the roles of chief political executive and chief party executive in the dominant Swedish Social Democratic Party. While serving as prime minister, Tage Erlander, Olof Palme and Ingvar Carlsson all functioned simultaneously as leader of the PPG and party leader.

Nonetheless, across the region as a whole, there has normally been a role differentiation between the leader of the party in government (the prime minister) and leader of the party in parliament. For example, when the Danish Social Democrats are in office, the leader (prime minister) continues as chair of the party's extra-parliamentary organisation, but resigns as chair of the PPG. (Bille 2000: 139)

The PPG of the prime minister's party normally constitutes the core support base of the government in parliament and for that reason alone cannot be taken for granted. The PPG has its own leader, rules and organisational structure and, though generalisation is treacherous, in the case of the Swedish Social Democrats at least, the PPG is less of a rubber stamp for the executive – the government's 'transport company' – than it used to be. The turning point was 1976, when after 44 years of virtually continuous involvement in government, the Social Democrats were finally dislodged from power. A former PPG leader recalled how "in the late 1960s, a large proportion of Social Democratic members of parliament were engaged in local government and viewed their work in the Riksdag as an extension of their activities at the sub-state level. The Social Democrats were dominated by these people, who were not full-timers. Intra-group democracy suffered in that there were few MPs who had the ambition to be part of the process of national policy-making". (Arter 2000: 106) All this changed when the Social Democrats were forced into opposition in 1976. The PPG was revamped with the *committee groups* constituting a horizontal power axis alongside the vertical authority stemming from the PPG leader and PPG executive downwards. The committee groups comprise the Social Democratic MPs (and their substitutes) sitting on a particular Riksdag standing committee and they inevitably possess a substantial body of knowledge of the policy area covered by the committee. Accordingly, they have been influential in determining the party line on issues within their field of competence. In opposition, in short, the Social Democrats' PPG became an increasingly autonomous legislative actor.

It is not clear how far this point can be generalised for PPGs in Scandinavia as a whole. In some cases, though not all, the prime minister does not have entirely free hands in appointing his/her party's slate of cabinet ministers. Frictions may be generated at the very outset if the norms guiding the recruitment of ministers are not fully observed. Knut Heidar identifies three cardinal unwritten rules in selecting ministers from the prime minister's PPG. First, the prime minister's party's allocation of ministers must reflect the different parts of the country. "A government without any minister 'representing' North Norway would be crippled from the outset" irrespective of its base in parliament. (Heidar 2001: 43) Second, there should be a fairly even gender balance and the presence of significant numbers of female ministers. Third, the government's relations with the Storting should be facilitated by the appointment of a number of experienced parliamentarians. (Heidar 2001: 43–44)

In presenting her list of Centre ministers after the March 2003 general election, Anneli Jäätteenmäki, the Finnish prime minister designate, announced five selection criteria – ability, individual expertise, public performance capability, team player capacity and reliability. However, when regional factors were ignored, regional lobbies within the PPG were active in pressing the case for particular individuals to be appointed to ministerial office. Ultimately, there were formal votes on no less than four of the six Centre ministers (excluding the prime minister).[12] Furthermore, even though, when the Social Democrats have been in power, the Swedish prime minister has had relatively free hands in appointing cabinet ministers, he has traditionally included one or more representatives of the central trade union federation LO. (Ruin 1991: 64) While generalisations about the PPGs of the prime minister's party are decidedly risky, it is clear that giving a convincing account of his or her actions and those of the government – that is, the successful management of relations with the PPG – is vital for an effective chief political executive.

There are inter-party, as well as intra-party challenges for the Scandinavian prime ministers. Indeed, the prevalence of minority governments has made the assertion of the former Riksdag Finance Committee chair Jan Bergquist – that "majority-building is the whole point of Swedish politics" – of particular relevance to the task of prime ministers in metropolitan Scandinavia. Widening the point, majority-building or coalition-building – either of the executive or legislative variety – will have implications for the role of the prime minister and his relationship with the parliamentary opposition. Moreover, in the case of coalition cabinets, the PPG of the junior coalition party(ies) will nominate its own ministers, with the result that, as the former Norwegian prime minister, Odvar Nordli, observed "if you cannot get the ones you want, you have to love the ones you get". (Olsen 1980: 218)[13] In the event of policy divisions within the coalition, the prime minister may well have to attend PPG meetings of the junior partners or, when it is a legislative coalition, forge good working relations with the party leaders of the support groupings.

From Clay Clemens' study of the German case, it is evident that even a long-serving Executive leader with strong individual views will need to work with and through both his own party and his coalition partners. It is not possible simply to dictate personal terms. Accordingly, Clemens characterised Germany under the long-serving Helmut Kohl (1982–98) not as a 'chancellor democracy', but a 'co-ordination democracy' in which the leader of the government served as "a moderator within and between parties". (Clemens 1994: 47) This appeared an admirable description of the Swedish prime minister's position in the first half of 2003. Certainly the strain on the legislative coalition between the ruling Social Democrats and its two opposition-based allies, the Leftists and Greens, in the early part of that year appeared to cast the Swedish prime minister in the role of conciliator.

First, a combination of reduced economic growth, high levels of sickness absenteeism and a sharp rise in early retirement rates necessitated cuts in the 2004 budget amounting to two and a half billion euros. Second, while a budget agreement was reached, the Leftist Party in particular was opposed to public spending cuts and badly split. Next, the resignation of the Leftist leader, Gudrun Schyman, and the apparent reluctance of anyone to replace her, negatively affected the personal chemistry of the legislative coalition. The fact that the Leftists and Greens were opposed to the euro, forced the Social Democratic prime minister to turn to the predominantly pro-EMU Conservatives and Liberals in the campaign leading up to the 14 September 2003 referendum. Finally, the evidence in July 2003 of an understanding, or at least a *rapprochment* between the prime minister, the Christian Democrats and Liberals on fiscal policy, prompted the acting Leftist leader, Ulla Hoffman, to threaten to pull out of the legislative coalition with the government for the budget deliberations in the Riksdag in the autumn.[14]

Yet the coalition constraint (executive or legislative) on the chief political executive should not be exaggerated. There is in fact little recent empirical support for Richard Rose's claim that since "in most Scandinavian countries the government is almost invariably a coalition of parties, there is a tendency for the prime minister to represent the lowest common denominator of interparty agreement. Instead of being a leader … instead of taking initiatives, the prime minister's job is to negotiate agreement when it can be found and to avoid issues appearing on the cabinet agenda that will split the coalition and cost him or her the top job". (Rose 1991: 16)

In fact, there are several obvious examples of Scandinavian prime ministers pursuing high-risk strategies on controversial issues and, by extension, putting their positions on the line in their determination to achieve a desired political outcome. Thus, having won a majority in favour of Finnish EU membership in his party only by threatening to resign as party chair, the Centre prime minister Esko Aho (1991–95) then effectively obliged the solitary Christian League minister, Toimi Kankaanniemi, to resign by insisting on unanimous cabinet support for a 'yes' vote in the October 1994 EU referendum. (Aho 1998: 131–134)

Having witnessed the way the question of EMU membership divided his Social Democratic Party, the Swedish prime minister, Göran Persson, pursued a high-risk strategy in appointing no less than five anti-EU cabinet ministers in his post-September 2002 general election 'reshuffle'. Persson had the authority of six years in the prime minister's post behind him and a reputation enhanced by his handling of Sweden's EU presidency in 2002. Ultimately, however, his challenge was to secure a vote in favour of EMU membership when his party was divided at all levels, his 'support parties' were opposed, the country sceptical and he himself was a relatively recent convert to the EMU cause.

In the event, Swedes rejected the euro by a resounding 55.9%–42.0% and probably under half of all social democrats voted in favour. (Widfeldt 2004: 503–514) Yet, ironically, while the EMU result represented a substantial personal defeat for Göran Persson, it ultimately did relatively little to diminish his authority as prime minister, either within his own party or indeed the country at large. There was strong criticism of his overbearing management style and his attempt to silence the EMU critics in his cabinet. Moreover, Persson appeared to make a number of tactical mistakes during the campaign. But Anna Lindh, a probable successor, had been murdered; all but Leif Pagrotsky of the anti-EMU ministers had been cleared out in the cabinet reshuffle of 3 October 2003; and, in his appointment of Laila Freivalds as foreign secretary, Persson signalled his intention to be active in 'European policy'. The referendum demanded by the 'support parties', the anti-EMU Greens and Leftists, had been held and gone in their favour and the legislative coalition (which did not include 'Europe') was not threatened.

Incidentally, criticism of Persson's autocratic leadership style as prime minister, frequently expressed during the EMU issue, reached a crescendo following the Asian *tsunami* on 26 December 2004 in which Sweden lost more citizens than any other country in the Western world. There were even more casualties than in the 'Estonia' car-ferry disaster in 1994. Exceptionally, Persson's critics included the King, who is not expected to make political statements, still less to criticise the government of the day. However, in an interview in the national daily *Dagens Nyheter* in January 2005, Karl Gustav XVI stated that, despite his best efforts, he had for two days been unable to glean any information about the catastrophe from either the foreign ministry or the prime minister's office.[15] The Swedish constitution expressly requires the prime minister to keep the monarch informed of current developments. Following the royal press interview, the opposition parties waded in, castigating the prime minister for his authoritarian style and inability effectively to deal with the crisis.[16]

Similar accusations of authoritarian leadership have, of course, been levied at the British prime minister, Tony Blair. Not only was there a personalisation of New Labour in Blair, but he has often seemed to by-pass the party altogether. Yet Blair's relative 'youth' – he was only 44 when he became prime minister in 1997 – and obvious charisma combined to bestow on him 'superstar status', especially after the successful 2001 general election. As Kenneth O. Morgan put it, "Blair seemed more than head of government, almost head of state. His assumption of authority in the wake of the death of Princess Diana, 'the people's princess' confirmed his own status as a kind of 'people's prime minister', obliged to pronounce on topics great and small from the attack on the World Trade Centre in New York to football and the death of pop stars. Here, under New Labour, was spatial leadership of a kind not seen hitherto". (Morgan 2004: 49) Interestingly, the year prior to the 2001 British general election, Jens Stoltenberg, a moderniser in the Blair mould, became at 41, one of the youngest prime ministers in Norwegian history. Yet, as John Madeley has noted, he ultimately failed to carry his party's old Labour Establishment with him and after a honeymoon period his government's popularity began to sink. (Madeley 2002: 213–214) Does this suggest a deep-seated Norwegian suspicion of prospective superstars? Alternatively, is there evidence of a trend in the Nordic region towards a measure of superstardom attached to the office of the prime minister?

The Nordic prime ministers – towards superstar status?

Despite the lack (outside Finland) of a detailed legal prescription of the duties of the post, the consensus among political scientists is that the power of the prime minister has [at very least] increased. A quarter of a century ago, Johan P. Olsen stated that "a Norwegian prime minister … is unlikely to achieve a position as superstar". (Olsen 1980: 213) The prime minister had to act in an environment dominated by formal organisations such as parties, the Storting, ministries and organised interest groups and he was unlikely to achieve a position of supremacy in these networks. Since then it appears things might have changed. Thus, according to Olof Ruin, "the office of the prime minister in Sweden has increased in importance over the decades since Tage Erlander [1946–69] first held it". (Ruin 1991: 80) In Iceland Svanur Kristjánsson comments that "in recent years the prime minister has become more powerful than before". (Kristjánsson 2004: 160) Heikki Paloheimo is similarly unequivocal. "As a result of the parliamentarization of the Finnish political system ... the role of the prime minister has clearly strengthened. The prime minister is the effective executive head and a kind of managing director of the state." (Paloheimo 2003: 233) A mix of common denominators and national factors appear to have conduced towards the increased importance of the position of prime minister in Scandinavia today. The following main points are indicative and make no pretence to being exhaustive.

First, the growing internationalisation ('globalisation') and 'Europeanisation' of politics have contributed to elevating the prime minister above the level of simply domestic politics. The Danish, Finnish and Swedish prime ministers occupy a strategic position as members of the European Council, which meets officially at least four times annually. In practice, of course, European Council members are in regular informal contact throughout the year. Certainly the duties of the prime minister appear significantly more demanding than before EU membership, since it is necessary to engage in important discussions without the aid of advisers and to create a network of effective working relations with the prime ministers of other EU member states.

Involvement in European Council meetings has allowed the Nordic EU prime ministers to appear international politicians rather than simply heads of government. By rubbing shoulders with the leaders of the large EU countries, staging press conferences in Brussels and pronouncing on strategic EU issues, the prime ministers of Denmark, Finland and Sweden have appeared to rise about domestic politics and, with extensive media coverage, to become the crucial opinion leaders on Union affairs. Moreover, across the region, the demarcation line between domestic and foreign ('European') policy has become increasingly blurred and the prime minister is extensively involved in the formulation and execution of foreign policy. The Swedish prime minister, Ingvar Carlsson (1986–91, 1994–96), estimated that at least one-third of his working time was devoted to foreign policy issues – and that was before Sweden's EU membership. (Ruin 1991: 70)

Clearly then, involvement at the EU level is likely to enhance the personal status of a prime minister. Thus, Danish television viewers saw the prime minister Anders Fogh Rasmussen successfully orchestrating the negotiations on EU enlargement at the Copenhagen summit in December 2002 and six months later being received at the White House. There President Bush thanked Rasmussen for Denmark's active stance as a US ally in the war against Iraq. The Swedish prime minister, Göran Persson, was never so popular as during the six months in 2002 that Sweden held the rotating EU presidency.

Second, it seems reasonable to hypothesise that a combination of longevity of tenure, the support of a regular parliamentary majority and the articulation of strong personal views will lead to a situation approximating 'prime ministerial government' (accepting of course the inherent simplification involved in this term). Davið Oððsson in Iceland illustrates the point. Oððsson, the leader of the largest parliamentary group, the Independence Party, became prime minister immediately on entering the Alþingi in 1991, having previously been mayor of Reykjavík. He became *the* dominant political figure in Icelandic politics, his unwavering opposition to EU membership based principally on the costs of the loss of self-determination rights in Iceland's fishing waters.[17] He also locked horns with the president over the media law of May 2004. Four months later, Oððsson took the unusual step (albeit one he announced he would take over a year earlier) of voluntarily handing the post of prime minister to the foreign secretary Halldór Ásgrímsson, the leader of the Progressive Party. Even so, it is a fair surmisal that Oððsson, albeit in his new post as foreign minister, was largely instrumental in the Alþingi's unanimous decision in spring 2005 to grant Icelandic citizenship to the American former world chess champion, Bobby Fischer.[18]

Both Oððsson and Steingrímur Hermansson (1983–87 and 1988–91) profited from the stable coalition of Independence and Progressive parties, which secured favourable working conditions for the prime minister to learn on the job. (Kristjánsson 2004: 160) Similarly dominant was Paavo Lipponen who, as Social Democratic party chair and prime minister of the 'surplus majority' 'rainbow coalitions' between 1995–2003 propelled Finland to the core of the EU. Finland became the first Nordic EMU member at its inception in 1999.

Third, the prime minister's right to 'hire and fire' – see for example, paragraph 6, articles 1–6 of the 1974 Swedish constitution – affords heads of single-party governments in particular a vital resource. In the case of recent Swedish Social Democratic governments, there has been a tendency for the prime minister to appoint ministers from outside the Riksdag – an incompatibility rule in Sweden and Norway anyway requires ministers to resign their parliamentary seats. In Göran Persson's 'cabinet reshuffle' after the 2002 general election, only two of the eight new ministers were MPs. The defence minister, Leni Björklund, came from the Social Democrats' christian wing *Broderskap*, while the deputy education minister had a background in the party's youth organisation SSU.[19]

Fourth, the major political parties in an era of 'electronic democracy' have increasingly focused their election campaigns on the claims of their 'prime minister candidates'. True, when Poul Nyrup Rasmussen, the Social Democratic prime minister, resorted to tearing up the Liberal leader Anders Fogh Rasmussen's book *From Social State to the Minimal State* in a live televised broadcast before the 2001 Danish general election, even the social democratic press described the act as 'silly'. But, as Mads Qvortrup has observed, the campaign was unusually presidential, focusing on the 'two Rasmussens'. (Qvortrup 2002: 207) In short, there has been a personalisation and 'centralisation' of elections and, as a corollary, a personalisation of the office of the prime minister. According to a *Suomen Gallup* poll, about 130,000 citizens decided to vote in the March 2003 Finnish general election so as to influence the outcome of the battle for the prime minister's post between the female opposition leader, Anneli Jäätteenmäki (Centre), and the long-serving Social Democratic prime minister, Paavo Lipponen. Without this personal contest, the turnout of 69.7% would have fallen to around 65%, well below the 1999 general election figure.[20] In connection with the personalisation of the office, the Riksdag Constitution Committee chair, Gunnar Hökmark, has suggested that the direct election of the prime minister should become part of the general election process.[21]

Fifth, the prime minister has in many ways assumed political responsibility for the coordination and management of the government's economic policy. He works closely with the minister of finance and may lend the status of the prime minister's office to initiatives to resolve particular economic challenges. These may include the achievement of an incomes policy package or convening a meeting between government officials and representatives of the main sectoral economic interest groups with a view to highlighting an acute problem such as long-term structural unemployment. In the 1950s, the Swedish prime minister Erlander's close contacts with the leaders of the trade union movement and employers' groups at the prime minister's country residence came to be known as 'Harpsund democracy' (see chapter 6). Regular meetings of the Nordic prime ministers also serve to identify a common agenda of problems and may lead to follow-up action. In February 2004 the prime ministers of Finland (Vanhanen) and Sweden (Persson) staged a joint seminar on the theme of the threat to the welfare state posed by a declining economically active labour force and an ageing population. In Persson's words, "it is no longer possible to solve the labour shortage in Sweden by sending a bus to Finland to recruit workers [as in the late 1960s]".[22]

Conclusions

Prime ministers of small states are unlikely to become household names around the world. While a six-month stint as head of the country holding the EU Presidency will give the prime minister of a small member-state intermittent global media exposure, he or she is unlikely to attain superstar status. This has certainly been true of Nordic prime ministers, although a few have acquired an 'international name'. Olof Palme first came to wider prominence in the 1960s as a vociferous critic of American involvement in Vietnam. During the

1970s and 1980s Palme became one of the world's leading spokespersons for oppressed peoples and for the growing international peace movement. (Hadenius 1988: 169) The Palme Commission produced a concrete plan for reducing armaments and increasing global security. In Sweden, Stig Hadenius has noted, there was a tendency to dismiss Palme's international role as media hyperbole. However, the extent of his global prominence became clear when a range of international statesmen "unprecedented in Swedish history" attended his funeral (following his assassination in February 1986). (Hadenius 1988: 170) In the 1980s the United Nations' World Commission on Environment and Development, headed by the Norwegian prime minister Gro Harlem Brundtland, pioneered terms such as 'sustainable development' and projected Brundtland's name onto the international stage. (Heidar 2001: 127) Moreover, as Heidar comments, "Mrs Brundtland shocked the world by bringing in nearly 50 per cent women into the Labour government in 1986"! (Heidar 2001: 44)

Other Scandinavian prime ministers have achieved the position of international statesmen (if only) in the eyes of at least a section of the national electorate. Paavo Lipponen did so when propelling Finland into EMU as a founder member in 1999. In the process the prime minister emerged from the shadow of the president (Martti Ahtisaari) as the dominant foreign policy actor. Furthermore, when Lipponen canvassed a pro-federal Union in a speech at the College of Europe in Bruges in November 2000, it was reported verbatim in the national daily *Helsingin Sanomat*, which fed readers with the image of Lipponen as a European statesman of substance. It certainly does not appear unreasonable to speak across the region of an expansion of the premier's role and of the existence of a prime ministerial agenda. This seems particularly to be the case on international questions where the prime minister has tended to usurp the foreign secretary's position.

On the domestic front, image, appearance and 'televisuality' have all acquired increased importance for prime ministers (and prospective prime ministers), although a slick television performance is by no means always a vote winner. Some prime ministers have dominated their governments (and the nation) for substantial periods and been viewed by critics as autocratic. Persson and Oððsson are cases in point. Others have made disastrous errors and forfeited office in short order. Such was the fate of Thorbjørn Jagland, the Norwegian Labour prime minister between 1996–97, who indicated that he would resign after the 1997 general election unless his party exceeded the 36.9% it had polled four years earlier. When it did not, he had no option but to go. Even shorter was the tenure of Finland's first female prime minister, Anneli Jäätteenmäki, when parliament suspected she had not 'come clean' about the sources of confidential information relating to exchanges between the (then) prime minister and President Bush. Equally, some prime ministers are 'survivors'. Kjell Magne Bondevik held together a three-party, non-socialist minority coalition with the backing of only 42 of the Storting's 165 seats for nearly three years between 1997–2000. He then returned to head another non-socialist minority coalition after the 2001 general election, which went the full distance to the September 2005 general election.

Bondevik is a valuable reminder of the supervisory skills needed to manage inter-party and indeed intra-party relations and which remain a sine qua non for all Nordic prime ministers. Few gave his minority cabinet, with its miniscule parliamentary base, a chance of lasting more than a few months. Yet despite announcing on television his decision to take time off to recuperate from nervous exhaustion – after which his popularity soared – Bondevik's government coped admirably until the controversial issue of gas-fuelled power plants in 2000. There has unquestionably been an internationalisation of the prime minister's role and, to an extent, this has led to a more international status as a politician. However, no Nordic prime minister can ignore the basic management skills, in particular, maintaining a solid support base in her or his parliamentary group.

A postscript on all this is in order. The high educational status of recent Nordic prime ministers – unlike the likes of Gerhardsen, Torp and the 'older generation' – has set them apart from the mass of the population. Yet – and it is admittedly a sweeping generalisation – the prime ministers in the region have tended to retain a certain 'ordinariness'. They have not 'stood on ceremony' and there has been little ceremony attached to the office. Symptomatically, until Olof Palme's assassination in February 1986, there were few special security arrangements for the prime minister. Paavo Lipponen, a water-polo enthusiast, regularly swam in a public pool as prime minister between 1995–2003, while his foreign secretary, Erkki Tuomioja pounded the pavements in marathon training without a huge security entourage. Indeed, despite the enhanced visibility of the Scandinavian prime ministers and the appearance of a growth in their powers, most of the incumbents have been imbued with a 'politics is work' ethic. Far from superstars, they have been able to operate rather ordinarily and retain a 'private life'. In an era of heightened international terrorism after '9/11' in New York and the suicide bombings in Madrid in March 2004 and London on 7 July 2005, this may of course have to change.

Notes

1 The Danish Prime Minister's Office was reorganised in 1994 and presently has a staff of about 70 persons.
2 In Denmark and Norway the Queen/King still presides over the formal meetings

of the Council of State (government). Constitutional reform in Sweden in 1974 precluded the monarch from cabinet meetings and from the beginning of 1975 he or she was also excluded from the cabinet formation process. Although the powers of the Finnish President have been significantly reduced, she (Tarja Halonen) still leads the 'presidential sittings' of the Council of State on Friday mornings.

3 The Bondevik government had a parliamentary base of only 42 of the Storting's 165 seats and it fell over the issue of building new gas-fuelled power plants. Knut Heidar comments that "the vote in parliament was historic, as it was the first time a Norwegian government had to leave office on an environmental issue". (Heidar 2001: 170)

4 As a disaffected minister, Johannes Virolainen, commented: "The president [Urho Kekkonen] always takes care to ensure that at any one time there is only one big tree in the forest; all the rest have been cut down". See Unto Hämäläinen, 'Pääministerin valta on valettu' *Helsingin Sanomat* 19.4.2003.

5 M. Jakobson, 'Pääministerin uusi rooli' *Helsingin Sanomat* 4.4.2003.

6 According to Jaakko Nousiainen, "it is evident that Finland has been moving closer to the parliamentary states of Western Europe and that there are hardly any grounds for the epithet 'semi-presidential'". Nousiainen 2001: 108).

7 Kristjánsson writes that "by skilful leadership, Grímsson has retuned to the *political presidency* as practised by Iceland's two first presidents. Grímsson has repeatedly emphasised the important and independent role of the president in the political system . It is clear that the political presidency is in principle supported by a sizeable majority of the people". (Kristjánsson 2004: 168, emphasis added)

8 'Islannin presidentinvaalia leimasi perustuslakikiista' *Helsingin Sanomat* 28.6.2004.

9 Several post-war Finnish prime ministers have held doctorates, most recently Mauno Koivisto (1968–70, 1979–82), who went on to become president between 1982– 94. This has been relatively rare elsewhere in the region. The most recent Swedish prime minister with a doctorate was the Conservative Ernst Trygger, who was a professor of law and led a short-lived, single-party minority cabinet between 1923–24.

10 'Suomalainen harvainvalta' *Helsingin Sanomat* 8.8.2004.

11 'Mies joka malttaa odottaa' *Helsingin Sanomat* 11.7.2004.

12 'Keskusta äänesti neljästä ministeristä' *Helsingin Sanomat* 16.4.2003.

13 Nordli headed a single-party Labour government between 1976–81 but his comment is even more apposite for the non-socialist coalitions in Norway and elsewhere in the Nordic region.

14 'Säästöbudjetista saatiin sopu Ruotsissa' *Helsingin Sanomat* 3.4.2003. See also Lars Bäckström's statement in the Riksdag's budget debate, 'Löftesbrott hettade till debatten' *Riksdag och departementet* 14, 2003, p. 25. Also 'Missnöjet gror i vänsterpartiet' *Riksdag och departementet* 14, 2003, p. 26. 'Euron vastustajien kannatuksen kasvu pani vauhtia Ruotsin kyllä-leiriin' *Helsingin Sanomat* 21.5.2003. 'V otydligt om fortsatt regeringssamarbete' *Dagens Nyheter* 7.7.2003. 'V hotar hoppa av regeringssamarbetet' *Dagens Nyheter* 5.7.2003.

15 'Järkytys kääntyi Ruotsissa poliittiseksi pyykinpesuksi' *Helsingin Sanomat*

14.1.2005.
16 Asko Sahlberg, 'Katkeraa siivousta kansan kodissa' *Helsingin Sanomat* 16.1.2005.
17 'Islannin ikipääministeri lähtee, mutta voi jäädäkin politiikkaan' *Helsingin Sanomat* 7.7.2003. 'Pääministerin vaihdos voi viedä Islannin kohti EU-jäsenyyttä' *Helsingin Sanomat* 7.7.2003.
18 Fischer had been jailed in Japan for travelling on an invalid passport and was also wanted in the US on charges of violating the sanctions against the former Yugoslavia (in 1992 he played against the Russian Boris Spassky in Belgrade). The Alþingi's decision was by no means popular with Icelanders, not least because of Fischer's stridently anti-Semitic views.
19 The reshuffle was generally interpreted in the media as representing a consolidation of Persson's power base. It was also suggested that the inclusion of five EMU opponents was an attempt to 'domesticate' them. If so, it scarcely worked. See 'Winberg kritisk till Pekguls ja till EMU' *Dagens Nyheter* 7.7.2003. Also 'Fullt eurokrig i regeringen' *Dagens Nyheter* 24.7.2003.
20 'Pääministerin kysymys tuskin ratkaisi eduskuntavaaleja' *Helsingin Sanomat* 5.6.2003. Nonetheless, only 30% of voters indicated that the persona of the next prime minister had had a significant impact on their choice of party. 'Pääministerivaali pakotti monet äänestämään puoluetta' *Helsingin Sanomat* 7.6.2003.
21 'Färre antal ledamöter skulle stärka riksdagens betydelse' *Från Riksdag och departementet* 21, 2003, pp. 32–35.
22 'Persson ja Vanhanen: Väestön vanheneminen uhkaa hyvinvointia' *Helsingin Sanomat* 10.2.2004.

References

Aho, Esko *Pääministeri* (Otava: Helsinki, 1998)
Alho, Arja *Silent Democracy, Noisy Media* (Helsinki University: Helsinki, 2004)
Arter, David 'One Ting Too Many: The Shift to Unicameralism' in Lawrence D. Longley and David M. Olson (eds) *Two into One* The Politics and Processes of National Legislative Cameral Change (Westview: Boulder, CO, San Francisco and Oxford, 1991), pp. 77–142
Arter, David 'Finland', in Robert Elgie (ed.) *Semi-Presidentialism in Europe* (Oxford University Press: Oxford, 1999), pp. 48–67
Arter, David 'Kekkonen's Finland: Enlightened Despotism or Consensual Democracy?' *West European Politics* 4, 3, 1981, pp. 219–234
Arter, David 'The Prime Minister in Scandinavia: Superstar or Supervisor?' *The Journal of Legislative Studies* 10, 2 & 3, 2004, pp. 109–127
Arter, David 'Change in the Swedish Riksdag: From a "Part-Time Parliament" to a Professionalised Assembly?' *The Journal of Legislative Studies* 6, 3, 2000, pp. 93–116
Bergman, Torbjörn 'When Minority Coalitions are the Rule and Majority Coalitions the Exception', in Wolfgang C. Müller and Kaare Strøm (eds) *Coalition Governments*

in Western Europe (Oxford University Press: Oxford, 2003), pp. 192–230

Bille, Lars 'A Power Centre in Danish Politics', in Knut Heidar and Ruud Koole (eds) *Parliamentary Party Groups in European Democracies* (Routledge: London and New York, 2000), pp. 130–144

Christensen, Jørgen Grønnegård 'In Search of Unity: Cabinet Committees in Denmark', in Thomas T. Mackie and Brian W. Hogwood (eds) *Unlocking the Cabinet* (Sage: London, 1985), pp. 114–137

Clemens, Clay 'The Chancellor as Manager: Helmut Kohl, the CDU and Governance in Germany' *West European Politics* 17, 4, 1994, pp. 28–51

Hadenius, Stig *Swedish Politics During the 20th Century* (Swedish Institute: Borås, 1988)

Heidar, Knut *Norway. Elites on Trial* (Westview: Boulder, CO, 2001)

Kristinsson, G. H. 'Iceland', in Robert Elgie (ed.) *Semi-Presidentialism in Europe* (Oxford University Press: Oxford, 1999), pp. 86–103

Kristjánsson, Svanur 'Iceland: Searching for Democracy along Three Dimensions of Citizen Control' *Scandinavian Political Studies* 27, 2, 2004, pp. 153–174

Kvavik, Robert B. *Interest Groups in Norwegian Politics* (Universitelsforlaget: Oslo, Bergen and Tromsø, 1976)

Lijphart, Arend *Patterns of Democracy* (Yale University Press: New Haven and London, 1999)

Madeley, John T. S. 'Outside the Whale: Norway's Storting Election of 10 September 2001' *West European Politics* 25, 2, 2002, pp. 212–222

Mattson, Ingvar 'Parliamentary Questioning in the Swedish Riksdag', in Matti Wiberg (ed.) *Parliamentary Control in the Nordic Countries* (Gummerus: Jyväskylä, 1994), pp. 276–356

Mayntz, Renate 'Executive Leadership in Germany: Dispersion of Power or "Kanzlerdemokratie"?', in R. Rose and E. N. Suleiman (eds) *Presidents and Prime Ministers* (Washington DC: American Enterprise for Public Policy Research, 1980), pp. 139–170

Miller, Kenneth E. *Denmark. A Troubled Welfare State* (Westview Press: Boulder, CO; San Francisco and Oxford, 1991)

Morgan, Kenneth O. 'United Kingdom: A Comparative Case Study of Labour Prime Ministers Attlee, Wilson, Callaghan and Blair' *The Journal of Legislative Studies* 10, 2/3, 2004, pp. 38–52

Narud, Hanne Marthe and Kaare Strøm 'Norway. A Fragile Constitutional Order', in Wolfgang C. Müller (eds) *Coalition Governments in Western Europe* (Oxford University Press: Oxford, 2003), pp. 158–191

Nousiainen, Jaakko 'Finland: Ministerial Autonomy, Constitutional Collectivism and Party Oligarchy', in Michael Laver and Kenneth A. Shepsle (eds) *Cabinet Ministers and Parliamentary Government* (Cambridge University Press: Cambridge, 1994)

Nousiainen, Jaakko 'From Semi-Presidentialism to Parliamentary Government: Political and Constitutional Developments in Finland' *Scandinavian Political Studies* 24, 2, 2001, pp. 95–109

Olsen, J. P. 'Governing Norway: Segmentation, Anticipation and Consensus Formation', in R. Rose and E. N. Suleiman (eds) *Presidents and Prime Ministers* (Washington DC: American Enterprise for Public Policy Research, 1980), pp. 203–255

Paloheimo, Heikki 'The Rising Power of the Prime Minister in Finland' *Scandinavian Political Studies* 26, 3, 2003, pp. 219–243

Qvortrup, Mads 'The Emperor's New Clothes: The Danish General Election, 20 November 2001' *West European Politics* 25, 2, 2002, pp. 205–211

Richardson, J. J. and G. Jordan *Governing Under Pressure* (Martin Robertson: Oxford, 1979)

Rose, R. 'Prime Ministers in Parliamentary Democracies' *West European Politics* 14, 2, 1991, pp. 9–24

Ruin, Olof 'Three Swedish Prime Ministers: Tage Erlander, Olof Palme and Ingvar Carlsson' *West European Politics* 14, 3, 1991, pp. 58–82

Tiili, Minna 'Hallituksen keskustelukulttuuri: kurkistus kollektiivisen ja kollegiaalisen ulkokuoren alle' *Politiikka* 46, 2, 2004, pp. 137–142

Widfeldt, Anders 'Elite Collusion and Public Defiance: Sweden's Euro Referendum in 2003' *West European Politics* 27, 3, 2004, pp. 503–514

Virolainen, Johannes *Pääministerinä Suomessa* (Kirjayhtymä: Helsinki, 1969)

8

The state of Scandinavian democracy: democracy 'in a state'?

The theme of the International Political Science Association (IPSA) World Congress in Fukuoka, Japan in summer 2006 is 'Is Democracy Working?' Yet, as its president Max Kaase has noted, that is not the only question. (Kaase 2004: 3) As important is the question 'How is democracy working?' and, through the specification of evaluative criteria, 'How well is democracy working?'[1] Constructing a *democratic audit* with a view to answering that question in the United Kingdom has been work closely associated with David Beetham and his colleagues, originating in the early 1990s. (Beetham et al. 2003). Concern with assessing the quality of representative democracy in Scandinavia, however, dates back over three decades. Moreover, publicly financed power studies are very much a Scandinavian phenomenon. There have been three recent ones, all set up in 1997. The commission entitled 'An Analysis of Democracy and Power in Denmark' was launched by the Folketing and reported in 2003. The 'Power and Democracy' commission in Norway, which was initiated by the Storting, also reported in 2003. The Swedish Democracy Commission's report 'A Resilient Democracy' (*En uthållig demokrati*, or EUD) came out in 2000.

The simultaneous operation of power and democracy commissions in the three 'metropolitan Scandinavian' states begs a number of obvious questions. Why were they needed? What were their main findings? What do they tell us about the state of democracy in Scandinavia? Does it appear to be healthy and vibrant or 'in a state' in the sense of experiencing a crisis of one sort or another? This chapter presents some of the main conclusions of the recent democratic audits in Denmark, Norway and Sweden. The central question is 'how well do the power and democracy commissions suggest that Scandinavian democracy is working? In other words, what has been the 'democratic diagnosis' of the Scandinavians themselves?

The background to the democracy commissions in 'metropolitan Scandinavia'

The backdrop to the creation of power and democracy commissions in Denmark and Norway was the diffuse feeling among many parliamentarians that there had been a decline in the legitimacy and legislative capacity of the national assembly. The loss of legitimacy was loosely linked in the eyes of MPs to evidence of declining electoral turnout and diminished civic involvement in parties and traditional social movements. The links in the democratic chain appeared badly worn and, as a consequence, the risk existed of an erosion of the legitimacy of the central institution of representative democracy, the national parliament. The loss of legislative capacity was reflected in the consensus among parliamentarians that things were not what they used to be. In Denmark, for example, MPs were said to be experiencing a sense of loss of control over the course of developments as a consequence of factors such as globalisation, decentralisation and the creation of government-owned corporations. It was also felt that the parliamentarian's task had been complicated by the fact that citizens were actively demanding greater influence over decisions affecting their personal lives. All in all, the Folketing was concerned about a loss of power. (Togeby 2003: 22) There was heightened sensitivity to this when the committee recommending the setting up of a democracy commission reported that, although there was not a democratic crisis in Denmark, the conditions for political governance and control were deteriorating.

In Sweden the background to the democracy commission was the trend towards declining political participation both through the political parties and more immediately the ballot boxes. Turnout has fallen consistently in every Swedish general election since 1982 and the 79% that voted in 2002 – two years after the democracy commission's report – was the lowest level during the entire period of the unicameral Riksdag since 1970 (see table 8.1) Initially, the cross-party Swedish democracy commission was given the very broad remit of examining the (changing) conditions and challenges confronting Swedish democracy on the eve of the new millennium. However, in November 1998 it received a supplementary directive asking it to explore the particular reasons for the declining electoral turnout – down to 81.4% in 1998 – and to suggest measures to increase civic participation and engagement in the democratic system. Bluntly, this was a response to a dismal Social Democratic general election performance in September that year – 36.4% of the vote – and saw the prime minister, Göran Persson, also create the post of Minister for Democracy. This went to a 33-year old single mother with two children, who was wholly inexperienced as a minister or indeed a politician and who assumed responsibility for revitalising Swedish democracy! (Arter

2004: 596–597) Incidentally, in addition to the publicly appointed and fi-
nanced Democracy Commission (1997–2000), the private and non-partisan
Centre for Business and Policy Studies (*Studieförbundet Näringsliv och Samhälle*
– SNS) has produced annual reports on the state of democracy in Sweden.

Table 8.1 Turnout in elections to the unicameral Swedish Riksdag, 1970–2002 (%)

1970	88.3
1973	90.8
1976	91.8
1979	90.7
1982	91.4
1985	89.9
1988	86.0
1991	86.7
1994	86.8
1998	81.4
2002	79.0

The three democracy commissions adopted contrasting methodological approaches. Managed by a board of academics, the Norwegian commission was
grounded in principal-agent theory. The quality of democracy was tested by
reference to the solidity of the democratic chain of command, which places
government (the cabinet, parliament and central administration as agents)
under the control of voters (the principal). There is a similar approach in a
special issue of *Scandinavian Political Studies*, edited by Torbjörn Bergman,
which focuses on analysing the changing nature of parliamentary democracy
in Scandinavia. (Bergman 2004) The central, albeit largely unstated presumption is that the greater the extent of citizen control, the healthier the state of
representative democracy. In Svanur Kristjánsson's words, "in a healthy democracy, the agents serve the wishes and interests of the principal. In an ailing
democracy, the agents of the people primarily serve themselves". (Kristjánsson
2004: 154)
The approach of the Danish commission, also coordinated by social scientists, was essentially normative and involved the evaluation of the state of democracy by reference to the extent to which it approximated five core ideals.
First, it was argued there should be *equal political rights* based on universal
suffrage, majority decisions and the protection of minorities. In other words,
all citizens should have equal opportunities effectively to influence political
decisions. Second, there should be the conditions for the *free formation of*

opinion based on open and diverse access to information. In other words, formal decisions should be preceded by a public debate in which all views have an opportunity to be heard. Next, there should be *broad and equal political participation* based on a broadly equal distribution of economic and social resources. Then there should be *effective and responsible governance* in the sense that the public sector is capable of solving collective problems in an acceptable and effective manner in line with politically formulated guidelines. Finally, society should be characterised by *trust, tolerance and regard for the community.*

The approach of the cross-party Swedish Democracy Commission was to proceed from a pragmatic rather than theoretical standpoint, consulting directly with civil society on ways of increasing levels of popular participation. Sixteen seminars were arranged around the country – they were taped and functioned like 'hearings' – and they attracted at worst 43 and at most 1153 participants. The majority of those in attendance represented interest groups, parties, local government authorities and the regional media, although there were some private individuals. The Swedish commission also had its own website, which contained a discussion forum.

The changing nature of political participation

In all three commissions, a good deal of importance was attached to examining the 'by the people' element in Abe Lincoln's classical formulation, although the question posed by Ylva Stubbergaard was neither directly addressed nor indirectly answered. Stubbergaard asks: 'What is the level of participation sufficient for a form of government to be characterised as democratic?' (Stubbergaard 2002: 201) It is a good question. After all, turnout in the two British general elections this millennium – that is, 2001 and 2005 – has not exceeded 60%. Moreover, for half a century and more turnout in Switzerland – "a system of government which is the very opposite of the Westminster model" – has hovered around the 50% mark. (Kriesi 2001: 59) It has not exceeded 50% in a federal election since 1975 and a national referendum since 1959. Can these two states then be described as democratic in any significant sense? Of course, the basis of representative democracy in the Nordic region (as elsewhere in Western Europe) is that political parties and groups are charged with aggregating and mediating societal demands and expectations to elected representatives. Parties in short are expected to mobilise voters. Yet all three commissions were in agreement that the traditional agencies of collective mobilisation – the basic linkage structures between state and society – have declined in recent years.

According to the Danish commission, the capacity of the parties for collective mobilisation has largely disappeared and many voters prefer to make up their mind on an issue-by-issue basis. (Togeby 2003: 16) Membership of political parties in the Scandinavian countries used to be exceptionally high, standing at a record 27% of the electorate in Denmark in 1947. (Goul Andersen and Hoff 2001: 252–253) However, it has declined sharply. In Denmark today just over 5% of the electorate are members of a political party and only approximately half of these members participate actively. Even in the 1960s, 20% of Danish voters belonged to political parties. (Damgaard 2004: 123) Strikingly too, the total number of party members in Norway is down by half since 1990 and parties have developed from mass parties to network parties. In 2001 in Norway only 8% of voters were party members. (Narud and Strøm 2004: 189)

In Sweden a study by *Kommunaktuelt* revealed that in 2003 the Conservatives lost nine thousand members to number less than 61,000 card-carriers in total and the Social Democrats lost a similar amount.[2] The Swedish commission spoke of a weakened identification with traditional collectivist norms and a tendency towards a "secularisation of politics". There are "fewer believers among voters and, therefore, fewer in church" (EUD 2000: 180) It concluded that, "in order to maintain and develop their significant role in representative democracy, the parties need to develop new 'meeting places', modernise their activities and design policies, which are relevant to citizens". (EUD 2000: 243) The SNS Democratic Audit in 1999 even predicted that if the decline in Swedish party membership continued at the same rate as in the 1990s, the parties would have no members at all by 2013. (Petersson 1999) All in all, as Andersen and Hoff concluded, it appears that "the era of Scandinavian exceptionalism with regard to class mobilisation in political parties is now coming to an end". (Goul Andersen and Hoff 2001: 254)

Along with the decline in party membership, all three commissions pointed to the fact that the era of mass popular movements is over. It is noted in Denmark that the trade unions and co-operative movement no longer mobilise workers and farmers in the way they did at the beginning of the twentieth century. Nor, it is said, do the social movements mobilise the well-educated to the extent they did in the 1970s and 1980s. (Togeby 2003: 17) The Norwegian power commission refers to a shift from popular movements to 'here-and-now organisations' (*øyeblikksorganisering*), with political participation increasingly channelled into issue-based action.[3] The 'here-and-now organisations' include self-help groups, community associations, neighbourhood action groups, bereaved groups, next-of-kin groups and so on. All in all, there appears to have been a shift towards more individualised forms of activism, including signing petitions and donating money to organisations.

While on the theme of political participation, the findings of the power commissions revealed marked differences between Denmark on the one hand and Sweden and Norway on the other. These related principally to the scale and structure of political participation. In Denmark levels of civic participation have been highest and the social structure of political engagement more homogenous than in Norway and Sweden.

Table 8.2 Turnout at Danish general elections, 1968–2005 (%)

1968	89.3
1971	87.2
1973	88.7
1975	88.2
1977	88.7
1979	85.6
1981	83.3
1984	88.4
1987	86.7
1988	85.7
1990	82.9
1994	84.2
1998	86.0
2001	87.2
2005	84.5

Unlike the two last-mentioned countries, Denmark has not witnessed a drop in general election turnout in recent years (see table 8.2). In fact, in every Danish general election since 1939 turnout has ranged between 80–90%, although never exceeding the latter as it did in Sweden between 1973–82. Electoral participation, moreover, has never been characterised by significant social differences and this remains the case. The gender gap has completely disappeared and, remarkably, young persons vote relatively more frequently than fifty years ago. The lowest turnout occurs among ethnic minorities and socially marginalised groups. Moreover, whereas earlier workers and farmers with the most elementary levels of education were the most active in political parties, they are now the least active. Nonetheless, the Danish commission concludes that "equality in participation has grown rather than declined in recent years, except in terms of party activity". (Togeby 2003: 41)

In Sweden electoral participation declined by ten percentage points from a record 91.4% in 1982 to 81.4% in 1998 (see table 8.1) while the class differential in turnout has grown substantially. At the 1976 general election the differential between working-class and middle-class turnout was 4.6% in favour of the latter; by 1998 the gap had widened to 12.1%. At the beginning of the 1980s the discrepancy in turnout between high- and low-income earners was 6.6% in favour of the former; by 1998 this had increased to 14.2%. In an empirical study by Jan Teorell and Anders Westholm, associated with the Swedish democracy commission, it was shown that voting constituted essentially expressive, norm-led behaviour. (EUD 2000: 179) Furthermore, the study made clear that older and more educated persons, more than younger and less educated, believed it important to express their views on political questions, even if they had no significance for the election result.

All in all, the Swedish commission concluded that civic participation, influence and involvement varied between social groups and that class, gender and age differences remained. It was stated that women cannot operate at all levels of society on the same terms as men. (EUD 2000: 243) There was a continued marginalisation of various groups of young persons, whose political interests were channelled through new social movements and into subcultures. Finally, persons with an immigrant and particularly non-European background and the unemployed, especially the long-term unemployed, exhibited the lowest levels of mobilisation and the gulf between these groups and the 'mainstream of society' had widened in the 1990s. The Swedish commission noted that "there are groups that are permanently outside the decision-making system". (EUD 2000: 244)

Table 8.3 Turnout in Norwegian general elections, 1969–2005 (%)

1969	83.8
1973	80.2
1977	82.9
1981	82.0
1985	84.0
1989	83.2
1993	75.8
1997	78.0
2001	75.1
2005	77.1

In Norway participation at the 1989 general election was 83.2% but in 2001 only 75.1%, the lowest level since 1927 (see table 8.3). The Norwegian commission linked falling turnout in part to the popular perception of a lack of clear governmental alternatives. It noted that it was possible to gain power in

Norway without winning an election. As a consequence of 'minority parliamentarism', it was stated, there is no direct connection between the election result and the composition of the subsequent government. Aside from the problems of electoral mobilisation, the Norwegian commission placed particular emphasis on inequalities in participation and new cleavage lines, quite distinct from what it describes as the 'old class society'

Norwegian society, it was argued, is in the process of witnessing the emergence of stronger class divisions following the lines of ethnicity. Substantial sections of the immigrant population do not participate in the Norwegian political system and they are gradually constituting a new underclass, either with low wage levels or located outside the labour market altogether. Equally, it was pointed out, there is a hierarchy among minorities in Norway: the Lapps have gained formal recognition as an aboriginal people. However, the immigrant groups are split into ethnic communities and this does not provide a ready base for 'class solidarity'. This distinguishes "the new class society from the old". The Norwegian commission concluded that, "an ethnically fragmented underclass, with a steady trickle of new groups from outside, cannot easily organise itself into a workers' movement". (Haugsvær 2003.3) In all three metropolitan Scandinavian countries there appears an obvious correlation between social and political exclusion.

The shift away from conventional, collective forms of mobilisation – through parties and social movements – and the downward trend in turnout in Norway and Sweden do not appear to have been a by-product of a declining civic interest in politics. The Norwegian commission noted that general interest in politics had not fallen over the last thirty years. Reinforcing the point, Ola Listhaug and Lars Grønflaten have observed elsewhere that "the decline in electoral participation at local elections in Norway and the low level of turnout at Storting elections from 1993 onwards has not been accompanied by a general weakening of political interest. Nor has there been a decline in political discussion about the election. Rather, the trend for these indicators has been in the opposite direction from that of turnout". (Listhaug and Grønflaten 2002: 11–12) Interest in politics has not, in short declined. Indeed, the evidence from the three democracy commissions points to the essential validity of Sören Holmberg's proposition that "it is parties that are the problem, not politics". (Arter 2004: 596)

In an EU perspective a distinctive feature of the Scandinavian countries in the 1990s was the low proportion of citizens claiming not to be at all interested in politics. In 1990 the figures ranged from a mere 4% in Norway to 11% in Sweden, compared with an EU average of 22%. (Goul Andersen and Hoff 2001: 18–19) By the new millennium, the Danish commission reported signs of a long-term *increase* in interest in politics. Voters, it stated, are knowledgeable and capable of grasping policy issues. They are better educated, possess greater self-confidence and make more demands. Their trust in politicians is growing not declining. "The 'power gap' in Danish society has narrowed. The state is no longer perceived as distant and superior." It was argued that Denmark had been transformed from an "authority state into an everyday state". (Togeby 2003: 19) In sum, political participation had not dropped and there was little evidence of a shift towards a passive *spectator democracy.* (Togeby 2003: 50)

In a 'spectator democracy' the citizenry is characterised by high levels of political interest but low levels of active participation and commitment (Goul Andersen and Hoff 2001: 251). In their study of *Democracy and Citizenship in Scandinavia,* Jørgen Goul Andersen and Jens Hoff note that in metropolitan Scandinavia "long-term political commitments, in particular active commitments, seem to be declining and participation is tending to become more particularized, more individualized. It is not at all directly related to the input side of the political system". "Without any pejorative connotations, the scenario of 'spectator democracy' with engaged and conscious spectators who, however, feel little opportunity or few incentives to engage actively in the 'big democracy' (elections, parties, trade unions etc) may catch quite a few of the tendencies" in the Scandinavian situation. (Goul Andersen and Hoff 2001: 257) The point has been laboured enough. Political interest does not appear to be declining and there appears a significant discrepancy between levels of civic interest in politics and levels of conventional political participation.

Both the Danish and Norwegian democracy commissions held that corporatism had weakened in recent years – that is, both 'routine corporatism' and 'peak corporatism' (in my terms) were on the wane. The number of preparatory bodies – commissions, committees and working groups – had been significantly reduced and the practice of incorporating groups into the policy formulation process had declined. True, the Danish commission noted that informal contacts between interest groups and civil servants and interest groups and the Folketing appeared to have become very extensive. However, it added that this shift from corporatism to 'lobbyism' had not necessarily betokened a significant loss of pressure group influence. Indeed, the Norwegian commission described the way interest groups had developed a more professional information and communications apparatus enabling them to target decision-makers in both the executive and legislative arms of the government and to work through the media.

It is evident from the findings of both the Danish and Norwegian commissions that the decline of corporatism should not be exaggerated. Particularly in Norway, peak corporatist practices persist. The Norwegian commission concluded that "the economic and labour-market groups remain strong and there are still central decisions, which are made in organs of corporatist co-operation". (Haugsvær 2003: 5) Co-optation is still practised although, as stressed in chapter 6, the minister lays down the terms of reference and time-table for commissions and, through his or her senior officials, the department will participate in their deliberations. In Denmark, developments, it is ar-gued, have meant that the larger interest groups have come to enjoy privileged access at the expense of smaller ones. In other words, interest group participa-tion in the policy process has become more unequal. In the commission's words, "corporatism in Denmark has always favoured the large and strong organisations, but the weakening of corporatism seems to have magnified this tendency". (Togeby 2003: 26)

Neither the Norwegian nor the Danish commission reaches an explicit con-clusion about the implications for democracy of the relative decline of corporatism. It is also difficult to deduce much of substance about the relative influence of pressure groups. They are clearly less of 'an extended arm of the state' than they used to be and, especially for the smaller groups, regularised access to formulating bodies cannot be taken for granted. On the other hand, the Danish commission notes that, at the implementation stage – that is, in the administration of current legislation – the position of interest groups has not deteriorated. Moreover, the ability of groups to adapt to changed circum-stances is emphasised. Thus, given the regularity of minority government, they have increasingly focused on the legislature, not least because parliament has the numerical means to amend bills, particularly at the committee stage. Groups also continue to possess sanctions and are able effectively to mobilise opposi-tion to measures that are perceived as detrimental to their members' interests. However, one of the members of the executive committee of the Danish com-mission has speculated – or at least implied – that the relative decline of corporatism has meant that the core institutions of representative democracy, namely government and parliament, have freer hands to determine policy than earlier. Modifying Stein Rokkan's celebrated maxim, Jørgen Goul Andersen has suggested that a possible conclusion on the basis of the Danish evidence might be that "resources count, but political leaders decide!" (Goul Andersen 2004: 16)

Although the wider democratic ramifications are not fully explored, the 'retreat of corporatism' is a theme running through the findings of the Danish and Norwegian commissions. The phenomenon referred to (less than felici-tously) as the *medialisation of politics* is given particular prominence in the Danish and Swedish reports. In a nutshell, they bring out the increased importance of the mass media as arenas for political discourse and as a means of communicating political messages. As the Danish commission concluded, "the increased political significance of the mass media is beyond all doubt". (Togeby 2003: 27)

The 'medialisation' and 'juridicialisation' of politics

Both commissions contend that the media affect the political agenda without necessarily having an agenda of their own. The Danish report stresses that "the decisive aspect is less the deliberate attempt of journalists to introduce single issues or engage in sensationalist journalism and more the influence of the media on the structure and form of political communication". (Togeby 2003: 27) In particular, since it is important to gain a high level of 'visibility', politicians are obliged to operate primarily on the electronic media's terms. This, in turn, has contributed, according to the Swedish commission, to a "secularisation of politics" – that is, to declining levels of partisan identification. "There are fewer [party] believers and, therefore, fewer [party faithful] in church." (EUD 2000: 180)

In this connection, it may be inferred from the Swedish investigation that the medialisation of politics has led to political messages suffering from something of a 'popularisation, trivialisation and simplification' syndrome. The desire to 'popularise' politics and get it across to a mass audience has seen politicians increasingly appearing on the likes of television 'talk shows'. Indeed, national election campaigns are principally contested 'on the box', alongside entertainment programmes and regular 'soaps'. The 'trivialisation' has been inherent in the proclivity to deploy 'sound bites' – resonant but essentially vacuous rhetoric – to minimise the perception that politics is dull and banal when judged from the standpoint of its entertainment value. The 'simplification' of the political message has been the consequence of a concern to render complex issues palatable to a large viewing public.

In a study attached to the Swedish democracy commission, Mats Ekström and Cathrin Andersson describe the way the medialisation of politics has involved politicians proceeding from the principle that 'caution is the better part of valour'. (EUD 2000: 180–181) Unlike the panacea-peddling of a handful of the more populist figures, the tendency of the mainstream politicians has been to avoid giving hostages to fortune. This in turn has meant that citizens have struggled to differentiate the various party political messages, a fact which has of course reinforced the tendency to a secularisation of politics. Ekström and Andersson point to the way in the period 1979–98 the parties became increasingly reluctant to take initiatives that could be construed as election commitments. They were concerned to avoid criticism in the media for making promises that could or would not be delivered on, but also risked criticism for not having solutions to the complex issues taken up by journalists. Clearly, in this type of situation, voters will have only a limited capacity to distinguish between diluted party political messages and to penetrate the war of words characterising media-oriented election campaigns.

It bears re-statement that the Danish and Swedish democracy commissions view the media as arenas rather than actors with an agenda of their own. The Danish commission concluded that "the media have increased their influence in recent years, but they have not taken over power". (Togeby 2003: 27) The Swedish commission is rather less sanguine. "The medialisation of politics has had consequences that have not been favourable to building a democratic awareness. When political debates form part of an entertainment channel (or programme), they are judged essentially by their entertainment value and this makes politics banal." (EUD 2000: 242)

Far more starkly than its Danish and Swedish counterparts, the Norwegian democracy commission spells out the deleterious implications for parliamentary democracy of the medialisation of politics. The medialisation phenomenon has contributed to a *loss of domain* for the central political institutions of parliament and government. The academic heading the Norwegian commission, Øyvind Østerud, has described the shift from the party-dominant media of the 1960s to the media-dependent parties of today. Østerud relates how three decades or so ago major newspapers were affiliated to political parties, while radio and television were public monopolies controlled by parliament. This is no longer the case and the media have achieved a much greater degree of institutional autonomy. Indeed, he goes well beyond the findings of the Danish and Swedish commissions to claim that in Norway the mass media are actors and not simply arenas – actors in that "they edit the public sphere". He concludes that the "medialisation of politics [in Norway] is partly the consequence of deliberate deregulation and partly a dynamic process with implications beyond the intention of deregulatory policies". (Østerud 2002: 2–3)

Another theme common to the democratic audits in Denmark and Norway is the *juridicialisation of politics* and its concomitant, an erosion of parliamentary sovereignty. It is argued that the separation of power between law makers and law interpreters has become increasingly blurred and that the non-elected courts have become more influential. The Danish commission noted that "the Danish judiciary has increasingly taken on a law-making role, shifting the traditional balance between the three branches of government. It is just one of the many indications that Danish society is becoming more 'judicialized'". (Togeby 2003: 24) The commission noted how the Supreme Court had become increasingly active in reviewing the constitutionality of legislation and it cited the Tvind case in 1999, which was the first time the Supreme Court had rejected a law on the grounds that it was not in line with the constitution.

A distinction has been drawn in the literature between supra-national juridicialisation and domestic juridicialisation. It is the nature and ramifications of the supra-national variant which are given most emphasis in the Danish and Norwegian reports. *Supra-national juridicialisation* involves a state adopting a body of supranational law and international covenants, which undermine the sovereignty of the national legislature. For example, as an EEA (European Economic Area) member, Norway has been obliged to adopt EU statutes and regulations without participating in the lawmaking process. This may not represent a *de jure* transfer of constitutional sovereignty because EEA membership is a treaty in international law, which can be unilaterally terminated. In practice, however, it is a substantial de facto transfer of sovereignty. Denmark has, of course, been a full EU member since 1973, but the Danish commission concludes that "with or without the European Affairs Committee, ceding sovereignty to the EU has weakened the Folketing". (Togeby 2003: 30)

In the field of human rights too, supranational juridicialisation has reduced the domain of the national legislature. Thus, in 1999, the European Convention of Human Rights was incorporated into Norwegian law, as it had been into Danish law seven years earlier. Denmark also signed up to the UN Convention on the Elimination of All Forms of Racial Discrimination in 1971.

Domestic juridicialisation followed in large part in the wake of the strengthening of welfare rights and services by legislation – that is, the enactment of laws guaranteeing certain basic standards of welfare. In Norway in the 1990s, for example, a new batch of laws reached the statute book granting legal rights to education and health care. The obligation to provide these services was vested in the local councils, albeit with a national supervisory commission. However, the failure to provide adequate central funding to facilitate the local delivery of these basic welfare rights has led individuals to turn to the courts to secure grievance redress.

Democracy in Iceland and Finland

Before proceeding to the sharply contrasting conclusions of the Danish and Norwegian democracy commissions, it might be noted that there has been no comparable history of the comprehensive investigation of the state of democracy in Finland and Iceland. Power and Democracy commissions have been absent in these two countries. Indeed, Svanur Kristjánsson has remarked that "instead of looking at the experience of other Western democracies, Iceland has become isolated from international discussions of democracy". (Kristjánsson 2004: 172) Things appear to be changing, however. We noted in the

Introduction that, during Iceland's Presidency of the Nordic Council in 2004, Siv Friðleifsdóttir, the Icelandic minister for Nordic co-operation, launched a Democracy Committee charged with analysing and improving democratic processes across the region as a whole. Moreover, the main findings of the Danish commission were also presented at a conference on 'Small States' organised by and in the University of Iceland in summer 2003.

Also influenced by the tradition of democratic auditing in the three metropolitan Scandinavian states, a Policy Programme for Citizen Participation (*kansalaisvaikuttamisen politiikkaohjelma*) was launched by the Vanhanen government in Finland in summer 2003.[4] The programme was designed to consolidate representative democracy and promote active citizenship – based on the notion of *citizens as partners* in OECD parlance – and it has two overriding aims.[5] First, there is concern to increase electoral turnout. Voting, it was argued, "is a good indicator of the state of democracy, civic participation and social capital" and declining turnout (as in Finland since the 1960s) may be viewed as a warning signal that all is not well in a democratic polity. Second, the policy programme is seeking ways of improving the citizen's scope for exerting influence between elections. The intention is to pay special attention to those groups manifesting low levels of civic participation – that is, the socially and politically excluded. Exploring and developing ways of strengthening representative democracy was to be the task of a *Democracy 2007* working group led by the former foreign secretary, Pertti Paasio. Thus far, this has focused on possible reforms of the electoral system, as well as ways of reversing the decline in party membership and public confidence in political institutions.

A feature of recent general elections in Finland, notwithstanding 'candidate voting' (see chapter 2) has been declining turnout. The downward trend has been longer and more accentuated than in Norway and 1972 was the last time more than three-quarters of the Finnish electorate voted (see table 8.4). In the 1960s the average turnout at Eduskunta elections was 85%; for the three general elections in the 1990s, the average was only 67.2%. As in Sweden and Norway, abstentionism has been particularly marked among young voters generally and among those young working class males who have moved to the concrete suburbs of Helsinki in search of work in particular. Unemployment is high in these areas and this, coupled with the difficulties of adjusting to life in the capital city, has spawned an acute sense of loss of community and by extension a diminished sense of class solidarity. Until the huge vote for Tony Halme at the 2003 general election suggested otherwise, the conventional wisdom was that the 'life cycle effect' was not really working in Finland. Younger age-cohorts were not entering the electorate later in life and Tuomo Martikainen adopted the 'spectator democracy' metaphor to describe the Finnish situation. (Martikainen 2003)

Table 8.4 *Turnout in Finnish general elections, 1970–2003 (%)*

1970	82.2
1972	81.4
1975	73.8
1979	75.3
1983	75.7
1987	72.1
1991	68.4
1995	68.6
1999	64.6
2003	69.6

As in the three metropolitan Scandinavian countries, party membership has declined in Finland and party members have become less active. In the 1960s, 18.9% of Finnish voters were members of a political party; by 1998 the proportion had fallen to 9.7% (Raunio 2004: 141) By 2005 only 7% of Finns belonged to a political party and a mere 3% of young persons between 18–29 did so.[6] There has been a particularly marked decline in the membership of the Centre Party, the only mass party in Finland in recent decades.[7] The combination of declining turnout and declining party membership would naturally point to a decline in partisan identification. However, while among many 'sofa voters' party allegiance is weak, this is not necessarily the case. True, the 2003 general election survey indicated that one-third of abstainers had no fixed party identification. But 29% reported that they had a fairly stable party identification and 12% a strong party identification. As Heikki Paloheimo has concluded, "among the 'sleeping voters' there are also those with a strong party allegiance, who for one reason or another did not vote". (Paloheimo 2003: 175–193)

In terms of conventional political participation, Iceland appears prima facie a strongly deviant case. Like Denmark, it has not experienced significantly declining turnout at general elections. There was a minor dip in the 1990s, but at the last general election in 2003 turnout rose to 87.7%, see table 8.5. (Hardarsson and Kristinsson 2004: 1025) Party membership has been high too and in the 1990s it stood at about one-quarter of voters. However, Kristjánsson has brought out the way this level is very deceptive. There is a low level of active membership and, since no membership fee is required, once members have joined they tend to become members for life. He notes that "except for a small number of activists, the political parties operate without active partisans". (Kristjánsson 2004: 166) Kristjánsson also brings out the way, since the 1970s, Alþingi elections have been characterised by high levels of electoral volatility and reduced levels of partisan identification. By the turn of the new millennium, only 30% of voters identified with a political party and "independent voters were just as numerous as loyal party supporters". (Kristjánsson 2004: 164)

Clearly, parliamentary democracy in the Nordic countries is confronting a variety of challenges that are common to many, if not most Western democracies. In his contribution to 'Democracy the Swedish Way – the Report from the Democratic Audit of Sweden in 1999' – Klaus von Beyme notes that, "in the majority of European countries, the notion that democracy is in crisis is widely held. Common symptoms are diminished party identification, falling turnout in elections, increased fragmentation of the party system and a decline in confidence in the 'political class'". (Petersson 1999: 23) It is not to accept that it signals the existence of a 'democratic crisis' none the less to note that, of von Beyme's checklist, it is a decline in partisan identification that has been *the* common factor challenging representative democracy in the Scandinavian states. Further evidence has come from the analysis of the 2002 Swedish general election, which showed that the proportion of the electorate boasting a strong party identification had fallen from 65% to 40% in the period 1968–2002. The drop was particularly marked among those persons who had little interest in politics – from 29% in 1968 to14% in 2002. (Ellis 2004: 8) Other factors challenging parliamentary democracy in Scandinavia, as elsewhere in Western Europe, have included the medialisation and juridicialisation of politics (discussed earlier), along with such 'veto players' as multi-national corporations and the money markets, which can twist the arm of domestic governments.

Table 8.5 Turnout in Icelandic general elections, 1971–2003 (%)

1971	90.4
1974	91.4
1978	90.3
1979	89.3
1983	88.6
1987	90.1
1991	87.5
1995	87.4
1999	84.1
2003	87.7

The state of Scandinavian democracy: 'in a state'?

So, how well do the recent power and democracy commissions suggest that Scandinavian democracy is working? Does the evidence suggest that democracy in the region is 'in a state', that is experiencing something of a crisis? Since the primary remit of the Swedish democracy commission – to analyse and suggest ways of reversing declining turnout – was narrower than its counterparts, this summing up section confines itself to the findings of the Danish and Norwegian commissions. They could not be more different. Danish democracy was reported to be flourishing whereas in Norway democracy was indeed 'in a state'!

According to the democracy commission, the Danes are still democratically active and the political institutions in the country are 'democratically robust'. The Danish people appear resourceful and capable. Political participation has not declined and participatory democracy has not been replaced by a passive 'spectator democracy'. The ability of the political parties to function as a link between the people and power-holders has declined, but they appear to have achieved a new stability with fewer members. "Compared with other political institutions, the Folketing has been strengthened more than it has been weakened." (Togeby 2003: 50)

The Norwegian commission came to two strikingly different conclusions. First, it argued that within Norway the democratic chain of command was weakening. There had been an attenuation in traditional forms of linkage, the democratic infrastructure was collapsing and Norway was a 'disintegrating democracy'. Second, it insisted that outside Norway a new chain of command was emerging, which constrained the Storting and eroded parliamentary sovereignty, but over which the citizenry and its elected representatives had virtually no control. The tone of the commission's report was generally pessimistic. For example, the commission noted that four out of five voters were wholly or partly of the view that Storting members did not pay particular attention to the opinion of ordinary people. It held that such figures amounted to a crisis of confidence in the representative system.

The Norwegian commission recognised that democracy is not simply based on power through popularly-elected bodies. It acknowledged that there are modes of participation outside elections, parties and popular movements – influence could be exerted as a user, consumer or activist in a pressure group. These different forms of what it called 'value-added democracy' complemented representative democracy, but they could not replace it. Indeed, the Norwegian commission commented that "when the meaning of democracy shifts from representative government as a formal decision-making system to different forms of value-added democracy, the disintegration of representative democracy is concealed and the distinction between democracy and non-democracy obscured". (Haugsvær 2003: 5)

The notable discrepancy in the main findings of the Danish and Norwegian democracy commissions raises the question of whether in Lauri Karvonen's words "the differential conclusions reflected differences in perspective or in fact?" He concludes that it was "a bit of both". (Karvonen 2004: 426) In Norway there was criticism of the commission on both empirical and normative grounds – the former particularly ironic in view of the weight of evidence collected. The 'empirical critique', largely from academics, focused on the interpretation of the evidence and the type of evidence generated, while politicians (ministers and parliamentarians) cast doubt on many of the central findings.

Significantly, two of the five academics comprising the Norwegian Power and Democracy Commission dissented from parts of the majority report. Hege Skjeie held that the evidence did not demonstrate conclusively that rule by popular consent was withering. She could well have alluded to survey work, which showed that, compared with other countries, confidence in the Norwegian political system has been very high. Citizens, it seems, have considerable confidence in the political process and the Storting as an institution. Indeed, Ola Listhaug has emphasised that this confidence is relatively stable and there has been no clear trend towards declining trust. (Listhaug 2004) For her part, Siri Meyer, the other 'dissenter', complained that there was insufficient evidence relating to popular perceptions of society and democracy, rather than narrowly democracy as a system of government. "My starting point for the analysis of the anatomy of power", she held, "is individuals and life forms. We know a good deal about the system, but what has happened to the people who live under that system?" (Ringen 2003: 8–9)

For several leading political figures, there was apparent incredulity at some of the main findings in the Norwegian report. For example, at the presentation of the commission's final report in August 2003, the prime minister Kjell Magne Bondevik's point of departure was that "the Storting's power has again increased". Hilmar Rommetvedt's recent work collected in the volume *The Rise of the Norwegian Parliament* suggested he had a fair point. In Rommetvedt's words, "the Storting at the turn of the new millennium is more active and Norwegian governments confront non-governmental majorities in parliamentary voting more often than they used to do. As a consequence, organised interests pay more attention to the Storting when they attempt to influence public policies". (Rommetvedt 2003: 12) As prime minister of a minority non-socialist coalition Bondevik doubtless completely concurred with Rommetvedt's remarks.

A challenging normative critique of the Norwegian commission's approach has come from Rune Sørensen, whose central thrust is that the chain of command from voters to representatives can be organised and formulated in different ways. The approach of the commission, he claims, is a society-oriented or collectivist one, which proceeds from the principle of the sovereignty of the people. This approach is characterised *inter alia* by the considerable discretion afforded elected representatives and the clear hierarchical lines of authority of elected representatives over the personnel of the central administration. The collectivist perspective leads to scepticism in respect of restrictions on the majority principle. In contrast, Sørensen outlines an individualistic democratic perspective, which proceeds from the sovereignty of the individual. Voters are more concerned with the content of politics than participating themselves and they view competition between the political parties as an important control mechanism. Viewed from an individualistic democratic perspective, the juridicialisation of decision-making – and the implicit control of the majority principle – would not be seen to be in conflict with the fundamentals of democracy. (Sørensen 2004: 156–176) Sørensen is critical of the narrow view of democracy held by the Norwegian commission. He concludes that researchers can have more or less sympathy with the 'individualistic democratic model'. But it is a variant of representative democracy, which has a basis in western democratic ideals, and cannot, therefore, be dismissed as a second-rate democracy.

Conclusions

A common denominator and point of departure for much of the substantial auditing work on Scandinavian democracy in recent years has been a concern among parliamentarians about an attenuation of the traditional inputs into representative democracy. They have seen that civic participation has declined through the ballot boxes, political parties and traditional social movements. The concern has been that this weakening in the 'by the people' element has challenged the legitimacy and undermined the legislative capacity of the democratically elected national assembly. Plainly, legitimacy and legislative capacity are not necessarily connected, but many parliamentarians were sufficiently persuaded of a loose link between the two to sanction the creation of democracy commissions.

The evidence from these commissions in metropolitan Scandinavia pointed up a striking paradox. There had been a decline in both membership in, and identification with political parties and a diminished engagement in traditional popular movements such as trade unions. But there was no decline in civic interest in politics or, generally, trust in politicians. There was strong evidence of a connection between social and political exclusion and immigrants, members of ethnic communities and indeed young, working-class men tended to remain outside the political decision-making system. Otherwise, political participation was taking new, issue-based forms – in 'here and now' organisations in Norway, for example.

For Scandinavian parliamentarians comparing the main findings of the democracy commissions and the cognate academic literature, the picture must have appeared contradictory and confusing. This was not least because there was a patent lack of consensus about the relative position and influence of the national legislature. The Norwegian commission reports that the decision-making power of the Storting is in decline. Kristjánsson claims that "in recent years the Alþingi has steadily been losing power". (Kristjánsson 2004: 159) However, Raunio, noting the reduction in the powers of the president and the demise of Soviet interference in government formation, insists that "Finland is probably the only West European country where parliamentary democracy has become less constrained since the 1980s". (Raunio 2004: 149)

In large part, such contrasting conclusions reflect the different methodological approaches and perspectives. Thus, in their introduction to the special *Scandinavian Political Studies* issue on 'parliamentary democracy', Bergman and Strøm distinguish the position of the legislature in relation to the executive and the position of parliament in its wider external environment. They conclude that "reforms have strengthened the constitutional parliamentary chain, but there is also a general deparliamentarisation of modern politics". (Bergman and Strøm 2004: 109) The Danish commission also differentiated legislative–executive relations from the wider constraints on the Folketing's decision-making authority. It acknowledged that Denmark's EU membership has meant that many important decisions are taken in a decision-making system over which citizens have only indirect influence. It states too that the increased strength of the judiciary at the expense of the legislature may reinforce the rule of law, but it weakens the sovereignty of the people.

Importantly, however, the Danish commission emphasised that the legislative–executive balance favoured the legislature more than earlier. "The Folketing has strengthened its control over the cabinet and hence the central administration, but it has also increased its influence on legislation." (Togeby 2003: 22) This brings us back to the *executive-parties dimension* in Lijphart's terms and the clear proposition in the Danish commission's report that the 'parties' – and mostly the opposition parties by definition – have an increased capacity to control and influence the 'executive'. The participation of the parliamentary opposition in the exercise of power is, of course, a central feature of Lijphart's 'consensus model democracy', which provides a timely cue to turn to the third central question in this book. 'Is democracy in Scandinavia consensual, majoritarian or mixed?'

Notes

1 Not well enough was the supposition underlying the theme of the 2005 American Political Science Association (APSA) annual meeting in Washington DC, which was 'Mobilizing Democracy'.
2 Anders Wettergren,'Förnyelse inget för partierna' *Göteborgs-Posten* 5.3.2004.
3 On the point of issue-based mobilisation, no less than 34,000 Icelandic voters – about 19% of the electorate – signed a petition in 1992 against the European Economic Area (EEA) Agreement. (Thorhallsson and Vignisson 2004: 43)
4 http://.om.fi/21390.htm.
5 The 'Policy Programme for Citizen Participation' is one of four cross-departmental programmes designed to counter the endemic sectoralisation of policy-making in the central administration. Directed by the minister of justice, Johannes Koskinen, the ministerial group also comprises the ministers of education, culture, finance and the interior.
6 'Suomalaisten käsitys politiikasta nuivempi kuin naapurimaissa' *Helsingin Sanomat* 8.3.2005.
7 'Apila-aate kaipaa lannoitusta' *Helsingin Sanomat* 21.11.2004.

References

Arter, David 'Parliamentary Democracy in Scandinavia' *Parliamentary Affairs* 57, 3, 2004, pp. 581–600

Beetham, David, I. Byrne, P. Ngan and S. Weir 'Democratic Audit: Towards a Broader View of Democratic Achievement' *Parliamentary Affairs* 56, 2, 2003, pp. 334–347

Bergman, Torbjörn and Kaare Strøm 'Shifting Dimensions of Citizen Control' *Scandinavian Political Studies* 27, 2, 2004, pp. 89–113

Bergman, Torbjörn 'Sweden: Democratic Reforms and Partisan Decline in an Emerging Separation-of-Powers System' *Scandinavian Political Studies* 27, 2, 2004, pp. 203–225

Damgaard, Erik 'Developments in Danish Parliamentary Democracy: Accountability, Parties and External Constraints' *Scandinavian Political Studies* 27, 2, 2004, pp. 115–131

Ellis, Andrew 'Relating Knowledge and Tools to the Practical Questions Facing Democratic Reformers' *Participation* 28, 3, 2004, pp. 6–10

Goul Andersen, Jørgen 'The Danish Democracy and Power Study: Danish Democratic Audit 1998–2003' Paper presented for the workshop on Small States, Reykjavík 17–18 September 2004

Goul Andersen, Jørgen and Jens Hoff *Democracy and Citizenship in Scandinavia* (Palgrave: Basingstoke, 2001)

Hardarsson, O.T. and G.H. Kristinsson 'Iceland', *European Journal of Political Research* 43, 7/8, 2004, pp. 1024–1029

Kaase, Max 'Is Democracy Working?' *Participation* 28, 2, 2004, pp. 3–4

Karvonen, Lauri 'Review of Scandinavian Power Studies' *Scandinavian Political Studies*

27, 4, 2004, pp. 423–427

Kriesi, Hanspeter 'The Federal Parliament: The Limits of Institutional Reform' *West European Politics* 24, 2, 2001, pp. 59–76

Kristjánsson, Svanur 'Iceland: Searching for Democracy along Three Dimensions of Citizen Control' *Scandinavian Political Studies* 27, 2, 2004, pp. 153–174

Listhaug, Ola 'Political Disaffection: Norway 1957–1997' (NOU 2004:1) Modernisert folketryd

Listhaug, Ola and Lars Grønflaten 'Trends in Political Involvement and Activism in Norway' Paper presented at the Scottish-Nordic Workshop, Ardoe House Hotel Aberdeen, 24–25 May 2002

Martikainen, Pekka, Tuomo Martikainen and Hanna Wass 'The Effect of Socio-Economic Factors on Voter Turnout in Finland: A Register-Based Study of 2.9 Million Voters' Paper presented at the Annual Meeting of the Finnish Political Science Association. Turku, 16–17 January 2003

Narud, Hanne Marthe and Kaare Strøm 'Norway: Madisonianism Reborn' *Scandinavian Political Studies* 27, 2, 2004, pp. 175–201

Paloheimo, Heikki 'Miten äänestäjät valitsevat puolueen?' *Politiikka* 45, 3, 2003, pp. 175–193

Petersson, Olof, Klaus Von Beyme, Lauri Karvonen, Birgitta Nedelmann and Eivind Smith *Democracy the Swedish Way* (SNS Förlag: Stockholm, 1999)

Petersson, Olof 'Den sista maktutredningen?' *Nytt Norsk Tidsskrift* 20, 2003, pp. 351–362

Raunio, Tapio 'The Changing Finnish Democracy: Stronger Parliamentary Accountability, Coalescing Political Parties and Weaker External Constraints' *Scandinavian Political Studies* 27, 2, 2004, pp. 133–152

Ringen, Stein 'Where Now, Democracy?' *Times Literary Supplement*, 13.2.2003

Ringen, Stein 'Wealth and Decay. Norway Finds a Massive Political Self-examination – and Funds Trouble for All' *Times Literary Supplement* 13.2.2004, pp. 3–5

Rommetvedt, Hilmar *The Rise of the Norwegian Parliament* (Frank Cass: London and Portland, OR, 2003)

Sørensen, Rune J. 'Et forvirret demokrati? Makt- og demokratiutredningens misvisende konklusjon om det norske demokratiet' *Norsk Statsvitenskapelig Tidskrift* 20, 2, 2004, pp. 156–176

Statens Offentliga Utredningar (SOU 2000:1) *En uthållig demokrati! Politik för folkstyrelse* (EUD)

Stubbergaard, Ylva 'Det politiska deltagandets mångfald' *Statsvetenskaplig Tidskrift* 105, 3, 2002, pp. 201–207

Tarschys, Daniel 'Democracy, Values, Institutions: the Use and Abuse of Governance' *Participation* 28, 3, 2004, pp. 12–13

Thorhallsson, Baldur and Hjalti Thor Vignisson 'A Controversial Step', in Baldur Thorhallsson (ed.) *Iceland and European Integration* (Routledge: London, 2004), pp. 38–49

Togeby, Lise, Jørgen Goul Andersen, Peter Munk Christiansen, et al. *Power and Democracy in Denmark. Conclusions* (Magtudredningen: Aarhus, 2003)

Østerud, Øyvind 'Judicialisation and Parliamentary Democracy' Paper delivered at a
Scottish-Nordic Workshop, Ardoe House Hotel, Aberdeen 24–25 May 2002

9

Analysing parliamentary opposition parties: both policy actors and policy arenas?

It was argued in chapter 1 that, from a rules-based perspective, all the Scandinavian states are majoritarian democracies rather than the consensual democracies they have been widely perceived to be à la Lijphart. Lijphart's approach to classification was viewed as conflating and confusing rules and behaviour, and the case for dropping the notion of 'consensus model democracy' was aired. However, when analysing *legislative behaviour*, Lijphart's claim that "most democracies have significant or even predominantly consensual traits" provides a useful point of departure. (Lijphart 1999: 7) We noted earlier Ganghof's assertion that "legislative majority rule, if combined with electoral proportionality, does not necessarily prevent behavioural patterns generally perceived as consensual. On the contrary ... it can contribute to them". (Ganghof 2005) Accordingly, the focus in the following chapters is on the legislative–executive relationship and, in particular, the question 'how consensual is legislative practice in the Nordic countries?'

There are two subsidiary questions. 1) How, and to what effect, does the parliamentary opposition participate in the exercise of power in the Scandinavian countries? 2) To what extent are non-veto players among the opposition parties – that is, those parties whose support is not strictly necessary to effect a change in the legislative status quo – able to exert influence in the legislative agenda-setting process? This last question may be regarded as the acid test of consensual legislative behaviour in the fullest sense of the term – that is, of extreme parliamentary consensualism.

In authoritarian systems, opposition parties, when permitted at all, have remained permanently in opposition. Thus, in Jerzy Wiatr's classic characterisation of the 'one-party hegemonic' Polish party system during the Cold War, the opposition parties never challenged the supremacy of the ruling Socialist Workers' Party. (Wiatr 1970: 312–321) They existed 'under licence', so to speak, merely to give a veneer of legitimacy to what was in practice a one-party "people's democracy". In contrast, one of the cardinal principles of liberal democracy is the legitimacy of political opposition and in principle all the opposition parties are eligible governing parties and possess varying degrees of 'governing potential'. Indeed, most opposition parties have entered government at some point in their history, even the larger, so-called 'anti-system parties' such as the French Communist Party. (Bell 2003: 24–37)

The first part of this chapter seeks to provide an analytical framework for the cross-national study of parliamentary oppositions in liberal democracies, albeit with particular reference to Scandinavia. Constructing an analytical framework is perhaps putting it too pretentiously. What I propose to do is to make a number of statements and suppositions regarding the modus operandi of parliamentary oppositions which, taken together, might provide the basic ground for comparative analysis. The second part of the chapter justifies the subsequent focus on comparing the parliamentary oppositions in Finland and Sweden by reference to a 'most similar case' design. The main characteristics of the two parliamentary oppositions are highlighted and the main opposition parties given a thumbnail profile.

Analysing parliamentary oppositions in liberal democracies: a basic framework

In Western democracies parliamentary oppositions comprise a number of political parties that operate severally and collectively within the framework of rules and procedures that make up the legislative environment of the national assembly. The structure of parliamentary oppositions and the interaction of the political parties constituting them will be dynamic and variable. The opposition will comprise more or less parties and there will be more or less cooperation between them. The extent of cooperation will vary between systems and within systems over time. Clearly, for example, there has been an increase in the number and diversity of parliamentary opposition parties in the Nordic region since the early 1970s and this might be expected to have had ramifications for the overall cohesion of the oppositions. As a general rule of thumb, Robert Dahl has noted that "the competitiveness of opposition depends in large measure ... on the number and nature of parties" – that is, on the extent to which opposition is concentrated. (Dahl 1968: 337)

Individually, parliamentary opposition parties will comprise autonomous policy sub-systems engaged in the process of generating and articulating policy alternatives. Those policy alternatives (outputs) will typically range from the production of an 'alternative budget' and the determination of a 'party line' on a specific issue to the decision to table an interpellation or submit a party motion. Parliamentary opposition parties will possess variable manpower and financial resources and a differential policy capacity.

The process of formulating and finalising opposition policy will involve the interplay between a variety of actors – individual MPs, committee groups, ad hoc working groups and members of the group secretariat – within the parliamentary party group. In other words, the parliamentary group will be both a policy actor *and* policy arena – an arena for the process of generating policy alternatives and an actor in promoting the outputs (increment) 'of the process in parliament at large.

The size of an opposition party's representation in the legislature will be likely to have implications for its policy capacity and policy output, as well as the policy processes in the parliamentary group. Larger opposition parties, it might be hypothesised, will possess greater resources than smaller ones to off-set the informational disadvantages of being out of government and so be in a position to formulate coherent policy alternatives. Size would be expected to impinge on the work practices of the parliamentary group. All things being equal, the larger the opposition's parliamentary group, the greater the scope for the decentralisation of policy responsibilities and the greater the potential for individuals and sub-groups of MPs to specialise in particular policy fields. The size of the opposition group will also have implications for the scope of its policy output, not least when there is a numerical threshold (a minimum number of MPs needed) for particular forms of legislative action (tabling an interpellation that leads to a vote of confidence in the government, for ex-ample).

Opposition parties will, albeit to varying extents, promote alternative poli-cies and ideas and seek to exert influence in the wider legislative environment. The extent of opposition party influence – its impact on the 'legislative agenda' – will reflect such factors as the rules of enactment and whether there are minority veto provisions; the legislative base of the executive and whether there is a majority or minority government; and the particular legislative cul-ture and whether a degree of consensual legislative practice is the norm.

In systems characterised by consensual legislative practices, there will be varying *modes of government–opposition consultation* on policy-related matters, although conclusions about the extent of opposition influence remain prob-lematical. First, and most obviously in the metropolitan Scandinavian con-text, where minority cabinets have become routine, there will be inter-party negotiations on aspects of a future policy programme, often leading to the formation of a *legislative coalition.* On the basis of the formalised – that is, written and detailed – nature of the legislative agreement between the govern-ing Social Democrats and their two 'support parties', the Greens and Leftist Party, Aylott and Bergman have referred to the phenomenon of 'contract parliamentarism' in Sweden. (Aylott and Bergman 2004)

Second, there may be negotiations between the government and one or more of the opposition parties leading to deals on specific policy measures or legislative packages prior to their introduction into parliament. Clearly, the functional logic of this type of *package deal parliamentarism* is likely to be greatest in relation to macro-economic policy when minority governments are in office. Thus, in Denmark, there has been a 'package deal' or *forlig* tradition, that is, a tradition of broad economic policy packages, negotiated prior to, or early in the new parliamentary year, and embracing one or more opposition parties. For example, in October 1986, one such *forlig*, quaintly known as the 'potato diet' (*kartoffelkuren*) because of an old holiday marking the end of the potato harvest, saw a minority non-socialist coalition under the Conservative Poul Schlüter agree an austerity package with the opposition-based Social Liberals. (Miller 1991: 126–127) When an attempted *forlig* has failed, minority governments have invariably resigned.

Third, there may be formal or informal *'leadership conferences'* between government and opposition leaders at any stage in the legislative process, although mainly before a major government policy statement to parliament. These conferences are most likely on matters of 'high politics' of immediate national concern and when there has traditionally been a broad, cross-party issue consensus. Such valence issues are typically in the foreign and security policy sphere – the practice of neutrality in Sweden, for example. Writing over thirty years ago, during the long era of single-party Social Democratic cabinet dominance, Donald Hancock described the Swedish tradition of government–opposition consultation on foreign policy. "Although the cabinet exercises the leading role in [foreign] policy initiatives, most issues are resolved through four-party consultations in informal party leadership conferences and the Riksdag's Advisory Council on Foreign Affairs" (*utrikesnämnden*) (Hancock 1972: 242). There has been no systematic examination of the party leadership conferences in Sweden and it is very possible that the brief references to them in the literature have served to inflate their real importance.

Finally, opposition party parliamentarians may be involved in *pre-legislative consultation* and represented on bodies engaged in the generation and formulation of public policy. We noted earlier in the book how Danish parliamentarians were extensively involved in the work of preparatory commissions and committees until the mid–1970s. In Sweden Torbjörn Larsson has been unequivocal in his assessment of the impact of opposition groups on commissions. "Participating in a commission is one of the best chances the political opposition can have to influence government policy". (Larsson 1994: 170)

The members of multi-party oppositions will compete among themselves in the electoral marketplace, as well as weighing the prospects of combining with other parties (in and out of government) in the post-election cabinet. The result will be the deployment of a range of short-term tactics, as well as the pursuit of longer-term strategies. The choice of opposition strategy will be dictated by a range of factors. Jean Blondel has posited that "the character of the opposition is tied to the character of the government". (Blondel 1997: 443) Yet it may not be unreasonable to extend Blondel's proposition. The character or strategy of the opposition is tied not only to the character of the government, but also to the character of the *next* government – or, more exactly, the desired combination of parties forming it. A strategic opposition party question, therefore is, 'is cabinet office a realistic prospect and, if so, how best can it be achieved?' Opposition parties may pursue a course of close cooperation – even to the point of producing a joint election manifesto – with a view to ousting the government in power and forming the next one. Equally, individual opposition parties may prefer a coalition arrangement with one or other of the present governing parties.[1] Moreover, an opposition party may pursue a different strategy in the electoral arena from the parliamentary. While the academic literature has identified three primary parliamentary strategies, these are to be regarded as complementary rather than mutually exclusive.

First, there is an *office-seeking strategy*. This describes the primary goal of a party, but not the means of achieving that goal. In other words, the nature of the office-seeking strategy or strategies must be viewed contextually. In multi-party assemblies, for example, an office-seeking strategy may involve bridge-building with one or more of the existing cabinet parties. It may also involve action designed to create (at least the appearance of) a more united opposition. A vigorously pursued office-seeking strategy may come at a price, by dividing the party leadership from the party group and rank-and-file activists who may, for example, fear the consequences of participation in government for the party's credibility as a radical force for change.

Second, there is a *policy-seeking strategy*. Kaare Strøm, it will be recalled, has argued that whether a party pursues an office-seeking strategy or not will depend largely on the electoral dividend and policy influence to be gained from remaining in opposition. (Strøm 1990). This suggests the distinction between 'opposition by design' parties and 'opposition by default' parties. For the former the choice reflects the application of a policy cost-benefit analysis and the calculation that there are significant advantages to be gained from remaining outside government.

Finally, there is vote-seeking, or what I would prefer to call in the parliamentary context a *profile-seeking strategy*. This may be pursued in particular by the smaller (and especially more radical) parliamentary parties, which have little or no chance of cabinet office and very limited means of influencing policy. They may well concentrate on single issues and, denied significant representation on parliamentary committees, they will tend to use the floor of the chamber to profile themselves and attract votes.

In presenting these three main opposition party strategies, it is, of course, important to acknowledge what Jørgen Elklit describes as a "vicious circle of instrumentalities". Elklit emphasises the way vote-seeking, office-seeking and policy-seeking "might be seen as instrumental to the fulfilment of at least one of the other two party objectives". He adds that the three party strategies are closely – and causally – connected, making it extremely difficult to separate the effects of the various independent variables. (Elklit 1999: 83)

Although the distinction may well be hairbreadth, it is probably fair to distinguish parliamentary opposition party *strategies* from parliamentary opposition party *styles*. For instance, it is not surprising in a Westminster-style system such as Ireland, where the opportunities for the opposition to exert policy influence are generally even more limited than in Westminster, that an adversarial opposition style has developed.[2] In contrast, during the heyday of social democracy in Norway and Sweden in the 1950s and 1960s, there was a strong presumption against an adversarial style of opposition. Instead, opposition parties sought to exert reasonable influence and to achieve what the Swedish Centre Party leader described as a "policy of results".[3] (Stjernquist 1968: 140) The adoption of a pragmatic, non-adversarial style does not, of course, guarantee parliamentary opposition parties influence proportionate to their numbers in the assembly. Moreover, pursuing a twin-track course of co-operation and combat can lead to the worst of all worlds. Nils Stjernquist captures the dilemma of the non-socialist parliamentary opposition in Sweden during the era of Social Democratic supremacy. "In trying to criticise the government in order to replace it and at the same time collaborate with it in order to participate in the decision-making process, the opposition has fallen between two stools." (Stjernquist 1968: 141)

Comparing parliamentary oppositions in Finland and Sweden: a 'most similar case' design

Since the last general elections in Sweden (2002) and Finland (2003), the two countries have witnessed contrasting governments, but strikingly similar oppositions (see table 9.1). Sweden has been governed by a minority Social Democratic government since 1994 whereas in Finland since 2003 a majority coalition comprising the Centre, Social Democrats and Swedish People's Party has been in office. The topography of the two parliamentary oppositions, however, has been remarkably alike. Since an overview of the common denominators in the two oppositions is integral to the analysis in the three following chapters, the main points are numbered below so as to give them the necessary emphasis.

Table 9.1 The composition of the parliamentary opposition in Sweden and Finland, 2002/03–2006/07

Sweden
Government: Social Democrats (144)
Opposition: Leftists (30*), Greens (17), Centre (22), Liberals (48), Christian
    Democrats (33), Conservatives (55), (205)

Finland
Government: Centre (55), Social Democrats (53), Swedish People's Party (9), (117)
Opposition: Leftists (19), Christian Democrats (7**), Greens (14), Conservatives
    (40), True Finns (3), (83)

---

*   Since the 2002 general elections, two Swedish Leftist Party MPs have resigned from the parliamentary group
** Similarly, two Finnish Christian Democrat MPs have defected from the party since 2003

1   In both Finland and Sweden since the last general elections there has been a situation of *pluralistic opposition*. Five parties have made up the opposition in the Finnish Eduskunta and six have made up the opposition in the Swedish Riksdag. The Swedish opposition has been numerically stronger with 59% of the parliamentary seats, compared with 42% in Finland. However, if the two 'support parties' of the governing Social Democrats are removed from the equation, the proportion of seats held by the two oppositions – now 45% in Sweden – is very similar.

2   The parliamentary oppositions in Finland and Sweden since 2002/03 have involved a *similar partisan composition*. Both comprise Conservatives, Christian Democrats, Greens and the post-communist Left. However, whereas in Finland the Centre is the largest governing party, it is one of the smallest opposition parties in Sweden. Furthermore, in contrast to Finland, where the Liberals do not have parliamentary seats, the Swedish Liberals, profiting from a notably volatile non-socialist electorate, are the second largest opposition party.

3   In both countries, the *structure* of the two parliamentary oppositions is very similar, both comprising predominantly small parties with under 10% of the vote. Out of a combined eleven parties in the two parliaments

between 2002/03–2006/07, eight polled under 10% – the Finnish Leftist Alliance managed 10.5% – and the True Finns gained only 2.8% of the national vote.

4   In both countries there is a good deal of *ideological distance* covering the opposition parties, which range from the Conservatives and a number of centrist groupings to the post-communist Left. On the subject of ideo- logical distance, there has been a similarity between Finland and Sweden on the one hand, and Denmark and Norway on the other, concerning the parliamentary radical right. In Denmark and Norway there have been sizeable radical rightist parliamentary groupings in the shape of the People's Party and Progress Party respectively. The only parliamentary right-wing populist party in Finland and Sweden since 2002/03 is the True Finns, which have only three of the 200 Eduskunta seats

5   In neither country is there, formally speaking, a leader of the opposition – that is Opposition with a capital 'O' as in Westminster. But in both the leading opposition party is the Conservatives and in reality – and cer- tainly in the media – their leaders are leaders of the opposition. In so far as both Conservative parties lost ground at the last general election, the po- sition of opposition leader has not gone entirely uncontested.

6   In both Sweden and Finland since 2002/03 the parliamentary oppositions have been *bilateral in character*. In Sweden, where the parliamentary op- position has a majority of seats, it comprises two 'support parties' of the ruling Social Democrats in the form of the Greens and Leftists. The four non-socialist parties in opposition clearly take this fact into account in their strategic considerations. In Finland, the Conservatives are poles apart from the Leftists and Greens, despite the fact that they were in govern- ment together under Lipponen between 1995–2003. In any 'most similar design' there are bound to be differences and two need to be noted, both relating to the internal dynamics of the parliamentary opposition.

7   In Sweden the 'bloc character' of political competition has become more accentuated in recent years and the non-socialist parties have at times achieved a greater unity of purpose (cohesion) than in Finland, where the opposition has been more disparate. Equally, given the evidence of intra- bloc volatility, there appears a greater degree of *direct* electoral competi- tion between the opposition parties in Sweden. Swedish non-socialist vot- ers switch rather readily between the Conservatives and Liberals on the one hand, and between the Christian Democrats, Liberal and Centre on the other.

8   Finally, there has been a striking 'across the blocs' character in Finnish

legislative–executive relations and the opposition parties have demonstrated remarkable *coalition versatility* in recent years. Since 1991, the Conservatives, presently the leading opposition party, have combined in government with every other parliamentary party except the miniscule True Finns. The True Finn Party in turn is the only one of the present Eduskunta opposition parties never to have entered government. Indeed, the complete absence of any bi-polarisation – or even the most elementary 'alternation of power' between government and opposition – has meant, it might be speculated, that Finnish opposition parties have displayed inherently individualised strategies rather than working en bloc to regain cabinet office.

The following thumbnail profiles of the parliamentary oppositions in Finland and Sweden between 2002/03–2006/07 clearly represent no more than a snapshot of a particular configuration of parties over a limited period of time. The exercise begs the question 'how typical is the composition of the two parliamentary oppositions in the period in question?' In Sweden, where there has been a dominant Social Democratic Party in power, the composition of the parliamentary opposition has not changed since 1994 when a general election marked the end of a non-socialist minority coalition. In Sweden, in short, the snapshot catches many of the essential characteristics of the parliamentary opposition. In contrast, since the 2003 general election and the demise of the Lipponen 'rainbow coalition', the composition of the Finnish parliamentary opposition has displayed several less typical features. For example, this is the first time in nearly twenty years that both the Conservatives and radical left have formed part of the opposition. Since both were part of the Lipponen cabinets between 1995–2003, the task of adapting to an opposition role would be expected to bring with it new challenges.

The parliamentary opposition parties in Finland and Sweden, 2002/03–2006/07

The only *radical rightist opposition party* among the Finnish and Swedish parliamentary oppositions in 2002/03–2006/07 is the True Finns (*perussuomalaiset*). This was founded by a 'gang of six'[4] in June 1995 and is the successor to the Finnish Rural Party, which ceased to exist shortly after the general election that year.[5] The True Finns gained 1.6% of the national vote in 2003 and elected three members of parliament. According to Timo Soini, its chair, the party is based on a 'positive populism' (*myönteinen populismi*), which is responsible and responsive to the people, the issues that concern them and those that the large parties fail to pick up or choose to ignore.[6] The True Finns, in short, are designed to provide a channel of influence for those ordinary ('true') Finns that are not tied to organised interests or big business. [7]

The *right-wing opposition parties* in the Finnish and Swedish parliamentary oppositions after the 2002/03 general elections have comprised the *Conservative parties*. Since 1979 the Swedish Conservatives (*Moderata samlingspartiet*), unlike their Finnish sister party, have been comfortably the largest non-socialist party. (Albinsson 1986) In the 1980s the Swedish party's neo-liberal advocacy of a 'shift in the system' – by redressing the imbalance between the public and private sectors in favour of the latter – was clearly influenced by the thinking of Ronald Reagan and Margaret Thatcher. But it made relatively little headway with voters. However, at the 1991 Riksdag election, the party's vote rose to 21.9% and Carl Bildt proceeded to form a Conservative-led minority non-socialist coalition with the Liberals, Centre and Christian Democrats.[8] The Swedish Conservatives increased their electoral support throughout the 1990s but in 2002, losing considerable ground to the Liberals, their vote plummeted to 15.1%, the lowest for thirty years. Following this weak electoral performance, Bo Lundgren was replaced as leader by Fredrik Reinfeldt.

Before returning to opposition in 2003, the Finnish Conservatives (*Kansallinen Kokoomus*) had the most distinctive post-war profile of any of the Finnish parties. Twenty-one consecutive years in opposition (1966–87) were followed by sixteen consecutive years in government (1987–2003), during which time the Conservatives shared power with every other party, including the post-communist Leftist Alliance. Between 1987–91 the party boasted the prime minister, Harri Holkeri, for the only time since the Second World War.[9] Since 2003 the Finnish Conservatives have faced the problems of adjusting to opposition after long years in government. Only four members of the party's parliamentary group have previous experience of being in opposition. The election of a new and young leader, Jyrki Katainen, in June 2004 clearly represented an attempt to replicate the considerably improved standing in the opinion polls achieved by Reinfeldt, the Swedish Conservative leader.

The *centrist opposition parties* in the Finnish and Swedish parliamentary oppositions after the 2002/03 general elections have been the Liberals and Centre in Sweden and the Christian Democrats and Greens in both countries. The Swedish Liberals (*Folkpartiet liberalerna*) are the third largest parliamentary grouping in the 2002–06 Riksdag, although their support has been the most volatile of all the non-socialist parties.[10] There were times in the months before polling when the Liberals looked at risk of plunging below the 4% national threshold to qualify for parliamentary seats and in 1998 they had managed a very modest 4.7%. However, on the strength of the party's striking gains four years later,[11] the Liberal leader Lars Leijonborg challenged the sitting

Social Democratic cabinet by attempting to form a minority coalition of centrist parties (Liberals, Centre and Christian Democrats) plus the Greens. This would have relied on tacit support from the Conservatives.

Early in the new millennium, the fortunes of the Centre (formerly Agrarian) parties in Finland and Sweden could not be more different. Whereas the Finnish party is the largest party for the second time in the last four elections, the vote for the Swedish Centre (*Centerpartiet*) declined in all three general elections in the 1990s. Although it recovered slightly to 6.2% at the 2002 Riksdag election, it is the smallest of the non-socialist parties.[12] In 1998 the Centre's poor performance was doubtless in part voter retribution for the party's legislative coalition with the Social Democrats on an unpopular austerity programme between 1995–97. Lennart Daléus resigned as party chair in 2001 and was replaced by the present leader Maud Olofsson.

The Swedish Christian Democrats (*Kristdemokraterna*) broke into the Riksdag with a vengeance, gaining 7.1% of the poll at the 'earthquake election' of 1991, when the party attracted much less media attention but, surprisingly, more votes than the populist New Democracy. The party's long-serving leader Alf Svensson's concentration on fundamental family values, put across in his familiar avuncular style, produced the Christian Democrats' best result of 11.8% in 1998. There were those who felt Svensson should then have taken the initiative and tried to form a Norwegian-style centre-based minority coalition. Indeed, the tentative evidence suggests that in hindsight Svensson rued a missed opportunity. In any event, four years later the Christian Democrats' support dropped, albeit not disastrously to 9.1%.[13] Svensson's subsequent departure as leader has posed fundamental questions about the Christian Democrats' future direction and strategy. Moves by the party board to remove the notion of 'christian ethics' from the party's rules were, however, thwarted by the new party leader, Göran Hägglund, at the Christian Democrats' fortieth anniversary conference in June 2004.[14]

The Finnish Christian Democrats, founded as the Finnish Christian League (*Suomen Kristillinen Liitto*) in 1957, have elected Eduskunta members continuously since 1970. The absence of an electoral threshold clearly facilitated the Christians' parliamentary breakthrough as in the latter year they managed only 1.1% of the national vote. (Arter 1980: 143–162) At the 2003 general election, however, the Christians polled their highest vote of 5.3%. During his time as Christian Democrat leader between 1995–2004 the bilingual Bjarne Kallis attracted significant numbers of Swedish-speaking Finns to the party's ranks.[15] This may prove much more difficult for his female successor, Päivi Räsänen.[16]

The Finnish Greens (*Vihreä Liitto*) began very much as a capital city movement and many of the pioneering figures were active in the so-called 'Helsinki

1976' movement.[17] The heterogeneous mix of souls who clambered on board the green movement had as their common denominator a reaction against the stultifying political climate of the 1970s, which suffocated the open debate of issues. The demise of the Liberal People's Party in the 1980s also opened up a space in the political centre, which the Greens could occupy.[18] In less than twenty years since their creation as a political party in 1988 the Greens have evolved from an anti-party to an Establishment party. They have boasted the longest parliamentary representation of any West European Green party and in 1995 the Finnish Greens became the first such party to enter a national government. However, having resigned from Lipponen's 'rainbow coalition' in spring 2002 in protest against the decision to authorise the construction of a fifth nuclear power station, the Greens contested the 2003 general election as an opposition party. The Greens' parliamentary breakthrough came in 1991 when the party polled 6.8% of the vote and gained ten Eduskunta seats. By 2003 this had risen to 8% of the vote and fourteen parliamentary seats.

The Swedish Green Party (*Miljöpartiet de Gröna*) was formed in 1981 by a disgruntled Liberal, Per Gahrton, and its founding elite comprised mainly a younger generation of environmentalists, which had lost faith in the Centre Party's commitment to oppose nuclear power development. In 1988 the Greens became the first new parliamentary party in Sweden since the breakthrough of the Communists in 1918. This was the 'greenest election' in Swedish history and the Greens recorded their best result so far of 5.5%. (Arter 1989: 84–101) By September 1991, the electoral mood was very different. The Berlin Wall had collapsed, the Swedish economy was plunging into recession, the Social Democratic government had applied to join the EU and green issues were subordinated to 'bread-and-butter' questions such as unemployment, taxes and food prices. The Greens became victims of the 1991 'earthquake election' and, with only 3.4% of the vote failed to qualify for Riksdag seats. Following the 1998 and 2002 general elections, in both of which the Greens polled 4.5%, the Swedish party has occupied a pivotal position between the socialists and non-socialists. Although never having participated in government, the Swedish Greens have formed part of a legislative coalition with the ruling Social Democrats since 1998 except on matters of European, foreign and defence policy.

The *left-wing parties* in the parliamentary oppositions in Finland and Sweden between 2002/03–2006/07 have been the *post-communist parties*. Unlike the radical left in Sweden, the Leftist Alliance in Finland (*vasemmistoliitto*) has spent more time in government (1995–2003) than in opposition (1991–95, 2003–) since its creation in April 1990. For nearly four decades after the second world war its predecessor, the Communist-dominated Finnish People's

Democratic League, had been one of the leading radical leftist parties in Western Europe, polling 23.2% in 1958 to become equal largest party with the Social Democrats. At the 2003 general election, the Leftist Alliance managed only 9.9% of the vote and appeared to be in slow, terminal decline. Under the female leadership of Suvi-Anne Siimes since 1997, the Leftist Alliance has given particular prominence to its 'eco-socialist' credentials, as well as to projecting a feminist image. The more traditional trade union wing of the party has been less than enamoured of this red–green formula and has resented in particular the way Siimes railroaded an anti-nuclear power position through party conference.[19]

Unlike its Finnish sister party, the Swedish Leftist Party (*Vänsterpartiet*) has never participated in government and it is presently led by Lars Ohly, a man who still describes himself as a communist! Yet in contrast to the Finnish communist movement, the Swedish Communists, and after 1967 Left Party Communists, had been a small, albeit stable element in the parliamentary party system. Between the introduction of the single-chamber Riksdag in 1970 and the collapse of the Berlin Wall in 1989, the Left Party Communists averaged 5.3% at general elections and the party was indebted to the so-called 'comrade vote' – tactical social democratic support – for consistently clearing the 4% barrier. The Leftist Party's strong growth in the 1990s – from 6.2% in 1994 to 12% in 1998 – occurred under the leadership of Gudrun Schyman. It saw the Leftist Party opposed to EU membership and advocating increased welfare spending at a time when the Social Democrats were managing Sweden out of recession. At the 2002 general election, the Leftist Party's vote dropped to 8.3%. Its legislative coalition with the Social Democrats and Greens meant it no longer contested the election as a fully-fledged opposition party, as it had four years earlier. Moreover, Schyman's resignation as party chair in 2003 and subsequent resignation from the party could prove electorally damaging to the Leftists in 2006.[20]

Dimensions of opposition behaviour

In the following chapters (10–12), three analytically distinct aspects or dimensions of opposition party behaviour will be examined and illustrated by reference to the Finnish and Swedish experiences in the period immediately after the most recent general elections in 2002/03. Chapter 10 views opposition party activity primarily from an internal *intra-group perspective*, exploring the role of the parliamentary party group as both actor and arena. Opposition parties are viewed as autonomous policy sub-systems possessing variable policy capacity, which will be deployed in a policy process and produce policy outputs. Perhaps the best example of collective policy-making in the parliamentary party groups when in opposition – certainly in the smaller ones – is the process of producing an 'alternative budget' since this draws on the policy capacity of the whole group. The parliamentary groups' 'policy capacity', 'policy process' and 'policy outputs' are examined in turn and some attempt made to penetrate the highly secretive world of parliamentary group politics.

Chapter 11 views opposition behaviour from the perspective of *the individual party's choice of strategy* or strategies. It is not easy or necessarily desirable to seek to categorise and compartmentalise an opposition party's strategy. Strategies may be shorter or longer-term and the immediate style of an opposition party may offer only limited insights into its underlying strategy. Both strategy and style are contingent, while vote-seeking, policy-seeking and office-seeking will often be overlapping in practice. It was suggested in chapter 7 that adversarial opposition is not exclusive to Westminster-style systems. Chapter 11 illustrates this with regard to Finland, a country that is widely regarded as an exemplar of 'consensus politics'. The focus is on the so-called 'decisive action strategy' (*tahtopolitiikka*) pioneered by the Centre chair Paavo Väyrynen in the early 1980s and which had its dramatic culmination in the 'Iraqgate strategy' pursued by the Centre leader Anneli Jäätteenmäki in the run-up to the 2003 general election. The wider question is 'how does one characterise a strategy designed to challenge and displace the Social Democrats as the hegemonic party in Finland?' By 2003 it was a case of office-seeking with a capital 'O' and to achieve that vote-seeking was critical and policies wholly incidental.

Chapter 12 views opposition behaviour from a collective *inter-party perspective* and concentrates on Sweden after the 2002 Riksdag election. The election demonstrated once again that the historic non-socialist parties remained primarily engaged in competition to gain relative electoral advantage, rather than cooperating to displace the Social Democrats from office. The internal balance of power among the non-socialists had swung in the Liberals' favour, largely at the expense of the Conservatives. The presence of the Christian Democrats since the early 1990s had meant an increased fragmentation on the centre-right of Swedish politics, while the Greens, holding the balance between the two blocs, lent the opposition heightened multi-dimensionality. The analysis focuses on the nature of the inter-party relations among the opposition groupings and the lessons to be learned from the Liberal leader Lars Leijonborg's abortive attempt to weld a post-election government of centrist parties and Greens. There is also discussion of the way in which in situations of minority government, as in Sweden, legislative majorities can involve various combinations of opposition parties – that is, multilateral oppositions and shifting winning coalitions.

The empirical work for these chapters is based on meetings with the leaders and senior figures in all the Finnish and Swedish opposition parties. The interviews were conducted partly to gain an authentic 'opposition perspective' – an insight into the 'opposition mindset' – but also to pick up any 'informal politics', that is interaction between the party leaders behind the scenes. The chapters are to an extent episodic and deal in some detail with particular events – attempts to form and indeed remove governments – that illuminate the bigger picture. The final chapter revisits the main question in the book – 'Are the Scandinavian democracies majoritarian, consensual or mixed?'

Notes

1 For instance, it was clear that the Austrian Socialist Party in opposition after 2000 preferred a return to a Grand Coalition with the People's Party to a 'red–green' coalition with its fellow opposition party, the Greens. Thus Müller and Fallend comment that the efforts of the Socialists and Greens to cooperate and coordinate their parliamentary activities did not exceed the minimum level required to avoid playing into the hands of the government. (Müller and Fallend 2004: 826)

2 It was much more surprising, therefore, that in September 1987 the new Fine Gael leader, Alan Dukes, committed his party to support the governing Fianna Fáil's budget. True, this was only marginally changed from the one drawn up by the previously governing Fine Gael, which had been delayed by a sudden general election. But the suspension of normal "Dáil warfare" and the departure from the highly combative style Fianna Fail had pursued in opposition between 1982–87 led to severe internal opposition to Duke's so-called 'Tallaght Strategy'. One backbencher stated bitterly that Dukes was the sort of leader "who would go out with a fork when it was raining soup"! (Marsh and Mitchell 1999: 52)

3 Writing on Sweden around the time of the shift to a unicameral Riksdag in 1970, Neil Elder captured in consciously idealised terms the essence of the expectation that opposition parties would conduct themselves responsibly. "Public business ... should be transacted in a spirit of cool objectivity with a minimum of partisanship and the co-operation of all. Opposition groups should seek to exert an influence on public affairs commensurate with their strength rather than act in between elections with the overriding aim of getting the government out at the first opportunity." (Elder 1975: 202)

4 The 'gang of six' comprised Raimo Vistbacka, Timo Soini, Kari J. Bärlund, Hannu Kauppinen, Rolf Sormo and Urho Leppänen.

5 The party's curious name resulted from a combination of factors. At the 1991 general election, the party's present leader, Timo Soini, had stood (unsuccessfully) for the Finnish Rural Party as a 'very ordinary Finn' (*tavallinen perussuomalainen*). Four years later, a group of right-of-centre urban liberals revived the name of the nineteenth-century Young Finn Party (*nuorsuomalainen puolue*) and elected two MPs. 'Finns', so to speak, were in the political air and hence the decision to 'cash

in' and name the successor party 'True Finns'. In the order of 60% of their members were also Finnish Rural Party members.

6 'Kansaa kuunteleva myönteinen populismi on tulevaisuuden tie' *Helsingin Sanomat* 8.6.2003.

7 'Perussuomalaiset on tuore vaihtoehto' *Perussuomalainen* 04/2004.

8 Before the election, Bildt and the Liberal leader, Bengt Westerberg, wrote a 'debate article' in the daily broadsheet *Dagens Nyheter* in which they formulated a joint programme for 'A New Start for Sweden'. Bildt also repeatedly exploited the fact that the Social Democratic minister of finance, Kjell-Olof Feldt, had resigned in spring 1990 and in his book *Alla dessa dagar* (*All Those Days*) had been critical of his own government's economic policy. (Feldt 1991)

9 President Mauno Koivisto has related how when the Conservatives finally entered government in 1987, plans for Finnish membership of the Council of Europe were shelved in case they raised concerns in Moscow about a change in direction by the Finnish government. (Koivisto 1995: 278–280)

10 In 1985, for example, under their youthful-looking leader Bengt Westerberg, the Liberals gained 8.3 percentage points to poll 14.2%, their second best result during the period of the unicameral Riksdag. Westerberg had replaced Ola Ullsten (the prime minister between 1978–79) and, although a previously unknown face to most Swedes, he had served as state secretary (broadly comparable to a British junior minister) in the Budget Department throughout the years of non-socialist government between 1976–82. (Lindström and Wörlund 1988: 252–278)

11 One of the seventeen points in the Liberals' new asylum and immigration policy in particular appeared to turn the tide quite dramatically in the run-up to polling. It stated that foreigners applying for citizenship should pass a Swedish language test, a requirement that had been abolished in the early 1980s. (Madeley 2003: 169) The Liberals held that while foreigners were welcome in Sweden, they would be obliged to leave after three months if they could not find employment. This was emphatically not conceived as an anti-imigration measure, but rather was intended to facilitate the integration of non-Swedes. Yet it clearly caught a mood of concern among a section of the electorate.

12 It has been the largest non-socialist party. In the late 1960s and early 1970s, the Swedish Centre both fed and exploited a growing popular reaction against urbanisation and centralisation and what was referred to pejoratively as 'removal van politics' (*flyttlasspolitik*). The talk was of a 'green wave' of protest that would sweep away the centralised decision-making that had characterised Swedish politics and Social Democratic government for decades. Capturing a 'New Left' mood sympathetic to decentralisation and environmental protection and grounded in an intuitive sense that 'small is beautiful', Thorbjörn Fälldin led the party to its best-ever result of 25.1% in 1973.

13 During the campaign the Christian Democrats embraced a number of issues which seemed to represent something of a return to the party's 'moral vigilante' days in the 1960s. For example, it canvassed the reversal of a Riksdag decision in June 2002 to allow homosexuals in a registered partnership to adopt children. The

party also announced its opposition to a proposed change in the law, which would extend to the protection of homosexuals against incitement to hatred. Shortly before polling day, moreover, the Christian Democrats came out in favour of 'chemical castration' for convicted rapists and paedophiles, if during the final third of their sentence, they wished to be considered for parole. (Madeley 2003: 169)

14 A large group, centred around the traditionalist and EU critic Lennart Sacrédeus, apparently believed that the party board was trying to distance the party from its christian heritage. 'Hägglund kämpar för etiken' *Dagens Nyheter* 1.7.2004.

15 Moreover, shortly after the 2000 presidential election, Kallis discussed with the (then opposition) Centre Party leaders the possibility of a merger of the two parliamentary party groups. The traditionalist-evangelical wing, however, has been highly resistant to change and almost certainly contributed to Kallis' decision to step down as leader in June 2004. 'Kristillset selvittävät Reinkaisen osuuden junttakirjeeseen' *Helsingin Sanomat* 20.6.2004.

16 'Kalliksen tilalle halutaan demokraatti' *Suomen Kuvalehti* 24.9.2004; 'Kristillisdemokraattien uusi ilme' *Helsingin Sanomat* 5.10.2004.

17 The present chair of the Helsinki City Council, Pekka Sauri, for example. 'Vihreä valta kurkotti kaupungintalolle' *Helsingin Sanomat* 30.5.2004.

18 'Liberaalien perilliset' *Helsingin Sanomat* 21.1.2003.

19 Siimes' frustration at not being able to take the party along a 'red–green' route boiled over at a seminar to discuss the Leftists' new programme early in 2005. "The Leftist Party is the first and only party to which I have belonged. I have never been a communist or indeed any sort of socialist", she declared. Siimes made it clear that she joined the Leftist Party not least because it stood aside from '-isms'. 'Puheenjohtaja Siimes kertoi olleensa viime ajat kuin kidutettavana' *Helsingin Sanomat* 6.2.2005.

20 In 1996 the Leftist Party officially adopted the suffix 'feminist party' and Schyman has throughout been an outspoken champion of feminist causes. For example, at the 2001 party conference, Schyman delivered her infamous 'Taliban Speech'. In it, she stated that discrimination against women took many different forms but "the same norms, the same structures, the same model are being replicated in Afghanistan as in Sweden". (Arter 2002: 101)

References

Albinsson, Per *Skiftningar i Blått* (Kommunfakta Förlag: Lund, 1986)

Arter, David 'A Tale of Two Carlssons: the Swedish General Election of 1988' *Parliamentary Affairs* 42, 1, 1989, pp. 84–101

Arter, David 'Change in the Swedish Riksdag: From a "Part-Time Parliament" to a Professionalised Assembly?' *The Journal of Legislative Studies* 6, 3, 2000, pp. 93–116

Arter, David 'Communists We Are No Longer, Social Democrats We Can Never Be: The Evolution of the Leftist Parties in Finland and Sweden' *The Journal of Com-*

munist and Transition Studies 8, 2, 2002, pp. 93–117

Arter, David 'The Finnish Christian League: Party or Anti-Party?' *Scandinavian Political Studies* 3, 2, 1980, pp. 143–162

Aylott, Nicholas and Torbjörn Bergman 'Almost in Government, But Not Quite: The Swedish Greens, Bargaining Constraints and the Rise of Contract Parliamentarism' Paper presented at the ECPR joint workshops, Uppsala, April 2004

Bell, David S. 'France: The Left in 2002 – The End of the Mitterrand Strategy' *Parliamentary Affairs* 56, 1, 2003, pp. 24–37

Blondel, J. 'Political Opposition in the Contemporary World' *Government and Opposition* 32, 4, 1997, pp. 462–486

Dahl, R. A. 'Patterns of Opposition', in R.A. Dahl (ed.) *Political Oppositions in Western Democracies* (Yale University Press: New Haven and London, 1968), pp. 332–347

Elder, N. C. M. 'The Scandinavian States', in S.E. Finer (ed.) *Adversary Politics and Electoral Reform* (Anthony Wigram: London, 1975), pp. 185–202

Elklit, J. 'Party Behaviour and the Formation of Minority Coalition Governments: Danish Experience from the 1970s and 1980s', in W.C. Müller and K. Strøm *Policy, Office or Votes?* (Cambridge University Press: Cambridge and New York, 1999), pp. 63–88

Feldt, Kjell-Olof *Alla dessa dagar. I regeringen 1982–1990* (Norstedts: Stockholm, 1991)

Flinders, Matthew 'Majoritarian Democracy in Britain: New Labour and the Constitution' *West European Politics* 28, 1, 2005, pp. 61–93

Ganghof, Steffen 'Retrieving True Majoritarianism. On Mapping and Theorizing Parliamentary Democracies' Paper prepared for presentation at the ECPR Joint Sessions of Workshops, Granada, 14–19 April 2005

Hadenius, Stig *Modern svenska politisk historia. Sjätte upplagen* (Hjalmarson & Högberg: Stockholm, 2003)

Hancock, M. D. *Sweden. The Politics of Postindustrial Change* (The Dryden Press: Hinsdale, Illinois, 1972)

Koivisto, Mauno *Historian tekijät* (Kirjayhtymä: Helsinki, 1995)

Larsson, T. 'Cabinet Ministers and Parliamentary Government in Sweden', in M. Laver and K.A. Shepsle (eds) *Cabinet Ministers and Parliamentary Government* (Cambridge University Press: Cambridge, 1994), pp. 169–186

Lewin, L. 'Majoritarian and Consensus Democracy: the Swedish experience' *Scandinavian Political Studies* 21, 1998, pp. 195–205

Lijphart, A. *Patterns of Democracy* (Yale University Press: New Haven and London, 1999)

Lijphart, A. 'Negotiation Democracy Versus Consensus Democracy: Parallel Conclusions and Recommendations' *European Journal of Political Research* 41, 1, 2002, pp. 107–113

Lindström, Ulf and Ingmar Wörlund 'The Swedish Liberal Party: The Politics of Unholy Alliances', in Emil J. Kirchner (ed.) *Liberal Parties in Western Europe* (Cambridge University Press: Cambridge, 1988), pp. 252–278

Madeley, John T. S. 'The Swedish Model is Dead! Long Live the Swedish Model! The 2002 Riksdag Election' *West European Politics* 26, 2, 2003, pp. 165–173

Marsh, M. and P. Mitchell 'Office, Votes and then Policy: Hard Choices for Political Parties in the Republic of Ireland, 1981–1992', in W.C. Müller and K. Strøm (eds) *Policy, Office or Votes?* (Cambridge University Press: Cambridge and New York, 1999), pp. 36–62

Miller, K. E. *Denmark. A Troubled Welfare State* (Westview: Boulder, CO, San Francisco and Oxford, 1991)

Müller, W. C. and F. Fallend 'Changing Patterns of Party Competition in Austria: From Multipolar to Bipolar System' *West European Politics* 27, 5, 2004, pp. 801–835

Pedersen, M. N. 'Consensus and Conflict in the Danish Folketing 1945–65' *Scandinavian Political Studies* 2, 1967, pp. 143–166

Sartori, G. *Parties and Party Systems* (Cambridge University Press: Cambridge, 1976)

Stjernquist, N. 'Sweden: Stability or Deadlock?', in R.A. Dahl (ed.) *Political Oppositions in Western Democracies* (Yale University Press: New Haven and London, 1968), pp. 116–146

Strøm, K. *Minority Government and Majority Rule* (Cambridge University Press: Cambridge, 1990)

Tsebelis, G. *Veto Players. How Political Institutions Work* (Russell Sage Foundation: New York, 2002)

Wiatr, Jerzy J. 'The Hegemonic Party System in Poland', in Erik Allardt and Stein Rokkan (eds) *Mass Politics. Studies in Political Sociology* (The Free Press: New York, 1970), pp. 312–321

10

Policy-making in the Finnish and Swedish opposition parties

It has become part of the accepted wisdom, both in Scandinavia and elsewhere in Western Europe, that power, or the centre of gravity, in political parties has increasingly shifted from the party organisation to the parliamentary party. Referring to Sweden, Magnus Hagevi states that "during the last few decades, the parliamentary party groups have become more important at the expense of other parts of the party". (Hagevi 2000: 159) The internal organisation of the party groups (PPGs) will, of course, differ. For example, the PPG statutes in Sweden specify that the internal division of labour should correspond to the Riksdag committee system (Hagevi 2000: 149), although, as we shall see later, this is not always strictly the case. In any event, a fundamental assumption in this chapter is that the PPG will be a central decision-making arena and that a variety of policy players will operate and interact within the PPG to finalise policy. Put another way, parliamentary opposition parties are viewed as autonomous policy sub-systems engaged in the process of generating and articulating policy alternatives. Importantly, the parliamentary party groups will not only be arenas in which decisions are reached, but also actors promoting those decisions in parliament as a whole. There are three elements in the analysis. The *policy capacity* of opposition parties refers to the PPG's 'resource bank', which in turn vests it with the capacity to generate policy. The *policy process* in the opposition PPGs involves the deployment of that capacity, that is, the mechanics of how policy is generated. The *policy output* of opposition PPGs refers, self-evidently, to the end-product or increment of the policy process, that is, the various decisions of the group.

The policy capacity of the opposition groups

In analysing policy-making in opposition parties, a basic premise is that the policy capacity of an opposition PPG will be related to the resources available to it for effective policy generation. Inevitably, much of an opposition PPG's activity will come into the category of reactive decision-making, that is formulating a position in response to a government bill or a ministerial statement to parliament. Some, however, will be pro-active, when the policy more or less originates in the party group. Of course, the PPG may on occasions work from, and then develop official positions emanating from an extra-parliamentary organ of the party. In any event, it seems reasonable to speak of three sets of overlapping policy resources. First, there are *financial resources*. Access to financial resources will permit the employment of a body of support staff. The PPG secretariat will be recruited so as to possess the relevant competencies (in law, economics or whatever) and will assist in policy-making, including consulting appropriate external actors. All things being equal, the larger the group secretariat, the greater the policy capacity of the PPG.

Second, while the level of financial resources is clearly part of the equation, the policy capacity of opposition PPGs will also relate to the *manpower resources* available to them. These will include not only the size of the group staff, but the number of parliamentarians in the group and, by extension, the policy knowledge at their disposal. This will not, of course, be readily amenable to quantification. However, opposition PPGs will vary, sometimes significantly, in terms of the educational and occupational backgrounds and interests of their members. At very least, the size of the PPG will have implications for its working practices.

Finally, opposition PPGs will have an informational disadvantage when compared with governing parties (or at least their cabinet elite) in that they will not have the backing of a large body of professional civil servants. Opposition PPGs in short will lack the access to the *resources of information and expertise* available to governing PPGs and the challenge is to narrow the gap as far as possible. An overarching hypothesis might be that "the greater the access to scarce resources of information and expertise, the greater the policy capacity of an opposition PPG". Financial resources and manpower resources are relevant here in so far as they contribute to generating a stock of information and expertise.

In both Sweden and Finland, the work of PPGs is funded out of the public purse and includes support for the work of a group secretariat. In Finland the subsidisation of PPGs dates back to the Party Law in 1969; in Sweden the party groups started to receive public monies in 1966 following legislation the previous year. In Sweden in 2004, the total support for the Riksdag parties amounted to 260.20 million Swedish crowns. Support for Swedish MPs and the work of PPGs takes three forms. First, there is 'general support'. Each party receives a basic annual apportionment. Governing parties receive the basic amount; opposition parties receive twice that amount. There is also an 'additional payment', which is paid in proportion to the number of members of parliament a party has. Second, support is provided to facilitate the employment of political secretaries for parliamentarians and this is calculated according to the norm of one political secretary per two MPs per month. Finally, support is available to allow MPs to participate in international conferences and undertake other foreign visits. This is based on a fixed (higher) rate for the first twenty MPs and a lower rate for the remainder. Table 10.1 sets out the public support paid to Swedish MPs and PPG work in 2004 in millions of Swedish crowns.

Table 10.1 Public support to Swedish MPs and PPG work in 2004 (millions of Swedish Crowns)

	SAP	M	FP	KD	V	C	MP
General support							
Basic sum	1.70	3.40	3.40	3.40	3.40	3.40	3.40
Additional sum	8.21	3.14	2.74	1.88	1.71	1.25	0.69
Political secretaries	31.71	12.11	10.60	7.27	6.60	4.84	3.74
Foreign travel	0.41	0.19	0.17	0.13	0.12	0.10	0.08

Source: Riksdagen: *De folkvalda: Partistöd*

SAP = Social Democrats; M = Conservatives; FP = Liberals; KD = Christian Democrats; V = Leftists; C = Centre; MP = Greens

With funding available, the size of the staff of PPGs has grown appreciably in recent years. In Sweden in 2004 the staff of the largest party, the Social Democrats, numbered eighty persons compared with twenty-one for the smallest group, the Greens. In Finland the size of the PPG secretariats is much smaller both in absolute and relative terms than in Sweden. The PPG secretariats nonetheless reflect the size of the PPGs, albeit not in a strictly proportional way (see table 10.2). The Finnish PPG secretariats are in fact approximately the same, in many cases slightly larger than the corresponding standing committee staffs. Table 10.3 presents data on the size of Finnish standing committee staffs in 2004. It should be noted that the figures include staff shared with other committees. For example, one of the staff of three on the Environment Committee shares his time with the Legal Affairs Committee.

Table 10.2 The size of the Finnish PPG secretariats in 2004

Party	Group secretariat	Eduskunta seats 2003–07
Centre	11	55
Social Democrats	9	53
Conservatives	9	41*
Leftist Alliance	5	19
Greens	5	14
Swedish People's	4	9
Christian Democrats	3	6
True Finns	1	3
		200

* Includes one defection (Lyyli Rajala) from the Christian Democrats in autumn 2003

Table 10.3 The size of the Eduskunta standing committee staff in 2004

Committee	Staff size
Grand committee	11
Foreign affairs	6
Finance	8
Administration	4
Legal affairs	4
Transport and communications	3
Agriculture and forestry	4
Defence	3
Cultural affairs	2
Social affairs and health	3
Economic affairs	4
Future	4
Workplace and equality	4
Environmental affairs	3
Constitutional affairs	5

While the size of the PPG secretariats has expanded in recent years and the larger parties have larger group staffs than the smaller ones, there are no research institutes attached to the parties, as in Holland and Germany, to boost the policy capacity of the Finnish and Swedish opposition parties. It may also be that the traditional linkages between the opposition PPGs and sectoral interest groups – the employers to the Conservatives or the producers' organisations to the Centre parties for example – have attenuated to a degree as groups seek to influence economic policy through dialogue with the government. Party leaders and individual parliamentarians may, of course, be members of outside think-tanks and policy institutes and, in this way, have access to resources of expertise.

The impact of the size of the PPG on its working practices – that is, on the policy process in the group – will be considered in some detail in the next section of the discussion. However, the policy capacity of a PPG is determined in not inconsiderable measure by the kind of parliamentarians that belong to it. Policy capacity is not solely or simply dictated by the size of the PPG. The Finnish Greens, which between 2003–07 have only 14 out of the 200 Eduskunta seats, will illustrate the point. Indeed, they bring to mind H.G. Wells' celebrated characterisation of British Liberals as "a diversified crowd that somehow achieves a common soul". The previous Green Party chair, Osmo Soininvaara, is in fact a former Liberal and has ministerial experience from the second Lipponen government between 2001–02. Another former party chair, Satu Hassi, was once on the hardline Sinisalo wing of the Communists and also has ministerial experience, this time from the first Lipponen 'rainbow coalition'. Nor can the other PPG members be described as typical MPs. *Helsingin Sanomat* depicted Tuija Brax as "a middle class lawyer with a social conscience", Jyrki Kasvi as a "technology enthusiast" and Rosa Meriläinen as "worried about the condition of the globe".[1] Erkki Pulliainen, moreover, nicknamed 'the wolf' because of his hawkish style, is a university professor, first elected in 1987, who has a reputation for working exceptionally long, gruelling days. Heidi Hautala, another previous party chair, is a former MEP who gained the highest individual vote of any candidate at the European Parliament elections in 1999.[2] Not surprisingly perhaps, the existence of such diverse, academically trained and strongly motivated MPs can be problematic in PPG meetings, which have become animated and protracted. The Greens' PPG, moreover, does not have formal whipping arrangements. However, it can scarcely be doubted that the quality of individual members substantially enhances the policy capacity of the Greens' group as a whole.

While it is a reasonable presumption that larger opposition parties will generally enjoy greater access to resources of information and expertise, the increment of the enterprise and initiative of parliamentarians in the smaller PPGs should not be underestimated. When the PPG staff is small, individual MPs can develop and deploy 'networks of expertise' to some effect. The Finnish Christian Democrat leader Bjarne Kallis described two ways in which this could happen. In Finland, unlike Sweden, there is a so-called 'expert stage' in a standing committee's deliberation of a bill. By inviting an expert to appear before a committee and by carefully briefing him or her beforehand – that is, asking for a particular point to be emphasised – it is not difficult to influence the content of a committee report or get an amendment approved. Kallis claimed he briefed experts in this way perhaps five or six times a year.[3] It can also be effective at the pre-parliamentary stage to brief an expert who will then tackle a ministry official on the need to change the content of proposed legislation.

On the subject of the networks of expertise cultivated by individual parliamentarians, anecdotal evidence suggests a tendency to something of an atomisation of the policy capacity of PPGs. Perhaps this is putting it too strongly, but there is tentative evidence of a growing 'privatisation' of parliamentary work at the expense of the PPG as an arena for collective deliberation. More research is needed and the point may apply most to the larger PPGs on the governing side. However, the former Social Democratic minister, Arja Alho, has related how, driving to the Eduskunta, she heard the dramatic news on the radio that it was the Legal Adviser to the President who had leaked confidential information on Iraq to the opposition leader, Anneli Jäätteenmäki (see chapter 11). Having dashed to the Social Democratic group's coffee room to catch up on, and chew over the implications of these developments (the train of events ultimately led to Jäätteenmäki's resignation as prime minister), she discovered there was nobody there! This confirmed her in the view that PPG meetings are no longer well attended and that MPs are increasingly pursuing their own agendas. Mostly under half of all Social Democratic group members were present at PPG meetings, she concluded.[4]

In discussing the policy capacity of opposition PPGs, a distinction must be drawn in the Swedish case between the 'pure' opposition parties (the four non-socialist parties) and the 'support parties' of the minority Social Democratic governments. In the case of the latter, their policy capacity has been enhanced both by the ease of access to ministers and ministry officials afforded their parliamentarians and the creation of a network of party-specific political experts or so-called *observers* in the ministries.

On the point about the ease of access, the Leftist Party group leader, Lars Bäckström, related how, during the brief legislative coalition between the Social Democrats and Leftists in 1994–95, his extensive contacts with the ministry officials were such that he was "in practice part of the Finance Department".[5] Similarly, the Green group leader, Helena Hillar Rosenqvist, described how, as part of the first legislative coalition between the Social Democrats, Greens and Leftists in 1998–2002, Green MPs had more direct contact with the government departments than Social Democratic backbenchers whom, she claimed, displayed signs of jealousy.[6] She likened the Green MPs to 'mini ministers', so good was their access to departments made possible by the three-party deal.

On the second point about the placement of 'partisans' from the 'support parties' in the central administration, the practice dates back to the mid-1990s. Indeed, during the Social Democrats' legislative coalition with the Centre between 1995–98, the latter as the 'support party' had been granted three designated political experts in the Cabinet Office. But the system of political experts or 'observers' was significantly expanded (both in its scale and scope) following the 2002 general election and the renewal of the legislative coalition between Social Democrats, Greens and Leftists. Each 'support party' gained eight 'observers', employed by the government, albeit it only for the duration of the co-operation between the three parties. From the minority Social Democratic government's standpoint, the observer system had a strictly utilitarian function. It was intended primarily to facilitate the passage of legislation through the Riksdag by keeping the PPGs of the 'support parties' informed and involved at the preparatory stage of policy-making.[7] In short, it was designed as part of the process of legislative majority maintenance.

When viewed from the standpoint of the 'support parties', the precise remit of the 'observers' has not always been at all clear and the Greens' group leader commented wryly that after two years in existence she was still unsure what their terms of reference were.[8] In practice though, the PPG leaders of the two 'support parties' were agreed that the 'observers' had made a substantial difference in terms of delivering information. Following the renewal of the three-party legislative coalition in October 2002, Leftist Party observers were placed in five government departments, Finance, Education, Industry, Environment and Justice. In contrast, the Greens' 'observers' were given both a Departmental base – several were located in the ministry of Industry – *and* a policy focus, concentrating in particular on social and economic policy questions. 'Observers' attend group meetings, brief PPG leaders daily by means of emails and telephone calls and generally "act as part of the group's backroom staff". Moreover, the flow of information provided by the 'observers' is not simply one way. They also transmit (if necessary negative) signals from the PPG leaders back to the ministries.

As noted several times earlier in this book, a distinctive feature of the Swedish policy process has been the participation of parliamentarians, including opposition MPs, in the work of the pre-legislative commissions of inquiry. Although the commission system has been substantially pruned since 1982, membership of a commission still represents a valuable socialisation exercise, especially for younger MPs, and it also facilitates the consolidation of policy expertise. An MP's specialist knowledge will be further reinforced by a position on the Riksdag standing committee corresponding to the subject matter of the commission.

The policy capacity of opposition PPGs then is integrally bound up with the resources of information and expertise at the disposal of the group. State funding has made possible the employment of a support team – political secretaries, personal assistants and a group secretariat – to underpin group activities. Individual MPs bring to their roles a body of substantive knowledge deepened by service on commissions and standing committees. Moreover, the 'support parties' during the recent periods of Social Democratic minority government in Sweden have enjoyed privileged access to the political executive and the various government departments. But how does an opposition PPG deploy its policy capacity? What are the mechanics and dynamics of the policy process in the group?

The policy process in opposition PPGs

PPGs are for the most part a secret world closed to outside scrutiny. However, the assumption made here is that the PPG will comprise a variety of policy actors – individual parliamentarians, committee groups, various other working groups and members of the group secretariat – that will act and interact in the process of policy-making within the group. Each parliamentary group will be to a certain extent different and have its own culture and style. Based on interviews and direct observation during the 1998–2002 Riksdag, Katarina Barrling Hermansson investigated the party culture in the seven Swedish PPGs (Barrling Hermansson 2004). She emphasised, among other things, the cultural differences between the opposition non-socialist groups. The Conservatives' group, for example, was hierarchical and collectivist whereas the Liberals comprised a group of individuals without an unthinking sense of conformity (*jantelag*). She concluded that the PPG culture can impinge on policy-making and both facilitate and complicate communication between the opposition parties.[9] The inference to be drawn from her work is that it is important to consider the *cultural distance* as well as the *policy distance* covering the opposition parties.

Whilst taking this point, it seems highly likely none the less that (the normative orientations of its members aside) the size of an opposition PPG will have an impact on its working practices. All things being equal, the larger the opposition PPG, the greater the scope for the dispersal of policy roles among members and the greater the potential for individuals and sub-groups to specialise in particular policy fields. There will be a two-way flow of authority, vertically from the group executive, but also horizontally from the sub-groups that present proposals to the full PPG meeting.

The PPG statutes in Sweden state that the internal organisation of groups should correspond to the Riksdag committee system. In practice, this is the case only in the Conservatives on the opposition side. The Conservatives' PPG comprises sixteen committee groups (*utskottsgrupper*), each containing the party's three full members of every Riksdag standing committee, together with the substitute members on the standing committee and some political secretaries. In the small opposition PPGs there are fewer sub-groups and they bring together members of several (broadly cognate) Riksdag committees, plus their substitutes. For example, the Christian Democrats' PPG, which has one full member and one substitute on each of the Riksdag's standing committees, has five internal policy groups. The Law policy group consists of the members of the Riksdag's Constitution, Justice and Legal Affairs committees. The Environmental policy group embraces the members of the Environment, Agriculture, Housing and Transport committees. The Economy policy group contains the members of the Finance, Labour Market, Taxation and Industry committees. The Social Affairs policy group has the members of the Social Security, Culture and Education committees; and the International policy group the members of the Foreign Affairs and Defence committees and the EU Council (*EU nämnden*). Each of these five internal policy groups is assisted by two or three political secretaries, meets weekly and is concerned both with the discussion of government bills and policy development. As the Christian Democrat group leader, Stefan Attefall, has noted, the policy groups have quite extensive contacts with experts and outside interests and only if a recommendation or proposal is not forthcoming will the matter be referred to the parliamentary group board (executive). The policy process in the Christian Democrats' group thus operates in accordance with a decentralised decision-making model.[10]

A similarly decentralised blueprint, which the small Liberal party group sought to implement in the 1998–2002 Riksdag session, however, conspicuously failed. Of the seven internal policy groups, only the one dealing with Social Affairs enjoyed any measure of success. With a significantly increased compliment of 55 MPs after the 2002 general election, 'supergroups' in the PPG have been created but, as the group leader, Bo Könberg conceded, they still have very little contact with the outside world.[11] The Greens, with only 17 MPs have four internal policy groups covering environmental policy, social policy, foreign affairs and defence and finance and taxation. The Centre, which has 33 MPs has five internal policy groups.

While the size of a parliamentary party group will inevitably have ramifications for its internal structures and processes, the organisation and dynamics of the larger parliamentary groups in particular may well reflect the shift to opposition after an extended period in government. There will be a premium on maximising the group's policy capacity, accommodating former ministers and mobilising rank and file activity so as to generate the policy output consonant with the ambition of a speedy return to power. The overhaul of the Swedish Social Democrats' PPG in 1976, when the party was consigned to opposition for the first time in 44 years is a case in point. There was a similar restructuring during the Social Democrats' next spell in opposition between 1991–94.

During the interlude of non-socialist coalitions between 1976–82, the Social Democrats' committee groups spearheaded the attack on government proposals, so enhancing their position in the party. The committee groups boasted their own chairman, secretary and whip, the latter to ensure a full attendance of members at the corresponding Riksdag standing committee meetings. (Arter 2000: 102) Organisational questions were also extensively discussed when the Social Democrats were next in opposition between 1991–94. In particular, the view was expressed that newly-elected MPs should be able to contribute to the formulation of party policy from the moment they took up their seats. In spring 1994 approval was given to the desire for a 'flatter organisation', that is a wider dispersion of duties and responsibilities in the group. The proposal that the PPG committee groups should assume greater responsibility was accepted and within the groups themselves it was stated that there should be a wider distribution of tasks. In sum, the new rules formalised a substantial decentralisation and democratisation of power within the Social Democrats' parliamentary group. (Arter 2000: 102)

After 16 years in government (admittedly barely one-third of Social Democrats' 44-year hegemony in Sweden), the Finnish Conservatives confronted the challenge, as the leading opposition party after the March 2003 general election, of structuring its PPG in such a way as to generate and project effective policy alternatives. Initially, there was discussion of whether to constitute a shadow cabinet. However, it was felt that for the first year in opposition at least it would be best left to the 'internal market' to see which individuals 'sold themselves' the most effectively. In other words, time would tell who emerged and/or which group members would be regarded by the media as the principal spokespersons on particular issues. Plainly, the former ministers had a head start in this respect.

Second, there was a concern to avoid a viscose, hierarchical structure that would not harness the group's full policy capacity. Rather, the ambition was to mobilise and capitalise on the activities of the committee groups. Committee groups, comprising the Conservatives' full and substitute members on each of the Eduskunta's 15 standing committees, had been in existence for years, but they had been relatively dormant during the party's long involvement in government. In contrast, after the 2003 general election, the PPG requested reports from the various committee groups, which were also asked over summer 2004 to review the part of the government programme that corresponded to their policy remit.

An innovative development was the group's decision to appoint rapporteurs (*selvitysmiehet*) to draft reports, which would subsequently be debated in the PPG. The idea was to harness and give incentives to the energies of new MPs who had some experience in cross-cutting policy fields. As one insider put it: "The PPG would be blind if it only looked at the work of the committee groups". By summer 2004 there had been two documents from rapporteurs. One from Jere Lahti, a 61 year-old 'newcomer' with a strong business background representing the Helsinki constituency, focused on the issue of opening up public services to competition. The other from Hanna-Leena Hemming, a 43 year-old language teacher representing Uusimaa, concerned children, youth and family matters (she has five daughters!).

Independent of the PPG's size and internal organisation, the process of generating policy outputs (whatever their form) will inevitably be linked, albeit in complex ways, to the extent of group cohesion. The 'group chemistry' in turn will be affected by a host of factors including ideological schisms (new or old), generational tensions, regional factors, the continuity of group membership, personal ambitions and antagonisms and the quality of group leadership. Clearly, however, the lower the level of PPG cohesion – that is, the more divided and the greater the strains among members – the more complicated the process of opposition policy-making will become.

Parties are internal coalitions and, as Bell and Shaw have observed, "models of party behaviour that assume the party or, indeed, the leadership and the rank and file to be homogenous single actors are not substantiated by the evidence". (Bell and Shaw 1994: 9) Richard Rose's classical analysis distinguishes between 'factions', 'tendencies' and 'non-aligned partisans' in parliamentary parties. (Rose 1964: 33–46) Apart from the populist-protest parties of the early 1970s – the likes of the Finnish Rural Party and the Danish Progress Party – which have in time split and splintered, only the larger PPGs in Scandinavia have occasionally experienced a measure of factionalisation. Even then, the notion of a faction in the strictest sense of involving a separate organisation within the PPG with its own membership, meetings and rules, is scarcely applicable. The Swedish Social Democrats have had easily the largest PPG in the Nordic countries. Yet, as Olof Ruin has brought out, Social Democratic prime ministers have not generally had to reconcile the differing party factions in their distribution of ministerial portfolios simply because factions as such have not really existed. (Ruin 1991: 64) Nonetheless, the last three decades have witnessed the emergence of new dimensions of conflict, which the Social Democrats' parliamentary party group has struggled to contain.

One was the split in the 1970s and 1980s between the 'concrete socialists' and 'eco-socialists' over the question of the future of nuclear energy. In connection with the nuclear power referendum on 23 March 1980 influential elements in the opposition-based Social Democrats favoured the rapid closure of all existing nuclear plants. (Arter 1994: 81) During the 1990s and into the new millennium, the questions first of EU membership and then EMU membership have divided both Social Democratic parliamentarians and the party at large. It was symptomatic of the split on the EU membership issue that at a joint meeting of the PPG and party executive on 19 January 1993, held to determine the appropriate conditions of Swedish entry and the party's overall EU strategy, a decision was simply deferred until 1994. It was agreed to call an extraordinary party conference in summer 1994 at which either a 'yes' or 'no' would be recommended to party supporters. However, it was stressed that the referendum result alone would determine the allegiance of the Social Democrats' PPG. (Arter 1994: 86)

Rather more clearly than in the case of the Swedish Social Democrats, the larger Finnish parties have witnessed the ephemeral existence of what might be described as *proto-factions*. In the 1970s, with the Conservatives in an 'offside position' in relation to coalition-building, a group called the 'renovators' (*remonttimiehet*) within the PPG sought, among other things, the normalisation of relations with President Kekkonen as a stepping-stone into government. Led by Harri Holkeri, the renovators' decision to back the Paasikivi-Kekkonen line of amicable Finno–Soviet relations was opposed by right-wingers like Tuure Junnila. (Arter 1987: 191–192) In the governing Centre Party, also in the 1970s, a rightist-inclined group of twelve parliamentarians, known as the 'dirty dozen' (*musta tusina*), opposed the propensity of the leadership to prioritise governmental co-operation with the leftist parties. In the post-communist Leftist Alliance, a minority of four or five hardliners, steeped in the Sinisalo neo-Stalinist tradition, has stuck together and, particularly when the party was a member of the Lipponen governments between 1995–2003, defied the group line to criticise aspects of government policy.

Rose's notion of 'tendencies' is more appropriate than 'factions' when depicting conflict in, and the strains on the cohesion of the Finnish and Swedish PPGs. A few examples must necessarily suffice. Thus, in the late 1980s, differences between 'fundo' and 'realo' tendencies in the Finnish Green movement led to a split and the creation by pragmatic 'realos' of the Green Party in 1988. In both the Finnish and Swedish Christian Democratic parties there have been longstanding differences between two tendencies. The *secularisers* have wanted to create a broad-based catchall party based in a general way on Christian values. The *evangelists* have viewed the party as predominantly a missionary organisation operating to spread the word of God in a world gripped by the twin evils of Satan and Mammon. The fortieth anniversary conference of the Swedish Christian Democrats in June 2004 mirrored the tensions between the two tendencies that were etched more starkly following the retirement of the long-serving chair, Alf Svensson. In the Finnish Christian Democrats, the leader Bjarne Kallis' decision to step down from that post, also in June 2004, was confirmed, if not solely caused by the adverse propaganda he received during the European Parliament election campaign that year. Kallis' candidacy was criticised in a circular distributed by an influential low-church clergyman in the party's ranks.[12]

Most of the members of the Finnish and Swedish PPGs are for most of the time 'non-aligned partisans'. Norms of group loyalty are strong and, although Westminster-style whipping is alien to Scandinavian practice, levels of PPG cohesion are high. As Torben K. Jensen has concluded, "in all the Nordic countries, only a miniscule share of all individual votes cast on parliamentary roll calls break with the party position". (Jensen 2000: 232) In a cross-national Nordic survey, 85% of parliamentarians stated that they were satisfied with the norm of adhering to the party line. (Jensen 2000: 222) Importantly, moreover, party discipline has more to do in Jensen's words "with coherence than with compliance". (Jensen 2000: 226) He attaches considerable importance to the growth in the workload of parliamentarians in explaining a long-term increase in group cohesion. The increased workload has resulted in specialisation and a more elaborate division of labour among parliamentarians, which in turn has made it impossible for individual group members to follow each and every legislative issue closely. "They are forced to rely on party experts and, as a general rule, MPs follow the party line unless special circumstances make breaking with the party line possible and desirable". (Jensen 2000: 233) This line of reasoning is perfectly compatible with a main finding of Magnus Isberg's interview survey of fifty-two Riksdag veterans conducted in 1991. Isberg argues that committee groups are the most important arena in determining the party line on an issue, although he adds that questions of recruitment to standing committees remain in the hands of the PPG leadership. (Isberg 1999)

The policy output of opposition PPGs

The size of opposition PPGs might be expected to have implications not only for their policy capacity and the process of policy-making in them, but also their policy output. This will be most clearly the case when there is a numerical threshold (a minimum number of parliamentarians needed) for particular forms of legislative action. For example, the Conservative Party was the only one of the Finnish opposition parties between 2003–07 that could in its own right command the twenty signatures necessary to table an interpellation (interpellations lead to a vote of no confidence in the cabinet). Similarly in Sweden between 2002–06, only two (the Conservatives and Liberals) of the six opposition parties (including the 'support parties') could contrive the thirty-five seats needed to table a motion of no confidence in the government. Of course, it could be objected that interpellations and motions of no confidence, although the product of a deliberative process in the party group, represent essentially demonstrative or *profile-seeking* action. They are primarily intended to point up the failings of the government rather than present clearly-defined opposition policy alternatives. Certainly, the policy outputs of the party groups will take a variety of forms.

First, individual MPs (by no means confined to the opposition PPGs) will table private members' motions, which are usually connected to government bills and to the annual budget in particular. In Sweden the government presents its annual budget to the Riksdag on 20 September (at the latest) and the fifteen days thereafter are known as the 'General Motions Period'. During this time MPs can submit motions either connected to the budget or so-called 'freestanding motions'. MPs can also submit motions in connection with other government bills within fifteen days of their being presented to parliament. In the five Riksdag sessions between 1998–2003, three-quarters of all private members' motions emanated from members of opposition PPGs (see table 10.4). Private members' motions are considered in the relevant standing committee, which reports on them and they then go to the plenary for debate and decision.

Table 10.4 Private members' motions emanating from opposition MPs in the Swedish Riksdag, 1998–2003 (%)

Year	Government	Opposition
1998/99	24.1	75.9
1999/00	22.7	77.3
2000/01	24.8	75.2
2000/02	22.1	77.9
2002/03	29.3	70.7
Period average	24.6	75.4

Private members' motions are usually drafted with the assistance of the PPG secretariat. Their number has increased exponentially, with the consequence that many will not be considered in the appropriate standing committee for some little time. They will invariably then be rejected and resubmitted year after year.

In Finland the new Parliamentary Orders (*Eduskunnan työjärjestys*), replacing those dating back to 1927, were introduced at the same time as the new constitution in March 2000. There were several innovative features – for example the enactment process was truncated from three plenary readings to two – and the rules relating to the various forms of private members' initiatives were systematically set out. Four types of members' initiatives are presented. First, there are private members' motions (*lakialoite*), which can be introduced by one or more MPs and propose legislation or an amendment to legislation. When the motion relates to an existing proposal – that is, it runs parallel to it and seeks to replace it – it is known as a 'parallel motion' (*rinnakkaisaloite*). Parallel motions undersigned by the whole PPG are referred to as 'group motions' (*ryhmälakialoite*).

Second, a 'budget motion' (*talousarvioaloite*) must be lodged at the latest by noon on the tenth day after the government's Finance Bill has been formally introduced into parliament. A 'supplementary budget motion' (*lisätalousarvioaloite*) must be submitted by noon on the fourth day after the government's Supplementary Finance Bill has been formally presented to parliament.

Third, when the Eduskunta is sitting, an MP may initiate various forms of action other than proposing a ready-made piece of legislation or 'parallel motion'. He may, for instance, ask the government to come up with draft legislation on a topic or solicit action from one of the parliamentary organs. Motions urging such action are known as 'request motions' (*toimenpidealoite* – previously *toivomusaloite*). It is the job of the Speaker's Council to determine whether a 'request motion' shall be sent to a standing committee.

Finally, there has been the recent introduction of the 'debate motion' (*keskustelualoite*). This is an initiative deriving from one or more MPs, which proposes that parliament should debate a topical issue unrelated to measures presently under consideration by the Eduskunta. As table 10.5 shows, there were thirteen 'debate motions' in the 2003/04 Eduskunta session.

Table 10.5 *Private members' initiatives in the (January–June) 2003/04 Eduskunta session*

Private members' motions	219
Request motions	157
Supplementary budget motions	55
Debate motions	13

Private members' motions (of whatever type) are usually the work of individual parliamentarians, possibly involving members of the group staff and the PPG is at best simply notified. However, Finnish opposition PPGs will on occasions introduce 'parallel group motions', lending their collective weight to an alternative to the content of a government bill presently before parliament. For example, in May 2004 the Greens forwarded a 'parallel group motion' in connection with the government's reform of the school matriculation examination (*lukiolainmuutos*). According to the cabinet proposal, only Finnish language was to remain a compulsory examination subject and, thereafter, students would choose three out of Swedish (the second national language), a foreign language, mathematics and general studies. The Greens' 'group motion' favoured in practice five compulsory subjects, including Finnish and Swedish. Since this corresponded closely with the position of the smallest coalition party, the Swedish People's Party (which had failed to retain Swedish as a compulsory examination subject),[13] it may be surmised that at least part of the Greens' motives involved seeking to drive a wedge between the governing parties. The suspicion that the 'group motion' was essentially a tactical manoeuvre is possibly confirmed by the fact that there was relatively little discussion of it in the PPG and, indeed, almost half the Green MPs were opposed to it. However, there was also doubtless sympathy for the point made by the Swedish People's Party minister of the environment, Jan-Erik Enestam, that it was scarcely a measure of a well-rounded education when students could graduate from school with examination grades in Finnish, English, mathematics and health care![14] In any event, the Greens' 'group motion' was roundly defeated in the chamber. Indeed, of the various private initiatives set out in table 10.5, 99.1% were either rejected or went unconsidered.

The equivalent of the 'group motions' in Finland are the 'party motions' (*partimotioner*) in Sweden, which are usually undersigned by the party leader and all or most of the PPG. 'Party motions' set out to emphasise the party line on a particular matter and are certainly not treated by the Riksdag standing committee staff in the cavalier manner of many individual motions. Rather, a nuanced response to party motions will be prepared by the standing committee staff, often in conjunction with the committee chair, and this may be debated in full committee. Party motions will often originate in one of the PPG committee groups.

A general feature of legislative politics in Finland and Sweden (and elsewhere in Scandinavia) has been the existence of responsible oppositions providing responsible policy alternatives, and a feature of this has been the production of 'alternative budgets'. All the opposition parties in Sweden come up with alternative budgets, as do several of the Finnish opposition parties. Janne Virkkunen has written that "because of the coalition governments, opposition politics in Finland has traditionally been difficult and particularly so for a small party. The party's publicity value decreases and its voice is not heard in national politics."[15] In a similar vein, Esa Erävalo, in the party organ *Kristityn Vastuu* has noted that the Finnish Christian Democrats had devised strong policy alternatives – comprehensive programmes covering criminal policy, human rights and the disabled – embracing the needs of the weakest in society. However, the problem, he added, was the party's low visibility in the media.[16] It is all the more remarkable, therefore, that small parties like the Finnish and Swedish Christian Democrats have eschewed a demonstrative, media-seeking style of opposition in favour of creating responsible policy alternatives.

In the Swedish Christian Democrats, the budget process begins over the summer and culminates in the presentation of an 'alternative budget' within the framework of the General Motions Period in late September and early October. The alternative budget is the work of the five internal policy committees and often involves bargaining between them, with one committee pushing for more resources in its particular area. There is also dialogue with those local Christian Democratic politicians likely to be affected by the budget allocations. The important point is that for the Swedish Christian Democrats – their sister party in Finland and other small opposition parties – the process of producing an alternative budget is an exercise in collective policy-making in the PPG. It draws on the policy capacity of the whole group and defines its policy for the coming parliamentary year. The party in turn will feed off aspects of the alternative budget throughout the year and thus have a costed alternative to that of the government.

In recent years, the approach of the two larger non-socialist opposition parties in Finland – the Centre before 2003 and Conservatives thereafter – towards the production of a detailed alternative budget has differed from the small opposition groups. True, the risk of giving hostages to fortune before a general election at which the leading opposition party has every prospect of becoming *the* governing party – the logic of Westminster – has a strictly limited application in Finland. Indeed, the distinctive feature in Finland, when compared with the other Nordic countries, has been the existence of three viable majority coalitions. These are a 'red-green' Social Democrat-Centre cabinet, a 'red-blue' Social Democrat-Conservative coalition, or a combination of the two non-socialist parties the Centre and Conservatives. Accordingly, probably the main risk for the Centre as the leading opposition party in the years before the 2003 general election was of distancing itself from prospective coalition partners. By producing a detailed alternative budget there was the danger of positioning itself (or being depicted as) outside the main or mainstream policy consensus. It did not take the risk and the Centre's 'alternative budget' was extremely broad-brush.

For the Conservative Party after the 2003 general election, the perceived risk was of damaging its credibility as the leading opposition party – particularly when faced with the challenge of the Greens – by being ready to criticise the main policy lines of the new government. These had not changed substantially from those of the outgoing Lipponen coalition and the cabinet contained the Social Democrats with which the Conservatives had cooperated for eight years. Making the party liable to charges of cynical, irresponsible opposition was essentially the concern of their group leader Ben Zyskowicz, who was opposed to the Conservatives formulating an alternative budget for the first two years in opposition. Ultimately, however, Zykowicz bowed to PPG pressure and, along with Johannes Koskinen, came up with a compromise and hastily-written alternative budget, which did the party few favours.

After sixteen years in government the Conservatives initially pursued an adversarial style of opposition politics, which stood in sharp contrast to their former coalition partners, the Greens and Leftist Alliance, now also in opposition. The combative style of the Conservative leader, Jaakko Itälä, represented in fact a strategic decision by the party, which was determined to confirm its chairman as informal leader of the opposition against the counterclaims of the Greens' chair to that position. At the party council in October 2003, Itälä delivered a broadside against his former cabinet colleagues, the Social Democrats, which seemed to position the Conservatives as a party opposed to the policy consensus. He insisted that the much vaunted consensus society in Finland simply meant that the central blue-collar federation SAK exercised too much power and, by extension, that its 'brothers' in the Social Democrats also had an excess of power. This, he exclaimed, was despite the fact that the combined electoral strength of the two leftist parties was only about 35%.[17] Itälä had tested (and gained a positive response to) this line of attack at meetings with the local Conservative branches the previous weekend. But the timing and content of his well-publicised speech at the party council meeting took the senior echelons of the party by surprise. It was not that there was disagreement over the diagnosis, but Itälä and the party elite were unprepared for the barrage of media questions about the Conservatives' alternative that followed. Itälä had a diagnosis, but no ready prescription. Early in 2004 he tendered his resignation as party leader and was ultimately replaced by Jyrki Katainen.

Ultimately, Itälä's *style of opposition* seemed misplaced in view of the Conservatives' long sojourn in government and his damning indictment of policies which had changed little from those his party had pursued in power. The style and strategy of the Centre Party, when it was the leading opposition party, will be the subject of the following chapter. During the Conservatives' leadership contest, one of the leading candidates, Ilkka Kanerva, canvassed the case for building support for a common opposition 'chancellor candidate' – an alternative prime minister backed by the opposition as a whole. Indeed, he went further to favour the formation of a single parliamentary party group (*yhteinen eduskuntaryhmä*) comprising all the opposition parties except the Leftist Alliance.[18] There were in fact serious talks between the Conservatives and Christian Democrats both before and after the 2003 general election. Kanerva's blueprint raises the wider question of relations between opposition parties – that is, the *inter-party opposition perspective*. This will be the focus of chapter 12, which concentrates on relations between the Swedish opposition parties.

Conclusions

It is not only governments that have programmes and initiate legislative change. So, too, do opposition parties. Indeed, parliamentary opposition parties should be viewed as autonomous policy sub-systems, which possess variable policy capacity and use that capacity to generate policy alternatives. The policy capacity of parliamentary opposition groups will be integrally bound up with their manpower resources and the resources of expertise at their disposal, although even the smaller parliamentary opposition parties can, and do develop specialist networks with relevant outside interests.

Parliamentary opposition parties should be viewed as dynamic internal coalitions of policy actors – individual 'issue entrepreneurs', committee groups, PPG staffers etc – which will interact, and at times compete to determine party policy. The process will mirror the existence of inter-personal tensions, as well as conflicting 'tendencies' (in Rose's term) in the PPG. Opposition PPGs as a whole, as well as committee groups and individual parliamentarians within them, can and do deploy mechanisms that seek to initiate legislative change ('motions' of various sorts). The policy output of opposition party groups will reflect a variety of factors, including the stage in the electoral cycle, the desired profile of the party and strategic decisions about the style of opposition.

By and large, there is a culture of responsible opposition in Sweden and Finland. However, it will be recalled that the Finnish Green leader, Osmo Soininvaara charged the leading opposition party – the Social Democrats between 1991–95 and Centre Party between 1995–2003 – with a highly irresponsible 'opposition for opposition's sake' approach. (Soininvaara 2002: 135–137) His inference was that this type of inveterate populism approximated the Westminster line of opposition with a capital 'O'. The next chapter deals with a particularly extreme and dramatic case of this type of adversarial opposition politics.

Notes

1 'Liberaalien perilliset' *Helsingin Sanomat* 21.12.2003.
2 'Vapiskaa, virkamiehet!' *Helsingin Sanomat* 22.2.2004.
3 Interview with Bjarne Kallis 12.5.2004.
4 Email information from Arja Alho 18.4.2004.
5 Interview with Leftist PPG leader Lars Bäckström 17.6.2004.
6 Interview with Swedish Green PPG leader Helena Hillar Rosenqvist 17.6.2004.
7 Konstitutionsutskottets betänkande 2002/03:KU 30. *Granskningsbetänkande* http://www. Riksdagen.e/debatt/200203/utskott/KU/KU30/KU 30000G.ASP.
8 Cf the very brief description of their role in Regeringskansliet: *Arbetet i departementen'*.
9 'Kulturkrockar försvårer borgerligt samarbete' *Dagens Nyheter* 29.2.2004.
10 Interview with the Swedish Christian Democrats' PPG leader, Stefan Attefall, 18.6.2004.
11 Interview with the Swedish Liberals' PPG leader Bo Könberg 17.6.2004.
12 'Reinikainen harkitsee luopumista politiikasta moitteiden jälkeen' *Helsingin Sanomat* 29.8.2004.
13 The cabinet voted by 14–2 to make Swedish a voluntary examination subject, but it would remain compulsory in the sixth form, or so-called '*lukio*'. 'RKP: n tuskainen tie' *Helsingin Sanomat* 18.4.2004; 'Haatainen: Ruotsiin ei luvassa lisätunteja' *Helsingin Sanomat* 14.4.2004.
14 'Yo-ruotsi äänestettiin valinnaiseksi' *Helsingin Sanomat* 16.4.2004.
15 Janne Vikkunen, 'Rkp: n tuskainen tie' *Helsingin Sanomat* 18.4.2004.
16 Esa Erävalo, 'Miksi oppositio laihtuu?' *Kristityn Vastuu* 22.1.2004.
17 'Konsensusyhteiskunta muuttui kokoomuksen maalitauluksi' *Helsingin Sanomat* 8.10.2003.
18 'Kanerva tarjoutuu yhdistämään porvarien voimaa' *Helsingin Sanomat* 8.5.2004.

216 Democracy in Scandinavia

References

Arter, David *Politics and Policy-Making in Finland* (Wheatsheaf: Sussex, 1987)

Arter, David 'The War of the Roses: Conflict and Cohesion in the Swedish Social Democratic Party', in David S. Bell and Eric Shaw (eds) *Conflict and Cohesion in Western European Social Democratic Parties* (Pinter: London and New York, 1994), pp. 70–95

Arter, David 'Change in the Swedish Riksdag: From a "Part-Time Parliament" to a Professionalised Assembly' *The Journal of Legislative Studies* 6, 3, 2000, pp. 93–116

Barrling Hermansson, K. *Partikulturer. Kollektiva självbilder och normer i Sveriges riksdag* (Acta universitatis upsaliensis: Uppsala, 2004)

Bell, David S. and Eric Shaw (eds) *Conflict and Cohesion in Western European Social Democratic Parties* (Pinter: London and New York, 1994)

Hagevi, Magnus 'Parliamentary Party Groups in the Swedish Riksdag', in Knut Heidar and Ruud Koole (eds) *Parliamentary Party Groups in European Democracies* (Routledge: London and New York, 2000), pp. 145–160

Isberg, Magnus *Riksdagledamoten i sin partigrupp* (Gidlunds Förlag: Södertälje, 1999)

Jensen, Torben K. 'Party Cohesion', in Peter Esaiasson and Knut Heidar (eds) *Beyond Westminster and Congress The Nordic Experience* (The Ohio State University: Columbus, 2000), pp. 210–236

Rose, Richard 'Parties, Factions and Tendencies in Britain' *Political Studies* 12, 1, 1964, pp. 33–46

Ruin, Olof 'Three Swedish Prime Ministers: Tage Erlander, Olof Palme and Ingvar Carlsson', in Jan-Erik Lane (ed.) *Understanding the Swedish Model* (Frank Cass: London, 1991), pp. 58–82

Soininvaara, Osmo *Ministerikyyti* (Werner Söderström: Helsinki, 2002)

11

The 2003 Finnish midsummer bomb and the Centre Party's 'decisive action strategy': a case of office-seeking with a capital 'O'

In my account of the 2003 general election in the journal *West European Politics*, I wrote that, "in the finest traditions of Finnish general elections, the campaign was as dull as ditch water – virtually an issue-free zone". (Arter 2003: 155) So it was until ten days before polling when the opposition leader played the 'Iraq card'. The present chapter is very different from the others in this book. It is an examination of a high-risk, office-seeking strategy – office-seeking with a capital 'O' – pursued by the first female chair of the leading opposition party, the Centre, Anneli Jäätteenmäki, in the months before the 2003 general election. The strategy had dramatic consequences, which culminated in the 'midsummer bomb'. A new cross-party agreement on the procedures relating to coalition-building, coupled with solid working relations between the two main governing parties, the Social Democrats and Conservatives, meant that office would be guaranteed only if the Centre emerged as the largest single party. Two consecutive periods in opposition, the longest in the Centre's history, placed an absolute premium on regaining office, but to be certain of doing so the Centre would need to displace the Social Democrats as the biggest party. But how was this to be achieved within the parameters of the broad cross-party policy consensus and with an electorate that was notably stable in its partisan allegiances? Failure to outperform the Social Democrats would almost certainly consign the Centre to a further stint in opposition and this, for a party which until the late 1980s had occupied a strategic role in coalition-building, was almost unthinkable. The weight of history bore heavily on the shoulders of the new Centre leader.

History, or at least the history of Finnish government-building until the late 1980s, was delightfully captured in a classic cartoon by *Kari* in the newspaper *Helsingin Sanomat* in 1966. It depicted a besuited and heavily perspiring Social Democratic prime minister elect [Rafael Paasio] tendering a bouquet of flowers to a decidedly 'sniffy' and very large farmer's wife representing the Agrarian-Centre. The text to this 'playing hard to get' scene indicates more about Finnish politics than many a weighty tome. It read: "I have heard that when a woman answers 'yes' it means 'perhaps' and when she answers 'perhaps' it means 'yes'. Is this the case?" – the prospective prime minister asks with some trepidation. The answer is, of course' 'perhaps'! Indeed, for long years the party of the rural producers, the Agrarian-Centre, and the party of the urban consumers, the Social Democrats, cooperated uneasily in government and confronted each other actively through the ballot boxes (hence the subsequent 'hard to get' syndrome). The staple Finnish coalition for half a century after the first 'red earth' cabinet of 1937 brought together the Agrarian-Centre and Social Democrats.

Yet by the start of the twenty-first century, the balance of power between these two parties had changed radically. In 1964 the Agrarian Party (*maalaisliitto*) – it did not change its name to 'Centre Party' until the following year – was the hegemonic party in Finland and controlled the political Establishment. There was an Agrarian prime minister, Johannes Virolainen, backed by the long-serving president and former Agrarian, Urho Kekkonen, the Agrarians were the largest parliamentary party, they had especially good friends in Moscow and the Social Democrats were badly split. By the early 1980s, the picture had changed markedly. There was a Social Democratic president Mauno Koivisto, a Social Democratic prime minister, Kalevi Sorsa, and the Agrarian-Centre had slipped behind not only the Social Democrats, but also the Conservatives to become only the third largest party at the polls. By 2003 the new Social Democratic hegemony was complete. Tarja Halonen, a former Social Democratic foreign minister, was president and there was a long-serving Social Democratic prime minister, Paavo Lipponen, a Social Democratic foreign secretary, a Social Democratic EU Commissioner and the Centre Party had been in opposition for eight years.

This is the backdrop to a chapter which takes on very much a life of its own. The events leading to the June 2003 'midsummer bomb' involved accusations, dismissals, secret informants, startling press headlines and, ultimately a highly-charged dénouement. I have edited the sequence of events quite strictly, albeit retaining the main developments. In the wider context, the chapter relates at one level to our earlier discussion of opposition party strategies and in particular the problems of separating out vote-seeking, office-seeking and policy-seeking strategies – Elklit's "vicious circle of instrumentalities". (Elklit 1999: 83) At the 1999 general election, the leading opposition Centre Party had presented itself primarily as a policy-seeking party. (Arter 2000: 180–186) Simplifying somewhat, vote-seeking and office appeared – or were presented – merely as a means of implementing radical policy change and in particular structural reforms to the economy. However, the Centre Party's detailed alternative policy package, the so-called 'work reform programme' was savaged by a combination of the Social Democrats and trade union movement. The party remained in opposition. In contrast, in 2003 the Centre pursued a line which, baldly stated, involved 'office-seeking for its own sake' or 'office-seeking at all costs'. Though never publicly stated, office was viewed as a necessary minimum condition for challenging the Social Democratic hegemony of power. In the Westminster mould, policy was incidental to attacking and bettering the leading governing party. Indeed, playing the 'Iraq card' was an alternative to the articulation of detailed policy alternatives. The Centre won the election albeit, as we shall see, at a high price.

'Midsummer madness' – Finnish style

Midsummer can be an explosive time in Finnish politics. The first 'midsummer bomb' was detonated by the parliamentary Speaker, Johannes Virolainen, who, interviewed in the weekly magazine *Suomen Kuvalehti* in June 1979, was asked why the Conservatives had remained in opposition following the best electoral performance in their history to date. The Conservatives emerged from the general election three months earlier as the second largest party with 21.7% of the vote and 46 of the 200 *Eduskunta* seats. Instead of intoning the familiar domestic factors, Virolainen inferred there were so-called 'general reasons' – a shorthand term for Soviet opposition to Conservative involvement in Finnish governments.[1] Shortly afterwards, the West German daily *Frankfurter Allgemeine* carried a piece about renewed Finlandisation and this prompted an irate Finnish president, Urho Kekkonen, to enlist radio time to rebuke the Speaker in the strongest possible terms. Virolainen was said to be guilty of "a complete falsification of the truth liable to cause incalculable damage to Finland's standing abroad". Ironically, Kekkonen had only recently returned from West Germany where he had sought to banish the bogey of Finlandisation!

Described as "the most dramatic day in recent Finnish history",[2] the second 'midsummer bomb' exploded on the floor of the Eduskunta on 18 June 2003 and brought down the country's first female prime minister, Anneli Jäätteenmäki, after barely two months in office. It also shook relations between the two leading governing parties, Jäätteenmäki's Centre and the Social Democrats to the very core. The sequence of events – sometimes referred to as 'Iraqgate' – began in January 2003 with the first of the big televised election debates involving Jäätteenmäki, then leader of the opposition, and the Social Democratic prime minister Paavo Lipponen. Jäätteenmäki claimed that, in private conversations with the American President George W. Bush, the previous month, Lipponen had given the impression that Finland was part of the US-led coalition against Iraq. An incensed Lipponen categorically denied the charge, but his party had to settle for second best, finishing narrowly behind the Centre at the general election on 16 March. Jäätteenmäki became prime minister, but found herself answering searching questions about the sources of her information on the confidential Bush–Lipponen exchanges in the White House.

As noted, for half a century until 1987, the Agrarian-Centre was the 'hinge group' of Finnish governments, routinely joining forces with the Social Democrats to form the 'red- green' core of Finnish cabinets. (Arter 1979: 108–127) However, between 1987 and the 2003 general election, the Centre had spent three electoral terms in opposition – 1987–91, 1995–99 and 1999–2003 – during which time the Social Democrats had joined forces with the Conservatives at the heart (a 'blue-red' heart) of broad-based coalitions. These two parties indicated they were ready to continue their governmental cooperation after the 2003 general election.

By the last-mentioned year, moreover, a combination of constitutional change and an informal understanding between the parties meant that only the largest party could be reasonably certain of leading the post-election government. The new constitution, which came into force in March 2000, excluded the head of state from the government formation process, except as a last resort, and elevated the role of the prime minister. (Paloheimo 2003: 219–243; Nousiainen 2001: 95–109) The president had previously coordinated the task of piecing together a new coalition and had nominated both a *formateur* and subsequently a prime minister (by no means always the same person). (Nousiainen 1994: 88–105) Today, an inter-party agreement (curiously there is nothing in law) affords the largest party the first shot at piecing together a new coalition. (Arter 2003: 153–162)

Uniquely among the Nordic family of Agrarian-Centre parties since the Second World War, the Finnish party had twice before the 2003 general election surpassed the Social Democrats in the polls. It did so in 1962, following Kekkonen's successful resolution of the so-called 'Note Crisis' in Finno–Soviet relations, and again in 1991, as Finland was entering the deepest economic recession in its history. The emergence of Jäätteenmäki as Centre leader boosted the party's standing among the electorate, but the Centre and Social Democrats were still running neck and neck in the polls as the 2003 general election approached. Jäätteenmäki thus faced the tactical dilemma of the leading opposition party in Finland of whether to pursue an adversarial line and risk alienating future coalition partners or simply 'sit tight', present moderate alternatives and hope the government would run out of favour with the voters.

Importantly, the structure and dynamics of the Finnish party system in recent decades have fuelled centripetalist tendencies in legislative–executive relations. In Janne Virkkunen's words: "The Finnish system of government, in which two of the three larger parties form the core of the post-election coalition and the other waits its opportunity in opposition, has meant that, inevitably, the main policy lines of the parties are very close to one another".[3] Indeed, unlike the other Nordic countries, there may be said to be three possible majority Finnish cabinets – Social Democrats and Centre, Conservatives and Social Democrats, and Centre and Conservatives.

In the run-up to the 1999 general election, the Centre under Esko Aho had tried to combine an office-seeking strategy and a strong policy-seeking strategy, urging in particular the need for a radical reform of work practices. The most highly publicised feature of the Centre's so-called 'work reform programme' was a local contract model for small firms, permitting those with a workforce of under five persons to be exempt from the binding national agreements on working conditions. This simply played into the hands of the Social Democrat–central trade union federation SAK axis, which claimed the Centre was seeking to destroy the foundations of the neo-corporatist Finnish model of industrial relations. Despite electoral gains, the Centre was left out in the cold and the Social Democrats and Conservatives continued to provide the core of a second 'rainbow coalition' under Lipponen. Reference was made in the press to the possible 'Siberianisation of the Centre' and the threat of the party finding itself in the same 'offside position' as the Conservatives between 1966–87 and especially after the first 'midsummer bomb' in 1979. (Arter 2001: 75) An editorial in the regional newspaper *Kainuun Sanomat* noted that the Centre may have to contemplate a long period in opposition for 'general reasons' – not its relations with the East (Moscow), but the trade union movement. (Arter 2000: 180–186) After the election Aho arranged a personal audience with Lipponen to try and smooth over relations with the prime minister and even offered to sacrifice himself and remain outside the cabinet if a 'red earth' combination could be pieced together. It was all to no avail. (Arter 2001: 78)

The Centre Party's highly adversarial office-seeking strategy under its new leader Jäätteenmäki in the run-up to the 2003 general election then reflected some very basic facts. 1) Unless it became the largest party the Centre was threatened with a third consecutive term in opposition. 2) The immediate electoral bonus of having a new leader, and a woman at that, had mostly worn off and the Centre and Social Democrats were approximately level pegging in the opinion polls. 3) Lipponen was a formidable prime minister who, after the terrorist attack in New York in September 2001, had contrived to reassure ordinary Finns about their personal security. However, the stakes were high and the challenge daunting in a deeper sense than pulling off a notable election victory. Though never expressed in public, the 2003 general election campaign for Jäätteenmäki and senior party figures was about breaking the social democratic hegemony of power in Finland. The Centre leader's highly confrontational style should be viewed against this wider power struggle and as an attempt to vindicate the line pursued by Centre leaders since the early 1980s.

The background to the 'midsummer bomb'

Jäätteenmäki, a lawyer and the minister of justice in a Centre-led non-socialist coalition under Esko Aho between 1993–95, was elected party leader in June 2002. She became the first female chair in the Centre's history. As a fresh face at the helm, the pressure on her to succeed was enormous and the early signs were auspicious. While deputising for the chair Esko Aho – who, having narrowly lost the presidential race in 2000, was licking his wounds on sabbatical leave at Harvard – Jäätteenmäki led the Centre to victory in the 2001 local government elections. Her popularity and that of her party considerably outstripped all others for most of the ensuing period until late autumn 2002. But nothing could be taken for granted. The challenge was to maintain her pre-eminent standing in the polls as she became a more familiar figure. In electoral terms, it was vital that she did not 'peak' too soon.

Jäätteenmäki's position as opposition leader was scarcely facilitated by the fact that since 1995 five parties, ranging from the former communists in the Leftist Alliance to the Conservatives and led by the Social Democrats, had cooperated in a so-called 'rainbow coalition'. This also included the Swedish People's Party and until 2002 the Greens. Since this 'surplus majority coalition' had the backing of about 70% of all parliamentarians and could contrive a broad-based consensus (or at least close ranks) around the main planks in the government's programme, it was not easy for the Centre to mount an effective opposition. It could not risk engaging in neo-populist electoral appeals, moreover, out of fear of burning its bridges to the other two large parties, the Social Democrats and Conservatives, one of which it would need to work with after the election, assuming the Centre emerged as the largest party. Equally, it was imperative that the Centre had a strategy to attract significant support in the 'deep south' – the urbanised triangle formed by the cities of Tampere, Turku and Helsinki – where most of the voters were situated. This was also the area where, as a former farmers' party, it had struggled to make inroads. Jäätteenmäki had previously represented a rural constituency in western Finland, but decided to chance her arm in the capital city Helsinki and the party also had strong candidates in the hinterland constituency of Uusimaa.

But what was to be the substance of the Centre's electoral appeal and how could it differentiate itself from its competitors?

The stakes could not have been higher. Accordingly, Jäätteenmäki, although (possibly because she was) inexperienced in the cut and thrust of televised leadership debates, clearly felt the need to seize the initiative and sustain an offensive against the defending prime minister Paavo Lipponen. This would not be easy since Lipponen had been premier for almost eight years and his avuncular, at times superior manner, was predicated on a special interest in foreign and EU questions. Indeed, he commanded a reputation outside Finland as a European statesman.

Foreign policy questions – until 2000 a presidential preserve – have rarely featured in Finnish general election campaigns. Nor has there been a tradition of Swedish-style party 'leadership conferences' on major foreign policy issues, so that the leading opposition party has been at a disadvantage in informational terms. It was, therefore, an extremely high-risk strategy for Jäätteenmäki to attack the prime minister on Iraq and one that can be comprehended only in terms of the opposition leader's determination to be seen to be 'slugging it out' with the prime minister in the run-up to a crucial election. The 'fresh face' wanted to show that she could 'go the distance' with the prime minister and secure a 'points victory'. The risk was that her point of attack would create an irreparable rift with the prime minister's party and rule out the type of 'red earth' coalition that had dominated Finnish politics for half a century until 1987.

The main sequence of events

The sequence of events that culminated in the 2003 midsummer bomb began with American preparations for a war against Saddam Hussein and the US circular of 21 November 2002 to about fifty states, including Finland, inquiring about their readiness to engage in the process of post-war reconstruction in Iraq. US coalition partners were also asked about their willingness to participate in military action. On 4 December the cabinet's foreign and security policy committee (Utva), chaired by the president, Tarja Halonen, considered the American request. It concluded that, in the aftermath of possible military conflict, "preliminary soundings would indicate that Finland has a reasonable capacity to take part in a *UN-led* reconstruction and humanitarian aid effort in Iraq."[4]

With the March 2003 general election rapidly approaching, the Centre leader went onto the offensive early in the new year. She accused the foreign policy leadership of differences over the sensitive question of NATO (Finland is not, of course, a member). Indeed, she claimed that the president, prime

minister, foreign secretary, chair of the parliamentary foreign affairs committee (all social democrats, albeit in Halonen's case now 'above party') and defence
minister were making conflicting statements on security policy questions. More
arrestingly still, on 11 January, Jäätteenmäki indicted the government with
promising too hastily to assist in post-war reconstruction in Iraq. "Never before has Finland made a decision on possible aid in a crisis before the UN has
requested it." (Ervasti 2004) To this charge Lipponen retorted that Jäätteenmäki
was blind if she could not see the preparations for war that were underway and
that Finland had not undertaken to participate in military conflict.

The feuding continued. In the first television election debate on 29 January
Jäätteenmäki reiterated that the prime minister and foreign secretary (Erkki
Tuomioja) had issued conflicting statements on Finnish participation in post-
war Iraq. This prompted Lipponen to state unequivocally that the Iraq situation should be resolved peacefully under the auspices of the UN Security Council, a line confirmed at a meeting of Utva on 14 February. It was stated that
possible military intervention would require a UN Security Council mandate.
On 28 February 2003, the Americans organised a 'coalition briefing' in Washington for those thirty or so states, that had in one way or another agreed to
help in the Iraq crisis. Finland attended and a memorandum about the meeting prepared by civil servants was subsequently leaked, adding fuel to the flames.

However, the fuse for the 'midsummer bomb' was really lit when, in an
MTV 3 election campaign broadcast ten days before polling, Jäätteenmäki
accused Lipponen of giving the US President too many promises in respect of
humanitarian aid and peacekeeping in post-war Iraq. Her thesis was that this
gave the Americans the impression that Finland belonged to the US-led coalition. The role of the UN should have been emphasised more. It later transpired that the Centre leader had got to know about the White House discussions between Lipponen and George W. Bush on 9 December 2002 from a
confidential foreign ministry memorandum. Jäätteenmäki posted verbatim
extracts from the document on her website in the run-up to the election and
they ended up being leaked to, and sensationalised by the afternoon press. On
11 March, for example, the headline in *Ilta-Sanomat* read: "Bush thanked
Finland for joining the coalition". The same day *Iltalehti* wrote that: "President Bush commended Finland as a partner and thanked the Finnish government for its stance on Iraq and for joining the coalition. Lipponen relayed the
decision of the president and government to respond favourably to the American request to engage in humanitarian aid and peacekeeping activity in Iraq
after a possible war".

It was not clear from the *Iltalehti* story whether Finland had joined Bush's
coalition against terrorism – as Lipponen and Tuomioja claimed – or the

coalition favouring war against Saddam. In any event, Lipponen, plainly irritated by Jäätteenmäki's claims, declared that the imminent general election was now about selecting the next prime minister. On the final day of campaigning, Jäätteenmäki was asked where she obtained her information about the private Bush–Lipponen conversation. She replied that "I have two ears and I have heard all kinds of things, things that I have told other people. I am not on the circulation list for foreign ministry reports". However, at a meeting of the inner sanctum of the Centre's party executive – its working committee, *työvaliokunta* – on 7 March, it later became apparent that Jäätteenmäki had *documentary* evidence to substantiate her claims about Lipponen, but had refused to reveal her sources.

At the general election four days before the US-led coalition invaded Iraq, the Centre narrowly bettered the Social Democrats' poll to become the largest Finnish party for the third time since the Second World War. For a former farmers' party to become the largest party in a 'high-tech', Nokia-led, post-industrial economy was indeed a notable achievement. Ominously, however, as the victorious Jäätteenmäki began the coalition-building process, the foreign ministry demanded a police investigation into the source of confidential documents that had been leaked to the afternoon press (the basis of the 11 March stories). The task of piecing together a new coalition progressed remarkably quickly, although the personal rift between Lipponen and Jäätteenmäki ultimately dictated that the former remained outside the new government. This was a minimal winning coalition of the Centre, Social Democrats and Swedish People's Party, which the president formally appointed on April 17. Jäätteenmäki became the first female prime minister in Finnish history, but her 'honeymoon period' was to last barely three weeks.

On 8 May MTV 3 reported that after one of the last election debates, the opposition leader had allowed members of its staff a glimpse of the Iraq-related documents in her possession. Jäätteenmäki, it seems, had denied having confidential material and claimed they were simply 'briefing papers'. However, there was growing surprise that extracts from the confidential foreign office memorandum were cited on Jäätteenmäki's website before they got into the press. Surprise quickly became outright suspicion and the story refused to lie down.

On 11 June, it emerged that a few weeks earlier, one of the Centre's deputy chairs, Hannu Takkula, had requested and received two faxed copies of the confidential minutes of his party executive's 'working committee' meeting on 7 March. This was the one at which Jäätteenmäki admitted having documents on the Iraq situation, but would not disclose her sources. Takkula had forwarded the faxed copies to two unnamed persons and subsequently *Ilta-Sanomat*

splashed the details on its front page. It was suggested that there was an element of *revanchisme* in Takkula's actions, since he had run against Jäätteenmäki
in summer 2002 for the leadership of the party, but was overlooked by the
prime minister designate in the selection of cabinet posts.[5] At parliamentary
questions on the same day (11 June), Jäätteenmäki confirmed having given a
statement to the police about the Iraq leak and telling them everything she
knew. However, she had been asked not to say anything in public. She did,
however, concede that her choice of words had on many occasions been unfortunate and promised to try and use a simpler, more precise vocabulary.[6]

In an interview in the Social Democratic newspaper *Uutispäivä Demari* the
following day 12 June, the president, Tarja Halonen (heretofore an apparent
supporter of Jäätteenmäki), stated that whilst foreign policy issues could le-
gitimately form part of an election campaign, the national interest should be
protected in giving personal opinions. She expressed the hope that the foreign
ministry leak would be clarified quickly and that confidence between politicians would be restored. She also underlined that the decisions in Utva relating to Finland's Iraq policy had been taken unanimously.[7]

The climax of the Iraqgate affair began on 16 June when *Helsingin Sanomat*
revealed on the basis of confidential sources that the person suspected of leaking the Iraq documents used by Jäätteenmäki was an official in the foreign
ministry.[8] That morning the prime minister met Paavo Lipponen, now
Eduskunta Speaker as well as chair of the Social Democrats, to report on the
latest developments in the investigation into the Iraq leak. Afterwards Lipponen
stated that during their short exchange "political questions had been aired"! A
momentous day ended with the results of a Marketing Radar poll commissioned by television's Channel 4, which revealed that 33% of respondents
believed that Jäätteenmäki had lied over the Iraq leak compared with only 8%
who believed she was telling the truth, and 46% felt that confidence in the
prime minister had been weakened whereas 52% believed that Jäätteenmäki
was still a credible prime minister.

The drama increased on 17 June. *Ilta-Sanomat* revealed that an adviser in
the President's Office, Martti Manninen, was suspected of being the source of
Jäätteenmäki's 'inside information' on Iraq. Manninen, a Centre appointee,
who had worked as a presidential adviser since 1984, admitted writing two
background briefings on the Iraq situation for Jäätteenmäki in which he cited
directly from confidential foreign ministry sources. But he denied leaking
material to the afternoon press (that is, the revelations of 11 March). The news
electrified the Eduskunta. A series of PPG meetings revealed that there were
those in the Social Democratic group who were demanding the prime minister's
resignation, although at this stage the Centre's party group remained loyal.

Ultimately, it was decided that the prime minister would make an announcement to parliament (*pääministerin ilmoitus*) the following day.

In her prime ministerial announcement, Jäätteenmäki denied having done
anything wrong and claimed that her hawkish stance had in fact contrived to
shift the emphasis of the Lipponen government's policy on Iraq. The importance of a UN Security Council mandate was stated more explicitly. She held
repeatedly and forcefully that, although her information was based on two
faxes from Manninen, she had not commissioned the material. Indeed, she
denied having requested or received foreign ministry documents and claimed
not to have realised that the material contained confidential information.[9] All
this did not satisfy parliament and one MP violated the members' code by
shouting out 'liar'![10] The Social Democrats' group leader, Jouni Backman,
intimated that his party had little confidence in Jäätteenmäki's version of events.
The main opposition party, the Conservatives, also suspected that the prime
minister knew about the press leaks. Jäätteenmäki engaged in inter-party negotiations to try to salvage the situation.

However, that afternoon Manninen stated that – contrary to what the prime
minister told parliament in her announcement in the morning – Jäätteenmäki
herself had requested the papers. Moreover, they had also met in a Helsinki
restaurant before the first televised election debate on 29 January. Jäätteenmäki
had asked for information on Iraq and had given Manninen her own private
and secret fax number.[11] Soon afterwards, he faxed Jäätteenmäki the first of
two Iraq briefings. The 'midsummer bomb' had exploded, the Centre Party
group knew the game was up for Jäätteenmäki, but sought to defer the
dénouement until after the midsummer weekend. The Social Democrats refused to acquiesce in this and after a two-hour meeting of the Centre group,
Jäätteenmäki announced her resignation.

Reflections on the 'midsummer bomb'

The events leading to the precipitous fall from grace of the first female prime
minister in Finnish history raise at least three general questions. The first relates to the origins of Jääteenmäki's Iraq offensive. Was it essentially a personal
tirade and/or crusade by the opposition leader or was this high-risk, office-
seeking strategy planned and supported by an inner circle – a core elite –
within her party?

The evidence is very limited and necessarily inconclusive. As noted,
Jäätteenmäki informed the party executive's 'working committee' that she had
substantiating evidence for her critique of Lipponen's handling of the Iraq
situation but wished to protect her sources. This suggested the Iraq offensive
did not emanate from the central decision-making organ in the party, which

seemed to be cast in an essentially reactive role. There were also leading figures in the party, who are known to have had major reservations about Jäätteenmäki's approach. Ten days before her resignation, Jäätteenmäki's predecessor as party chair, Esko Aho, claimed in an interview in *Hämeen Sanomat* that the only advice he gave her was not to play the 'Iraq card' in the election. He continued that while there were different views in the party, he believed that what Lipponen had said to Bush was consonant with Finland's security policy line.[12] All in all, it is probable that at no point in the Iraqgate crisis did the Centre's parliamentary group or core elite support Jäätteenmäki and, ultimately, she was isolated among her party colleagues.[13] The tough, adversarial challenge to Lipponen on Iraq appears to have been largely a personal decision of the Centre leader rather than the senior party management and it personalised the campaign as a battle between the prime minister and the leader of the opposition.

A second general question raised by the whole episode relates to the electoral success of Jäätteenmäki's hawkish line on Iraq. Did playing the 'Iraq card' make any difference to the outcome of the election or was the Centre heading for a victory anyway? Rephrased, was the cost of aggravating relations with the Social Democrats – and to a lesser extent the Conservatives – offset by crucial gains at the polls, which allowed the Centre to become the largest party?

Again, the evidence is not conclusive. The opinion polls in the weeks before 16 March showed the Centre and Social Democrats running neck-and-neck and, ultimately, only two parliamentary seats separated them. There was absolutely no certainty of an electoral victory and for a party out of power for eight years the Centre had not benefited from a significant anti-government backlash (as in 1991). In short, the election had to be won on merit. Equally, it is reasonable to speculate that it was less the substance and/or accuracy of Jäätteenmäki's allegations against Lipponen, than the impression created by these attacks, and their impact on Jäätteenmäki's image as a future prime minister, that might affect floating voters.

Shortly after the election, the deputy Speaker, Seppo Kääriäinen (now defence minister), stated publicly that the Iraq card had attracted the decisive votes that accounted for the Centre's narrow victory.[14] There is reason to doubt this. True, a *Suomen Gallup* poll, conducted after the general election, revealed that about 130,000 citizens, who had initially intended to abstain, ultimately voted specifically to influence the outcome of the contest for prime minister between Lipponen and Jäätteenmäki. This may safely be said to have increased turnout to (a still modest) 69.7%.[15] But this is not to confirm that Jäätteenmäki's decision to play the 'Iraq card' swayed voters her way, still less was the decisive factor in separating the two leading parties at the polls. Both the Centre and

Social Democrats *gained ground* on their performances at the 1999 general election.

The third general question raised by the exceptional turn of events was why did Iraqgate precipitate Jäätteenmäki's fall after only two months as prime minister and could her resignation have been avoided? Could she have acted to nip the problem in the bud or did she contribute to her own downfall by allowing events to escalate into a fully-blown crisis of confidence in her credentials as a politician and prime minister? Several points are in order.

There was clearly a rapid loss of confidence in the ranks of the Centre's main coalition partner, the Social Democrats – especially among those parliamentarians in its PPG who had been overlooked for cabinet office – and residual bitterness over the way Lipponen had been misrepresented and mistreated during the election campaign. It was hardly surprising when Lipponen doggedly rejected Jäätteenmäki's overtures and declined a post in the new government. One possible interpretation of the 'midsummer bomb', therefore, was that it was detonated by backbench Social Democratic parliamentarians – particularly those who stood to gain from a new prime minister and a new ministerial team – for whom the Iraq affair constituted ammunition in a revenge attack on Jäätteenmäki. Such an explanation, however, needs qualifying by the fact that only the prime ministership changed hands – the Centre's deputy chair, Matti Vanhanen, the defence minister, assuming the office – and the Social Democrats' ministerial team remained intact. Unlike the disgruntled elements in the Social Democrats' party group who had lost out in the allocation of ministerial portfolios, it is a fair bet that there were Social Democrats in the cabinet who wished to maximise their opportunity now that Lipponen was sidelined.

The climax of events on the floor of the Eduskunta also led to a manifest lack of confidence in Jäätteenmäki in the Conservatives' ranks. Their leader, Jaakko Itälä, contemplated tabling an interpellation – which would have led to a vote of no confidence in the government – but, ultimately, left the coalition parties to do their own dirty work.

Ultimately, when Manninen countered Jäätteenmäki's version of events by describing their meeting in a Helsinki restaurant, the Centre's PPG, which had been loyal until then, was obliged to face the reality that the prime minister's position had become untenable. Jäätteenmäki had misled parliament, lost the confidence of parliament and had to go.

Nonetheless, there were those at the time who held that Jäätteenmäki's resignation could have been avoided. One variant of this view was that she could have acquired the same information on Finland's Iraq policy by other means. It was argued that from the time of Mauno Koivisto's presidency (1982–94) it had become customary to give the opposition leader background information on major foreign policy questions (presumably on request). Koivisto himself claimed that Jäätteenmäki could in any event have received confidential information as a member of the Eduskunta's foreign affairs committee, although as such she would have had a duty to keep things secret.[16]

The view was also expressed that in a fashion not dissimilar to Bill Clinton in the Monica Lewinsky affair, Anneli Jäätteenmäki came unstuck not so much because of what she did as what she said about what she did (or did not do). Clearly, many MPs felt she had misled parliament throughout the spring when insisting that she did not have in her possession confidential foreign ministry documents. Strictly speaking, however, the argument ran, she was telling the truth because she only had Martti Manninen's briefing paper, although this drew on confidential foreign office minutes. Similarly, Jäätteenmäki could claim to be truthful (in the strictest sense) in saying that she had not requested confidential foreign office documents, merely Manninen's briefing based on them. It was argued that if she had come clean at the outset about what she had done, events might not have spiralled towards an enforced resignation. Challenging the prime minister on Iraq using foreign ministry information would not in itself have led to her fall from office.[17]

In the aftermath of the 'midsummer bomb', several letters to the editor from members of the public insinuated that Jäätteenmäki had sacrificed herself and her career in order [successfully] to save Finland from involvement in war. Two of the Centre's regional newspapers even pushed the case for Jäätteenmäki, who stood down as party chair soon after her resignation as prime minister, to assume a post as deputy chair. In short, there were voices who sought to exonerate and 'rehabilitate' the former prime minister whom, it was implied, had had a raw deal as a result of a conniving and conspiring Social Democratic Party.

In the vanguard of these 'conspiracy theories' were the newspapers *Ilkka* and *Keskisuomalainen*, which had supported Jäätteenmäki in the campaign for the party's chair post and, thereafter, for prime minister. According to *Ilkka*, the Social Democrats and Lipponen pressurised Jäätteenmäki into resigning as prime minister because she sided with the president Tarja Halonen against Lipponen in what were portrayed as divisions over Finnish foreign policy (not least NATO). The deputy editor Seppo Keränen claimed there was evidence of the Jäätteenmäki–Halonen axis in the president and her husband's visit to Jäätteenmäki's home during the Iraq storm in domestic Finnish politics and *before* the opposition leader got in touch with Martti Manninen in the President's Office.[18]

At the extraordinary Centre Party conference in October 2003 – at which the prime minister Matti Vanhanen was unanimously elected the new party chair – Jäätteenmäki appeared to perpetuate a version of the conspiracy theory. She stated that, at the Centre's parliamentary group meeting on the afternoon of 18 June, she had received a note, which stated that if she did not resign by the evening the Social Democrats would withdraw their ministers from the cabinet.[19] Jäätteenmäki's clear inference was that she had sacrificed herself on the altar of sustaining the 'red earth' coalition, which, against the odds, she had succeeded in building two months earlier. She resigned in the national interest and in the interests of her party.

The evidence largely undermines the 'martyrdom myth'. First, there was nothing in Jäätteenmäki's own evidence to the police investigation that implicated president Halonen in her Iraq offensive.[20] Second, it was indeed evident that it was principally Social Democratic pressure that had obliged Jäätteenmäki to resign. However, the content of the Social Democrats' note did not contain a threat to withdraw the party's ministers.[21] Rather, the note held that urgent decisions on the position of the prime minister were needed before the midsummer recess of parliament later that same day and that no other ministerial changes were necessary.[22] Intriguingly, however, it appears that the Social Democrats' party executive had decided at their meeting on the previous evening that Jäätteenmäki should resign and that this decision had been communicated to the Centre leadership, which, of course, included the prime minister.[23]

When, six months later, the Social Democratic Party leadership published its analysis of the March 2003 election result, it was critical of the Centre for its unscrupulous use of the 'Iraq card'. It held that the Centre "sought with vague allusions to create the impression that Anneli Jäätteenmäki was on the side of peace whilst Paavo Lipponen was on the side of war". The report did, however, concede that the prominence given the Iraq question during the campaign deflected attention away from policy issues on which Jäätteenmäki was even less well informed. Put another way, the Social Democrats had not been able sufficiently to expose the opposition leader's Achilles heel – a patent difficulty in mastering the detail of policies.[24] Equally, individual Social Democrats openly expressed their surprise that Lipponen had not defended himself more effectively against Jäätteenmäki's Iraq offensive.

Office-seeking with a capital 'O' and the Centre's 'decisive action strategy'

Three main conclusions stand out from the events leading to the 'midsummer bomb' of June 2003. First, the episode brought out into the open the 'dirty linen' of practices, which had persisted from the era of Finlandisation three decades earlier. In a real sense, Iraqgate had its roots in the past and served as a reminder of the persistence of a *sotto voce* patronage system that became endemic through the dark years of the Kekkonen presidency in the 1970s and into the 1980s. As the two leading coalition parties before 1987, the Social Democrats and Centre operated a 'spoils system' and fought over, and carved up senior administrative appointments between them. The critics of the party politicisation of the senior echelons of government departments claimed that the patronage system contributed to an institutional inertia, since sections within ministries were headed by appointees of parties opposed to one another. But the clientelism, it seems, extended even to the staff of the President's Office. In an interview in the Swedish-language daily *Hufvudstadsbladet*, the former Centre chair, Paavo Väyrynen (1980–90), acknowledged that when he led the party he was in regular contact with Manninen, although he received no written transmissions from the President's Office. Väyrynen stated that Manninen was a politically motivated appointment designed precisely to provide the Centre with access to the President's Office at a time when the President and his senior adviser were social democrats.[25]

In this light, Manninen during the Iraqgate affair was just doing what he had always done – and what was standard practice – albeit this time putting 'pen to paper' and the paper(s) into the fax machine. Manninen's attorney stated publicly that what Manninen had done in providing (partly confidential) material was accepted practice, but that Jäätteenmäki had broken the rules of the clientelist system – respected by her predecessors, Väyrynen and Aho – by using the information, and citing from it (on her website) during the election campaign.[26]

Second, although her adversarial line on Iraq and the Iraqgate aftermath ultimately isolated Jäätteenmäki from her party, the strategy should not be seen in isolation. Rather, it should be viewed as the culmination of a concerted challenge on the Social Democrats' hegemony of power, which the Centre had pursued for the previous twenty years. While Jäätteenmäki's Iraq offensive was a high-risk course of action, the strategy of challenging the Social Democrats for the status of leading party in Finland dated back to soon after Väyrynen's accession as party leader in 1980. In the 1970s, the Social Democrats and Centre combined regularly in government under the chairmanship axis of Kalevi Sorsa and Johannes Virolainen. However, the retirement in 1981 on health grounds of the long-serving president, Urho Kekkonen, who had worked to maintain the power stronghold of his former party (the Agrarian-Centre), ushered in what the Centre Party secretary at the time, Seppo Kääriäinen, has described as the party's "danger years". (Kääriäinen 2002: 230) The following year, 1982, a social democrat, Mauno Koivisto, was elected president for the first time; the Conservatives had for a decade surpassed the Centre as the largest non-socialist party; and there were still residual intra-party divisions deriving from the selection of Centre's presidential candidate. The party leadership had opted for Ahti Karjalainen whereas the rank-and-file had successfully backed former chair Johannes Virolainen. He came in third behind Koivisto *and* the Conservative candidate.

Against the backdrop of pessimistic prognoses about the Centre's future expressed by members of its executive, the party chair Väyrynen set out aggressively on a two-stage strategy designed to reunite the party and revive its electoral fortunes. First, there was to be the creation of a centrist bloc of parties – the Liberals joined the Centre, while the Centre, the Swedish People's Party and Finnish Rural Party coordinated their activities in government. (Arter 1987: 326–358) The opposition-based Finnish Christian League later joined this 'centre bloc'.[27] Second, the centrist bloc was to challenge the Social Democrats and, in league with the Conservatives, displace them from power.

Väyrynen's so-called 'decisive action strategy' (*tahtopolitiikka*) ultimately led in rather unseemly circumstances to the collapse of 'red earth' cooperation in 1987. In December the previous year, Väyrynen did a secret deal (*kassakaappisopimus*) with the Conservative opposition leader, Ilkka Suominen, and the Swedish People's Party chair, Christoffer Taxell. It was agreed that if the non-socialist parties gained a majority at the March 1987 general election, they would form a coalition government. Both Väyrynen and Taxell were at the time ministers in a 'red earth' coalition led by the Social Democrat Kalevi Sorsa! In the event, despite a conducive election result, president Koivisto scuppered the secret plan and appointed the Conservative Harri Holkeri to lead a Conservative-Social Democratic based coalition.[28] Väyrynen's successor Aho did manage to piece together a non-socialist coalition when he became the youngest prime minister in Finnish history in 1991. Having steered Finland through the worst economic recession in its history, however, Aho's Centre was soundly beaten at the polls in 1995, although at the general election four years later, Aho came within six thousand votes of defeating the Social Democrats.

It is imperative, therefore, not to see Jäätteenmäki's Iraqgate strategy in isolation. It was in the same assertive mould as her two predecessors as party leaders. The election was presented and broadly perceived as a two-party contest for the prime minister's post between the Centre and Social Democrats. When these two main rivals subsequently formed the core of the new Jäätteenmäki-led coalition, the political science professor, Tuomo Martikainen, complained *inter alia* that this showed scant respect for the will of the electorate.[29] More interestingly perhaps, it appeared to represent significant *party system change* in Peter Mair's sense of change in the nature of elite inter-party relationships (see chapter 3). The Conservatives were consigned to opposition for the first time in sixteen years, all but four of them with the Social Democrats, and the leading governing party, the Social Democrats, and the leading opposition party, the Centre, joined hands in government. This new red–green partnership withstood the crisis of confidence provoked by Iraqgate, if only just!

A final conclusion relates to the future of adversarial opposition – 'office for the sake of office' – strategies in a multi-party system, which has lacked the bipolarity of Westminster or even Swedish politics. The Centre leader and new prime minister, Matti Vanhanen, appeared to set his party on a diametrically different course. Vanhanen had been the architect of the 'work reform programme' in 1998 which, although containing much solid substance, had been exploited by the ruling Social Democrats and ultimately watered down before the 1999 general election campaign began. Much to the astonishment of most, and dismay of many in the Centre, an apparently chastened Vanhanen had even suggested before the 2003 general election that, if the Centre became the largest party, a reasonable price of coalition cooperation with the Social Democrats would be to allow Lipponen to continue as prime minister. For him a viable office-seeking strategy meant abandoning the combative 'decisive action' line of Väyrynen and his successors and, possibly too, serious hopes of smashing the Social Democrats' power base in Finland.

Vanhanen exploited the Centre's period of post-Jäätteenmäki convalescence, and his own unanimous elevation to party chair, to declare a change in party strategy. There was to be a discarding of 'decisive action thinking' and a return to the less adversarial approach of the Virolainen years. Vanhanen set out his thinking in the party organ *Suomenmaa*. "Without doubt the strategy of challenging the Social Democrats has kept the Centre on its toes and produced some of the party's best results. But, ultimately, success in politics is measured by how much a party is able to influence policy decisions. If the strategy leads mainly to exclusion from government, it cannot be regarded as particularly successful."[30] It was important to be able to take part in government and so influence policy without necessarily being the largest party, Vanhanen concluded. Vanhanen reiterated the point following his election as Centre chair in October 2003. "We will challenge the problems of the day and not our competitors. Negotiate, compromise and manage the affairs of state – that is my philosophy in a nutshell."[31] Vanhanen's chosen direction implicitly recognised that in practice ruling coalitions in Finland require Social Democratic involvement. Clearly, this policy-seeking strategy, designed to facilitate the Centre Party's participation in government in the longer term, is not without risks.

If the Centre prime minister and his party's cabinet colleagues are seen to be the Social Democrats' lapdogs, the Conservatives could make real electoral hay.[32]

Notes

1 'Hallituksen teko oli hallan torjuntaa' *Suomen Kuvalehti* 25, 15, 1979, pp. 20–22.

2 Atte Jääskeläinen 'Jäätteenmäen eron syy oli luottamuspula' *Helsingin Sanomat* 7.10.2003.

3 Janne Virkkunen, 'Kokoomus vielä tuuliajolla' *Helsingin Sanomat* 1.5.2004.

4 'Halonen: Vaaleissa saa käyttää aseena ulkopolitikka mutta varovasti' *Helsingin Sanomat* 16.6.2003.

5 'Keskustan vuotajan epäillään löytyvän puoluejohdosta' *Helsingin Sanomat* 12.6.2003. Takkula, who represented the Lapland constituency, insinuated that he believed he warranted a ministerial portfolio on the basis of the considerable size of his vote.

6 'Jäätteenmäki katuu sananvalintojaan' *Helsingin Sanomat* 13.6.2003. This prompted an exasperated SDP chair of the parliamentary foreign affairs committee to exclaim: "Wouldn't it be simply honest of the prime minister to acknowledge that the campaign moped had run out of control and that your Iraq policy was pure opportunism. Then the book could be closed on this whole Iraq business".

7 'Halonen: Vaaleissa saa käyttää aseena ulkopolitiikka mutta varovasti' *Helsingin Sanomat* 14.6.2003.

8 'Irak-vuodosta epäilty on ulkoministeriön virkamies' *Helsingin Sanomat* 16.6.2003.

9 'Näin Jäätteenmäki kertoi eduskunnalle' *Helsingin Sanomat* 19.6.2003.

10 'Hurja päivä Arkadianmäellä' *Helsingin Sanomat* 19.6.2003.

11 'Uusi paljastus laukaisi Jäätteenmäen pakkoeron' *Helsingin Sanomat* 19.6.2003.

12 'Aho varoitti Jäätteenmäkeä Irak-kortista' *Helsingin Sanomat* 8.8.2003.

13 Atte Jääskeläinen, 'Lappu peitti poliittiset strategiat' *Helsingin Sanomat* 11.10.2003.

14 'Komeasti korkealle, nolosti alas' *Helsingin Sanomat* 20.6.2003.

15 'Pääministeri kysymys tuskin ratkaisi eduskuntavaaleja' *Helsingin Sanomat* 5.6.2003.

16 'Komeasti korkealle, nolosti alas' *Helsingin Sanomat* 20.6.2003.

17 The Green leader, Osmo Soininvaara put the case. "At the outset it was probably a matter of a fairly innocent exchange of information on Jäätteenmäki's part. Finland is the type of consensus society in which one or other politician receives confidential information from time to time. But we have got a type of Skiing Federation mentality [referring to the dogged denial until the very last minute by the Federation's executive body of doping offences committed by its Olympians]. We admit things only when we are caught in the creel." Laura Pekonen, 'Juristit kompastuivat kieleensä' *Helsingin Sanomat* 20.6.2003.

18 'Ilkka: Jäätteenmäen ero johtui asettumisesta Halosen tueksi' *Helsingin Sanomat* 28.8.2003.

19 'Jäätteenmäen jäähyväiset: "Rakastan teitä"' *Helsingin Sanomat* 6.10.2003.

20 'Jäätteenmäen kuulustelut eivät sisällä paljastuksia Halosesta' *Helsingin Sanomat*

29.8.2003.

21 'Jouni Backman lappukohusta: Olen kertonut nämä asiat useaan kertaan' *Helsingin Sanomat* 26.10.2003.

22 Jouni Backmanin mukaan kohutun viestilapun sävy on töksäyttävä' *Helsingin Sanomat* 8.10.2003.

23 'Demarit päättivät Jäätteenmäen kohtalosta jo edellisiltana' *Helsingin Sanomat* 25.10.2003.

24 'Sdp:n vaalianalyysi ei peitä katkeruutta keskustaa kohtaan' *Helsingin Sanomat* 26.9.2003.

25 'Hbl: Manninen oli keskustan lähde jo Väyrysen aikana' *Helsingin Sanomat* 12.10.2003.

26 'Asianajaja Wuori: Jäätteenmäki tönaisi hyvä veli-jarjestelmää' *Helsingin Sanomat* 15.10.2003.

27 The Liberal People's Party left the Centre Party's organisation to become an independent party again in 1986.

28 Unto Hämäläinen, 'Kun punamulta rapistui' *Helsingin Sanomat* 23.3.2003.

29 Tuomo Martikainen, 'Vaaleissa ei saa pelata kaksilla korteilla' *Helsingin Sanomat* 5.4.2003.

30 'Matti Vanhanen aikoo lopettaa Sdp:n haastamisen' *Helsingin Sanomat* 4.10.2003.

31 'Vanhasen keskusta hakee yhteistyötä' *Helsingin Sanomat* 5.10.2003.

32 In late March 2004 the Helsinki Magistrates Court ruled that the presidential adviser, Martti Manninen, had wittingly provided the leader of the opposition with confidential material and was thus guilty of contravening the official secrets act. He was fined. However, there was insufficient evidence to convict Anneli Jäätteenmäki of the charge of aiding and abetting Manninen to disclose confidential material. The court none the less stated that it found Manninen's version of events to be more reliable in many particulars. But it could not be proven that Jäätteenmäki actively pressed Manninen for confidential material and she was acquitted. 'Jäätteenmäen syytteet nurin', Manniselle 80 päiväsakkoa' *Helsingin Sanomat* 20.3.2004.

References

Arter, David 'The Finnish Centre Party: Profile of a 'Hinge Group' *West European Politics* 2, 1, 1979, pp. 108–127

Arter, David 'Liberal Parties in Finland: From Perennial Coalition Actors to an Extra-Parliamentary Role', in E. Kirchner (ed.), *Liberal Parties in Western Europe* (Cambridge University Press: Cambridge, 1987), pp. 326–358

Arter, David 'The Finnish Election of 21 March 1999: Towards a Distinctive Model of Government?' *West European Politics* 23, 1, 2000, pp. 180–186

Arter, David 'The Finnish Centre Party: A Case of Successful Transformation?', in David Arter (ed.) *From Farmyard to City Square?* The Electoral Adaptation of the Nordic Agrarian Parties (Ashgate: Aldershot, 2001), pp. 59–95

Arter, David 'From the "Rainbow Coalition" Back Down to "Red Earth"? The 2003

Finnish General Election' *West European Politics* 26, 3, 2003, pp. 153–162

Elklit, Jørgen 'Party Behaviour and the Formation of Minority Coalition Governments: Danish Experience from the 1970s and 1980s', in Wolfgang C. Müller and Kaare Strøm (eds) *Policy, Office or Votes?* (Cambridge University Press: Cambridge, 1999), pp. 63–88

Ervasti, Pekka *Irakgate – Pääministerin nousu ja ero* (Gummerus: Jyväskylä, 2004)

Kääriäinen, Seppo *Sitä niittää, mitä kylvää* (Gummerus: Jyväskylä, 2002)

Nousiainen, Jaakko 'Finland: Ministerial Autonomy, Constitutional Collectivism, and Party Oligarchy', in Michael Laver and Kenneth A. Shepsle (eds) *Cabinet Ministers and Parliamentary Government* (Cambridge University Press: Cambridge, 1994), pp. 88–105

Nousiainen, Jaakko 'From Semi-Presidentialism to Parliamentary Government: Political and Constitutional Developments in Finland' *Scandinavian Political Studies* 24, 2, 2001, pp. 95–109

Paloheimo, Heikki, 'The Rising Power of the Prime Minister in Finland' *Scandinavian Political Studies* 26, 2, 2003, pp. 219–243

12

Minority government, shifting majorities and multilateral opposition: Sweden in the new millennium

According to the Riksdag Speaker, Björn von Sydow, "non-socialist opposition in Sweden is weak whereas Social Democratic opposition is strong".[1] His inference is clear: the non-socialist opposition has been weak because it has been divided, lacking in cohesion and, by extension, unable to dislodge the ruling Social Democrats from power. Unlike Finland, Swedish politics has been characterised by a fundamental bipolarity and governments have comprised *either* the Social Democrats *or* the non-socialist parties. Yet while there has been an alternative government option, an alternation of power in Sweden has been relatively rare. Only between 1976–82 and 1991–94 have there been short interludes of non-socialist government. Indeed, Sweden has probably come as close to having a *permanent opposition* as is possible in a liberal democracy. This chapter seeks to present an inter-party opposition perspective. The first part examines relations between the Swedish non-socialist parties and, in particular, the Liberal leader's attempt to build a non-socialist coalition of centrist parties and Greens following the 2002 general election.

In situations of minority government, the opposition parties have by definition a majority of parliamentary seats and for the government, therefore, majority-building is a pre-requisite for the enactment of a legislative programme. In Sweden since 1998 majority-building has involved the minority Social Democratic cabinets forging a legislative coalition with the Greens and Left Party. The second part of this chapter analyses the way on a number of questions – notably the intended imposition of transitional restrictions on immigrant workers from the new East European EU countries – not covered by the legislation coalition, Sweden has witnessed the politics of shifting majorities and multilateral oppositions. The final section considers the evidence of heightened inter-party co-operation between the non-socialist opposition parties in the build-up to the 2006 Riksdag election. Have they finally digested von Sydow's point about the structural weakness of non-socialist opposition and learned the lessons of history?

The non-socialists' dilemma

From a Swedish non-socialist perspective, the lesson of history is unmistakable. There has been an endemic fragmentation on the centre-right of Swedish politics and the three traditional non-socialist parties, the Agrarian-Centre, Liberals and Conservatives, have primarily been engaged in competition to gain relative electoral advantage rather than co-operating to displace the Social Democrats. The 'balance of power' between the old non-socialist parties has varied over the decades and each 'dog', so to speak, has had its day. The Liberals were pre-eminent in the late 1940s and early 1950s, the Centre in the late 1960s and most of the 1970s and the Conservatives in the 1980s and 1990s. There has been ephemeral talk of a merger between the Centre and Liberals, but this has come to nothing.[2] Rather, the Swedish non-socialists have been 'wilderness parties', their decades in the opposition wilderness broken by only two short periods in government in the late 1970s and early 1990s. Oversimplifying only a little, it could be said that non-socialist cooperation has been seen as a last resort rather than a first option – something to contemplate when all else fails. True, when it came to the crunch it was possible in 1976 finally to dislodge the Social Democrats. But this type of 'crunch co-operation' has been the exception and it has not been able to 'paper over' a number of deep divisions (on energy and taxation questions, for example) between the non-socialists in office.

Moreover, the brief periods of non-socialist government have coincided with difficult economic times, lending the Social Democrats in opposition ready material with which to discredit the centre-right as a competent government option. After forty-four years of virtually unbroken Social Democratic rule between 1932–76 there was a heavy irony in the way, during a period of economic recession, Thorbjörn Fälldin's coalition between 1976–78 felt obliged to bail out such ailing traditional industries as shipbuilding and steel. Carl Bildt's non-socialist coalition between 1991–94 fared even worse and was required to manage the economy during the worst recession in Swedish history. This was a period characterised by what was known as 'the Swedish disease' of a bloated public sector, along with bankruptcies, mass unemployment and a spiralling national debt. Not surprisingly, therefore, a basic electoral premise of the Social Democrats has been that the non-socialists are incapable of running the economy and should not be trusted with power.

Since their return to office in 1994, the Social Democrats under Ingvar Carlsson (1994–96) and Göran Persson (since 1996) have formed single-party, minority cabinets, which have functioned on the basis of legislative coalitions with one or more of the opposition parties. The 'support party' between 1994–95 was the post-communist Leftist Party, which was summarily ditched in

favour of an arrangement with the Centre between 1995–98, designed to put
Sweden's economic house back in order. This legislative coalition 'across the
blocs' was viewed in some quarters as evidence of the classic Social Democratic 'divide and rule' strategy towards the non-socialist opposition. The idea,
it would be argued, has been to undermine non-socialist unity and heighten
intra-bloc rivalries by identifying, isolating and working with a non-socialist
party 'in the national interest'. There was a similar Social Democratic arrangement with the Liberals in 1990, though never as yet with the Conservatives.
Since 1998 the legislative coalition has been 'bloc based', the Social Democrats working with the Greens and Leftists (except in matters of foreign, security and defence policy). This has been a sub-optimal solution for both 'support parties', which have pressed hard to enter government.

Following the 2002 general election, the traditional fragmentation in the
non-socialist camp was heightened – as it had been since 1991 – by a solid
showing from the Christian Democrats. There were now four rather than three
non-socialist parties to be reckoned with. The internal 'balance of power' had
swung in the Liberals' favour, largely at the expense of the Conservatives, while
the Greens held the balance between the two blocs and possessed obvious veto
potential. Could they be attracted into government by Lars Leijonborg's attempt to form a post-election coalition of centrist parties and Greens? Furthermore, would 'crunch co-operation' suffice to oust the Social Democrats?
Although improving their electoral performance on 1998, the Social Democrats had narrowly failed to reach the symbolic 40% mark. Persson, their leader,
was characteristically bombastic, but they would need 'support parties' either
as part of the government or from opposition.

Building an opposition-based alternative to Social Democratic govern-
ment: the Leijonborg initiative of September 2002

During the final days of the 2002 general election campaign, the four non-
socialist parties contrived a strong show of unity. Their leaders shared a plat-
form together at a big outdoor rally on the eve of polling and played down
their differences in public. This was particularly noticeable in the televised
'party leaders' debate', which was broadcast two days before voting. There
were also suitably evasive responses to the question of which of the non-socialist leaders would be best equipped to become the next prime minister. In the
event, the election result markedly shifted the distribution of seats in the non-
socialist bloc. The Liberals won 48 seats and almost tripled their parliamentary representation to become the third largest party behind the Social Democrats (144) and Conservatives (55). The Conservatives' poor result – they lost
27 seats – handed the initiative to the Liberal leader Lars Leijonborg who,

already on election night, made it clear that he would do everything in his power to prevent another Social Democratic government. The onus was on the non-socialist opposition, however, since, according to the constitution, the Social Democrats could sit tight until such time as they received a vote of no confidence.

The strategic player in the coalition-building process was the Green Party, which with 17 seats held the balance of power between the two blocs in the Riksdag. The combined tally of the two left-wing parties, the Social Democrats and Leftists was 174 seats, while the Conservatives, Liberals, Christian Democrats and Centre had a combined 158 seats altogether. Two things became apparent when the election dust began to settle. First, the Green Party intended to exploit its pivotal position to the full and announced it would not support any government in which it did not have seats. Equally, one of its two party spokespersons, Maria Wetterstrand, was clearly directing her comments at the prime minister Persson when stating that the Greens could not contemplate supporting a non-socialist coalition, especially not one that contained the Christian Democrats and Conservatives.

Second, it quickly became evident that the early post-election negotiations between the government and the Greens were not proceeding smoothly. On 22 September, the second Greens' spokesperson, Peter Eriksson, publicly expressed irritation at the arrogant attitude of the Social Democrats. At the same time he announced the Greens' decision also to enter coalition negotiations with the centre-based Liberals, Christian Democrats and Centre. On Monday 23 September, talks between these parties began in earnest on what was a wholly new construct in Swedish politics, a minority cabinet of the aforementioned parties. This would rest on the tacit support of the Conservatives. It was decided to concentrate the coalition talks on three policy areas, the economy, family policy and infrastructure. For the Greens the prospect of three ministerial posts provided the real spur.

At this stage the Green Party was involved in parallel negotiations with both government and opposition parties. It had entered talks with the centre-based non-socialist parties but negotiations with the Social Democrats, although strained, had not completely broken down. Moreover, it appeared that cooperation with the Social Democrats and Leftists was the Greens' preferred option, although the personal chemistry between the Green and Social Democratic leaderships was anything but good. Equally, there were obvious pitfalls in the way of a coalition with the centrist parties – divisive issues such as EMU, family policy and NATO.

Although heading the largest non-socialist party, albeit it one drastically reduced in size, the Conservative leader Bo Lundgren found himself potentially marginalised by developments. His position was scarcely facilitated by the insistence of a Youth Organisation figure, Tove Lifvendahl, that the Conservative Party should detach itself from the other non-socialists and profile itself as 'a party of ideals', that is as an 'opposition of principle'.[3] The Conservatives would, however, hold the balance in the event of Leijonborg's initiative coming to fruition and this would be an unprecedented position for the party. Nonetheless, there was a good deal of internal unrest and criticism of Lundgren's unconvincing peformance during the election campaign.

At this juncture, the Leftist Party began publicly to question the 'two timing' of the Greens. According to its leader, Gudrun Schyman, any association with the centrists would be "to betray the [Green] voters". Like the Greens, Schyman was actively pressing for cabinet seats, although her party's vote had fallen back on its record performance in 1998.

For their part, the Social Democrats reiterated that foreign, defence and security matters would continue to fall outside the scope of any new legislative coalition with the Greens and Leftists and were non-negotiable issues. On Tuesday 24 September 2002 the Social Democratic government presented its two previous 'support parties' with the basis of a legislative coalition to replace the 1998–2002 arrangement. It seemed business as usual. However, in a dramatic turn of events the following day (see table 12.1) Persson suspended negotiations with the Greens. He called it "a pause in negotiations". "We will not become engaged in an auction in which our offer becomes the basis for talks with others", Persson added at a well-attended press conference[4] at which he also made public the details of the proposed deal with the Greens and Left Party to cover the period 2002–06. However, the Greens were neither bullied nor chastened and continued to negotiate with the centrists. In yet another dramatic turn of events, the Centre Party on 27 September, pulled out of the talks on the Leijonborg initiative, which, as a result, was stillborn.

In seeking to examine the failure of Leijonborg's attempt to realise a Liberal-led minority non-socialist coalition with the Greens, four main questions will serve as an analytical framework. First, was the Leijonborg initiative principally a case of 'posture politics' – a show of doomed defiance against the inevitable continuation of Social Democratic rule – or was there a genuine belief among all, most or at least some of the participants that a non-socialist coalition could be formed?

To accept that the Liberals, the primary architects of the coalition initiative, proceeded from the standpoint of 'almost nothing to lose' is not to argue that the whole project was merely 'gesture politics'. On the Liberal side, it may well have represented "a serious attempt to gain power"[5] and one which undoubtedly took the Social Democrats by surprise.[6] Leijonborg was probably encouraged to swallow some of his prior scepticism towards the Greens by statements made by the latter's spokesperson Eriksson, who claimed over the summer months to be well disposed towards cooperation with Centre and possibly even the Liberals.[7]

Table 12.1 Lars Leijonborg's attempt to form a Centrist-Green minority coalition, 23 September 2002–2 October 2002

September 23	The Greens begin to negotiate with the Liberals, Christian Democrats and Centre on a minority coalition under the Liberal leader, Lars Leijonborg
September 24	The Social Democratic prime minister, Göran Persson, presents the content of a package designed to renew the legislative coalition with the Greens and Leftists
September 25	Persson suddenly suspends negotiations with the Greens.
September 26	The Greens continue talks with the centre-based parties. Meanwhile, the Leftists engage in wider discussions with the government
September 27	The Centre announces its decision to pull out of the Leijonborg talks.
September 28	The Social Democrats put a new legislative deal to the Leftists and Greens
September 29	The Greens and Leftists reject the Social Democrats' offer
September 30	Roll-call in the newly-elected Riksdag. The Conservatives put down a motion of no confidence in the prime minister, which is tabled for the first time
October 1	The opening of the new Riksdag and the presentation of the Government's Declaration. The vote of no confidence is tabled for a second time. Later that evening the government and Greens meet up and reach an agreement.
October 2	The Conservatives' vote of no confidence is defeated by 174 (Social Democrats and Leftists) – 158 (the entire non-socialist bloc) with the 17 Greens abstaining.

Source: Från Riksdag och Departementet 29, 2002, p. 7

The Christian Democrats' and Greens' approach to the Leijonborg project was probably best characterised as 'all right, let's see how it goes'. True, the Christian Democrats had initial doubts about its viability and were somewhat lukewarm at the outset. But the feeling grew that something might come out of it and the party leader, Alf Svensson, was in fact one of the most active in pushing for the start of formal negotiations. Political commentators were critical of Svensson in 1998, following the Christian Democrats' strong electoral gains, for not approaching the Greens with an arrangement that would have replaced the Social Democratic government. Four years later he was possibly mindful of this criticism. As for the Greens, while never disguising their preference for governmental cooperation with the Social Democrats, the prospect of minis-terial seats in a Leijonborg-led coalition meant the talks with the non-socialist parties far exceeded 'posture politics'.

Nor did the Leijonborg initiative merely go up in a puff of rhetorical smoke, so to speak. Negotiations proceeded a long way down the road – in fact as far as a government declaration and a detailed sketch of the budget. Three sub-stantive policy working groups were set up – on economic policy, family policy and communications and infrastructure – and, according to one participant, "there was a good feeling in all these groups".[8] The Leijonborg project in short gathered a momentum of its own, talks reached an advanced stage and the Centre's decision to withdraw was, therefore, regarded as extremely disappoint-ing. Yet it was perhaps less the latter's withdrawal, as the timing of the with-drawal, that was so surprising. A member of the family policy working group in the negotiations has related how at the end of a session of that group the Centre's representative was unaware that his party had turned its back on the whole project!

So, secondly, why did the Centre leave the negotiations on a unique 'cen-trist parties + Greens' minority non-socialist coalition? It was certainly not because of any opposition in principle towards such a governmental alterna-tive to the Social Democrats. It was the Centre, then led by Olof Johansson, that had mooted the possibility of a coalition of the centrists and Greens in the run-up to the 1998 general election. Following a three-year legislative pact with the ruling Social Democrats on economic reforms (1995–98), Johansson plainly felt unable to swap cooperation with the governing party for participa-tion in a possible non-socialist coalition headed by the Conservatives, the leading party of the right. There was plainly a premium on projecting an inde-pendent Centre Party identity in the approach to the election. Accordingly, modelled in part on the creation in Norway in 1997 of a centre-based minor-ity coalition under the Christian Democrat, Kjell-Magne Bondevik, Johansson mooted the idea of a three-party centrist cabinet in Sweden. Significantly, later versions of this blueprint also included the Greens. Moreover, irrespec-tive of their motives, the Green spokespersons indicated shortly before polling day that a 'centrist government' was in fact their 'ideal scenario'.[9] The Liberal and Christian Democrat leaders, Leijonborg and Svensson, however, poured cold water on the possibility. In addition to the weak numerical base of such a cabinet, Leijonborg in particular was sceptical about the prospects of reaching agreement with the Greens on a comprehensive governmental programme when such divisive issues as EMU and nuclear power remained on the agenda.

Moreover, there is irony in the fact that the new Centre leader Maud Olofsson undertook much of the groundwork for the Leijonborg initiative. Six months before the 2002 general election, she attempted to breath new life into co-operation with the Liberals by referring to the notion of a 'non-socialist left' (*en borgerlig vänster*). Furthermore, at the Centre Party conference in June 2002, the solidarity between the two parties was cemented in a number of key policy areas. Indeed, when Olofsson's party arrested its [apparently terminal] electoral decline and picked up a few Riksdag seats in September 2002, it seemed prima facie that the Leijonborg initiative would be an option worth pursuing.

At the press conference on 27 September 2002 at which the Centre announced its withdrawal from the Leijonborg negotiations, Olofsson noted that "the dialogue has been very constructive. I have been surprised that we have a common standpoint on many issues. It has been good for Swedish democracy to discover there are alternatives to Social Democratic government".[10] Such apparently sanctimonious sentiments were given short shrift by the Centre's negotiating partners. Alf Svensson countered that had a comprehensive will existed, a non-socialist cabinet would have materialised. The Green Åsa Domeij, a member of the economic policy working group in the negotiations, noted scathingly that the Centre had plainly calculated that it was more in its interests to remain in opposition than to take part in government in the existing circumstances.

Although the Centre was divided over the Leijonborg project, several main threads appear to have combined to win the argument for withdrawal. First, a minority 'centre parties + Greens' coalition would have rested on the goodwill of the Conservatives, which, it could not be assumed, would have been well disposed towards this type of support role. Nursing electoral bruises, every single Conservative member of the Riksdag would be a prospective veto player.[11] Second, although Sweden had largely recovered from recession, welfare spending, the Centre contended, was still unacceptably high. Yet there were serious doubts whether the Greens in particular shared the Centre's goal of reducing it to approximately the same level as the other Nordic countries. Third, there were salient policy differences between the negotiating partners. For example, the Liberals were pro-EU and pro-USA whereas the Green Party was opposed to the EU and certainly Swedish membership of EMU and was also against an American-led invasion of Iraq. Finally, there were doubts about Leijonborg's leadership capacity and, by extension, the sustainability of the proposed cabinet.[12] Risking the electoral cost to a small party of participating in a short-lived coalition, it might be speculated, was considered not worth it. However, a senior Centre figure has related how the internal discussion was less about the risk of participation than the probability of the Leijonborg government succeeding.

In the media it was stated that the Centre had claimed the Greens were not a responsible party and, therefore, not a reliable partner in economic policy matters. This was mainly pretext. However, despite Maud Olofsson's express denials at the time, there were unquestionably elements in the Centre that feared the electoral consequences of governmental co-operation with the Greens. The two parties competed in the same vote market and, as a Christian Democratic parliamentarian put it: "the Centre did not want to give the Greens a helping hand into government".

While challenging the Greens' economic policy credentials was essentially tactical, the Centre's sceptical attitude towards the Conservatives' willingness to play the role of 'support party' was on altogether more solid ground. True, the Liberals' intention, it seems, had been to apply pressure on the Conservatives over the weekend before the start of the new Riksdag on 28–29 September 2002. Earlier that week, moreover, there had been telephone contact between the negotiating parties and the Conservative leader Lundgren, who had reported the substance to senior figures in his party. However, the perception in the Conservatives' party group was that the primary goal of the Leijonborg initiative was to oust the Social Democrats and reservations were expressed about this fundamentally negative logic. It is not inconceivable that the Conservatives would have lent consistent support to a Centrist-Green coalition had it been presented with a well-coordinated and carefully articulated programme. However, following a disastrous election result, which led to calls for a change in the leadership, the Conservatives were in no mood to sustain a minority cabinet, which it believed lacked a cohesive policy base.

A third basic question in the whole episode relates to Social Democrats' attitude towards the abortive Leijonborg project and, in particular, the reasons why Persson suspended negotiations with the Greens on 25 September. The prime minister's reaction to the Leijonborg move was undoubtedly one of surprise and very probably irritation. His reaction to its ultimate collapse was doubtless one of relief. The relief was evident in his commendation of the Centre, following its withdrawal from the talks, for being a party with a responsible approach to economic management and one with which the Social Democrats had worked closely in the past. There was conceivably the hinted suggestion also that cooperation between the two parties might be renewed in the future. The sub-text possibly read that if a deal with the Greens could not ultimately be concluded, the Social Democrats might revert to their classic 'divide and rule' strategy by forming a legislative coalition 'across the blocs' with one of the non-socialist parties.

Persson's irritation was evident when confronting the reality that the Greens, who were playing 'fast and loose', held the balance of power in the new Riksdag. They were also demanding cabinet posts and would need to be accommodated one way or another if a secure left-wing legislative majority was to be built. Persson's temperament, however, was hardly well suited to achieving compromises in such situations. As one opposition party leader put it, "Persson is not a consensus man". He was seen by the Greens as a high-handed, zero-sum operator, whose approach was an all or nothing 'support me or not' line. Nonetheless, his decision to suspend talks with the Greens on 25 September was surprising. Several factors probably contributed to it.

Persson might well have felt that the Leijonborg negotiations were going too well and that he had perhaps misjudged the Greens' intentions. While there has never been a German-style split in the Swedish Greens between 'realos' and 'fundos', the existence of internal factions or at least tendencies meant that Persson could not be entirely sure which grouping or approach held sway at the time. The evidence clearly suggests that the Greens entered the Leijonborg negotiations in a constructive spirit and, understandably, were attracted by the prospect of cabinet posts. Equally, Persson probably calculated that, since the majority of Green parliamentarians and voters were to the left of centre, the party leadership would experience difficulties in selling involvement in a predominantly non-socialist coalition to the grassroots of the movement. Viewed in this light, the carefully orchestrated press conference to announce the suspension of talks was designed to use the media to apply pressure on the Greens to come back into line. Ultimately, concessions were made – political experts or more commonly known as 'observers' in the ministries – although these fell short of granting the Greens cabinet seats. Unlike Finland, in short, the Swedish Greens have not yet enjoyed cabinet status.

Finally, what does the Leijonborg episode indicate about relations between the opposition parties in recent years? Since the Social Democrats returned to power in 1994, the four non-socialist parties have been, in the words of a leading journalist, "a long way from [the prime minister's office at] Rosenbad" and have appeared to work from a presumption of permanent Social Democratic government.[13] Individual non-socialist parties have tended to seek influence, as the Riksdag Speaker suggested, as "bargaining partners of the Social Democrats" – the legislative coalition with the Centre between 1995–98 is a case in point – rather than creating and uniting behind a clear alternative.[14] Put extremely crudely, the non-socialist opposition parties in this version of events have tended to compete with one another for Social Democratic favours rather than rallying behind a single leader and a well-defined alternative programme. *Dagens Nyheter* described the Leijonborg initiative as a "useful exercise", and it was useful in the minimal sense of mounting a serious challenge to the Social Democrats' governmental hegemony in Sweden. Like Jäätteenmäki's 'decisive action' approach in Finland the following year, it was an office-seeking strategy with a capital 'O'. Policy was strictly incidental. However, despite the late show of non-socialist unity as the election approached, there had been a lack of any prior coordination and harmonisation of policy and the absence of a viable alternative government programme. It proved difficult to paper over the cracks at the last minute.

The opposition defeats the government over immigration controls on East European EU workers

The failure to build a legislative majority in favour of transitional rules to control the expected influx of migrant workers from the new East European EU countries, meant that on 1 May 2004 Sweden became the only existing Union member not to impose temporary restrictions on their entry. This was both ironic and paradoxical, since both the minority Social Democratic government under Göran Persson *and* the two leading opposition parties, the Conservatives and Liberals, favoured the introduction of transitional rules. All four remaining opposition parties, in contrast, opposed any special entry conditions.

For years Persson had stated that he did not want any restrictions on the entry of migrant workers. However, in autumn 2003 he completely shifted his stance and spoke of the threat of 'welfare tourism' and the lure of the generous state benefits in Sweden. The government changed its mind when one 'old' EU country after another decided in favour of transitional regulations. The government bill none the less seemed broadly to reflect the mood of the country and especially the concerns of organised labour. It proposed that those seeking jobs in Sweden should acquire a work permit in their home country, a condition of which would be that the applicant had an offer of 'something permanent', preferably full-time employment. He or she would also have to have an approved salary (this was to become a real bone of contention) and to have organised accommodation in advance. A large *Sifo* poll published in *Svenska Dagbladet* at Easter 2004 indicated that a majority of 54% of Swedes supported the enactment of rules limiting the influx of immigrant workers from Eastern Europe.[15] Whereas only one-third of respondents were opposed to transitional rules, it was significant that Social Democratic supporters and members of the central trade union federation LO were the most supportive of them.

The two leading opposition parties also favoured transitional regulations for migrant workers. True, the Conservatives and Liberals opposed the acquisition of a work permit, but they insisted on evidence that the migrants could provide for themselves. In return, child benefits and housing support would be paid to the worker's family during his time in Sweden. The other opposition parties were against all special regulations for new EU citizens. They charged the government with fishing in the waters of racial prejudice and pointed to surveys, which suggested that there would not be a flood of migrant workers into Sweden.

The rift between the government and opposition on the issue was mirrored at the committee stage of the bill. In its statement to the lead committee, the Social Security Committee, a majority on the Labour Market Committee, comprising all six opposition parties, came out against the government's transitional rules. It warned of the dangers of creating a two-tier Europe and emphasised the importance of all EU citizens being able to travel, work and live in the Union under the same conditions. In the Social Security Committee there were three dissenting statements or 'reservations', and an opposition majority of nine to eight against the government bill (see table 12.2). The joint four-party 'reservation' from the Christian Democrats, Greens, Leftists and Centre held that the same rules should apply to all EU countries. The Conservatives' reservation argued that workers and their relatives should receive a residence permit on condition they could earn a living in Sweden. The Liberals favoured temporary restrictions for 2004 only. They believed, like the Conservatives, that a residence permit should be granted as long as the worker could demonstrate he had the means to provide for himself. Significantly, the Conservatives, which had initially announced they would abstain in the plenary vote – leaving the outcome at the whim of absentees – changed their mind.

Table 12.2 The party balance on the Riksdag's Social Security Committee in 2004

	Committee seats	Chamber Seats
Social Democrats	8	144
Christians, Leftists, Centre, Greens	4	102
Conservatives	3	55
Liberals	2	48

The political temperature rose as the decisive chamber debate and vote approached. On the eve of the plenary session, in a letter to the parliamentary group leaders of the four smaller opposition parties, the Conservative group leader, Mikael Odenberg, responded to media speculation about the possibility of tactical voting. In particular, he averred to the possibility of the Social Democrats voting strategically to defeat the reservation from the four smaller opposition parties in order to bring together the government bill and the reservation from his party in the final vote. Both, of course, favoured some conditions on the free entry of migrant workers. Odenberg noted that such an eventuality would violate all the unwritten norms of parliamentary behaviour but if, contrary to his expectations, it did come about, he urged support for the Conservatives' reservation.[16] By the same token he emphasised that if the Social Democrats and the four small-party reservation were paired in the final vote, the Conservatives would support the latter.

Ultimately, on 28 April 2004, the government bill, introducing transitional restrictions on the admission of migrant workers, lost out to the joint four-party reservation from the Christian Democrats, Leftists, Centre and Greens on the Social Security Committee by 182–137. The press described it as Persson's most significant domestic defeat since the negative majority in the EMU referendum. Both the Conservatives and Liberals, who favoured transitional arrangements voted against the government.

Yet while the government was roundly defeated, the two larger opposition parties in particular were far from united. Ultimately, fourteen Liberals refused to back their own party's proposal and opposed all restrictions. Conversely, two Leftists went against their party's line and supported the government bill in the final plenary vote. The immigration minister placed the responsibility for the government's defeat firmly at the door of the Conservatives and Liberals. They both wanted a degree of regulation, but voted with the four parties which had opposed transitional rules. "It is absurd", she declared, "that a majority in the three largest parties favoured regulations and yet there was a negative outcome. Party tactics and party egoism were allowed to prevail."[17]

At one level, the failure of majority-building between the Social Democrats, Conservatives and Liberals was an expression of the adversarial character of Swedish politics under Persson. The governing party simply did not try to create a legislative majority before putting its proposal before the Riksdag and might well have succeeded had it done so. Equally, the Conservatives and Liberals, in the words of one commentator, "were afraid of appearing Persson's poodles". It was all about posturing to their respective constituencies.

Majority-building was also complicated by divisions in the two largest opposition parties, while the governing party's position was a tricky one. It was under pressure from the blue-collar federation LO to use the issue to introduce wide-reaching labour-market reforms, including the stricter monitoring of the wages paid by employers. A significant proportion of LO members already comprised migrant workers and the government legislation sought improved wage conditions for them, as well as ensuring acceptable wage rates for East European arrivals. While appearing to act to prevent 'welfare tourism', the government was in fact serving the interests of its core trade union constituency.

The Social Democrats did contrive to maintain an uneasy unity on the issue. The Liberals in contrast were divided on the principle of restricting the free movement of labour and a significant minority favoured a policy of no regulations. In many ways, the Conservatives faced the most difficult task. They were confronted with the virtually impossible job of reconciling the sentiments of their ordinary voters, who feared 'welfare tourism' and favoured temporary controls, and the interests of the employers, for whom the legislation would remove the incentive to employ immigrant workers.

The Conservatives proved more adept than the Liberals at concealing their differences. The Liberals' split was openly publicised when the party's policy spokesperson and a former leader, Bengt Westerberg, produced a joint article in a leading newspaper opposing restrictions. It was clear, moreover, that the fourteen parliamentarians who took a similar view were not acting simply on the basis of conscience and principle, but rather were bound by the decisions of their local party boards. Grassroots' sentiment in the Liberals, in short, was divided. Interestingly, although Persson did not engage in majority-building prior to putting the bill before parliament, representatives of the governing party did try to negotiate a deal with the Liberals at the committee stage. When the Social Democratic chair of the Labour Market Committee tried to do so, however, it became evident that the two Liberal committee members were opposed to their own party line on the issue. Significantly, Bo Könberg, a senior Liberal member of the lead committee, the Social Security Committee, has stated that he thought he could have reached an agreement with the Social Democrats, but that the support of only two-thirds of his party group would have been insufficient to get the legislation through.

The Conservatives' divisions, or at least tensions over the bill were less public and the party's opposition to the government in a way less 'principled' than the Liberals. It was not a matter of the principle of the free movement of labour, but rather the practical dilemma of squaring the views of ordinary supporters and the particular needs and interests of the employers, a small but vital element on the political Right. The big business sector had engaged in vigorous lobbying on the issue across the Nordic region. For example, the large industrial employers' interest groups in Denmark, Finland and Sweden undersigned a joint letter, which appeared in *Dagens Nyheter* on the eve of the decisive plenary vote, opposing transitional rules. The industrial leaders insisted that the Nordic region would need a million migrant workers to sustain the welfare sector, particularly in view of the growing number of persons over retirement age.[18]

When Persson presented the immigration rules as an attempt to forestall 'welfare tourism', it was obvious that the vast majority of Conservative voters sympathised with the thrust of the legislation. This significantly raised the prospective electoral cost of opposing the government. However, the Conservative leadership believed Persson had adopted a populist position in public, but had simply pandered in the bill to his party's allies in the trade union movement. Ironically, LO, which contained a sizeable immigrant membership, had not argued for transitional controls. Instead, it pushed for legislation giving the trade unions the powers to ensure that *all workers* – not just those from the new East European EU countries – were not being underpaid. Accordingly, the government proposal argued, among other things, that many immigrant workers stood to be exploited by employers and that trade unions should be empowered to ensure this did not happen (including gaining the right of access to the books of private companies to check the salary levels being paid). In somewhat simplified form, the legislation appeared from a Conservative perspective to protect and promote the interests of organised labour at the expense of business and industry in a way that was unacceptable to the political Right. As a very senior Conservative figure put it in private: "If employers have to pay non-Swedes as much as Swedes, the incentive to employ immigrant labour will disappear completely".

The Conservative parliamentarian, Gunnar Hökmark, made the same point in the chamber, albeit in coded form. Referring to the perceived duplicity of the Social Democrats, Hökmark pulled no punches. The Social Democrats, he argued, are presenting themselves as protectionists, who are ready to erect new barriers to the internal market instead of completing the work of making the EU the world's most competitive economy. They have turned their back on the vision of European cooperation and freedom and surrendered to the unions and the other special interests that are promoting obstacles to the free movement of EU citizens.[19]

All in all, the failure of majority-building between the three largest Riksdag parties that favoured imposing at least some controls on the free entry of migrant workers was because there was no majority to build. It is possible, though by no means certain, that negotiations between the Social Democrats and Liberals at the pre-parliamentary stage might have led to a deal. However, Persson's initial deployment of a 'zero-sum' strategy, effectively saying to the Conservatives and Liberals 'support the government proposal or there will be no transitional regulations' was hardly conducive to inter-party compromise, even if there had not been wider and conflicting interests at stake. Ultimately, the government bill was defeated by ad hoc multilateral opposition from all four non-socialist parties, along with the Social Democrats' two 'support parties'. Yet with the opposition parties in practice divided, the defeat for the government did not threaten its position and the prime minister made it clear that the position would be reviewed and fresh measures introduced in the autumn if the flow of migrant workers demanded it. At very least it was a setback for Persson because it was very much his personal initiative. More disconcertingly, the whole issue brought anti-immigrant sentiment in Sweden out of the closet.

From 'crunch cooperation' to greater non-socialist cohesion?

When the four non-socialist opposition leaders met at Maud Olofsson's summer cottage at the end of August 2004, a *Temo* poll put the Conservatives on 23.5%, comfortably more than the combined total of the three centrist parties. The so-called 'Leijonborg effect', which had propelled the Liberals to within two percentage points of the Conservatives at the 2002 general election, had dissipated and the differential between the two parties was nearly fourteen percentage points in the Conservatives' favour. Their leader, Fredrik Reinfeldt, had emerged as de facto leader of the Swedish parliamentary opposition.[20]

The decisions taken at the Olofsson meeting were designed to lay the foundations for the creation of a cohesive and credible non-socialist opposition at the 2006 Riksdag election. The aim was to build an *Alliance for Sweden*. There were to be regular meetings of the four parliamentary party groups (the first was held on 15 February 2005), joint working groups to fashion the main lines of a non-socialist election manifesto and various pre-election events and seminars, commencing in 2005. Early evidence of the new non-socialist unity was to be found in the rejection of the government's defence policy package for 2005–07 only three weeks after the Olofsson meeting. Defence policy programmes are conventionally agreed across party lines, but negotiations with the opposition collapsed over the amount of the savings and the deployment of Swedish divisions on the international stage. In June 2004, the Centre and Christian Democrats had indicated their support for the government but, as the defence minister, Leni Björklund, remarked dismissively, "non-socialist co-operation is now more important for these two parties than defence decisions".[21]

Still more strikingly, or at least more visibly, a joint non-socialist party press conference, called to give details of their deepening cooperation, was strategically timed so as to detract attention from the prime minister's announcement of a cabinet re-shuffle the same day. Indeed, the reshuffle at the end of October 2004 could be seen in no small measure as Persson's response to heightened non-socialist cooperation and, although there were only three new ministers, there were some significant shifts in portfolio. These included the appointment of Pär Nuder as finance minister and thus the minister with primary responsibility for maintaining cooperation with the Leftists and Greens. Persson claimed the ministerial changes represented "a new start" for Sweden. However, exactly two hours before his announcement – in a type of pre-emptive *coup* – the four non-socialist leaders revealed further steps in the process of coordinating opposition policy. Six policy working groups would provide the basis for a joint election manifesto. The press described developments as giving Swedish politics "an injection of vitamins" and commented that, for the first time, there were not just two alternative programmes but two alternative teams.[22] The chairs of the six 'programme groups' were regarded as 'shadow ministers'[23] who, with the four non-socialist leaders, could reasonably be expected to make up the core of a non-socialist cabinet after the 2006 general election.

The Conservative leader Reinfeldt has done much to relocate his party more towards the political centre. Gone is the commitment to sweeping tax cuts. Instead, in its 'shadow budget' in autumn 2004 the party espoused a type of 'welfare conservatism' – conserving the welfare state by spending more on health, education etc. In an interview in *LO-tidningen*, the organ of the central trade union federation, Reinfeldt even claimed that the Conservatives were a party for low-paid trade union members. Polls that autumn indicated that the Conservatives were stronger than the Social Democrats among 18–44 year old men and also in the big cities. Moreover, at least 10% of those voting Social Democrat at the 2002 general election now regarded a non-socialist party as their first choice.[24] By Easter 2005, the Conservatives (with 31.5%) had narrowly edged ahead of the Social Democrats in the opinion polls for the first time since 1997, while total non-socialist support outstripped the combined backing for the government and its 'support parties'.

The two-bloc character of Swedish politics appears as pronounced in summer 2005 as at any time earlier and there is at least the real possibility of an alternation of power and the advent of a non-socialist government in September 2006. A note of caution is none the less in order. There are still important policy differences between the non-socialist parties on issues such as NATO, nuclear power and alcohol taxation and the risk that any joint election manifesto could be – or might be perceived as – a case of consensualism of the lowest common denominator. Clearly, in view of the non-socialists' unfortunate previous experiences of governing during periods of economic recession, the

need to formulate a responsible economic policy may be regarded as a necessary condition of their return to power.[25] There appears no room in Sweden
for the traditional ploy of Westminster oppositions of eschewing detailed policy
commitments so as to avoid tying their hands when in government. Yet in a
multi-party market place, the non-socialist opposition parties are bound to be
electoral competitors (as well as allies) and the need to profile themselves will
be greater for small parties (like the Christian Democrats) sinking towards the
4% threshold for Riksdag representation. There has also yet to be agreement
on a 'chancellor candidate', that is, the presentation of Reinfeldt as the "alternative prime minister".

The opinion poll ratings in spring 2005 that showed the Conservatives
marginally ahead of the Social Democrats coincided with a particularly 'bad
patch' for the governing party. There was residual criticism of the prime
minister's handling of the *Tsunami* disaster, while the Social Democrats had
acquired an increasingly murky image, with allegations of membership irregu-
larities in the party's Youth Section. A group of prominent journalists and
researchers had also compiled a volume entitled 'Power above all else' (*Makten
framför allt*), which was highly critical of Persson's authoritarian leadership
style and lack of vision. Yet the events of 1991 and the last non-socialist success might be instructive. The balance was tipped not so much by the joint
Conservative-Liberal manifesto 'A New Start for Sweden',[26] as New Democracy's
promise of massive tax reductions and its populist critique of immigration
policy, which managed to attract vital votes from the Social Democrats.

Conclusions

Since 1994 the Social Democratic minority governments in Sweden have faced
six opposition parties in the Riksdag and have proceeded on something of a
'divide-and-rule' basis. Legislative majority-building has involved negotiating
legislative coalitions 'across the blocs' (with the Centre on the economy between 1995–98 for example), but mainly with the Left Party and the left-of-
centre Greens (excluding foreign and defence policy).

For much of this period of Social Democratic government, the non-socialist parties have lacked the cohesion to appear a credible governing alternative.
The abortive Leijonborg initiative immediately after the 2002 general election
reflected the existence of bilateral non-socialist opposition. A centrist grouping of parties aspired to govern with support from, but not the formal involvement of the Conservatives. This would have been the Norwegian model plus
the Greens. It was essentially an office-seeking strategy, which had a symbolic
value. But as an exercise in 'crunch co-operation' it failed ultimately because
when it came to the crunch there were doubts about its viability and concern

about the electoral costs of its failure.

The government's defeat over the imposition of transitional immigration controls pointed to the reality of multi-dimensional opposition in the Riksdag. The four smaller opposition parties, including the Social Democrats' two 'support parties' opposed all controls. The two larger opposition parties, the Conservatives and Liberals, the latter badly divided, supported controls (albeit of different types), but opposed the Social Democrats' proposed legislation.

The Greens have enjoyed a pivotal role – and considerable veto power – between the two blocs. Unlike Finland, they are regarded as a left-of-centre party rather than a non-socialist grouping, but have combined to form legislative majorities on Riksdag committees with the non-socialists. However, the question of Green involvement in a possible non-socialist governing coalition has divided the centre-based opposition groups from the Conservatives.

Since the later part of 2003 there has been a move from internal pluralism to a greater degree of cohesion among the non-socialist parties. Accordingly, the bloc character of Swedish legislative–executive relations has become more accentuated and the non-socialists have sought to co-ordinate their challenge to the Social Democrats earlier and more thoroughly than ever before. Persson acts much in the manner of the prime minister of a majority government and Reinfelt parades as the *de facto* leader of the opposition and the prime minister of a future non-socialist cabinet.

Notes

1 Interview with Björn von Sydow 18.6.2004.
2 At a meeting of the Centre Party's executive board – the so-called 'Uppsala meeting' – in November 1973, the Centre leader Thorbjörn Fälldin argued for a merger with the Liberals. However this was met with internal resistance, particularly from the young wing of the party, and Fälldin did not receive a mandate to negotiate. (Hadenius 2003: 154)
3 Staffan Thulin, 'Valrörelsen som inte ville ta slut' *Från Riksdag och Departement* 29, 2002, p. 8.
4 Staffan Thulin, 'Valrörelsen som inte ville ta slut' *Från Riksdag och Departement* 29, 2002, p. 8.
5 Interview with the Liberal PPG leader, Bo Könberg, 17.6.2004.
6 Interview with the Riksdag Speaker, Björn von Sydow 18.6.2004.
7 Hans Norrbom, 'Mittenregering aktuell även 1998' *Från Riksdag och Departement* 29, 2002, p. 11.
8 Interview with Stefan Attefall, Christian Democrat PPG leader, 18.6.2004.
9 Hans Norrbom, 'Mittenregering aktuell även 1998' *Från Riksdag och Departement* 29, 2002, p. 11.
10 Staffan Thulin, 'Valrörelsen som inte ville ta slut' *Från Riksdag och Departement*

29, 2002, pp. 6–9.
11 Interview with Henrik Sjöholm, Centre Party Board member 17.6.2004 and Åsa
   Torstensson, the Centre Party's Parliamentary Group Leader, 17.6.2004.
12 Interview with Åsa Torstensson, 17.6.2004.
13 Interview with Leader writer on *Dagens Nyheter,* Barbro Hedvall, 16.6.2004.
14 Interview with Björn von Sydow 18.6.2004.
15 'Övergångsreglerna ned – S, v och mp vill ha skärpta regler' *Svenska Dagbladet*
   29.4.2004.
16 'Moderaterna uppmanar kd, v,c och mp att rösta ned regeringens övergångsregler'
   Moderaternas pressmeddelande 27.4.2004.
17 'Enda EU-landet utan övergångsregler' *Göteborgs-Posten* 29.4.2004.
18 'Suomenkin työnantajat siirtymäsääntöjä vastaan' *Helsingin Sanomat* 29.4.2004.
19 'Socialdemokraterna vill ersätta gamla gränser med nya regler och hinder'
   Moderaternas pressmeddelande 27.4.2004.
20 In autumn 2003 Leijonborg endeavoured to revive his flagging leadership profile
   by instigating two policy working groups between the Liberals and Greens. One
   dealt with the issue of choice in the welfare state and the other with immigration
   questions. However, a stumbling block to a future non-socialist coalition might
   well be the role of the Greens. Leijonborg's governmental blueprint includes them
   whereas Reinfeldt appears opposed to their participation. Arvid Lagercrantz, 'Ett
   revolutionärt mittenparti' *Från Riksdag och Departement* 29, 2002, pp. 10–11.
21 'Porvaripuolueet eivät tue Ruotsin puolustuslinjauksia' *Helsingin Sanomat*
   23.9.2004. The Left Party's opposition to the defence package in the decisive vote
   in December 2004 is discussed in the concluding chapter.
22 'För första gången finns två tydliga alternativ' *Dagens Nyheter* 21.10.2004.
23 Mikael Odenberg (M), the convenor of the economic policy working group, was
   viewed as vital in ensuring a fully costed set of alternative economic policies'.
   'Hopp om borgerlig enighet' *Dagens Nyheter* 22.10.2004 .
24 'Väljarflykt från de rödgröna' *Dagens Nyheter* 24.9.2004.
25 Interview with the Conservative leader Fredrik Reinfeldt 18.6.2004.
26 'Missnöjesröster avgör om Persson blir schack matt' *Dagens Nyheter* 30.8.2004.

References

Hadenius, Stig *Modern Svensk Politisk Historia* (Hjalmarson & Högberg Bokförlag, 2003)

Conclusion

Democracy in Scandinavia: consensual, majoritarian or mixed?

The point of departure for this book, it will be recalled, was the widespread perception, indeed reputation of the Scandinavian states as the home of consensus politics and the Mecca of consensual behaviour. They have even been viewed as a block of distinctive consensual democracies. It was something approximating Scandinavian-style consensus – it was called 'new politics' – that the architects of the Scottish Parliament sought to import 'north of the border' following devolution in 1999. Yet the consensus among political scientists about the consensual nature of Scandinavian politics does not in itself make the case. Confusingly, moreover, the literature is replete with references to terms such as 'consensual policy style' and 'policy consensus', often with different meanings, which have not lent themselves to measurement or operationalisation.

In the introductory chapter, it was noted that a rules-based approach to classifying democracies, in line with the work of McGann and Ganghof, among others, yielded three main types. *Supermajoritarian democracies* combine an electoral system based on proportional representation with the existence of minority veto provisions in the legislative process. For example, in Hungary, the most important legislation during the early phase of democratic transition required a two-thirds majority to be enacted. (Ágh 2001: 96) However, in 1998, a simple majority rule was introduced, marking a shift to what Attila Ágh refers to as 'quasi-majoritarian democracy' under the national-conservative government. (Ágh 2001: 102)

Ganghof regards Switzerland as a case of a supermajoritarian democracy. It is certainly true that the so-called *konkordanz* model – a system anchored in the mutual accommodation of interests – has meant that decisions are not made on the basis of majority rule, but following a protracted process of negotiation involving all the relevant actors. (Klöti 2001: 19–34) In other words, legislative supermajorities are commonplace and underpinning these broad-based parliamentary coalitions has been two types of popular initiative. If 50,000 voters sign a petition opposing a bill ninety days after its passage in the bicameral federal parliament, the bill must gain majority approval in a referendum in order to be enforced. Moreover, if 100,000 signatures are collected within a period of eighteen months proposing a constitutional amendment, a referendum must be held. The outcome will be binding, provided a majority of voters and cantons support the proposal. (Papadopoulos 2001: 36)

Clearly, the provision for citizens to challenge enacted legislation and oblige it to gain the backing of a majority in a referendum has contributed significantly to the practice of building legislative supermajorities. These supermajorities in turn reduce the likelihood of a referendum challenge being launched. Since the 1960s the proportion of bills challenged by a referendum has fallen to just under 7%. Nonetheless, in the strictest sense, the provision for a popular initiative on most ordinary legislation does not require parliament to pass laws by more than a simple majority. Indeed, more controversially, Simon Hug and George Tsebelis have argued that the initiative effectively eliminates all other veto players from the process, thus making it a perfect majoritarian instrument. (Hug and Tsebelis 2002: 465–516).

True majoritarian democracy combines a PR electoral system and legislative majority rules. Several of Lijphart's 'consensus model democracies' should be placed in the majoritarian camp if the distinction between rules and behaviour is strictly observed. Typically, in analysing the Netherlands, Theo Toonen refers to "governing a consensus democracy" and focuses on the interplay between "pillarisation and administration". (Toonen 2000: 165–178) However, in the absence of minority veto provisions, Holland would appear a clear case of a true majoritarian democracy.

Pluralitarian democracy combines a simple plurality voting system and legislative majority rules and the UK appears its archetype. The extent of the violation of the fundamental principle of political equality ('one vote one value') inherent in the British electoral system was given striking expression at the May 2005 British general election. The Labour Party gained an overall majority of 65 seats with only 36% of the vote. It was the lowest-ever vote share for a winning party and for the first time lower than the 39% of the 'sleeping party' (abstainers).[1] True, there may be a broad policy consensus between the main parties in line with Richard Heffernan's analysis – see the introductory chapter of this book (Heffernan 2002:742–762). But the Westminster model has been characterised by the absence of consensual parliamentary practice, the supremacy of adversary politics and opposition with a capital 'O'. In short, pluralitarian democracy is associated with exclusionary legislative–executive relations.

On the basis of the institutional rules, all the Scandinavian states are majoritarian democracies, which witness varying degrees of consensual legislative behaviour. Accordingly, the generic question in the final part of this book has been 'how consensual is legislative practice in the Nordic countries?' This has been broken down into two sub-questions. First, how, and to what effect, does the parliamentary opposition participate in the exercise of power in the Scandinavian countries and in the contrasting cases of Finland and Sweden in particular? Second, to what extent are non-veto players among the opposition parties consulted by the political executive and thus able to exert influence in the legislative agenda-setting process?

We have noted that the identification of veto players and the calculation of their relative veto power is no straightforward task. *Institutional veto players* need not involve the existence of qualified majority voting rules in the national parliament. We have noted the role of the popular initiative in Switzerland. The 1920 Estonian constitution also provided through the popular initiative (and referendum) a means by which citizens could both introduce and enact legislation and overturn decisions of the 100-seat, unicameral Riigikogu. If the latter situation occurred, it was deemed a vote of no confidence in the Riigikogu and fresh elections had to be called. (Parming 1975: 8) The Standing Orders of the Italian Parliament until 1988 permitted secret voting. There was no official record of how each MP voted; only the number and names of those present and voting were recorded and counted. The outcome of secret voting was often to veto executive legislation.

The identification of *partisan veto players* is also not without problems. Veto players may be members of the government and/or members of the parliamentary opposition. At times factions, even individuals within the parliamentary party groups may function as veto players. Indeed, Tsebelis raises the pertinent question of the degree of internal cohesion among partisan veto players. It is clearly erroneous to assume that parties function solely as unitary actors. It may be, as Michael Laver has argued, that "it is almost never the case that only a section of a party joins a government, whilst another section stays outside". (Laver 2002: 203) But this is precisely what happened in Finland in the early 1980s, since the 'Eurocommunist' wing of the Finnish People's Democratic League participated in the broad-based, centre-left governments, while the hardline Stalinist minority wing remained in opposition. Laver has also argued that "electoral systems in which people cast votes for individual candidates ... allow legislators to build their own power bases and thereby insulate themselves from the potential sanction of party leaders". (Laver 2002: 221) Although this may have only a limited general application in Scandinavia, it has been certainly true for the former hardline Finnish Communist, Esko-

Juhani Tennilä. He has built a power-base in the Lapland constituency from which he has been able to thwart the best efforts of the (post-communist) Leftist Alliance leader to create parliamentary party unity. On the subject of Finland and veto players, the CPSU operated as an *exogenous veto player* in relation to government-building in Finland during the Cold War years.[2] The repeated exclusion of the Conservatives is testimony to this fact. (Isaksson 2001: 40–54) More widely, the EU may be regarded as an exogenous veto player in relation to the national parliaments of the Nordic member states. (Jääskinen 2000: 114–134; Raunio & Wiberg 2000: 344–364)

It is also worth noting in connection with the discussion of parties as unitary actors and veto players that while parliamentary party group decisions may be collective and cohesive on the surface – that is, free of factional division – it is unlikely that the decisions will have been collective in any real sense. We noted in our earlier discussion (chapter 10) of PPGs as autonomous policy sub-systems that in practice decision-making followed horizontal rather than simply vertical lines of authority. The committee groups were crucial actors, while individual MPs could be assigned important duties as *rapporteurs*. Magnus Isberg's work on the Swedish PPGs indicated that, in substantive policy terms, it was the horizontal axis that was decisive and that the PPG generally simply rubber-stamped the line formulated in the committee groups. (Isberg 1999)

Findings from other countries point in the same direction. Commenting on Norway, Hilmar Rommetvedt has noted that "on a day-to-day basis I would expect the committee groups (*komitefraksjoner*) to be more influential in relation to most specific issues than the group boards" of the Storting parties.[3] In the same vein, Gerhard Loewenberg has written of the German Bundestag that "it is in the working [committee] groups (*Arbeitskreise*) of the PPGs that the substantive positions of each party are formulated". (Loewenberg 2003: 24) Moreover, on the basis of extensive participant observation, Jürgen von Oertzen has related how full Bundestag PPG meetings will normally approve committee group decisions and most will not even be discussed in the PPG as a whole (von Oertzen 2005). Oertzen adds that the much-vaunted Bundestag committees are not particularly powerful and that if a parliamentarian seeks an influential position he or she will choose to be a chair of a committee group in his or her party rather than the chair of a standing Bundestag committee.

Henrik Jensen's analysis of the Danish PPGs follows complementary lines. Jensen argues that decision-making in the parliamentary party groups, as in the legislative process as a whole, is dispersed in both time and space. It is an atomised process, where the work, responsibility and influence on a PPG's day-to-day decisions are spread out and devolve first and foremost to individual policy spokespersons and (when the party is in government) ministers. They in turn will invariably have contact with a network of external actors – the party in the country, interest groups, experts, journalists etc – and there will be a two-way flow of communication between them. Consequently, decision-making is an incremental process, moulded in a variety of forums such as the full chamber, Folketing standing committee rooms, PPG rooms and government ministries. The implicit thrust of Jensen's submission is that the genesis of majority-building in Denmark should be sought in the relevant policy community – comprising outside actors and the responsible parliamentarians in the various PPGs – which combines to construct the necessary support for legislative change. Jensen concludes that, as a consequence of the dispersion of decision-making in time and space, it has become increasingly difficult to distinguish a PPG's working procedures from its decision-making structures. (Jensen 2002: 216–218)

While all the Scandinavian states are majoritarian democracies, the essential, and indeed differential nature of government–opposition relations in these countries can be analysed by reference to a continuum of consensual legislative practice. *Ad hoc parliamentary consensualism*, it will be recalled, is characterised by fluctuating legislative coalitions, negotiated primarily on an issue-by-issue basis, which manifest a low degree of formalism, variable majorities and have a generally short duration. *Binding parliamentary consensualism* entails policy-making on the basis of more or less formalised legislative coalitions, often described in a binding document, which will embrace a spectrum of policy areas and usually be minimal winning in character. *Extreme parliamentary consensualism* will typically witness the inclusion of non-veto playing opposition parties into 'surplus majority legislative coalitions', of both shorter or longer duration, albeit most typically negotiated on specific pieces of legislation.

Finland: from supermajoritarian to majoritarian democracy and exclusionary legislative–executive relations

Unlike Sweden, but in common with countries like Holland and Switzerland, Finland has a multi-party system without a dominant party in electoral terms. True, the Social Democrats have gained the largest share of the popular vote in all but three post-war elections. But their advantage over the second-placed party has never been more than a few percentage points. There are in fact three middle-sized parties (or at best larger parties) in Finland: the Centre, Social Democrats and Conservatives – each claiming in the range 20–25% of the electorate – two of which at any one time have comprised the core of governing coalitions. The core of the present Vanhanen cabinet, formed in June 2003, consists of the Centre and Social Democratic parties.

The English word 'consensus' has been taken directly into the Finnish language – albeit spelt with a 'k' rather than a 'c' – and used extensively by the media and political scientists alike to capture the essence of Finnish politics over the last three decades or so. Yet the widespread reference to the consensus tradition in Finland should not be confused with the existence of inclusionary legislative–executive relations. Rather, it must be related primarily to the size and structure of governments and, in particular, the frequency of 'surplus majority' coalitions 'across the blocs' (that is, involving socialist and non-socialist groups). In other words, partisan veto players have been located *within the political executive*, although the sheer size of governing coalitions – the Lipponen 'rainbow coalitions' of 1995–2003 for example – has tended to reduce their effective veto power. The Greens left the government in 2002 over a matter of principle – opposition to the decision to approve the construction of a fifth nuclear power station – without it materially affecting the stability of the government.

The strategic goal of returning to government has meant that the middle-sized (and leading) party in opposition has *generally* sought to build bridges to, and not to antagonise the two middle-sized parties in government (obviously Jäätteenmäki's 'Iraq offensive' involved throwing caution to the wind). A by-product of the search for working inter-elite relations between the three middle-sized parties has thus been a broad policy consensus. But this has co-existed with the virtual absence of consensual parliamentary practices. Neither the institutional rules nor the dynamics of the parliamentary party system have necessitated consultation across the divide between government and opposition and this has in fact been rare in recent years.

The policy consensus (convergence) between the three medium-sized parties (although it should not be exaggerated, especially as general elections approach) may be contrasted with the opposition block as a whole, which has tended to cover a much greater degree of ideological ground. Following the 2003 general election, the Finnish opposition comprised the former communists in the Leftist Alliance, the Greens, Christian Democrats, Conservatives and True Finns. Equally, all the opposition parties (except the miniscule group of True Finns) have participated in government since the early 1990s and all are office-seeking. Consequently, the opposition has lacked cohesion and relations between the opposition parties have largely been competitive. In addition, the individual opposition parties have at times lacked internal unity. The Leftist Alliance has been deeply split between the traditional trade union wing (some even favouring a merger with the Social Democrats)[4] and the 'modernisers' spearheaded by the party chair, Suvi-Anne Siimes, who have pursued a red–green mix of policies. The Christian Democrats have been divided between a conservative evangelical wing and the more secular approach of the former chair Bjarne Kallis.

Summing up, the Finnish opposition does not constitute an alternative government and recently has lacked both cohesion and partisan veto players.[5] The profile of its members is generally low and virtually its sole weapon of attack is the interpellation, which requires a minimum of twenty signatures. At present only the Conservatives have the necessary number of parliamentarians in their own right to table an interpellation and the smaller opposition parties must combine forces to do so. Only infrequently, in the lifetime of the present Eduskunta have the opposition parties united behind an interpellation. They did so in spring 2004 when the Greens put down an interpellation on the question of employment levels and welfare state spending. However, when the Conservatives tabled an interpellation on exactly the same matter in September 2004, only the three True Finns and two of the Christian Democrats' parliamentary group backed it. In the parliamentary debate it was evident that the Greens and the Leftist Alliance objected not only to the Conservatives' proposed tax reductions, but also their chairman Katainen's attempt to present himself as leader of the opposition.[6] Plainly, the Conservatives' interpellation was so timed as to attract a measure of publicity prior to the local government elections the following month. Interpellation debates are usually televised and attract several column inches in the national press. Publicity was also probably the primary motive for a Leftist Alliance interpellation on social service provision and a combined opposition interpellation on local government finances.[7] The latter was the sixth interpellation in the lifetime of the Vanhanen government, which none the less survived the subsequent 'no confidence vote' by the comfortable margin of 106–76.

Not commanding the number of elected members necessary to table an interpellation on its own, a small opposition party may well use the floor of parliament to raise its profile. The reporting of parliamentary proceedings in the media is much less detailed than it used to be. But for a small party there may be little alternative. Thus, in the first two years of the 2003–07 Eduskunta, the True Finn chairman, Timo Soini, made over three hundred plenary speeches.[8]

Running a presidential candidate has also attracted some media attention to the opposition parties. All the opposition parties – except the Leftist Alliance, which is backing the incumbent Tarja Halonen – are running candidates in the 2006 presidential election. For the Conservatives, who are putting up their former leader and former long-serving finance minister, Sauli Niinistö, this is clearly part of a strategy of challenging the Centre for the position of leading non-socialist party. A good campaign will in any event prepare the ground for a further challenge at the 2007 general election. For the smaller opposition parties, a presidential candidate will provide a means of getting its policies across, raising its profile and attracting extra votes. For example, the Green Heidi Hautala, who also ran in the 2000 presidential contest, will clearly challenge the Conservative and Centre candidates on issues such as gender equality and the challenges stemming from globalisation.[9] In this connection, a routine complaint of leading opposition party figures has been that their parties have 'good policies but low visibility'.

All in all, however, legislative practice in Finland today is not consensual and the parliamentary opposition does not participate in the exercise of power. None of its members is a veto player. Re-stated, legislative–executive relations are exclusionary, relations between the opposition parties competitive, at times even adversarial and the opposition both numerically and politically weak. Legislative majority rules and majority coalitions, combined with a fragmented and ideologically disparate opposition, have meant that Finland is executive-dominant (in Lijphart's terms) and the position of the government has been strengthened by the reduction in the powers of the president contained in the 2000 constitution.

Importantly, the position of the parliamentary opposition has weakened over the last decade or so. Put another way, a change in the institutional rules and the abolition of most of the historic qualified majority rules in 1992 meant that Finland shifted from being a supermajoritarian democracy to become a 'true majoritarian democracy', so denying the opposition its former veto power. Before 1992 one-third of MPs could postpone ordinary legislation over a general election, while one-sixth could prevent a measure being declared 'urgent' – 'urgent measures' could be enacted in the lifetime of a single parliament. These minority veto provisions meant in practice that the size of a minimal winning coalition was 'two-thirds plus one' of Eduskunta members. This in turn meant that the government would be obliged to consult with at least the leading opposition party (mostly the Conservatives) in respect of most important economic legislation (including the budget). A modicum of consensual legislative practice in short became a functional necessity since negotiation with the opposition was usually a sine qua non for achieving the qualified legislative majority. The legislative rules had an obvious impact on legislative behaviour. (Cox 2000: 169–192)

Yet too much should not be made of the impact of the qualified majority rules as an institutional veto player. Governments were often sufficiently broad-based in their own right to deny the opposition its suspensive veto. Moreover the Conservative Party, which was in opposition continuously between 1966–87, sought through a cooperative strategy both prospective involvement in government and, as a means to that end, acceptance in Moscow. It rarely played hard to get. Consultation there was, but concessions to the opposition over matters such as the budget tended to be minor. Nonetheless, legislative–executive relations were to a limited extent inclusionary. This is no longer the case. The era of 'rainbow coalition' between 1995–2003 was an interesting instance of 'supermajoritarian behaviour' without the necessity of supermajoritarian rules, although consensual practice was confined to members of the governing coalition. Since 2003, however, Finland has been a majoritarian democracy with the only 'surplus' governing party, the Swedish People's Party representing the national language minority.

Sweden: inclusionary legislative–executive relations in a majoritarian democracy

Sweden has a multi-party system with a dominant party in the form of the Social Democrats. However, although polling little short of twice the percentage poll of its nearest rival the Conservatives, the Social Democrats have not gained an absolute majority of Riksdag seats since the shift to unicameralism in 1970. Accordingly, minority governments have been the norm and they have rested on legislative coalitions, which, like government–opposition relations, have largely followed socialist–nonsocialist bloc lines. The 'bloc character' of Swedish parliamentary politics has become more pronounced in recent years and stands in contrast to the 'across the blocs' nature of the Finnish experience.

Nonetheless, for several decades Sweden has witnessed inclusionary legislative–executive relations in so far as minority governments have relied on 'support parties' in opposition for a legislative majority. The relationship between the minority Social Democratic governments and their 'support parties' – since 1998 the Left Party and Greens – has recently been described as 'contract parliamentarism' (Aylott and Bergman 2004). Contract parliamentarism should be viewed as a variant of *binding consensualism*, since a formalised legislative pact has afforded minority governments a reliable legislative majority across a broad spectrum of agreed policy areas.

Contract parliamentarism has not neutralised the 'support parties' as veto players. Thus, the legislative coalition between the government and the Leftists and Greens has not covered foreign and defence policy and in the latter field the Leftists have proved something of a thorn in the Social Democrats' side. In fact, the government's defence package, which went before the Riksdag on 15 December 2004, seemed in practice to herald the end of the celebrated Swedish post-war policy of 'armed neutrality'. The bill stated that Sweden no longer perceived any serious threats to its national territory and the emphasis would therefore be placed on the training of its defence forces for engagement in international crisis management activity. One-third of its thirty regiments would be wound up, the number of submarines and fighter aircraft substantially reduced, and the size of the defence staff cut by one-quarter. Formally, Sweden would retain military service. Yet only about 8–10,000 of the 60,000 men reaching call-up age every year would be needed and those who did 'volunteer' would undertake the standard eleven months and then have the option of a further three to five months' special training for international duties. Interestingly, it was less the principle of the 'rationalisation' of Sweden's military capability that divided the Riksdag parties than the extent of the cuts (the non-socialists favoured less) and which regiments would be abolished.

As noted in chapter 12, the traditional type of broad cross-party defence agreement between the government and the opposition was ruled out at an early stage. Under Reinfeldt's leadership, the four non-socialist parties were more united than for a long time and the Centre and Christian Democrats, which earlier had indicated they might support the government, ultimately backed out of any deal. This meant that the prime minister would be obliged to build a legislative coalition with his two 'support parties', something which was complicated when four rebellious Leftists threatened to vote with the non-socialists to defeat the defence package. In particular, they expressed strong objections to the proposed closure of the infantry garrison at Arvidsjaur in Swedish Lapland, which was said to be vital to the economy of the region.[10]

There were indications that Göran Persson would have called an early election if the Left Party had voted to defeat the defence package. Indeed, on 7 December the Social Democrat tabloid *Aftonbladet* voiced the case for a premature dissolution. Three days later, it seems, Persson, in negotiations with the Leftists, did indeed threaten to 'go to the country'. It was widely believed that it was this threat that brought the latter to heel. After a marathon debate in the Riksdag, the defence package was ultimately approved by 167–138 votes on 16 December 2004.[11] Nonetheless, two Leftists, both from districts affected by closures, voted with the non-socialist opposition. The regional imperative proved stronger than a commitment to the party line.[12]

The Swedish opposition parties since 1994, ranging from Leftists to Conservatives, have covered a similar amount of ideological ground to the Finnish opposition. Ironically, unlike Finland, however, two of their number, the government's 'support parties' have never participated in government. Moreover, unlike Finland, all the (four) non-socialist parties are presently in opposition and contriving a greater unity of purpose as the 2006 general election approaches.[13] Relations between the minority Social Democratic government and the non-socialist parties in opposition have been essentially adversarial. Persson has appeared to conduct himself in the manner of the leader of a majority government and Reinfeldt in the manner of the leader of a government in waiting.

Yet Sweden appears a good example of McGann's proposition that legislative majority rule, if combined with electoral proportionality, does not necessarily prevent behavioural patterns generally perceived as consensual. Sweden is a majoritarian democracy in which legislative majority building is the perennial challenge and this has dictated legislative coalitions with 'support parties'. However, this type of 'binding consensualism' has not extended beyond the functional dictates of majority-building. 'Surplus majority' legislative coalitions in short – an indicator of 'extreme parliamentary consensualism' – have been exceptional in recent years.

Nonetheless, exceptionally in Sweden, it might not be far-fetched to allow for the possibility of *surplus majority pre-legislative coalitions*. Put another way, it might be hypothesised that the more extensive the participation of the parliamentary opposition – both 'support parties' and non-veto players – in the policy-making process at the pre-legislative stage, the more distinctive Sweden's form of binding consensualism. In this connection, Larsson, it will be recalled, held that involvement in a commission of inquiry was one of the best opportunities the parliamentary opposition has to influence government policy. (Larsson 1994: 170) A snapshot of commission activity during the 2002/03 Riksdag session will serve to illustrate the point.[14]

First, while in the aforementioned 2002/03 Riksdag session parliamentarians not infrequently chaired commissions of inquiry, it was highly exceptional for members of the opposition parties to hold the post of chair. The Riksdag's 2002/03 Commission Report listed eleven parliamentarians acting as commission chairs and all but one was a Social Democrat. Interestingly, chair posts on commissions were not distributed to the government's 'support parties'.

Second, in the 2002/03 Riksdag several parliamentarians were appointed, or continued to serve as special investigators/researchers (*särskild utredare*) on one-person commissions, albeit supported by a team of experts, advisers and secretarial staff. This was particularly common for commissions in the Department of Social Affairs, where the special investigator was often a member (or previous member) of the corresponding Riksdag standing committee on Social Affairs. However, it was less common for an opposition parliamentarian to be nominated a special commission investigator.

A notable exception was Kerstin Heineman, a Liberal member since 1994, presently Second Deputy Speaker and a member of the Riksdag's Social Affairs

Committee with particular responsibility for health, the handicapped and the elderly. In May 2002 she became special investigator for a new commission examining ways of improving knowledge of various forms of misinformation. The Conservative parliamentarian, Christel Anderberg was the special investigator for a commission examining the capacity of local and regional councils to deal with "extraordinary peacetime events in society" (floods, power cuts, accidents involving chemicals and explosives etc). The former Centre Riksdag member, Anders Svärd, was appointed the special investigator on a commission dealing with security of information, while the former Green member, Gudrun Lindvall, assumed a similar role on a commission examining the transportation of animals. However, of the ten Riksdag or former Riksdag members listed as special commission investigators/researchers in the 2002/03 session of the Swedish parliament, 60% were Social Democrats.[15]

Third, a parliamentarian's experience and/or expertise in a particular policy area may lead to his or her nomination as a commission member or special adviser, although in 2002/03 at least this appeared true primarily for members of the governing party. An example of an MP serving as a special adviser was the Social Democrat Ronny Olander, a former builder who had worked in the construction industry in the Malmö area. He served as an expert to a commission charged with devising an action plan for increasing health in the workplace. As a case of a parliamentarian appointed to a commission on the basis of her special knowledge, mention might be made of the Social Democrat Agneta Lundberg, a member of the Riksdag's Education Committee. She served between 1996–2002 as the only parliamentary member (aside from the chairwoman) of a commission examining advanced vocational training. There were relatively few comparable examples from the non-socialist ranks. Indeed, the evidence from 2002/03 suggests that opposition parliamentarians will only rarely chair commissions of inquiry and are significantly less likely than a member of the governing party to be named as the special investigator/researcher. Individual opposition parliamentarians are also less typically recruited onto a commission on the basis of particular expertise than members on the governing side. Importantly, however, opposition MPs *are* routinely involved on commissions with a broad parliamentary membership.

In 2002/03 there were twenty-eight Swedish commissions of inquiry comprising at least three members of parliament and all of them were 'cross-bloc' in composition – that is, they brought together socialist and non-socialists. For example, *SENIOR 2005* was a commission set up in 1998 to devise a policy programme for an increasingly ageing population, and by 2002/03 a total of twenty-two members had served on the commission. Of these, there were thirteen members or former members of the Riksdag – seven Social

Democrats, three Conservatives and one each for the Centre, Liberals and Left Party. A commission on 'Working Time, Holidays and Paid Leave', set up in the Ministry of Industry, comprised nine members, of which six were Riksdag members – two Social Democrats and one each from the Greens, Conservatives, Centre and Christian Democrats. The much smaller commission to develop public transport systems set up in the Ministry of Industry in May 2001 comprised only four parliamentarians. But the membership 'crossed the blocs'. There was one Riksdag member each for the Social Democrats, Greens, Leftists, and the Centre.

Several commissions comprised members of all or nearly all the parliamentary parties. Such 'surplus majority pre-legislative coalitions' included a commission reviewing the state of the police and public prosecutor network and another preparing a new law on the treatment of offenders. A national commission for the implementation and further development of Agenda 21 and Habitat Agenda, set up in June 2000 comprised almost exclusively ministers and parliamentarians and embraced representatives of all seven Riksdag parties. Yet the Swedish system of legislative-executive power-sharing in the preparation of public policy, and the involvement of Riksdag members from both the government and opposition side in the work of commissions, should not be viewed as radically compromising the government's capacity to govern. In appointing the chair, laying down the terms of reference and determining the composition, the government is generally able to control the commission system (see chapter 6). None the less, commissions routinely include parliamentarians from those opposition parties that cannot be regarded as veto players at the stage when government bills come before the Riksdag. All in all, Sweden is a majoritarian democracy with consensual legislative practice concentrated on, albeit not confined to the pre-parliamentary stage of policy formulation.

Denmark and Norway: contrasting forms of parliamentary consensualism in majoritarian democracies

Although Denmark and Norway were covered in full in the thematic chapters (1–8) of this book, the detailed empirical work, including interviewing the opposition leaders, was confined to the 'most similar design' cases of Finland and Sweden. However, a few very brief observations on legislative–executive relations in Denmark and Norway are in order. In both countries in recent years minority centre-right governments have been dependent on support from the radical right – the People's Party in Denmark and Progress Party in Norway – and traditionally the largest party, the Social Democrats, have been in opposition. Yet while minority coalitions have been dependent on opposition support for a legislative majority, the patterns of legislative–executive behaviour in the two countries appear to have differed somewhat.

Since 2001 the Liberal-Conservative minority governments in Copenhagen have relied on support from the Danish People's Party in getting the Annual Finance Bill (budget) through the Folketing. But they have blocked the attempts of the radical right to enter the cabinet (Venstres Landsorganisation 2004: 153). Instead, policy-making has proceeded along the traditional lines of 'package deal' agreements. Importantly, moreover, approximately two-thirds of the increasing number of Danish package deals negotiated between the minority government of the day and the parties in opposition have been 'oversized'. They have been *surplus majority legislative coalitions*. Frequently too, the deals are committed to paper and have become more detailed. Flemming Juul Christiansen has noted how the average length of the text of a 'package' between 1984–87 was 550 words, whereas this rose to 2650 words for the period 1998–2001 (Christiansen 2005). The practice of broad-gauge package deals, backed by 'surplus' legislative majorities across the government–opposition divide, makes a strong prima facie case for regarding Denmark as a limiting type of extreme parliamentary consensualism.

In contrast, the recent non-socialist minority governments in Norway until 2005 have tended to rely on ad hoc parliamentary support rather than Swedish-style formalised agreements or medium-term Danish-style package deals. As in Denmark there was no formal agreement between the Bondevik government and radical rightist Progress Party – except on the state budget – and legislative majority-building appeared to proceed more on a short-term, flexible basis – that is, *ad hoc parliamentary consensualism*.

While minority governments have become the norm in the three 'metropolitan Scandinavian' states in recent decades, the term 'minority parliamentarism', widely used by Scandinavian political scientists to characterise legislative–executive relations in these three countries, appears both unhelpful and misleading. Thus, writing in the early 1990s, Hilmar Rommetvedt described a shift to "dissensual minority parliamentarism" in Norway. He added that "coalition and minority governments cannot expect automatic support for their proposals in the national assembly in the same way as during the single-party majority Labour governments in the 1950s". (Rommetvedt 1992: 96) Parliament (the Storting) and the opposition parties, it was inferred, mattered. Similarly in Denmark, widely regarded as the home of minority governments, Erik Damsgaard has stated that "even opposition parties can influence important political decisions. They do not have to oppose the government all the time, they can actually make or influence policies". (Damsgaard 1992: 48) Moreover, in Peter Esaiasson and Knut Heidar's survey of the Nordic parliaments, a somewhat surprising statistic is reported, namely that an average of

28% of opposition party parliamentarians in the five countries of the region have weekly contacts with ministers. It is not made clear what sort of contacts these are, i.e. in the cafeteria, standing committee, commission of inquiry, floor of the chamber or wherever. Nonetheless, Heidar writes that this may "reflect a system of negotiations, power-sharing, power integration ... which makes Nordic parliamentarism clearly different from that in Westminster". (Heidar 2000: 199)

The regularity of minority governments in Denmark, Norway and Sweden is notable in a comparative perspective and the government's dependency on parliament (opposition parties) to implement a policy programme is an obvious concomitant. But the term 'minority parliamentarism' is simply not appropriate. Apart from article 42 of the Danish constitution, there are no special rights/protection for legislative minorities in metropolitan Scandinavia. Norway, to be sure, has a curious type of qualified unicameralism – the Storting divides into two internal 'chambers' to consider proposed 'laws' – and the *Lagting* was originally designed to provide institutional checks and balances against the tyranny of the (peasant) majority before the breakthrough of parliamentarism in 1884. Iceland had a broadly similar arrangement until 1991. But since the overall partisan balance in the Storting is replicated in the two internal 'divisions', the Lagting has (and has had) in practice little veto power. Rather, Denmark, Norway and Sweden (with proportional electoral systems and legislative majority rules) are majoritarian democracies in which minority governments are obliged to engage the opposition in the legislative majority-building process. Of course, patterns of opposition influence and involvement will vary between the three states, but the term 'minority parliamentarism' is of little intrinsic value in capturing or indeed understanding the essence of legislative–executive relations in metropolitan Scandinavia.

A final point warrants emphasis. It is possible that there is a measure of consensual legislative practice – largely unaffected by the mathematics of the legislative–executive balance – that falls full square into the realm of informal ('invisible') politics. This was not picked up by my leadership interviews, but that is not to say there are not significant and routine backbench-to-backbench and backbench-to-minister contacts across the government–opposition divide. This is perhaps most likely to be the case in respect of regional and moral questions, fostered by the cross-party groups in parliament. Clearly, at very least, the relative frequency of the contacts between opposition MPs and ministers is in need of more detailed and systematic investigation. But the precise extent of consensual legislative practice will always be dynamic and changing. Above all, all five Nordic states – to reiterate the response to the question posed in the title of this book – are majoritarian democracies. It is time to proceed from this simple de-mythologizing proposition. The Scandinavian states do not comprise a regional group of 'consensual democracies', although they exhibit varying degrees and types of consensual legislative behaviour – most in metropolitan Scandinavia and least in Finland and Iceland. While this situation could conceivably change, any future re-assessment will need to maintain the basic distinction between rules and behaviour. This book has favoured a rules-based approach to classifying democracies and on this basis only Finland has shifted from the 'supermajoritarian' to the 'majoritarian' class of democracies in recent times.

Notes

1 A Labour MP needed only 26,858 votes to be elected, a Conservative MP 44,241 votes and a Liberal Democrat MP 98,484. 'Government's record low share of the vote and system's bias fuel reform demands' *The Guardian* 7.5.2005.

2 A highly respected journalist has written in *Helsingin Sanomat* that "during the Cold War the Communist Party of the Soviet Union was Finland's most signifi-cant party, although its name did not appear on the register of parties in the ministry of justice". 'Voittaja, joka hävisi' *Helsingin Sanomat* 12.4.2003. The 1970s have been described as "the revolutionary decade" in Finland. Recent evidence suggests that twice, in 1970–71 and 1976–77, the Soviet Communist Party sought to engineer things so that power would shift to the Finnish Communists. In short, during these "danger years", Finland was threatened with a communist revolution initiated from Moscow. 'Tutkija: Nkp yritti Suomessa kumousta kahdesti 1970-luvulla' *Helsingin Sanomat* 12.4.2003.

3 Email correspondence with Hilmar Rommetvedt 23.5.2005.

4 'Vasemmistoliiton johto tyrmäsi taas puolueiden yhdistämispuuhan' *Helsingin Sanomat* 23.4.2005.

5 In running for the Conservative Party chairmanship in 2004, the Eduskunta Deputy Speaker, Ilkka Kanerva, argued for opposition party cooperation leading to a common presidential candidate in 2006 and an alternative government programme at the 2007 general election. 'Kanerva tarjoutuu yhdistämään porvarien voimaa' *Helsingin Sanomat* 8.5.2004.

6 'Eduskunta kiisteli työllistämiskeinoista' *Helsingin Sanomat* 13.10.2004.

7 'Kuntien tilasta ei saatu selvää välikysymyskeskustelussa' *Helsingin Sanomat* 13.10.2004.

8 'Kahden herätyksen mies' *Helsingin Sanomat* 15.5.2005.

9 'Keskustelu on Hautalalle tärkeämpää kuin vaalitulos' *Helsingin Sanomat* 24.4.2005.

10 Ironically, the Leftists' prospective veto power was increased by the obvious lack of cohesion in their parliamentary ranks. This was because the Leftists' original line – agreed with the government – was to abstain en bloc and so allow the govern-ment to carry the day.

11   The Social Democratic government made concessions on Arvidsjaur in order to secure Leftist support. Extra money was to be available to secure some jobs and a military presence would be maintained in the form of facilities for running a variety of civic and military tests in a 'sub-arctic environment'. *Från Riksdag och Departementet* 40, 2004, pp. 6–7.

12   They were Peter Pedersen from near Kristinehamn and Camilla Skold Jansson from Östersund.

13   By summer 2005 the Swedish non-socialists stood on 53.5% in the polls, compared with 42.3% for the three parties in the government's legislative coalition. This was the biggest lead for the non-socialists since 1991.

14   The empirical material includes both commissions set up in the first post-election year 2002/03 *and* those already in existence and still to complete their deliberations.

15   All the data in this section on pre-legislative Swedish commissions of inquiry can be found in *Regeringens skrivelse 2002/03:103 Kommittéberättelse 2003, Kommittéernas sammansättning* (Stockholm 2003).

References

Ágh, Attila 'Early Consolidation and Performance Crisis: The Majoritarian-Consensus Democracy Debate in Hungary' *West European Politics* 24, 3, 2001, pp. 89–112

Aylott, Nicholas and Torbjörn Bergman 'Almost in Government, But Not Quite: The Swedish Greens, Bargaining Constraints and the Rise of Contract Parliamentarism' Paper presented at the ECPR joint workshops, Uppsala, April 2004

Christiansen, Flemming Juul 'Inter-Party Co-operation in Scandinavia. Minority Parliamentarism and Strong Parliaments' Paper presented at the ECPR joint workshops, Granada, 14–19 April 2005

Cox, Gary W. 'On the Effects of Legislative Rules' *Legislative Studies Quarterly* 25, 2, 2000, pp. 169–192

Damgaard, Erik 'Denmark: Experiments in Parliamentary Government', in Erik Damgaard (ed.) *Parliamentary Change in the Nordic Countries* (Scandinavian University Press: Oslo and Oxford, 1992), pp. 19–49

Heffernan, Richard '"The Possible as the Art of Politics" Understanding Consensus Politics' *Political Studies* 50, 2, 2002, pp. 742–760

Heidar, Knut 'Parliamentary Party Groups', in Peter Esaiasson and Knut Heidar (eds) *Beyond Westminster and Congress: The Nordic Experience* (Ohio State University Press: Columbus, 2000), pp. 183–209

Hug, Simon and George Tsebelis 'Veto Players and Referendums Around the World' *Journal of Theoretical Politics* 14, 4, 2002, pp. 465–516

Isaksson, Guy-Erik 'Parliamentary Government in Different Shapes' *West European Politics* 24, 4, 2001, pp. 40–54

Isberg, Magnus *Riksdagledamoten i sin partigrupp* (Riksbankens Jubileumsfond & Gidlunds Förlag: Södertälje, 1999)

Jääskinen, Niilo 'Eduskunta. Aktiivinen sopeutaja', in Tapio Raunio and Matti Wiberg (eds) *EU ja Suomi* (Edita: Helsinki, 2000), pp. 114–134

Jensen, Henrik *Partigrupperne i Folketinget* (Jurist- og Økonomforbundets Forlag: Copenhagen, 2002)

Klöti, Ulrich 'Consensual Government in a Heterogeneous Polity' *West European Politics* 24, 2, 2001, pp. 19–34

Larsson, T. 'Cabinet Ministers and Parliamentary Government in Sweden', in M. Laver and K. A. Shepsle (eds) *Cabinet Ministers and Parliamentary Government* (Cambridge University Press, 1994), pp. 169–186

Laver, Michael 'Divided Parties, Divided Government', in Gerhard Loewenberg, Peverill Squire and D. Roderick Kiewiet (eds) *Legislatures. Comparative Perspectives on Representative Assemblies* (The University of Michigan Press: Ann Arbor, 2002), pp. 201–223

Loewenberg, Gerhard 'Agenda-Setting in the German Bundestag: Origins and Consequences of Party Dominance' *The Journal of Legislative Studies* 9, 3, 2003, pp. 17–31

Oertzen, Jürgen von 'Some Caveats on Numbers' Paper presented at the ECPR joint workshops, Granada, 14–19 April 2005

Papadopoulus, Yannes 'How Does Direct Democracy Matter? The Impact of Referendum Votes on Politics and Policy-Making' *West European Politics* 24, 2, 2001, pp. 35–58

Parming, Tönu *The Collapse of Liberal Democracy and the Rise of Authoritarianism in Estonia* (Sage: London-Beverley Hills, 1975)

Raunio, Tapio and Matti Wiberg 'Parliaments' Adaptation to the European Union', in Peter Esaiasson and Knut Heidar (eds) *Beyond Westminster and Congress: The Nordic Experience* (Ohio State University Press: Columbus, 2000), pp. 344–364

Rommetvedt, Hilmar 'Norway: From Consensual Majority Parliamentarism to Dissensual Minority Parliamentarism', in Erik Damgaard (ed.) *Parliamentary Change in the Nordic Countries* (Scandinavian University Press: Oslo and Oxford, 1992), pp. 51–97

Toonen, Theo A. J. 'Governing a Consensus Democracy: The Interplay of Pillarisation and Administration' *West European Politics* 23, 3, 2000, pp. 165–178

Venstre ved du hvor du har (Venstres Landsorganisation: Copenhagen, 2004)

Index